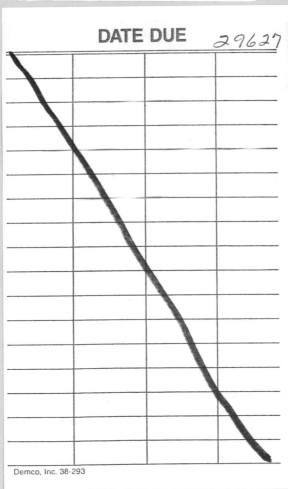

DATE DUE *29627*

Demco, Inc. 38-293

DISTANCE TRAINING

DISTANCE TRAINING

How Innovative Organizations Are Using Technology to Maximize Learning and Meet Business Objectives

Deborah A. Schreiber
Zane L. Berge

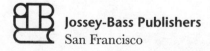
Jossey-Bass Publishers
San Francisco

Jossey-Bass books and products are available through most bookstores. To contact Jossey-Bass directly, call (888) 378–2537, fax to (800) 605–2665, or visit our website at www.josseybass.com.

Substantial discounts on bulk quantities of Jossey-Bass books are available to corporations, professional associations, and other organizations. For details and discount information, contact the special sales department at Jossey-Bass.

For sales outside the United States, please contact your local Simon & Schuster International Office.

 Manufactured in the United States of America on Lyons Falls Turin Book. This paper is acid-free and 100 percent totally chlorine-free.

Library of Congress Cataloging-in-Publication Data

Schreiber, Deborah A., 1953–
    Distance training : how innovative organizations are using
technology to maximize learning and meet business objectives /
Deborah A. Schreiber, Zane L. Berge.
        p.   cm.
    Includes bibliographical references and index.
    ISBN 0-7879-4313-4 (hardcover)
    1. Distance education—United States—Case studies.
    2. Occupational training—United States—Case studies.
    3. Telecommunication in education—United States—Case studies.
    I. Berge, Zane L. II. Title.
    LC5805.S35   1999   98-40416
    371.3'58—dc21

FIRST EDITION
HB Printing 10 9 8 7 6 5 4 3 2 1

CONTENTS

PART TWO: BUILDING SKILLS (TECHNICAL AND CRITICAL THINKING)

TABLES

FIGURES

EXHIBITS

This book is dedicated

To my husband, Rick.

Deborah A. Schreiber

To my mother, Iva Berge, who with my father started my training,
and after 45 years still inspires my education from a distance.

Zane L. Berge

PREFACE

It is a daunting task to maintain an educated, high-performance workforce in today's global economy. Increased competition, regulatory bodies, changing technology, and process re-engineering conspire to disrupt traditional employee practice and capability. The need for training, retraining, and lifelong learning by professionals demands that continuing education and staff development accommodate diverse learning environments, including the home, office or offsite conference room. To meet such demands, organizations and businesses are relying on communications technology and distance learning to deliver training.

Trainers and education specialists in business, nonprofit organizations, and government agencies traditionally looked to developments in communications technology to strengthen distance learning. Following a century of dramatic change and innovation, it appears that the integration of telecommunications and satellite technology are poised to support significant improvement in the interactivity, collaboration, and real-time delivery of distance education and training. There is an ever-increasing explosion of interest now in corporate videoconferencing, electronic performance support systems, and online web-based courses by business and industry.

Deciding what technology to use, however, and how to use it effectively are probably the two biggest questions faced by organizations as they attempt to design delivery of distance training. And once implementation begins, a company wrestles with how to institutionalize its efforts so that distance learning becomes part of the profile of the organization.

Purpose

The purpose of this book is to describe how corporations, non-profit organizations, and government may apply education and training at a distance to best meet business objectives. The goal is to illustrate, through case studies, how to maximize utilization of organizational technology to implement effective distance and distributed learning. Each case summarizes the organizational and technical barriers encountered as well as the pitfalls and limitations that were overcome in meeting business goals and objectives through distance training.

To help address these issues, a set of guiding principles has been identified that provide a framework for discussing distance learning in corporations, nonprofit organizations, and government agencies. These principles are derived from the theories of conceptual models of learning and instructional systems development. The guiding principles are not "standards" of operation established to meet criteria of accreditation or funding. These principles represent systems engineering strategies for design, development, and implementation of distance training "processes."

Audience members should keep in mind this set of guiding principles when reading the book. These principles may be used to guide analysis and discussion of the case studies as the authors discuss such issues as the strengths and weaknesses of distance learning technology, relating distance training performance objectives to business needs, or developing an effective corporate distance learning implementation strategy. This book is unique for its richness in business-focused experiences and simultaneous consideration of learning issues.

Audience

The intended audiences for this book include organizational managers, performance consulting professionals, and practitioners charged with the training functions in corporations, non-profit organizations, and government agencies. Additionally, this book may be used as a primary textbook for students and professionals studying to enter the distance training field.

Readers would use this book mainly to analyze how others have successfully integrated distance training into their organizations and the pitfalls and limitations that were overcome in meeting business goals and objectives. As a text, this book is most suitable for courses in business management, government training, and college graduate classes. Students should use this book to analyze case studies in distance training and discuss various perspectives on alternative solutions.

Guiding Principles

A set of principles has been developed that guides planning and preparation of training tailored to meet business-driven distance and distributed learning. The goal is to follow these principles to identify the organization's business needs and objectives, determine performances that meet these needs, and deliver distance training events and programs that facilitate the desired performance outcomes.

The editors distinguish here between a distance learning "event" and a distance learning "program." A *distance learning program* is not a program of instruction, such as a curriculum of courses or modules. A distance learning program refers to an organizational process, consisting of policies and procedures specific to departments' or divisions' functions and responsibilities. In contrast, a distance learning event does represent an independent course or module. The *distance learning event* is often an isolated and separate delivery exercise.

The following *guiding principles* represent a model for developing distance training. This model employs a reiterative process of analysis and design and is derived from the theories of instructional systems development and conceptual frameworks of learning. The goal is to maximize utilization of technology and institutionalize an organization's distance training efforts:

1. Analyze business needs,
2. Identify strategic distance training events and programs,
3. Apply conceptual frameworks of learning to distance training,
4. Identify and select delivery tools (develop organizational technology plan),
5. Correlate distance learning instructional materials to technology delivery tools,
6. Secure implementation support,
7. Implement a balanced roll-out strategy, and
8. Evaluate distance learning processes and measure transfer.

(See Chapter Three for more information on the *Instructional Design Model for Distance Training*, which is an embellishment of these guiding principles.)

Organization of the Book

This book begins with Chapter One's discussion of the history of distance training and explains how trainers and education specialists traditionally looked to developments in communications technology to strengthen distance learning. Chapter One also describes corporate and government cultures and how they influence policy and management issues regarding an organization's technology capability for distance learning. The various roles and personalities of information systems and human resource personnel are discussed as well as the impact such diversity has on the interdisciplinary efforts necessary for successful distance training.

Chapters Two and Three focus on the conceptual frameworks for distance learning and discuss some of the more salient instructional design principles as applied to distance training.

Regarding models of distance learning, Chapter Two explains that essentially there are two frameworks from which to view training and education. In the first, content and knowledge determined by someone else is transmitted to the learner (for example, lecture, textbook, videotape). In the second, a learner transforms information, generates hypotheses, and makes decisions about the knowledge he or she is constructing or socially constructing through interpersonal communication with others. Successful distance training occurs when instructional events are consistent with the characteristics of the selected learning model.

Chapter Three illustrates how the application of instructional design theory to distance learning enables a systems processing approach to be used to develop and implement training at a distance. The systematic application of the processes of analysis, design, and development to the implementation of distance learning ensures identification of each contributing factor and accounts for the associated impact of each component. Components of the distance learning process are interrelated and include the learner, instructor, primary instructional goal, performance objectives (driven by business needs of the organization), the learning environment, instructional delivery technology, and organizational culture. The focus of organizational culture includes discussion of corporate facilitators and institutional constraints affecting the design and development of distance learning.

Description of Case Studies

Chapters Four through Eighteen contain fifteen case studies that illustrate distance training in corporate, non-profit organizations, and government. Each case reviews the organizational and technical barriers encountered as well as the pitfalls and limitations that were overcome in meeting business goals and objectives through distance learning. The distance training applications range from dissemination of information and building skills in critical thinking and problem solving to changing attitudes and affecting organizational culture. Content areas addressed include technical and electronic systems development, safety operation and maintenance, general healthcare and specific nursing tasks, managerial and policy issues, and organizational restructuring and new business development. While at one time some types of learning may have been considered inappropriate or "undoable" at a distance (such as mechanical or electronic skill development), the current corporate, non-profit, and government cases demonstrate this is no longer so.

The case studies help organizations answer such questions as how to maximize utilization of technology to deliver distance training and what organizational processes and procedures may aid in institutionalizing distance training efforts.

The case studies are organized into three sections, categorized by the primary type of learning that is facilitated by the distance training event or process: Part One (*Distributing Information and Increasing Knowledge*), Part Two (*Building Skills [Technical and Critical Thinking]*), and Part Three (*Changing Attitudes and Enhancing Motivation*). The editors utilized this categorization for two reasons: first, it dispels any lingering misconception that certain types of learning are undoable at a distance; and second, it illustrates that mastery of performance outcomes is dependent upon understanding what knowledge, skills, and attitudes facilitate the desired behavior. Each section describes case studies that fulfill business needs with specific types of learning delivered via a distance training event or process. The technologies[1] selected for delivering distance training include a combination of computer-based training, electronic-performance support systems and online courses over the intranet/extranet, and live two-way video conferencing via satellite and fiber optics networks.

The authors of the case studies discuss the pitfalls and limitations that were overcome in meeting business goals and objectives with distance training and refer to the aforementioned guiding principles with varying degrees of detail. Employing this model for developing distance training, the contributing authors describe associated issues, including the following:

---

[1]Due to the rapidity with which technology is changing, the case studies focus on the processes and events of distance training and not the industry standards for hardware and software configurations.

- Relating performance objectives to an identified business need
- The rationale for selecting specific distance training instructional strategies (events or processes) to facilitate mastery of the performance objectives
- The strengths and weaknesses of technologies selected to deliver distance training
- The development of an implementation plan (coordinating and maintaining support for delivery of distance training)
- Integrating formative and summative evaluation of the distance training event or process

Part One: Distributing Information and Increasing Knowledge

Disseminating information to increase knowledge is a most appropriate type of learning to facilitate at a distance when time and application are critical. This often occurs in content related to marketing information, operational processes, new business regulations, and life-saving techniques and other health issues. The body of information distributed includes facts, names, principles, and generalizations.

Part One contains five case studies that demonstrate distance training activities that disseminate information and increase knowledge. The chapter contributed by Dennis Fukai and others, "Building Customer Relations: Web-Based Training for the Home Improvement Industry," illustrates how an in-store web-based application delivers information about construction materials that are purchased for home improvement projects. The application serves as a marketing tool for retail sales personnel, identifying and describing the hardware and manufactured materials available for sale as well as explaining the use of equipment and tools needed for successful completion of projects.

The next two case studies, provided by Barry Howard ("Increasing Employee Knowledge and Understanding of Operational Systems: Integrating Multiple Technologies at NYNEX") and Lissa Klueter ("Disseminating Time-Sensitive Information: Using Interactive Distance Learning to Deliver Training and Education in the American Red Cross Biomedical Services"), also demonstrate distribution of information to increase knowledge. However, in these cases the performance outcomes are driven not by marketing but by business needs related to operational processes, including new rules and regulations. The NYNEX case integrates several technologies (including business television, live interactive videoconferencing, and computer-based tutorials) to provide information to staff to increase knowledge and understanding of the company's operational systems (for example, processes associated with the core business-telecommunications operations). Information is distributed on order-entry, maintenance scheduling, and accounts inquiry.

The case study by Lissa Klueter describes distance training employed by the American Red Cross Biomedical Services that includes dissemination of time-sensitive information about new FDA regulated procedures in the areas of collecting, manufacturing, and distributing blood components. The case describes in detail the roles and responsibilities of the members of the core distance learning team as well as the differences between two delivery tools: business television (BTV) and interactive distance learning (IDL) via satellite technology.

The last two case studies in Part One are provided by Therese Monahan ("Disseminating Time- and Regulation-Sensitive Information: Mortgage Bankers Association of America") and Michelle Warn and others, ("Graduate Programs at a Distance: A Partnership Between the California Department of Rehabilitation and San Diego State University"). In the case study described by Therese Monahan, the Mortgage Bankers Association conducts two distance training seminars to distribute time- and regulation-sensitive information regarding banking processes and procedures. The content is intended for loan originators and underwriters and includes information about loan origination, underwriting, and appraisal review.

The case study provided by Michelle Warn and others describes a partnership between the California Department of Rehabilitation and San Diego State University to provide training to fulfill state-mandated continuing education requirements. The goal of the training is the dissemination of information to increase knowledge and understanding in the field of rehabilitation, including issues surrounding people with disabilities, events that sway policy and social outcomes, and the overall community services and support systems available. The instructional technologies examined by this case study include online courses, teleconferencing, desktop conferencing, and compressed video conferencing.

Part Two: Building Skills (Technical and Critical Thinking)   Skills-based training at a distance is becoming increasingly successful due to the application of improved distance learning instructional strategies. Well developed activities are being designed and employed to engage participants in group discussions, role-play, and online review of demonstrated techniques. Extended practice in the workplace is also employed to build and reinforce skill development with follow-up evaluation by online experts and/or clinical advisors.

Skill-building at a distance may include development of intellectual skills, motor skills, or interpersonal and communication skills. Distance training of intellectual skills includes the application of rules and solving problems, as well as the development of cognitive strategies for self-learning and independent critical thinking. Manual or psychomotor skills involve coordinated and accurate execution of muscle-controlled performances (such as production and maintenance of machines and technical or electronic systems). Interpersonal and communications skills (often considered intellectual skills) include the application and interpretation of verbal and nonverbal cues for social and political implication.

Part Two contains six case studies that demonstrate distance training activities designed to facilitate building technical skills and developing critical thinking. The first case listed, submitted by Mick Mortlock and Ed Dobrowolski, is titled "Reskilling Employees for Competitive Advantage: Reinventing at Unisys Corporation." This case study describes computer-based training and electronic performance support systems designed for distance learning in information management and re-engineering. The goal of the Unisys training is to develop critical thinking and problem-solving skills in employees so they may redirect current expertise to new and innovative areas of applications. The target audience for the distance training is interdisciplinary, cross-cultural, and multi-generational. The company's business need is to retain and sustain its human intellectual resource as the organization restructures and develops new business.

The next two case studies included in Part Two are "Delivering Technical Training to Advance Mechanical Skills: Interactive Video Teletraining in the Federal Aviation Administration" and "Delivering Clinical-Based Training in a Public Health Setting," contributed by Lynn W. Payne and Henry E. Payne, and Janet Place and others, respectively. Both cases describe distance training activities that facilitate physical or psychomotor skill development.

The case study provided by Payne and Payne illustrates that technical training can be delivered and mechanical skills successfully developed via interactive videoteletraining (IVT). One of the first courses at the Federal Aviation Administration to be converted from resident-based training to IVT was the Cockpit En Route Inspection course. Safety operators and maintenance staff successfully developed skills for using the new equipment. The case study illustrates that there was no statistically significant difference in learning between the resident-based and distance training courses. The FAA case study also describes evaluation of several components that contribute to the success of IVT events, including effective instructional strategies that enhance participant-instructor interactivity during teletraining.

The case study by Janet Place, Tim Stephens, and Patricia O'Leary Cunningham also describes technical or, more specifically, clinical-based training via distance learning. The instructional strategy combines interactive video at six remote sites to guide clinical training in physical assessment for patient screening and referral. A proficiency-based model is followed that requires learners to perform a series of actual client exams for exercise and practice. Physical assessments may include breast exams, PAP tests, and prostate exams. Follow-up evaluation is provided by clinical advisors.

The fourth case study in Part Two describes development of interpersonal and communication skills via distance training. The case, titled "Skills-Based Distance Training for a Global Environment: Malaysia's Virtual University," was submitted by Patrice Sonberg and Manon Ress and describes a cross-cultural partnership between the Malaysian government and an educational technology firm in the United States. The objective of the described case was to develop and implement a web-based distance training program that is skills-based and designed to meet the corporate and political needs of an evolving world economy. Although one of the training objectives was to build intellectual skills in content areas of "high technology" (computer and information systems capabilities and international business practices), the primary goal was to build student interpersonal skills for participation in a global environment. This includes building skills in language, communication, and cultural procedures and protocol.

The last two cases described in Part Two are "The Value of Building Skills with Online Technology: Online Training Costs and Evaluation at the Texas Natural Resource Conservation Commission" by Scott Walker and "Building Intranet Courseware Using Multidisciplinary Teams: The Story of Quantum Solutions, Inc. and Columbia/HCA Healthcare Corporation" by Ann D. Yakimovicz. These case studies describe distance training activities intended to build critical thinking and problem-solving skills in using online technology and in managing multi-disciplinary teams for development of web-based courseware, respectively.

The case by Scott Walker describes the application of distance learning by the training academy of the Texas Natural Resource Conservation Commission, a state environmental regulatory agency. The agency utilized multiple distance learning technologies to deliver training, including videoconferencing and internet-based online courses (with email and web-based delivery of instructional materials). After briefly describing the strengths and weaknesses of the various attempts at distance training, including the coordination of nine remote sites throughout a heavily-used videoconferencing network, Walker focuses on building skills in using online technology. The strategy employed includes piloting and evaluating the internet-based course "Online Training: Net Tools for Work." The intended audience for the distance training was highly technical in their areas of expertise (environmental management and legislation) but very novice with this delivery medium.

Finally, the case study by Ann D. Yakimovicz describes the design of intranet-based courses that build skills in healthcare management and policy issues. Course topics target senior healthcare executives of the Columbia/HCA Healthcare Corporation and cover content areas related to shifts in managed care, for-profit hospitals, and patients covered by HMOs and other insurance contracts that provide a fixed monthly payment for services. The training was designed to facilitate problem-based learning. The author provides significant information on the development of multi-disciplinary teams, the roles and responsibilities of each member, and the team's affect on design, development, and delivery of distance training.

Part Three: Changing Attitudes and Enhancing Motivation   The final section of case studies includes four chapters, each describing distance training activities that are designed to change attitudes or enhance motivation for desired behaviors.

Attitude may be considered a personal or emotional perspective, preference, or value. Attitudes guide social and organizational interactions and affect performance. Enhancing motivation of staff is appropriately facilitated through distance training when personnel and business perspectives are adversely affecting overall productivity and return.

The first case study presented in Part Three, "Eliciting Community Beliefs and Changing Attitudes Through Education: Interaction Distance Training at the Columbus Center," was submitted by Regina Bento and others. This case study in distance training represents a just-in-time application developed to serve the information and emotional needs of high school students and teachers, as well as a broader public, regarding the pfiesteria microorganism associated with a critical problem of fish lesions in Chesapeake Bay. The study describes distance training activities that elicit the beliefs and feelings of the participants about pfiesteria, the fish lesion problem, and the broader societal impacts and allows them to examine these feelings in a supportive environment. The latest scientific evidence is available during the distance event to provide information and answer questions. The goal is to quiet "pfiesteria hysteria" and facilitate the immediate and extended audience to make informed decisions about the use of Chesapeake Bay seafood and waters, as well as to motivate these participants to later seek, on their own, further information about the subject.

The second case study presented in Part Three, "Measuring Existing Attitudes to Assess Training Transfer: The Interactive Distance Learning Group Looks at Learning and Transfer from Satellite Training," was submitted by Joan Conway Dessinger and others. This case study is different from the one submitted by Bento and others in that Dessinger and others describe distance training that does not change attitudes but rather "measures existing attitudes" of participants toward a particular distance training event as an indicator of transfer of learning. This case evaluates self-efficacy, perception of utility, and course satisfaction to determine the effectiveness of a distance training event to facilitate learning transfer back on the job. Although this case study also measures increased understanding from newly distributed content information, as well as improved skill development, it is the measure of affective characteristics by the Interactive Distance Learning (IDL) Group that is unique to this chapter. (Note: The IDL Group, Inc. is a subsidiary of the nonprofit organization National Center for Manufacturing Sciences. Companies and agencies participating in this case study include Eastman Kodak, Ford Motor Company, General Motors, EDS, Texas Instruments, and the United States Airforce.)

The third case study presented in Part Three is "Unanticipated Attitudinal Change: The Progression Toward Self-Directed Distance Training at H.B. Zachry," submitted by Larry M. Dooley, Kim E. Dooley, and Keith Byrom. This case study is similar to the first chapter in this section by Regina Bento and others except that the significant change in attitude of Zachry company staff was unplanned. The improved attitude toward distance training was an unexpected (but welcomed) outcome of the distance training activities themselves.

The H.B. Zachry corporation originally identified its business goal to standardize training on the customs and procedures of supervisors by designing and institutionalizing a distance learning program. The intent was to provide information on company and industry regulations and guidelines, including corporate history and culture, procedures for hiring, discipline, and termination, labor law compliance and human relations, and employee benefits. And although the intended outcomes for increased knowledge and skill development occurred, the most significant, albeit unexpected, outcome was a major shift in attitude of the traditional, conservative, family-owned company toward self-directed distance learning. Classroom-based, instructor-led training appears no longer to manifest the only effective training approach for this company!

The final case study of the book was submitted by Jim Suchan and Alice Crawford and is titled "Utilizing Telelearning as a Strategic Media Choice to Enhance Executive Development and Affect Organizational Perspective: The U.S. Navy's Bureau of Medicine and Surgery." This chapter describes a distance training model that focuses on telelearning as strategic media choice, not merely a conduit that passes information from instructor to student. This distance training model is designed to guide the Navy Bureau of Medicine and Surgery Executive Management Education administrators' thinking about distance learning applications to executive development modules and to change the organizational discussion about learning, interactivity, and the capabilities of new telelearning media. The case study by Suchan and Crawford is similar to the H.B. Zachry chapter in that the authors hope to see a change in attitude about distance training as a result of participation in distance training activities themselves. Also, Suchan and Crawford identify the strategic contributions of the distance training events and discuss how this information may be used to enhance motivation of executive management toward support and institutionalization of telelearning.

Conclusion

The final chapter of the book provides a summary of best practices of distance training as represented by the case studies. A discussion of the lessons learned includes the strengths and weaknesses of distance training efforts as related to the guiding principles outlined in Chapter One.

Following the final chapter, a Glossary is included to standardize usage of distance learning terms and vocabulary relative to the case studies presented. The editors' intent is to avoid ambiguity which may result due to use of organization-specific references, as well as to clarify potential misconceptions about technologies. Online resources for additional terms and phrases in distance learning are also provided in the Glossary.

A key to implementing successful distance training events is the integration of instructional methodology, instructional materials, and the technology utilized to deliver the instruction. A consistency or complementation must exist among these components for successful distance learning to occur. The discussions of the conceptual frameworks of learning and instructional design model for developing distance training facilitate the process. Following this strategy, organizations begin to answer such questions as how to maximize utilization of technology to deliver distance training and what organizational processes and procedures may aid in institutionalizing distance training efforts.

Acknowledgments

We would like to acknowledge the reviewers of this book: Diane Gayeski, Barry Howard, Ellen D. Wagner, and Tom Clark. We greatly appreciate their time and contribution on this book.

Washington DC   Deborah A. Schreiber, Ed.D.
September 1998   Zane L. Berge, Ph.D.

THE AUTHORS

DEBORAH A. SCHREIBER is president of DAS, Inc., a consulting firm that is recognized for corporate applications of distance learning. She possesses fifteen years experience in instructional systems development, needs analysis, and delivery of computer-assisted education and training. She has designed, developed, and staffed continuing education programs for scientists and engineers, technical managers, and nontechnical personnel. Dr. Schreiber demonstrates significant skill in the effective use of organizational technology for onsite instruction and distance learning.

In addition to consulting, Dr. Schreiber teaches in the Training Systems Program at the University of Maryland Baltimore County. Her courses include computer-based training and corporate distance learning. Dr. Schreiber also maintains an active schedule as a member of the United States Distance Learning Association (USDLA) and is a regular participant in the National Science Foundation's panel review of Small Business Innovation Research (SBIR) program proposals.

Dr. Schreiber received her B.S., B.S.Ed., and M.Ed. from the University of Cincinnati and her Ed.D. from Boston University. Dr. Schreiber can be reached at debs@schreibinc.com.

ZANE L. BERGE is Director of the University of Maryland Baltimore County (UMBC) Training Systems graduate program. He is widely published in the field of computer-mediated communication used for teaching and learning. His most notable books are: *Computer-Mediated Communication and the Online Classroom* (Volumes 1–3) (1995) and a four-volume series, *Wired Together: Computer Mediated Communication in the K12 Classroom* (1998). Before joining the faculty at UMBC, Berge founded the Center for Teaching and Technology at Georgetown University. He consults and conducts research internationally in distance education. Dr. Berge can be reached at berge@umbc.edu.

David Aurelio was born in upstate New York and has been actively involved in the home improvement industry all his life. He grew up in his father's hardware store and started working in the family's remodeling and construction business as a teenager. David moved to Florida in 1987 and worked on various commercial and residential projects for a number of companies. Realizing that the home improvement industry is in his blood, he soon started work in the millworks and building materials department for Home Depot in Gainesville, Florida, where he has acted as a customer service representative, helping teach people how to complete their own home improvement projects. After helping to build countless home improvement projects, Mr. Aurelio recently decided to return to school to pursue a degree in construction management and is currently a senior at the M. E. Rinker Sr. School of Building Construction at the University of Florida. He can be reached at Djaurelio@aol.com.

Regina Bento is the Yale Gordon Distinguished Teaching Professor at the Merrick School of Business, University of Baltimore. She received a Ph.D. in management from the Massachusetts Institute of Technology (1990) and an M.D. degree, with a specialization in psychiatry, from the Federal University of Rio de Janeiro, Brazil (1977). Dr. Bento's published works include an award-winning book, chapters in books published by Sage and the Harvard Business School Press, several articles in journals such as *Human Resource Management Journal, Journal of Managerial Psychology, Information and Management,* and others, as well as numerous business cases, proceedings, and other publications. Her scholarly work has followed four inter-related research streams: behavioral issues in the management of end-user computing; unintentional bias in the allocation of organizational rewards; and values, culture and organizational rewards; teamwork and information technology in higher education. Dr. Bento has received numerous teaching awards, including the top teaching awards at the Merrick School and at the University of California Riverside (where she worked prior to joining UB). She is chair of a university-wide committee for teaching enhancement at UB and coordinator of distance education efforts at the Merrick School. She can be reached at rbento@UBmail.ubalt.edu.

Kenneth G. Brown is a doctoral candidate in the Industrial and Organizational Psychology Associates. He earned a B.S. in psychology (1993) from the University of Maryland, and a M.A. in psychology (1996) from Michigan State University. He has published articles on training, learning, and motivation in both scientific and professional journals, including *Journal of Applied Psychology* and *Human Resource Planning.* Current research and consulting projects include the influence of motivation on learning processes in self-paced training, the effects of feedback and guidance on learning outcomes in web-based training, and the influence of work environment on the utilization of desktop learning. He can be reached at Brownke6@pilot.msu.edu.

Keith Byrom is Senior Manager, responsible for recruiting and employment development, for H.B. Zachry Company, one of the country's premier industrial and heavy constructors. He became interested in distance learning when as doctoral candidate in Education Administration, he took a course on distance education concepts at Texas A&M University. The professor for this course was Dr. Larry Dooley. Subsequently, under the leadership of Byrom and Steve Hoech, Vice President of Human Resources, Zachry has become a leading advocate and innovator in distance education in the construction industry. Distance education initiatives at Zachry include employee education, core management training, craft skills training, and training on costs and scheduling. Keith Byrom can be reached at Byromk@Zachry.com.

Charles Compton is a resources specialist for the California Department of Rehabilitation. He also worked as a rehabilitation counselor and a senior rehabilitation counselor with the department prior to his present position. He earned his B.A. degree (1987) in English literature from California State University Stanislaus. He earned a certificate in Rehabilitation Administration (1994) from San Diego State University and is currently one of the students in the distance education Master of Rehabilitation Counseling program discussed in this chapter.

Compton's main research activities include analysis of the functions of the Staff Development Section within the Department of Rehabilitation in California, and the development and implementation of a comprehensive personnel development program within this agency. He can be reached at ccompton@inreach.com.

Alice Crawford is a Senior Lecturer at the Naval Postgraduate School. She earned a B.A. (1970) and a M.A. (1972) in experimental psychology from San Diego State University. Before coming to the Naval Postgraduate School, she conducted research and development in the areas of organizational effectiveness and instructional technology for fourteen years.

Her primary research interests have been in technology-mediated training and education, simulation, and militery leadership. She currently serves as program manager for a unique master's degree program in Leadership Education and Development which is offered by the Naval Postgraduate School at the United States Naval Academy. She can be reached at acrawford@nps.navy.mil.

Patricia O'Leary Cunningham is the director of the Public Health Training and Information Network (PHTIN) of the North Carolina Department of Health and Human Services. She holds a bachelor's in Nursing from Mercy College in Detroit (1974) and a master's in public health from the University of North Carolina at Chapel Hill (1979). Prior to directing the PHTIN, she was Director of Research and Education for the state Office of Public Health Nursing and served as a regional health director. O'Leary Cunningham has taught for more than twelve years in the University of North Carolina's Schools of Nursing and Public Health and has used the statewide video network to teach classes in eight of those years.

O'Leary Cunningham is North Carolina's designated distance learning coordinator to Public Health Training Network of the Centers for Disease Control and Prevention in Atlanta. She also serves on the North Carolina governor's Health and Medicine Applications Task Force and the Connectivity Task Force of the North Carolina Information Highway. She can be reached at Pcunning@sph.unc.edu.

Joan Conway Dessinger holds a B.A. in journalism, an M.A. in reading education from Marygrove College, and an Ed.D. in instructional technology from Wayne State University. Prior to becoming a training and development consultant, she designed, implemented, and evaluated reading and writing workshop programs for adult learners at the Adult Basic Education, high school completion, and college levels. In 1989 Dr. Dessinger founded The Lake Group, Inc., a consulting firm that provides needs assessment, design, development, implementation, and evaluation of training and non-training performance interventions. She is president and senior consultant for The Lake Group and specializes in needs assessment, as well as design and evaluation of distance learning programs.

Dr. Dessinger also teaches graduate courses in instructional systems planning, needs assessment, program evaluation, instructional systems design, and adult learning in the Instructional Technology Department at Wayne State University. In addition, she teaches a course on health care education program administration for the University of Detroit-Mercy.

Since 1980, Dr. Dessinger has made presentations and facilitated workshops for over fifty state, national, and international conferences, including conferences sponsored by Michigan Council on Learning for Adults, Michigan Association for Adult and Continuing Education, American Association of Adult and Continuing Education, American Society for Training and Development, National Society for Performance and Instruction, and the International Coalition on Technology in Education. Her topics have ranged from the learning disabled adult to planning, designing, and evaluating programs and products for adult learners.

Dr. Dessinger is active in American Society for Training and Development and The International Society for Performance Improvement and Kappa Gamma Pi National Honor Society. Dr. Dessinger and Dr. James L. Moseley have co-authored several articles on the adult learner. Most recently, they co-authored a chapter in Volume 2 of the *Performance Improvement Pathfinders Series:* "Classic Performance Interventions," published by ISPI. The chapter features their 360° Performance Intervention Evaluation Model. She can be reached at JDessinger@aol.com.

Edward Dobrowolski is a senior consultant in worldwide human resources at Unisys Corporation. He leads the Learning Technologies group, which is part of the Worldwide Professional Development Organization.

Mr. Dobrowolski has over twenty years of experience in the design and development of technology-based training tools, including instructional design and project management experience from Applied Data Research Corp. and Planning Research Corp. He joined Unisys in 1987 to lead an interactive video courseware development team. Since then he has held increasingly responsible positions within Unisys, managing numerous multimedia and computer-based training (CBT) development projects. The topics for this courseware range from mainframe operating systems to instructional systems design concepts. Mr. Dobrowolski and his team also created an electronic support tool for the company's performance management system.

In 1996, he was selected to manage the development of the first human resources intranet web site at Unisys. After a successful launch, his team went on to develop the Career Fitness Centre, an interactive career development web site for Unisys employees.

Mr. Dobrowolski received a Bachelor's degree in communications and a master's degree in educational media, both from Temple University in Philadelphia, Pennsylvania. He has spoken at a number of conferences on developing computer-based training and human resources intranet sites. He can be reached at Edcdobrowolski@unn.unisys.com.

Kim E. Dooley is an assistant professor in the College of Agriculture and Life Sciences at Texas A & M University. Her Ph.D. is in educational human resource development from Texas A & M University with a specialization in Distance Learning.

Dooley's major responsibilities include mentoring, coaching, and supporting faculty who are teaching at a distance. She facilitates faculty training and instructional design for all programs designed for dispersed audiences, oversees the design and implementation of distance interactive video classrooms, and acts as a liaison with other university and state entities. Dr. Dooley's teaching and research specialization is in technological change and effective use of computer technology and telecommunications for teaching scientific principles. She can be reached at k-dooley@tamu.edu.

Larry M. Dooley is an associate professor and assistant department head of the Department of Educational Human Resource Development at Texas A & M University. Moreover, he is also an associate professor with the Center for Distance Learning Research at Texas A & M University. He earned his B.S. (1975) in Agricultural Economics, his M.S. (1982) in Educational Administration, and his Ph.D. (1989) in Higher Education Administration, all from Texas A & M University in College Station, Texas.

In the department of Educational Human Resource Development, Dooley is coordinator of the master's and doctoral degrees in distance learning and is also responsible for the master of science degree in educational human resource development that is delivered completely by a distance (the first one to be approved by the state to be offered to multiple sites). Dooley is also in his fifth year as chair of the National Distance Education Conference sponsored by the Center for Distance Learning Research at Texas A & M University.

He currently serves as the chair of the Distance Education and Technology Unit of the American Association for Adult and Continuing Education and consults widely at both the state and national levels in the areas of technology integration, distance education, and human resource development. Moreover, his papers have been presented at conferences and scholarly meetings both domestically and internationally. He can be reached at dooley@tamu.edu.

Lauri E. Elliott is president of The Performance Consulting Group, Inc., a consulting firm that specializes in organizational development, performance improvement systems, and technology applications. She received her masters of education in corporate training from Regent University. She is currently working on a doctorate degree in instructional technology at Wayne State University. Her areas of research are multimedia application development and distance learning.

Ms. Elliott has performed a wide variety of performance technology services, including conducting training needs assessment and performance analyses, designing and developing training curriculum, designing and developing organizational development and non-training performance improvement interventions, and implementing evaluation strategies. Her most recent projects include conducting training needs analysis and developing courses for both web/intranet-based and interactive satellite mediums.

As a corporate trainer, Ms. Elliott has successfully facilitated courses in technical and soft skill areas. She is also a certified distance learning instructor for the Interactive Distance Learning Group. In addition to her corporate training background, she has served as an adjunct professor in the Human Resource Management Graduate Program at Siena Heights College, as well as a computer technology instructor at both Eastern Michigan University and Cleary College. She can be reached at lelliott@tpcginc.com.

Dennis Fukai was a contractor and licensed architect for twenty years before returning to the University of California, Berkeley to earn a Ph.D. in Architecture in 1994. He received a Center for Latin American Studies research grant to Mexico in 1991, a CJAAA scholarship in 1992, and a Fulbright fellowship to Chile in 1992–93. While completing his graduate studies, Dr. Fukai worked as a high school, community college, and continuing education teacher in the San Francisco Bay area and central California. He is currently an assistant professor of construction management at the M.E. Rinker Sr. School of Building Construction, College of Architecture, at the University of Florida, where he teaches graphic and computer communications. Dr. Fukai uses the Internet extensively in all of his classes and has directed a number of graduate studies on the use of the World Wide Web. His research centers on integrated technical data systems and the delivery of construction information on local and wide-area networks. He has also completed a number of grants exploring the viability of the World Wide Web for conference, training, and educational purposes. He can be reached at drdeny@gator.net.

Barry Howard was the director of Computer & Distance Learning Centers for the NYNEX Corporation through 1997. NYNEX's experience with electronic education tools spans almost ten years of business planning, trial implementation, and expansion into production for a wide variety of tools. NYNEX's strategy was to embrace each tool for its specific advantages, maximizing its contribution on a wide scale. NYNEX rarely was an "early adopter," preferring to learn from the experiences of others and then applying them on a macro scale. The process required creative vision, driving management, and a team of enthusiastic managers to keep all of the systems operational. As NYNEX approaches the year 2000, it is well positioned to absorb the next revolution of electronic education tools.

Mr. Howard has left NYNEX to assist other organizations in their transition to electronic education as a member of QED Consulting, a New York-based organization that has specialized in human resource change management. He was the director of General Electric's Computer Training School in New York. He is also an adjunct professor in Computer Science at Baruch College in New York City and has taught college-level management and marketing courses using two-way video for the Center for Distance Learning (State University of New York).

His responsibilities at NYNEX include all computer-related training for the NYNEX Corporation as well as all distance learning efforts for all training disciplines. Video, multimedia, computer-based training, electronic performance support systems, and intelligent tutors are included in the responsibility. In previous positions he was responsible for automation, marketing, the NYNEX Corporate College, and telecommunication operations. He developed NYNEX's Strategic Training Vendor plan.

He has a bachelor's degree in mechanical engineering from the City College of New York and a master of business administration in computer science from Baruch College.

Mr. Howard has spoken at the Training Director's Forum (1996,1997); the Society for Applied Learning Technology (1993–1996); the Computer and Training Support Conference, Training '95 & '96; Data Training (multiple years); Synergy '92; Metropolitan System Educators and Trainers (METROSET—multiple years); ITTC (93–95); the Management Development Forum; and the National Conference on Workforce Development on a variety of subjects from distance learning to trainer's career development. He has written articles for a number of training publications and has been quoted by the media on electronic education, strategic outsourcing and computer training subjects. He can be reached at ceec2000@aol.com.

Elizabeth Kalweit has coordinated interactive distance learning programs for the American Red Cross business television network for three years. She has also appeared in several business television broadcasts and in an educational video which she co-wrote. Prior to that she managed a national training database for the American Red Cross Biomedical Services and managed local area networks for ARCBS. She has developed numerous quick reference guides, policy manuals, and other job aids for American Red Cross Biomedical Services. She earned her B.A. degree (1993) in English (writing) at George Mason University in Virginia. She can be reached at Lizkalweit@aol.com.

Lissa Klueter has fifteen years of technical expertise producing materials for various instructional technology systems including business television, interactive business television (such as One Touch), educational video, online distance learning, and multimedia. She earned her B.A. (1984) in management at the University of South Florida and her M.A. (1994) in human resource development with a graduate certificate in instructional design at Marymount University.

Ms. Klueter became interested in distance learning when she was the director of a large project for the Department of Defense Dependent Schools (DODDS) Office of Distance Education. The focus of the project was to teach DODDS K-12 teachers multimedia, Internet, and distributed learning teaching skills. As a program manager of training technologies for the American Red Cross Biomedical Services, Ms. Klueter has designed a series of IDL programs in the area of transfusion medicine and promotes ways to use intranet technology for delivering training to ARCBS staff. Ms. Klueter is seeking her doctorate in instructional technology and distance education at Nova Southeastern University. She can be reached at Lklueter@aol.com.

Susan Levine is an instructional designer at the Center for Research in Mathematics and Science Education (CRMSE) at San Diego State University. She is also a clinical psychologist practicing psychotherapy in San Diego. She obtained her B.A. in psychology at Brooklyn College and her Ph.D. in Clinical Psychology at California School of Professional Psychology, San Diego. She is currently completing an M.A. in education (educational technology) at San Diego State University.

Dr. Levine's interests focus on distance education, constructivist learning methods, user centered interface design, web design, and usability. She designed the practicum course for the distance learning master of science in rehabilitation counseling at San Diego State University. At CRMSE, she is working on a National Science Foundation-funded project to develop constructivist-based biology lessons for publication on the web. She has recently published an informational and promotional web site based on a self-help book, *Peace After Abortion*. She has also published guidelines for coaching and advising novice computer users. She can be reached at levine@mail.sdsu.edu.

Therese L. Monahan is director of distance learning for the Mortgage Bankers Association of America (MBAA). She earned her B.S. (1981) in business administration at Oregon State University and her M.Ed. (1997) in instructional technology at George Mason University, Fairfax, Virginia. Prior to joining the MBAA in 1996, she was responsible for the development and implementation of an accreditation program for federal thrift regulators at the Office of Thrift Supervision, U.S. Department of the Treasury.

Ms. Monahan's main interests lie in promoting strong instructional design concepts to conventional and unconventional distance learning delivery mechanisms. She is currently a member of the United States Distance Learning Association, Society for Applied Learning Technologies, and the American Society of Association Executives. She can be reached at tmonahan@earthlink.net.

Mick Mortlock is a senior consultant at Unisys Corporation. He is currently on the start-up team for Unisys University and is the worldwide director for People-Soft training.

Mr. Mortlock recently joined Unisys from Intel Corporation where he was Intel University's worldwide director of multimedia and alternative training technology and the director of the Center for Interactive Technology. He developed Intel's first computer-based training applications, performance support systems, and intranet training solutions. His Internet radio program *The Freshwave Radiozine* was an early entry in the field of internet radio.

Mr. Mortlock is the co-founder of the Learning Solutions Lab at Arizona State University and was co-producer and Intel Project Manager for "Designing Instructional Media," the first masters' level distance learning program. He took a hiatus between Intel and Unisys to work on a novel and develop interactive training programs for high school English and Literature students. He holds a degree in philosophy from Portland State University and has done post-graduate work at City University. He may be reached at mickmortlock@unn.unisys.com.

Henry E. Payne is manager of the Federal Aviation Administration's (FAA) Interactive Video Teletraining (IVT) program. He earned both his B.S. (1973) in speech and his M.S. (1975) in secondary education with emphasis in educational technology at Oklahoma State University, Stillwater. He earned his Ph.D. (1998) in educational leadership and policy studies at the University of Oklahoma, Norman.

Dr. Payne is responsible for implementing the FAA's compressed digital satellite network. This network is used to conduct general, technical and managerial training to the FAA's widely dispersed workforce. He also developed a White Paper that became the FAA's distance learning strategy, guiding such distance learning programs as correspondence course study and computer based instruction, in addition to IVT.

Dr. Payne currently serves as president of the Federal Government Distance Learning Association, a chapter of the United States Distance Learning Association, also known as the FGDLA. He also serves as president of the Government Alliance for Training and Education (GATE) since its creation in March 1995.

GATE is an official organization of government agencies interested in sharing video teletraining resources.

Before coming to the FAA, Payne worked for the Department of the Army as a civilian Instructional Systems Designer for thirteen years. While with the Army, he served as Chief of the Futures Training Division at the US Army Training and Doctrine Command. He was responsible for the development of such projects as voice recognition technology used in computers for foreign language refresher training in the field, the development of Army 21, the Army's long range training strategy into the twenty-first century, and the Army's distance learning strategy, called distributed training. He can be reached at Hank_Payne@mmacmail.jccbi.gov.

Lynn W. Payne is assistant professor of marketing and management at Langston University. She earned her B.S. in business administration from James Madison University, an M.B.A. in management from Golden Gate University, a Ph.D. in management from La Salle University, and a Ph.D. in educational leadership and policy studies at the University of Oklahoma.

Dr. Payne is responsible for developing marketing curriculum and integrating computer and distance learning technology into the classroom. Her academic appointment at Langston University includes teaching responsibilities in the areas of marketing strategies, marketing research, international marketing, business communication, and managing complex organizations. As a Walton Fellow, Payne oversees the activities of the Langston Chapter of Students in Free Enterprise (SIFE).

Dr. Payne currently serves as a judge and member of the Board of Advisors for the Oklahoma Quality Foundation. She provides leadership and develops team leader training for lead examiners based on the Malcolm Baldridge National Quality Award criteria. The Governor of Oklahoma presents the Oklahoma Quality Award each year to exemplary organizations in business, education, health care, and government.

Before going into higher education, Dr. Payne worked for GE Government Engineering and Management Services as contract manager for government contracts. Before moving to the civilian sector, Payne spent seven years as a Finance Officer in the U.S. Army serving in such roles as Resource Manager for the Training Technology Agency at the U.S. Army Training and Doctrine Command, managing budgets and contracts for the development of educational technology, and Cash Control Officer for the Ninth Infantry Division and I Corps. Prior to military service Payne installed custom software, trained customers, and performed computer related trouble shooting for Allied Data in Lacey, Washington, and taught computer programming for Waynesville Vo-Tech in Missouri.

Janet L. Place is a distance learning specialist and director of the Enhanced Nurse Training Program, School of Public Health, University of North Carolina at Chapel Hill. She earned her BA in anthropology at Lawrence University (1982) and masters in public health in behavioral science at the University of California, Berkeley (1996). Prior to coming to the university, she was a program officer for the Henry J. Kaiser Family Foundation's program for health and development in South Africa.

Ms. Place has over fifteen years of global experience in community health with a special emphasis on increasing access and quality of health care for poor and underserved populations. She has consulted widely in the area of health and poverty. Her current work involves training public health nurses throughout North Carolina to meet the special needs of health department clients. In addition to Adult Physical Assessment, she directs training courses in women's health, family planning, maternal health and sexually transmitted diseases, all of which are taught in a distance learning format. She can be reached at jplace@sph.unc.edu.

Alberto Ramirez is currently a consultant in science education and educational technology, working with the Association of Science-Technology Centers and various science museums.

During 1997 he worked as director of public programs at the Hall of Exploration in Columbus Center, where he led the implementation of distance learning programs in marine science and marine biotechnology. He has over eight years of experience working in the development of original programs in science centers. As a science and technology coordinator and later as the director of youth programs in the Miami Museum of Science, he developed a series of programs in marine science, computer technology, and work skills development for underserved inner-city youth that promoted the museum to a leadership role under the "YouthALIVE!" National Initiative. With the support of the State of Florida and National Science Foundation, he conducted for seven consecutive years a marine science enrichment summer camp for middle school minority and female youth, recognized with several awards.

Mr. Ramirez received his B.S. in biology from the National University of Mexico, his M.S. in biological oceanography from the Scripps Institution of Oceanography, and has pursued advanced studies in marine biology at the Rosenstiel School of Marine and Atmospheric Science, University of Miami. He developed the University of Mexico's Mazatlan Marine Research Station and was its first director and associate professor for six years, while conducting research on billfish migration in the Eastern Pacific Ocean. He can be reached at aramirez@bellatlantic.net.

Manon Anne Ress is an education consultant based in Washington, D.C. She earned her B.A. (1980) and M.A. (1983) in history at the Universiti de Lettres de Nice (France), an M.A. (1985) and her Ph.D. (1992) in romance languages and literature at Princeton University.

Ress was assistant professor of French at Temple University where she taught 17th-century French literature and French theater. She served on the university's Teaching Learning and Technology Committee and the College of Arts and Sciences Committee on Teaching and Technology. She was selected as a Lilly Fellow to study the use of technology in teaching. She held various research and teaching positions as a lecturer at Princeton University.

From February 1996 to October 1997, she was a member of a team working with KUB Malaysia, to create Universiti Tun Abdul Razak (UNITAR), a virtual university in Malaysia. She was responsible for the selection and evaluation of educational partners and curricula, adaptation of course contents for Malaysia, analysis of modes of delivery and teacher training, human resources planning, course content selection and integration, memorandums of understanding with American academic institutions, and negotiation over copyright and other intellectual property issues. She was the owner of the team Internet discussion list, EDUTECH@ibm.net, which focused on issues relating to the development of UNITAR and other distance education programs. She can be reached at mress@essential.org.

Tamara Salganik is the project manager for the Distance Learning Lab and Audiovisual Specialist at the Columbus Center, where she helped launch the new Distance Learning Lab. Salganik earned her B.A. from the University of Maryland Baltimore County and has extensive experience in film and video direction, production, and teleconferencing. Prior to her position at Columbus Center, she served as the multimedia specialist at the Johns Hopkins School of Health and worked as an instructor of independent film making. She has also overseen the video teleconferencing department at the Aberdeen Proving Ground Army Installation and has worked as the long-distance learning technician at the School of Medicine and School of Nursing at the University of Maryland at Baltimore.

Ms. Salganik won an Award of Excellence in 1995 from the U.S. Army Center Optical Engineering Branch for her video and teleconferencing work. In addition, Salganik won a place in a juried exhibition for her film animation in 1994, and she received academic honors from the Fine Arts Gallery at the University of Maryland Baltimore County in 1993. She wrote, produced, directed, and edited an animated promotional film entitled *95-Alive* for Development Design

Group, Inc., Baltimore's third largest architectural firm. She can be reached at Salganik@columbuscenter.org.

Cindy Schuster is a media specialist in the Network Information Resources Department at the Langsdale Library, University of Baltimore. She provides technical and facilitator support to University of Baltimore's interactive video classrooms using IVN (Interactive Video Network) and MIDLN (Maryland Interactive Distance Learning Network). She also coordinates the scheduling of UB distance education classrooms and the training of faculty, staff, and students on the use of these systems and other iterations of electronic classrooms.

Ms. Schuster is also an adjunct faculty member in the Information and Quantitative Sciences Department in the Robert G. Merrick School of Business. She participates in the University System of Maryland Institute for Distance Education and LATA Users Group. She received her M.A. in publications design in 1989 from the University of Baltimore. Research interests include the use of the web/Internet in an electronic classroom and the use of the web as a vehicle for providing distance education online courses and/or services. She can be reached at cschuster@ubmail.ubalt.edu.

Patrice Anne Sonberg has a B.A. in communications with a minor in psychology from George Washington University (1992) and an M.A.T. degree in teaching English to speakers of other languages from the School for International Training (1998).

Ms. Sonberg specializes in English as a Foreign Language (EFL), distance education, and cross-cultural communications. She currently serves as an adjunct faculty member at George Washington University in the EFL Department where she teaches academic reading and writing to graduate and undergraduate students. Sonberg is a member of the national association of Teachers of English as a Second Language (TESOL) and the local Washington-area chapter (WATESOL).

She was a senior project manager and EFL specialist on the Malaysian Virtual University Project Team. She evaluated software, conducted research, wrote on trends in distance training, participated in strategic planning, and advised on issues related to EFL. Prior to this project, Ms. Sonberg held a one-year teaching position in Japan where she taught English to high school and college students, adults, and business executives. She has taught EFL courses in business English, public speaking, american culture, and newspaper production at several language institutions throughout the U.S. She has worked with students from Asia, South America, Europe, and the Middle East. In addition to her academic background, Ms. Sonberg has worked in public relations and journalism. She served as account executive at a Washington, D.C.-based public relations firm, The Kamber Group, and as a stringer for *The New York Times*. She is currently the editor of the newsletter for the association of Washington Area Teachers of English as a Second Language (WATESOL.) She can be reached at sonberg@gwis2.circ.gwu.edu.

Tim Stephens is acting director of Distance Learning at the University of North Carolina at Chapel Hill School of Public Health. He earned his B.A. (1986) in film studies and literature at the University of Warwick, England and a masters in communications (1991) from the University of North Carolina at Chapel Hill. Before joining the School of Public Health five years ago, he worked for a statewide videoconference distance learning network in North Carolina.

Mr. Stephens has consulted widely on distance learning and public health educational outreach and training with national and state public health and educational agencies. He presently serves on the North Carolina Information Highway Policy Board, and represents the SPH on the joint Centers for Disease Control and Prevention/Association of Schools of Public Health Distance Learning Taskforce. He can be reached at tim_stephens@unc.edu.

Jim Suchan is associate professor of management at the Naval Postgraduate School in Monterey, California, where he teaches courses in managerial communication, and organization and management. Jim received his B.A. (1971) in English literature and his M.A. in humanities (1973) from the State University of New York at Buffalo. He received his Ph.D. (1980) from the University of Illinois, Urbana.

Dr. Suchan's research focuses on organizational metaphors and the effect they have on organizational communication. In addition, he is doing research on communication patterns in various forms of telelearning. He has published his work in *Management Communication Quarterly, The Journal of Business Communication, The Journal of Business and Technical Communication, Business Horizons,* and *Personnel Administrator,* among others. Prior to coming to the Naval Postgraduate, Jim taught at The University of Alabama and The University of Arizona. He can be reached at JSuchan@mntry.nps.navy.mil.

Scott Walker is instructional technology specialist at Our Lady of the Lake University in San Antonio, Texas. He earned his B.A. (1987) in photography from Sam Houston State University, Huntsville, Texas, and his master of applied geography (1997) from Southwest Texas State University, San Marcos, Texas. Before joining the staff at Our Lady of the Lake University he was an instructional designer with the Texas Natural Resource Conservation Commission for four years.

Mr. Walker's work includes demonstrating the uses of technology and applying technology in educational settings and international development situations, as well as incorporating technology in instructional design for both training and education. He has facilitated several online conferences and teaches a variety of classes over the Internet. He has also initiated distance training/education programs in government agencies and higher education institutions.

Mr. Walker works with non-governmental organizations, government agencies, research institutes, schools, teachers collaboratives, and web volunteers around the world to incorporate and utilize technology in education, training, and participatory development. He can be reached at sw24316@swt.edu.

Michelle M. Warn is the project manager for the Interwork Institute Distance Education Program at San Diego State University (SDSU). She earned her M.A. in 1995 in education (education technology) at SDSU and will receive her doctorate in education from Claremont Graduate University in 1998. She is a member of the International Interactive Communications Society, the Association for Computing Machinery, and the Phi Beta Delta Chapter for International Scholars.

Before coming to the field of education, Ms. Warn spent several years with Apple Computers as a systems analyst. She worked internationally with Apple implementing database and systems solutions. Ms. Warn is also a human interface design consultant and teaches multimedia courses to students at the University of California, San Diego.

Ms. Warn is presently researching the evolution of online communities in the distance classroom. She is also developing and refining universal instructional design principles which would be applicable across cultures, learning styles, and physical and cognitive disabilities. She can be reached at warn@mail.sdsu.edu.

Sandra Whitteker is an instructional designer for the Interwork Institute Distance Learning Project at San Diego State University (SDSU). She earned her B.A. (1969) in speech and hearing, her teaching credential (1970) in elementary education (minor in deaf education), and her M.S. (1995) in rehabilitation counseling at SDSU, San Diego. She is currently pursuing a second graduate degree in Education Technology. Before joining the staff at SDSU Interwork Institute, she was a teacher of the deaf for nine years and lived outside the United States for six years.

Recent research efforts have concentrated on distance learning with a special focus on electronic communication media and strategies (synchronous and asynchronous), implementation of learner-centered and constructivist paradigms in distance education, effective web page design for online coursework, and accessibility for individuals with disabilities in online education.

Ms. Whitteker served on a number of committees throughout her teaching career that were involved with education of the deaf and special education, developed projects such as an internationally known mime troupe composed of elementary deaf students, and served on or headed committees for non-profit fundraising organizations such as Make-a-Wish Orange County and MS of San Diego. She is currently a member of the Association for Educational Communications and Technology and Association for the Advancement of Computing in Education. She can be reached at swhit@interwork.sdsu.edu.

Ann D. Yakimovicz is president and chief executive officer of Aprendio Inc., a distance learning company specializing in design, development, implementation, and evaluation of web-based training and continuing professional education. She currently presents workshops on designing web-based training and on writing for online reading and learning. She earned a B.Sc. in landscape architecture (1986), followed by an M.S. in industrial education (1993) and a Ph.D. in educational human resource development (1995), all from Texas A & M University, where she researched computer-mediated communication and creativity. She has presented and published numerous articles and papers on distance learning.

Before founding Aprendio, Dr. Yakimovicz was director of interactive distance learning for Columbia/HCA Healthcare Corporation. Using Columbia's intranet, she initiated company-wide training for employees from senior management to front-line staff, and she started an online knowledge management system, Healthcare Educators Forum, to share education and training knowledge among all of Columbia's facilities.

Dr. Yakimovicz has been designing innovative courses including classroom and teleconference-delivered training since the 1970s when she developed some of the first "soft skills" training for police officers in southern Oregon. As a consultant, she has created training programs for major clients such as Schlumberger Wireline & Testing NAM, Tenneco Gas Company, and Houston Community College's Small Business Program. She served as coordinator of the Training & Development Certification Program while at Texas A&M University and has been listed in *Who's Who in American Women* since 1989. She can be reached at annyak@aprendio.com.

DISTANCE TRAINING

INTRODUCTION

CHAPTER ONE

ORGANIZATIONAL TECHNOLOGY AND ITS IMPACT ON DISTANCE TRAINING

Deborah A. Schreiber

There has been an explosion of interest in corporate videoconferencing, electronic performance support systems, and online Internet/intranet courses by business and industry in the past few years. This is in response, Portway and Lane conclude, to an evolving workforce crisis in the United States, in which an estimated four out of ten workers who are on the job today require training to meet the demands of the economy (1994). Steve Eskow agrees (1997). Increased competition, regulatory bodies, changing technology, and process reengineering conspire to disrupt traditional employee practice and capability. It is a daunting task to maintain an educated, high-performance workforce. As a result, organizations are reaching out to an array of technological supports to meet this need.

Today's business environment is one of increased training need and lifelong learning, yet also one of diminished resources. Operating in a global economy, employees interact worldwide. The idea of individuals primarily *coming to* training is obsolete (Fitzsimmons, T., personal conversation, 1997). Staff development must move out into the workplace, reaching geographically dispersed employees. To close the training gap, organizations must become effective and efficient in providing education and training at a distance (Portway and Lane, 1994).

Trainers and education specialists traditionally have looked to developments in communications technology to deliver distance learning (Tiffin and Rajasingham, 1995). As is often the case with complex phenomena, however, no one solution provides a silver bullet. It appears that the most effective strategy for meeting the needs of distance education and training is to employ a variety of forms of instructional technology and electronically mediated instruction (DiPaolo, 1996; Franklin, Yoakam, and Warren, 1996).

Instructional technologies include satellite broadcasts, interactive compressed video, and the Internet. The Internet may provide web-based interactive multimedia (computer-based training) or the intranet/extranet for communication, data services, and electronic performance support systems. Computer-based training is also packaged independently on CD-ROM.

Deciding what technology to use and how to use it effectively probably rank as the two biggest questions faced by organizations as they attempt to design delivery of distance learning. Deutsch (1997) recognizes that many companies procure new technology but often see limited return because they do not know how to best utilize it. And for the organization that is mature in its technological capabilities, effective implementation of distance learning events may occur; however, the company wrestles with how to institutionalize its efforts so that distance training becomes part of the profile of the organization.

In the following paragraphs, Chapter One discusses the history of distance training and explains how trainers and education specialists traditionally looked to developments in communications technology to strengthen distance learning. This chapter also describes corporate and government cultures and how they influence policy and management issues regarding an organization's technology capability for distance learning. The various roles and personalities of information systems and human resource personnel are discussed, as well as the impact such diversity has on the interdisciplinary efforts necessary for successful distance training.

History of Distance Training and Business

Pick up a current training journal or business weekly magazine, and you may see the following headlines:

Hewlett-Packard saves over $5 million with distance learning!

H-P spends $1.5 million to train nationwide 700 engineers on a new electronic chip in 30 days. In comparison, the company's original estimate for conventional "onsite classroom" training totaled $7 million and required a year of trainers' time (Picard, 1996).

or

Sprint has been "chunking" and "streaming" multimedia computer-based training on the company's intranet for over a year now!

Newly hired salespeople access online training to learn effective ways to get appointments with clients, as well as remediation training for basic marketing and sales skills development. And whereas Sprint's sales force used to struggle to keep up with the new product changes (new product material may be obsolete in as little as 30 days), they keep informed and knowledgeable of the most recent product developments via the intranet (Filipczak, 1996).

The effects of such headlines are varied. Some readers feel "Everybody's Doing It!" (*"and I'd better hop on the bandwagon before it's too late"*), while others may feel despair and hopelessness (*"my training budget is only $300K; I'm not in the same league as those spending, as well as saving millions of dollars"*) or (*" 'chunking' and 'streaming', I don't even know what that is?!"*). Both reactions may result in hasty, uninformed decisions about purchase, production, and implementation of distance training.

Discussions of business applications of distance training have reached lofty heights. No longer do conversations center on correspondence courses or Public Broadcasting Services and educational television. Today, trainers and education specialists debate the size and capabilities of satellite dishes, the impact of fiber optics, and the benefits of Integrated Services Digital Network lines for online courses and compressed video! *How did we arrive at such technology-driven practices of distance learning?*

1900–1930

As early as the turn of the century, nontechnical correspondence courses became available which provided self-paced, independent study. The mining industry possessed a need to provide instruction on mine safety to scattered populations separated by rugged topography, and the Colliery Engineer School of Mines provided the course materials (Tiffin and Rajasingham, 1995; Moore and Kearsley, 1996). Also, with the advent of railroads and the call for industry standards and procedures, the International Correspondence Schools (ICS) provided home study courses to employees of 150 railroad companies throughout the country (Moore and Kearsley, 1996).

Initial correspondence education integrated limited instructor-learner interaction, however (Tiffin and Rajasingham, 1995), and educators and trainers looked to evolving communications technology to strengthen distance learning. One of the first applications of technology to deliver distance education and training was the use of radio and film. Moore and Kearsley (1996) report that in 1925 the State University of Iowa conducted five radio courses for credit; and by the late 1920s, over 10 percent of all broadcast radio stations were owned and operated to deliver educational programming (Lane, 1994).

1940–1970

The late 1940s through the 1970s witnessed the rise, fall, and rise again of instructional television (Tiffin and Rajasingham, 1995). Early applications provided a one-way medium for disseminating information and were embraced by educational and public service organizations. Iowa State University went on the air in 1951 with WOI-TV (Lane, 1994), and Stanford University's Stanford Instructional Television Network began broadcasting in 1969 (Moore and Kearsley, 1996). In the late 1970s, PBS Adult Learning Service was established (Lane, 1994).

The strengths and weaknesses of instructional television as a delivery medium were not initially understood, however, and early efforts to adapt broadcast technology to distance learning were disappointing (Lane, 1994). Programmed courses were poorly produced and offered at odd times of the day and night (Ivey, 1988). Minimal to no interaction was incorporated into the program design. Soon educational television became simply a delivery medium rather than an instructional medium. With the development of audiovisual and videocassette recordings, educators and trainers began relying on independent viewing of taped programs.

Businesses and corporate organizations focused on the increasing availability of audiovisual tapes and videocassette recordings in the 1960s and 1970s to support distance learning. During this time, Reuters owned and operated its own in-house video facility that produced video materials to complement classroom printed materials (Cook, 1997). Abbey National, a financial organization in the United Kingdom, integrated videocassette products to facilitate management development training at a distance (Wakeley, 1997).

1980–Present

The 1980s represent the decade of desktop (personal) computers in homes and offices. With availability of personal computers, development of computer-assisted instruction, computer-managed instruction, and computer-based training materials followed. Xerox and Motorola in the United States (Griffiths, 1996; and Adams, 1995; respectively), as well as the Trustee Savings Bank and Abbey National in the United Kingdom (Brown, 1997), all incorporated computer-based training into their repertoire of distance learning capabilities. Computer-based multimedia and laser disks were particularly popular during this period.

In addition to the introduction of personal computers, there was an explosion of development in communications technology in the late 1980s and throughout the 1990s. Satellite communications, originally launched in the mid-1960s, matured and became readily available in the 1980s to those organizations and businesses that could afford them. Corporations, including Xerox, Hewlett-Packard, and the National Technological University, used commercial and proprietary satellite networks to successfully broadcast seminars and training courses globally. Nonprofit organizations, including the American Association of Retired Persons, became proficient in broadcasting regularly scheduled distance training events to staff and volunteers nationally (Schreiber, 1996).

Finally, continuing advances in telecommunications technology have also significantly influenced corporate distance training. The installation of fiber-optic cables worldwide and evolving satellite networks enable digital transmission of video, voice, and data simultaneously (Tiffin and Rajasingham, 1995; Saettler, 1990). Telecommunications and computers now use the same language. Local-area networks [LAN], wide-area networks [WAN], and the Internet link personal computers and telephones for web-based interaction (Moore and Kearsley, 1996). And as the *Sprint* newspaper headline illustrated at the beginning of this section, such online dissemination of information and skills training at a distance is current, real, and effective.

Integration of Computers and Telecommunications Technology (Collaborative Delivery of Distance Training)

The evolution of digital electronics has paved the way for convergence of traditionally separate technologies. Computers, cable television, videocassettes, satellites, and lasers have come together to produce a hybrid of new media configurations (Saettler, 1990; Sheehan, 1982). Examples include teleconferencing and the Internet. Teleconferencing integrates traditional television broadcasting with computer networks. The Internet and electronic mail integrate database technology and text management with word processing and distributed work stations.

The merging of communications technologies and computers, however, has brought with it organizational environments that are more complex than ever before. For example, traditionally an organization's television broadcasting experts focused on production and delivery. Now, teletraining organizations have had to decide whether broadcasters and production staff become experts also in instructional design, or whether instructional systems development expertise is provided from another department. And as interdisciplinary teams are established, the phenomenon of group dynamics must be addressed.

Corporations and businesses are restructuring. Boundaries between jobs and responsibilities are becoming less distinct. It is a time when cooperation and collaboration across organizational functions are critical to meeting business needs of the corporation or agency.

Interdisciplinary Efforts to Deliver Distance Training

The development and delivery of effective distance training today depends on contributions from both technical and nontechnical staff. Employees from management information systems (MIS), broadcasting, and integrated technology (IT) functions must collaborate with instructional designers and training specialists from human resource management (HRM) departments and learning centers. The need for sophisticated and strategic distance training demands that telecommunications experts and specialists from computer services and business operations, as well as instructional designers and training specialists, no longer function separately or isolated from one another.

The roles and responsibilities of technical and nontechnical staff are many and varied in the collaborative effort to design and deliver effective distance training. Telecommunications experts and computer specialists develop the distributed networks for automation and electronic mail, as well as provide ongoing maintenance and support of work stations. These technical staff also mechanically and electronically integrate personal computers and interactive video systems, including auxiliary hardware and software. The technical staff provides access to advanced data bases and collaborative shareware, as well as synchronous communication environments.

The nontechnical staff who participate to ensure effective strategic distance training includes instructional designers, trainers, content experts, and organizational development professionals. These individuals conduct performance needs assessments, consider psychological factors of learning, and assess utility aspects of technology. Instructional designers and content experts identify learning objectives and determine instructional methodology as prerequisites to design and development of distance training events and activities.

And finally, it is the operations and business specialists who work to provide funding and financial services to support overall distance training efforts.

Knowledge of the roles and responsibilities traditionally exhibited by staff helps to improve collaborative efforts among diverse experts for new efforts such as business-driven distance learning. However, even with the availability of prescribed models for design and implementation of distance training, there is continuing difficulty on the part of employees and organizations to participate in cooperative efforts that are systematic and rational. This may be attributed to the diverse background experiences and intellectual perspectives that make up the personalities of the individuals involved (Dipboye, 1997).

Personality Characteristics of Diverse Experts Involved in Distance Training

A potential barrier to collaborative efforts by interdisciplinary teams involved in developing distance training is the diverse and sometimes diametrically opposed personal and professional background of the participants. For example, research indicates that as recently as 1994 human resource management personnel viewed the best trainers as team-oriented, warm, outgoing, positive and humanistic (Dipboye, 1997). Effective training is characterized as people-oriented and focused on individual employee development. Consistently, these individuals may pursue the design and development of distance training with a very humanistic, rather than scientific, approach (Schreiber, 1996).

In contrast, technical staff (including information systems engineers, operations staff, and production personnel) suggest that successful distance training is defined by task-focused and job-specific activities (Schreiber, 1996). These individuals tend to design training from a very analytical viewpoint, with a primary concern for financial and other bottom-line objectives (Dipboye, 1997). Think of the fireworks that may ignite when such opposing perspectives are put together in an interdisciplinary effort to design and deliver distance training!

Recent research by Dipboye (1997) identifies several phenomena that impact collaboration and the ability of individuals to participate in cooperative efforts that are systematic and rational. Four of these include (a) personal attitudes, (b) contextual factors, (c) the *raison d'être* for the activity, and (d) individual reaction to power and politics. Research by Schreiber (1996) suggests that these phenomena account significantly for the difficulties encountered during interdisciplinary efforts to design and deliver distance training.

For example, personal attitudes about training (specifically, distance training) may be expressed as scientific or humanistic (as stated previously). The individual with a scientific perspective maintains a very analytical viewpoint and is objective and often impersonal. The humanistic perspective is characterized by examining the emotional and psychological disposition of the learner. When engaged in an interdisciplinary effort to design and deliver distance learning, the staff member operating with a humanistic approach would focus on personal learning styles and be anxious to facilitate relaxation and enjoyment during the training. The individual with a scientific point-of-view would scrutinize operations, focus on expertise of content specialists, and perhaps make judgments regarding delivery technology based on costs rather than instructional effect.

A second phenomenon that impacts collaboration and the ability of individuals to participate in cooperative efforts similar to developing distance training is the context of the training itself. Contextual factors are those that define the organizational, social, and psychological environment (Dipboye, 1997). The context of training may be viewed as job-specific or as part of an interpersonal relationship with the organization. Interviews with technical and financial staff involved in team efforts to design and deliver distance training reveal that some think of themselves as objective, data-querying, code-crunching personalities who are task-driven and concerned only with the bottom-line (Schreiber, 1996). This contrasts with feedback provided by some staff development professionals who see themselves as more concerned with group synergy and organizational citizenship (Dipboye, 1997). As participants in designing and delivering distance training, these individuals focus on exhibiting and facilitating the current values and culture of the organization (Schreiber, 1996).

The perceived *raison d'être*—the reason or justification for training—is another factor contributing to personality characteristics that affect interdisciplinary efforts to design and deliver distance learning. The *raison d'être* of training may be perceived in one of two ways: from the perspective of the bottom line or from the perspective of public presence (Dipboye, 1997). Individuals who maintain a perspective of public presence are concerned with designing distance training that facilitates learning yet simultaneously portrays the company or agency as an organization concerned with individual employee development, diversity, quality, and customer relations. Individuals operating from the perspective of the bottom line view organizational symbols as extravagant, unrelated to the task at hand, and even a waste of time (Dipboye, 1997).

The final personality factor considered which affects collaborative distance training efforts among diverse experts is one's individual reaction to power and politics. Power is defined as "the ability to achieve desired outcomes," and politics refers to the "activities taken within an organization to acquire, develop and use power" (Dipboye, 1997).

Power and politics can have a negative impact on collaborative distance training activities when the interdisciplinary team tasked with the effort is perceived (by themselves and others) as redundant, ineffectual, and operating in name only. Under these conditions, the team as a whole may "seek situations that are sufficiently ambiguous that their actions cannot be closely scrutinized" (Dipboye, 1997). Further, both technical and nontechnical staff involved with this type of distance training effort will begin to behave negatively: technical members may withhold information and access to organizational technology to deliver distance training; human resource staff may try to build coalitions to control decisions driving distance training outcomes. In the end, the phenomenon is a self-fulfilling prophecy.

In summary, it is only through positive, diverse, and interdisciplinary contributions that distance training programs will be implemented that contribute strategically and become institutionalized as part of the profile of the organization. The goal here has been to provide some insight into the dynamics that affect organizational technology capability for distance learning, which is described in the next section. Please note that much of the discussion is derived from professional interviews and anecdotal experiences of the author while visiting sponsor sites. The purpose of the discussion is to explain the need for technical and nontechnical team members to recognize and understand their varying views about training so that the strength of each perspective is harnessed during the design and delivery of distance learning activities.

Organizational Technology Capability for Distance Training

Trainers and education specialists in business, nonprofit organizations and government agencies traditionally looked to developments in communications technology to strengthen distance learning. Following a century of dramatic change and innovation, it appears that telecommunications, computers, and satellite technology are poised to support significant improvement in the interactivity, collaboration and real-time delivery of distance education and training.

Researchers caution, however, that extraordinary upheaval in the communications industry, technology, and legislatures may affect distance learning in ways still unknown. Continuing changes in services, pricing, and packaging are daunting (Cullen, 1997). Hardware and software processing capabilities double roughly every eighteen months (Brown, 1997). And state, local, and often federal regulations are not clearly defined nor understood regarding information technology and communication (Cullen, 1997).

Businesses and corporations also are experiencing one of the fastest rates of transition regarding organizational change and evolution (American Council on Education, 1996, *Guiding Principles*). There is a shift from manufacturing to service-based businesses; where products are still manufactured, the shelf-life may be as short as one year (Franklin, Yoakam, and Warren, 1996). Competition is global. Just-in-time knowledge and retraining are common expectations of staff and management. Lifelong learning may be a necessity, but how effectively it is experienced depends on a company's goals and objectives, as well as the overall culture of the organization.

Designing and implementing distance training that contributes strategically to the organization requires not only a new organizational chart but often a transformation of the corporate culture itself (Cronin, 1994). Maximizing utilization of technology to deliver distance and distributed learning is not dissimilar to reengineering processes in that there is a redefining of roles and responsibilities. Compelling influences from technology and education experts, as well as executive management, requires that the traditional corporate hierarchy evolve into a more flexible institution that facilitates teamwork, collaboration with business partners, and distributed decision-making.

Consequently, the primary cultural characteristic of a corporation, agency, or institution that significantly impacts effective implementation of distance training is the organization's level of capability to utilize technology. This concept of *organizational technology capability* describes an organization's degree of sophistication with which technology is applied to distance learning to resolve business needs.

The stages of organizational technology capability for distance learning are illustrated in Figure 1.1. These stages are best described by the level of maturity an organization exhibits in understanding, acquiring, and using technology to deliver distance training. The maturity level discussed here is similar to that researched by Paulk and others (1993), which referenced data information systems. Paulk describes maturity level as "a well-defined evolutionary plateau toward achieving a systematic and systemic process" (p. 7). (For more information about maturity levels, see Paulk and others [1993] Capability Maturity Model℠ for Software, Version 1.1, *Technical Report CMU/SEI-93-TR-024.*)

There are four primary stages of capability that an organization may experience when using technology to deliver distance and distributed learning. The first stage represents an organization that is just *beginning* to implement distance learning. The organization currently delivers separate and sporadically planned distance education and training events. Each event is sponsored and budgeted by an individual function or department. And one area of the organization is unaware of what another area is doing. The application of distance training is fragmented at this stage.

The second stage of organizational technology capability is manifested by distance education and training events that are repeated or duplicated by the organization. The organization is now considered somewhat experienced with distance training. The corporation or agency often forms an interdisciplinary team at this time, and the participating members respond to staff and management inquiries and recommendations regarding distance training.

The ultimate capability stage for implementing distance training is illustrated by the organization that understands the strengths and weaknesses of various delivery tools, correlates instructional materials development to these strengths and weaknesses, and truly maximizes utilization of the technology. This organization also has successfully institutionalized its efforts in distance and distributed learning.

As an organization evolves from a level of immaturity to a level of sophistication in its application and utilization of technology to deliver distance learning, however, it experiences a point of transition that is pivotal to its evolutionary progress. This stage of corporate development is defined by the establishment of organizational policy and procedure regarding distance and distributed education and training. These policies and procedures are driven by organizational vision and mission, and subsequent distance learning events and programs are recognized for strategic contributions and response to business needs.

FIGURE 1.1. STAGES OF ORGANIZATIONAL TECHNOLOGY CAPABILITY FOR DISTANCE LEARNING.

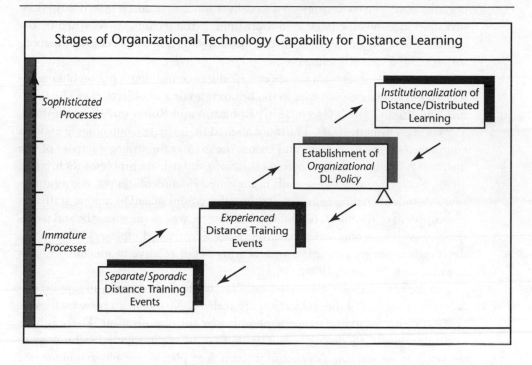

Figure 1.1 illustrates the stages of organizational technology capability for implementing strategic distance and distributed learning. Following this diagram, further explanation is provided of the various maturity levels an organization experiences and the significant and unique influence each bears on an agency's or institution's ability to effectively deliver, support, and sustain distance training efforts.

Separate/Sporadic Distance Training Events

An organization's initial attempt at distance learning often includes a single-training event, with a migration toward multiple events that are sporadically planned and separate or unknown from one sponsor (or department) to another. An event's target audience is identified, however, and individual characteristics are analyzed. The designers and developers of each distance training event define clearly the instructional goals and generally meet expectations of the participants.

In the first level of the maturation process, an organization's capability to technologically support distance and distributed learning is limited. Each distance training event is spearheaded by an individual staff member or an individual department, independent of input or collaboration from other functions in the organization. The technology used to deliver the instruction is rented, leased, or procured in some other way for a short time. If the technology is owned by the company or agency, its access is often controlled (or greatly influenced) by the sponsor(s) of the distance training event.

Research indicates that the success of distance training relies on linking intended performance outcomes to the business goals and objectives of the organization (Eskow, 1997; Green, 1997; Robinson and Robinson, 1996; Steward, 1995; and Newman, 1997). The more aligned performance outcomes are with a company's corporate mission and vision, the greater the strategic impact of the distance training event in providing solutions to business problems (Schreiber, 1996). Such alignments also result in improved documentation of an organization's distance learning activities and broader communication among staff and management of the effects of distance learning, as well as the strengths and weaknesses of various technologies to deliver distance learning. Employees begin to understand corporate education and training needs relative to specific business requirements (Steward, 1995).

In the early stages of an organization's technological capability to support distance learning, few of these objectives are realized. No link exists between the distance training event and strategic planning by the organization. There is little understanding of the strengths and weaknesses of organizational technology to deliver distance learning. Absence of a technology plan also results in uninformed and often expensive decisions regarding procurement of hardware and software to deliver distance education and training. And finally, because the distance training event occurs in relative isolation of other business activities, communication about distance learning throughout the organization is minimal, and collaboration is overlooked.

Experienced Distance Training Events

As an organization's experience increases in delivering distance training, its technological capability to support distance learning matures. The initial distance education and training events become standard practice, and replication occurs. At this stage of organizational technology capability for distance learning, a corporation or agency often forms an interdisciplinary team, and the participating members respond to staff and management inquiries and recommendations.

Members of the interdisciplinary team represent the diverse content expertise needed to enhance an organization's capabilities to provide distance learning. Consequently, the distance learning team may include one or two individuals from each of the following organizational functions: executive branch, information technology, network systems, broadcasting, communications, instructional design, and training or performance consulting. This team contributes as a core steering committee for the organization's distance learning efforts. The primary strength of the team is its ability to facilitate collaboration among diverse content experts. (See Chapter Three for discussion of the contribution of each content expert in the analysis, design, and delivery of distance training. Refer to the previous section in this chapter for further explanation of personalities of diverse expert and group dynamics of interdisciplinary distance learning teams.)

Collaboration among diverse content experts (including information systems engineers, performance consulting professionals, and executive management) is a recognizable characteristic at this level of organizational maturity. The impact of successful collaboration on distance learning ensures a higher probability that the distance training event (and subsequent distance learning programs) will yield the organization's intended outcomes to meet business needs. Robinson and Robinson (1996) explain that the phenomenon of collaborative efforts can result in the following: (a) increased accuracy of analysis, (b) effective identification and accountability for processes and procedures associated with the task or event, (c) increased investment of time and ownership in support of team effort, (d) improved diagnosis and documentation of strengths and weaknesses of task or event, and (e) development of relationships based on trust and respect. It is the significant collaboration that becomes critical to ongoing maturation by the organization for technological capability to support distance learning.

Establishment of Organizational Distance Learning Policy

The first step in establishing organizational policy and procedure for technological support of distance and distributed learning is to develop a technology plan. It is the role of the interdisciplinary distance learning team to collaboratively develop a plan that aids the organization in the identification and selection of technology to deliver distance training (Schreiber, 1996; Green, 1997).

An organization's technology plan provides a stable and predictable process to facilitate the identification and selection of appropriate distance learning delivery media. It establishes access to diverse delivery media, accounts for flexibility, and aligns utilization of organizational technology with company priorities and business objectives. (See Chapter Three for further discussion of organizational technology plans.)

Broad access to diverse distance learning technology critically affects organizational distance learning policy and procedure. It prevents rigid or demanding delivery strategies that may constrain implementation or result in missed opportunities (Cronin, 1994, p. 247). Planning for flexibility facilitates strategic acquisition of distance learning delivery tools and avoids potentially insurmountable financial commitments (Cronin, 1994, p. 247; Brown, 1997). And finally, aligning utilization of organizational technology with company priorities regarding distance training facilitates internal cooperation and collaboration and increases communication of associated business objectives. Opportunities are recognized, and innovation is embraced (Cronin, 1994).

As an organization evolves from a level of immaturity to a level of sophistication in its application and utilization of technology to deliver distance learning, it experiences a stage of transition that is pivotal to its evolutionary progress. To successfully move to the next level of technology capability for distance learning, an organization must effectively engage all members of the organization. Individuals will not buy into or support evolving distance learning policies and procedures if they lack confidence in the system, see limited pay-off, or disagree with values and concepts propagated by the core steering committee (Schreiber, 1996; Robinson and Robinson, 1996).

The following practices and processes facilitate the establishment of organizational policies for distance learning and engage staff and management support during transition (extrapolated from Robinson and Robinson, 1996; Bridges, 1988; and Moss-Kanter, 1983): (a) increase parameters within which individuals may contribute ideas and suggestions regarding technology for delivering distance training; (b) increase parameters within which individuals can make decisions regarding development and implementation of distance learning; (c) develop policies and procedures that provide accurate and timely information about commercial products, services, and current corporate technological capabilities; (d) modify work processes that inhibit broad-based collaboration across disciplines; and (e) ensure that associated administrative tasks are directly focused on processes of design, development, and delivery of the distance training events.

Institutionalization of Distance and Distributed Learning Efforts

The existence of corporate policies and procedures regarding distance training and the communication of associated business objectives facilitate the phenomenon of whole-company ownership for distance learning. Cronin identifies "*whole-company*" ownership as an organizational attribute that guides transition and growth (1994, p. 250). The corporation or agency that exhibits Stage 4 behaviors has established a distance learning identity and conducts systematic assessment of distance training events with an organizational perspective.

Traditional evaluation of distance learning includes assessment of student interaction, instructor capabilities, degree of knowledge acquisition and skills development, and overall return on investment. Evaluation of distance learning from an organizational level (or whole-company perspective) may include assessment of the following additional characteristics: learner-learner and learner-instructor interactions, learner motivation, quality assurance, business-driven performance objectives, organizational support, contributions of interdisciplinary design and implementation teams, hardware and software usability, access to multiple delivery media, impact of organizational culture on implementation of distance learning, impact of distance learning on organizational culture, organizational costs and benefits, and evidence of institutionalization of efforts. (Cronin, 1994; Newman, 1997; Steward, 1995; Schreiber, 1996).

The ultimate level of technology capability for implementing distance training is illustrated by the organization that understands the strengths and weaknesses of various delivery tools and maximizes utilization of the technology. This organization is then able to successfully institutionalize its efforts in distance and distributed learning.

Conclusion

Trainers and education specialists traditionally have looked to developments in communications technology to deliver distance learning. As is often the case with complex phenomena, however, no one solution provides a silver bullet. It appears that the most effective strategy for meeting the needs of distance education and training is to employ a variety of forms of instructional technology and electronically mediated instruction. Deciding what technology to use and how to use it effectively probably rank as the two biggest questions faced by organizations as they attempt to design delivery of distance learning.

It is recognized that many companies procure new technology but often see limited return because they do not know how to best utilize it. And for the organization that is mature in its technological capabilities, effective implementation of distance learning events may occur; however, the company wrestles with how to institutionalize its efforts so that distance training becomes part of the profile of the organization.

Designing and implementing distance training that contributes strategically to the organization requires not only a new organizational chart but often a transformation of the corporate culture itself. Maximizing utilization of technology to deliver distance and distributed learning is not dissimilar to reengineering processes in that there is a redefining of roles and responsibilities. Further, significant collaboration among diverse experts becomes critical to ongoing maturation by the organization for technological capability to support distance training.

To understand the impact that such diversity may have on the interdisciplinary efforts necessary for successful distance training, one must examine the various roles and personalities of information systems and human resource personnel involved. It is also necessary to understand corporate and government cultures, as they greatly influence policy and management issues regarding an organization's technology capability for distance learning.

Even with the availability of prescribed models for design and implementation of distance training, there is continuing difficulty on the part of employees and organizations to participate in cooperative efforts that are systematic and rational. This is due to the phenomenon of group dynamics associated with interdisciplinary teams.

Overcoming barriers to interdisciplinary efforts, however, is critical to successful implementation and institutionalization of distance training. Some strategies for facilitating and enhancing interdisciplinary efforts include the following: increased communications (vertically and horizontally within the organization), clear explanations regarding cause-and-effect, and defined standards of performance and accountability. Successful manifestation of these behaviors enhances organizational growth and technology capability for distance training.

CHAPTER TWO

CONCEPTUAL FRAMEWORKS IN DISTANCE TRAINING AND EDUCATION

Zane L. Berge

The field of distance education is experiencing a change, a change sufficient enough in scale and breadth to move us to search out new conceptual frameworks.

MORRISON AND LAUZON, 1992, P. 6

A model of instruction, training, or education is a description or prescription of a learning environment. There are dozens of models and approaches to teaching and learning. But essentially, there are two major frameworks from which to view training and education. In the first, content and knowledge determined by someone else is *transmitted* to the learner (for example, lecture, textbook, videotape). In the second, a learner *transforms* information, generates hypotheses, and makes decisions about the knowledge he or she is constructing or socially constructing through interpersonal communication with others.

Each instructor, trainer, or designer of instruction values these frameworks with different weights. Therefore, this valuation causes the design of instructional interventions used in teaching to take on characteristics common to the umbrella of guiding principles held by the designer. Of course, it is rare that any of these is used in a pure form in any training program of significance or that the instructor can articulate many of his or her underlying assumptions. Still, these overarching frameworks are found throughout teaching and learning in all contexts and with all ages of learners.

Training, Development, Education, and Leadership

Training is mainly concerned with developing the skills people use to solve problems within an already existing, well-defined system of knowledge. Education broadens understanding by persons to problem solving outside existing models and to ill-defined systems of knowledge. The development of both of these areas is important. It takes leadership and certain well developed attitudes about an area of endeavor for a person to make judgments about when it is appropriate to use an existing knowledge system or when it is more appropriate to create alternatives to traditional activities, actions, and thought processes. Often we develop a collective intelligence when dealing with solving problems that we face together, either in a training paradigm or an educational context.

Campfires, Watering Holes, and Caves

David Thornburg (n.d.) speaks of three venues for learning. For thousands of years the storytelling around the campfire has been used as a venue for persons to sit at the feet of their elders and sages to become informed. This sharing of knowledge, skills, and wisdom continues to be a critical element in teaching and learning. A large amount of training involves an information transmission model for its efficiency and effectiveness.

The watering hole is a learning space that is greatly different from the campfire. Historically, people shared information with their neighbors and travelers who happened to be there. This is often a much more informal gathering, with stimulating conversation about the news, gossip, or other mutually interesting topics. But the essence is a shared culture and social learning.

Still another venue for learning occurs when one wants to take what he or she has learned from and with others and "make sense of it." What becomes important then is the seclusion of a cave, a personal space, where one can internalize knowledge and make it one's own. These caves today may be the solitude of a walk in the woods, the kitchen table, or closing one's office door.

Transmission and Transformation Frameworks

In the case mentioned previously, in which the primary goal is to transmit the expert knowledge of one person to the more novice person, the framework is based on *positivism* (training by objectives, emphasis on competence, focus on context, and role conception as expert instructor) and *behaviorism* (a focus on behavioral changes in which a new behavioral pattern is repeated until it becomes automatic).

In the second major framework, called *constructivism* by many educators, what is thought to be critical is the active participation and reflection by the learner, while recognizing the flexible and dynamic nature of knowledge. As a part of a constructivist orientation, many educators find *social interaction* important in learning. To embrace one of these paradigms does not mean one has to nor should reject the other.

Information Transmission

The key concept is that a teacher can transmit a fixed body of information to students. Sherry explains:

> [The teacher] represents an abstract idea as a concrete image and then presents the image to the learner via a medium. The learner, in turn, perceives, decodes, and stores it. . . . The learner then develops his own image and uses it to construct new knowledge, in context, based on his own prior knowledge and abilities.
>
> (p. 3, Sherry, 1996)

Essentially, the student interacts with pre-packaged content as a response to stimuli provided by the instructor. In training, manifestations of this are approaches that are didactic, often linear, "recipe-type," and workbook-focused. This is referred to in the literature as teacher-centered because the focus is on what the teacher does in selection of the content and in the teaching styles used to get a *specific* outcome from the students. The philosophers and psychologists most often cited leading to behaviorism include Ivan Pavlov, John Watson, Edward Thorndike, B. F. Skinner, and more recently Robert Gagne, Benjamin Bloom, and Robert Mager.

Transformation (Constructivism)

Over the last five or six decades, instructional design theory has developed theory and practice incorporating principles of cognition. Constructivism covers a wide range of beliefs about cognition (Jonassen, 1991). Traditional (cognitive) constructivists, who most often cite John Dewey, Jean Piaget, Jerome Bruner, and more recently John Seely Brown (Brown, Ford, and Milner, 1989), Howard Gardner (1993), and Howard Rheingold as sources of their reasoning, emphasize individual thinking and construction of meaning. Training under this approach is more tentative, flexible, multiple-perspective, experiential, project-based, and holistic—what is often referred to as student-centered. Through the processes of assimilation and accommodation, old concepts are adapted and altered to fit a logical framework (Bentley, 1993). The resulting outcomes are not completely predictable. Joyce and Weil (1996) state that if students learn within a discipline, it is *not* so they will know exactly that discipline as known by others but rather this awareness is to help them create a way of framing the problem to be solved.

Social Constructivism

A community of learners will often influence each individual's learning through interpersonal interaction. When people work together, there may be a synergy that is created that causes a team to be more effective than the sum of the individuals' efforts. One reason may be that the production of knowledge of value to others, rather than only for personal achievement, demonstrates strong engagement of the learner (Scardamalia, 1997, p. 16). Many constructivist educators incorporate ideas regarding culture and social learning in their designs of the learning environment, with antecedents from several sources including Lev Vygotsky (1962; 1978), Albert Bandura (1971), and Allan Collins (1991). Social constructivism marries a constructivist's strong focus of the dynamic nature of knowledge with an interactionist's focus on creating understanding through requiring learners to explain, elaborate, and defend the position they hold to others. Participants interact by interpreting, evaluating, and critiquing peers' comments and by sharing information.

Varying Conditions, Methods, and Outcomes

Depending upon the specific context (conditions and environment) of learning and teaching, various methods and strategies are selected by the instructor to teach or facilitate learners to certain outcomes. There are characteristics of a learning environment that naturally lead themselves to certain teaching styles and models. For instance, early childhood educators may be particularly interested in developing models of how learners mature. Persons involved in training of adults are not as keenly interested in that particular factor but are interested in such things as prior experience of the learner and how that experience affects present training. In all cases, however, attention must be paid by persons developing the learning environment to both of these paradigms.

Teaching Methods

In general, the difference between the transmission model and the constructivist and interactionist frameworks is that the former is highly teacher-centered and the latter are student-centered approaches to learning and teaching (see Figure 2.1). Instructors have implicit or explicit personal theories of what constitutes good instruction that describes education under their usual teaching conditions.

FIGURE 2.1. TEACHING METHODS CONTINUUM.

TEACHING METHODS CONTINUUM
Teacher-focused
lecture
questioning/recitation
drill and practice
guided discovery
demonstration/modeling
discussion
collaborative learning activities
authentic learning activities
self-assessment/reflection
Student-focused

To learner-centered teachers part of teaching well means to encourage self-direction and learner-control in their students. To do this they use the spectrum of teaching methods. In Figure 2.1, I have listed selected teaching methods to show a relative relationship along a teacher-centered to student-centered continuum. I believe teachers will select teaching devices, methods, and techniques and communication/media channels that are consistent with the theoretical basis that they hold, when given the choice. Often, when teaching many facts, rules, or procedures, new constructions are not necessary and would be ineffective or at least inefficient. Appropriate times during instruction for direct (teacher-centered) instruction include the need to

- Disseminate information not readily available from texts or workbooks in appropriately sized pieces according to a teacher-determined structure
- Arouse or heighten student interest
- Review previously learned skills and knowledge
- Give feedback and corrective guidance

There are times when direct instruction is not effective, efficient, or appropriate compared to inquiry or problem-solving methods. This is because not all outcomes require responses that resemble the stimulus material. Times direct instruction may be less desirable include instances when the outcomes of instruction are to analyze, synthesize, and evaluate; when ill-defined, authentic problems are focused on; when multiple perspectives are desired; or when the content needs to be learned gradually over an extended time period (Borich, 1996, pp. 246–249, 291–293).

Different Models for Distance Training and Education

The predominant factor overarching the two philosophies of transmission and transformation in practice is the degree to which the instruction is teacher- or student-centered. As may be expected from the previous discussion, the biggest differences in various models of distance education center around the assumptions underlying the educational philosophy of the model builder. Some models are designed for industrialized or pre-packaged knowledge (Peters, 1989), and others are more flexible, customized to the individual, and organic (Bagnara, 1994).

While there are many variations of distance training mainly differing by the types of technologies used (Institute for Distance Education, 1996), basically the difference rests in the control aspect. In some models, the trainer and organization have primary control, and in others the control resides with the trainee. There is a continuum of models along a line from technologically mediated learning that supplements traditional classroom training to a model in which all teaching and learning is done with no face-to-face component. A second dimension involves whether or not the model used involves distributing instruction to groups of participants at a given place or is designed for individual participation with some type of asynchronous communication medium being used.

Issues Common to All Models

There are certain issues that need attention regardless of what model is used in distance training. Organizations wishing to bring distance education into the mainstream of their corporate culture may need to address a broad range of policy issues. These will vary from one organization to the next, but they may include

- Strategic planning
- Technological Infrastructure
- Employee rewards and incentives
- Trainer access and technical support for technology
- Trainee access and technical support for technology
- Centralization versus decentralization of technology and support
- Cost—who pays
- Evaluation
- Acknowledgment of the risk of innovation and reduction of costs to innovators

FIGURE 2.2   THE SECRET OF INSTRUCTIONAL DESIGN.

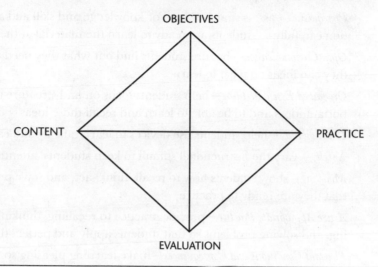

Source: Yelon, S. L. and Berge, Z. L., 1988.

Figure 2.2, The Secret of Instructional Design, shows another set of elements common to all instruction (Yelon and Berge, 1988). The idea is that regardless of the conditions, there must be alignment among the content, instructional objectives, the practice in which the trainee is encouraged to involve him or herself, and the evaluation that is used. Methods will vary according to the outcomes, conditions, and instructor's philosophy, but regardless of the methods used, these must match the practice and evaluation students receive, with all these elements at the end point of training matching the environment in which the student will be required to perform outside of the training situation.

Principles in Effective Teacher-Centered Training

Yelon, in his recent book *Powerful Principles of Instruction* (1996), identified excellent teachers as defined by such things as winning teacher awards and peer or student evaluations. He interviewed these teachers and found four common attributes. These teachers (a) were concerned about their subject matter, (b) were concerned about their students, (c) liked the job of teaching, and (d) put into practice ten powerful instructional principles. He went on to identify those instructional principles:

Meaningfulness—motivate students by helping them connect the topic to be learned to their past, present, and future

Prerequisites—assess students' level of knowledge and skill and adjust instruction carefully so students are ready to learn the material at the next level

Open Communication—be sure students find out what they need to know so they can focus on what to learn

Organized Essential Ideas—help students focus on and structure the most important ideas and to be able to learn and recall those ideas

Learning aids—help students use devices to learn quickly and easily

Novelty—vary the instructional stimuli to keep students' attention

Modeling—show students how to recall, think, act, and solve problems so that they are ready to practice

Active Appropriate Practice—provide practice to recalling, thinking, performing, and solving problems so that students apply and perfect their learning

Pleasant Conditions and Consequences—make learning pleasing so that students associate comfort with what is learned and make learning satisfying so that students keep learning and using what is learned

Consistency—make objectives, tests, practice, content, and explanation consistent so that students will learn what they need and will use what they have learned outside of the instructional setting

Compare these to the following summary of principles involved in online teaching that is overall a more constructivist learning environment (Berge, 1997).

Principles in Student-Centered Training

The essence of inquiry is when the student is personally challenged by being faced with a problem to solve, a project to complete, or a dilemma to resolve. This challenge causes the inquiry to be personally meaningful for the student, and through individual or group investigation, this curiosity leads to explicit formulation of the subject to be investigated and the process that will be used for solving the problem or project. Both the process and the tentative solutions are studied, reflected upon, and thereby improved. Through discussion and interaction with others, the students share their experiences, try out different ways of looking at their own experiences, and explore multiple perspectives and views that often conflict with their own. All this occurs while students respect and value other students' experiences and individually and socially construct new knowledge—adjusting and augmenting prior knowledge. Through continuing, first-hand experience using authentic problems and projects, reflection, reorganization of concepts and attitudes, and stimulation catalyzed by interaction with others, students generate and co-generate solutions, implement them, and build new knowledge—often discovering new lines of inquiry as well.

The instructor can provide the student with a problem or project, but often the simple giving of a problem believed by the instructor to be important does not produce the desire to know and learn within trainees necessary to motivate them during the process of inquiry. The trainee must develop a self-awareness about the personal meaning in the inquiry he or she is about to embark upon in order to sustain the drive and interest in meeting the challenge with the best individual and collaborative work possible. In an environment that contains low structure and high dialogue, that fosters trust, respect for a variety of viewpoints, flexibility, and risk-taking, students will assume responsibility for their learning and become less dependent on direct instruction from the instructor. Through such processes as application, analysis, synthesis, evaluation, and attention given directly to these experiences, more powerful ways of knowing are created, new questions are discovered, and significant learning within each student is fostered—an indication that significant teaching has occurred.

Important Factors In Technology-Mediated Training and Education

Among the important factors to consider in training is the type of *interaction* students should engage in (Moore, 1989), the *synchronicity* of that interaction when it involves interpersonal communication, and the amount *of control over the content and pace of instruction* maintained by the instructor or student. As the instructor encourages interaction, learners can become personally involved (Hackman and Walker, 1990). Such interaction is essential to effective learning. Current technology allows for very flexible communication in the training environment. The instructor is able to design training that takes place at the same or different times, and that allows trainees to participate at the same or different places.

Interaction with Content

For learning to occur either alone or in a group, the student must interact with and process the content of the course. The content cannot merely pass before students' senses but must be cognitively processed (Bower and Hilgard, 1981). Typically, in formal schooling much of the content quickly becomes "inert" (Gagne, Yekovich, and Yekovich, 1993) as it has little relevance to the life circumstances of the student and eventually becomes "lost" to retrieval. Hence, instructors, especially in business, are exploring the advantages of just-in-time learning. It appears that knowledge and skills acquired immediately prior to a need may reduce the need for retraining later.

Interpersonal Interaction. The importance of interpersonal interaction in learning is well documented (Fulford and Zhang, 1993). When students have the opportunity to interact with one another and their instructors about the content, they have the opportunity to build within themselves and to communicate a shared meaning, to make sense of what they are learning. Much learning inevitably takes place within a social context, and the process includes a mutual construction of understanding (Bruner, 1971). Interpersonal interaction offers the opportunity for the student to gain the motivational support of fellow students and instructors, develop critical judgment, and participate in problem-solving. Also, it often has the potential for other incidental learning (Chacon, 1992).

Synchronous and Asynchronous Communication

Synchronous communication occurs in real time—as in a course delivered via video or audio conferencing. All participants in the interaction must be present although not necessarily at the same physical location. Asynchronous communication among students and instructor is in some way technologically mediated and is not dependent upon the student(s) and instructor being present together at a specific time to conduct learning-teaching activities. Besides the potential convenience of students being able to work when and where they want, students can also control the pacing of instruction (Berge, 1996b).

Figure 2.3 shows selected media distributed along the dimension of a synchronous-asynchronous communication continuum and an interaction continuum. Synchronous/asynchronous continuum was chosen because while a printed textbook is clearly asynchronous and the telephone operates in real-time, there are varying degrees of rapid asynchronous communication, such as fax or email, that at times can appear as synchronous conversation.

Use of real-time and asynchronous communication channels often serve different purposes or are used in solving different instructional problems. For instance, real-time, two-way video usually is more efficient if not more effective than asynchronous discussion in team building, which may be important in such things as forming common language, indoctrination into the culture of the organization, and more immediate feedback to the instructor from the trainees. On the other hand, asynchronous computer conferencing offers advantages for such purposes as allowing participants time to reflect upon responses to questions posed (Berge, 1994).

FIGURE 2.3. MEDIA SELECTION BASED UPON CHARACTERISTICS SHOWING TYPES OF INTERACTION AND COMMUNICATION MODE OF SELECTED MEDIA.

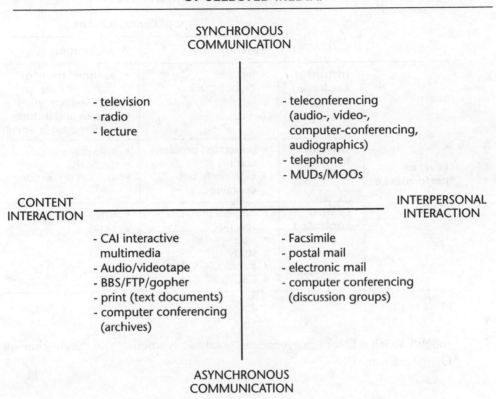

Teacher vs. Student Control

The teacher control level of performance in Table 2.1 is didactic, completely guided, generally deductive, introductory, and informing. It is similar to Bloom's "knowledge" category or Gagne's "know." The guided learner-control level is generally inductive, guided, drill-practice-apply, and somewhat contrived. It is similar to what Bloom would call "application" or Gagne (Gagne, Briggs and Wager, 1992) would categorize as "use." The learner control level of skill is inductive, experimental, problem-centered, culminating, realistic, and complete. It corresponds

TABLE 2.1.   TECHNIQUES (AND DEVICES) FOR DIFFERENT LEVELS OF COGNITIVE SKILLS USING SYNCHRONOUS AND ASYNCHRONOUS COMMUNICATION.

		Type of Communication	
		Synchronous	Asynchronous
Level of performance	**Instructor controlled**	• lecture • demonstration	• assigned readings (hard- or softcopy) • audio/video taped • demos and lectures • mail (postal or email)
	Guided learner controlled	• annotated problem-solving • case study/self-contained	• role play • tutorials • guided simulations
	Learner controlled	• original problem-solving • open-ended case study • interactive video • CBI	• open-ended case study

roughly to what Bloom categorizes as "analysis, synthesis," and "evaluation" or Gagne calls "find."

Changing Roles of Students, Instructors, Curriculum, and Organizations

Given the demographic, social, and economic reasons for desiring distance or distributed training today and the higher-order performance outcomes expected of participants, there is support for instruction that is technologically mediated. Distance education is not new. A major reason distance training is getting a second look now by trainers and educators is the ability of the technology to add value in the speed of two-way interactive among participants and between participants and the instructor.

But shifting to a distance or distributed learning environment often precipitates significant changes along all dimensions of training (Berge and Collins, 1995a). For example, shifting from a teacher-centered to a student-centered orientation usually means one must "let go of hierarchical politics" and forces one's hand on the issue of empowerment (Finney, 1997, p. 69).

Table 2.2 (Avis, 1993; Berge, 1996a; Raggatt, 1993; Reigeluth, 1997; Symes, 1995; Wilson, Teslow, and Osman-Jouchoux, 1995) summarizes some of the different characteristics in a teacher-centered or student-centered environment. Since distance education using many of the two-way communication technologies that

TABLE 2.2. SELECTED FACTORS DISTINGUISHING THEORIES AND PHILOSOPHIES UNDER THE DIFFERENT EDUCATIONAL PARADIGMS.

Factor	Transmission	Transforming
	• centralized • early differentiation/ selection • standardization • mass production, long production runs providing economies of scale • small range of products • fixed automation • centralized planning, bureaucratic, hierarchic organization, vertical integration • specialized division of labor • workforce mostly full-time • lay-offs and turnover provide flexibility/ economies, labor viewed as variable cost • direct labor costs tightly controlled • arms-length outside purchasing based on competitive pricing, many suppliers • no supplier training • centralized control	• decentralized • late differentiation/ selection • specialization • short production runs for specialized markets • wide variety of products • flexible automation • intelligent organization, decentralized decision making, flatter hierarchies, partial vertical integration • multi-skilled workers operating in teams, job rotation, few job classifications • smaller core of full-time workers plus part-time, temporary, and contract workers providing flexibility • core workforce regarded as an investment, management seeks to reduce turnover • economics through just-in-time production and greater reliance on buying in outside services as required • outside purchasing based on price, quality, technology, fewer suppliers • suppliers may receive training • autonomy with accountability
Nature of how the organization does business		

(continued)

TABLE 2.2. (CONTINUED).

Factor	Transmission	Transforming
Nature of learning environment	• one-way • teachers having total control of the teaching environment • just-in-case • cultural uniformity • education and training completed during teens • hierarchical • one-way communications • compartmentalization • CEO as "king" • mass production • standardization • bureaucratic organization • autocratic decision making • conformity • parts-oriented • autocratic • maximal division of labor	• two-way; many-to-many • teacher relinquishing some control to student as learner • just-in-time • cultural diversity • life-long education and training • non-hierarchical • networking • holism • customer as "king" • specialized production • customization • team-based organization • shared decision making • diversity • process-oriented • democratic • minimal division of labor
Nature of learning outcomes	• individual intelligence • single-skilled • restricted range of skills required by individuals • prescribed tasks	• both individual and collective intelligence (teamwork) • multi-skilled • wider range of skills, includes interpersonal and communication skills • stochastic tasks
Nature of curriculum	• rigid subject divisions • fragmented • limited provision, on-the-job training predominates, some specialist/technical training for specialist workers • rigid • task standardization	• integrated core studies • integrated • on and off-the-job training, substantial off-the-job training in new technologies for core workers • flexible • task variety
Students' role	• work is closely supervised; teacher directed • adversarial relationships • usually individual effort	• work autonomously; self-directed • cooperative relationships • usually group work or team work, collaborative

(continued)

TABLE 2.2. (CONTINUED).

Factor	Transmission	Transforming
Teachers' role	• communicator of a fixed body of information • having total autonomy • information is a scarce resource doled out by teacher • supervision • controlling complexity and simplifying content for initial consumption by novices • usually individual faculty member designs, develops, and delivers the course • focus on delivering instruction	• facilitator of learning • activities that can be broadly assessed • information is unlimited resource available to students and teachers alike • coordination • managing the complexity and helping novices find their way around it • team approach in designing, developing (e.g., computer author; video producer; site facilitator • focus on access to learning resources

have emerged for distance training use the past several decades is more student-centered, the following descriptions are couched in terms of shifting from a transmission to a transformation model. It should be noted that as described previously, there is need for a balance between the two, and it is especially important that the conditions and outcomes are considered when deciding the methods to employ in a particular learning system.

Changing Students

As the learning environment becomes more technology-rich, trainers and educators can encourage and guide students in using available information resources toward appropriate, collaborative work with other students (Twigg, 1994). Given this, tomorrow's students may learn in ways more like today's apprentices and researchers, developing qualities of increased independence and self-reliance.

It is likely that there will be more technologically mediated interaction and less face-to-face contact between learners and instructors in the corporate training and educational institutions of the future. Twigg (1994) considers one of the explicit goals of the design of technology-rich learning environments to be that students will learn more independently, using materials that meet their own individual learning needs, abilities, preferences, and interests, and spend more time in small discussion groups or working on collaborative projects with their peers (when appropriate).

Changing Instructors

Instructors often seem to take the attitude of "prove that technology will work for me, in my classroom, and I may give it a try (if I have time)." While those persons whose mission it is to promote technology in the classroom try their best to demonstrate its capabilities to trainers and managers, success takes, as we will discuss later, support and direction from the highest levels of the organization. Integrating technology into course delivery involves shifting to unfamiliar materials, creating new types of assignments, and inventing new ways to assess learning (Ehrmann, 1995) often using new techniques and devices. While it is almost impossible for an individual instructor to find the time and resources to implement the changes needed, instructors must take a more proactive approach to changing their roles and teaching style. Yet as the role of the instructor changes from expert and controller to facilitator and coach, the teaching-learning process can move out of the direct control of the instructor, an often painful and disconcerting change, so much so that veteran trainers might resist the technologies that allow more natural learning and that can accomplish important goals for students (Jette, 1994).

Technology can help instructors manage their most valuable resource—their time. They can have virtual meetings with students, extend their office hours to times convenient to both parties in many cases, or allow students who have missed classes to review materials, online notes, or demonstrations. This "time-shifting" permits learning and instruction to take place even when the teacher and student are not in the same place nor necessarily communicating at the same time (Klaphaak, 1994).

Many instructors are concerned about changing their teaching methods as in most cases the instructor alone can no longer develop all the learning materials and activities in a technology-rich learning environment. It takes a team of people, usually with the instructor (subject-matter expert) directing and guiding the team. While frightening in some ways, this is analogous to a model of using technology that is quite old in training and development. Even though instructors *can* write, most of them do not develop their own textbooks, videos and so on. Why should developing multimedia be different?

Changing Curriculum

Changes to curricula can be facilitated by a technologically rich learning environment. For example, Ehrmann (1995) points out that instructors are more inclined to ask students to "do it over again." When technology lessens the mechanical effort, the instructor is free to use models that permit students to edit, revise, and try again—that is, to take a more authentic approach to problem-solving than before

(Berge and Collins, 1995b). Example problems can become messy and use more realistic demands for calculations. When using project-and problem-based learning, technology helps the problem to be situated in context(s), and students can then work in stages to plan, draft, discuss, redraft, and submit. Each of these stages offers a chance for trainees to rethink, expand, re-articulate and generally improve upon their problem-solving efforts. In this way technology may enable important changes in the curriculum and program without changing the content.

Word processors, databases, spreadsheets, and communication and presentation packages are tools enabling students to plan and revise complex projects, conduct team discussions, and gather resources from around the world. It is when a technology-rich environment exists across all problem-solving and project areas available to be used in a seamless way throughout training that the power of technology to change the curriculum will be realized. When trainees begin to practice what experts in the discipline do each day, the true nature of curriculum change due to technology will be seen.

Changing Organizations

In far too many cases, managers and leaders in the organization have not examined the role technology plays in organizational change—at least not in the strategic planning for applying technology to the problems of changing learning and teaching (Ehrmann, 1995; Twigg, 1994). Using technology for place-based and distance teaching is generally brought about by the efforts of individuals for individual assignments or for an individual course. It will take more of a reengineering effort on the part of human development managers at the highest levels to have their organizations reflect ongoing technological and socio-cultural changes.

Conclusions

Instructors have implicit or explicit ideas about epistemology and about underlying psychology. These notions affect their pedagogical philosophy. Still, when given a choice instructors usually select the more comfortable way of teaching to meet the instructional goals and objectives. By comfortable, I mean he or she will choose the conceptually familiar, "tried-and-true" methods, techniques, and teaching style. The challenge is to find the right mix of teaching methods under the conditions presented to help to learner meet the outcomes desired. The interactions planned by the designer of instruction need to combine a teacher-centered focus (with content and sometimes with the teacher) and more student-centered approaches (interaction with content, sometimes with the teacher, and more often with peers).

This designing needs to be done regardless of whether one of the conditions is that the learning is to occur at a distance or be distributed.

The overarching frameworks for teaching and learning involve a learner constructing knowledge through someone else determining what is important to know, at other times through their individual constructing, or from social construction with other persons. It is the balance of these avenues for learning that is important. We each have preferred styles of learning or teaching (for those of us who teach). Regardless of those preferences, we can not expect effective or efficient construction of meaning to take place if there is a mismatch between the instructional goals, content, methods, and evaluation and the practice, activities, and interpersonal interactions planned for learning.

Historically, distance education has been defined as a way of providing access to instruction when students were physically and temporally apart from the instructor. Students at a distance often worked in isolation on pre-packaged materials, independent of faculty and other students. However, that conception of the boundaries of distance education is too limited and limiting. Information technology allows access to a rich, interactive distance training experience which can in some cases exceed the interactivity in a traditional classroom (Boettcher and Conrad, 1997). The proper mix of various distance training models by the instructional design collapses boundaries to learning that have existed. Boundaries of time and space have no meaning. Other more subtle boundaries are evaporating too, such as accreditation, geographic monopolies by universities or by regional units within an organization, and methods of assessment—indeed, the classroom itself.

Many of the barriers that have previously isolated training and education from the rest of the workplace and society are being dismantled. We need to develop ways to think about learning and the infrastructure to support new interactional frameworks of learning in the changing business environments that exist today and will exist tomorrow (Levin, 1997). One challenge may be to discover what models of support are needed to promote and expand the use of these frameworks by a very diverse set of learners. It is with this in mind that the cases involving distance training found in this book are provided for your analyses and reflection.

CHAPTER THREE

INSTRUCTIONAL DESIGN OF DISTANCE TRAINING

Deborah A. Schreiber

This chapter describes a systems processing model for developing and implementing distance and distributed education and training. The model employs a reiterative process of analysis and design and is derived from the theories of instructional systems development and conceptual frameworks of learning. The *guiding principles* presented in the Preface represent an outline of this instructional design model for distance training.

The goal of the proposed model is to maximize utilization of technology and institutionalize an organization's distance learning efforts. Instructional needs and performance outcomes of a distance training event or program are defined by business goals and objectives. The impact of organizational culture, as well as internal corporate dynamics, are also discussed within the model.

The author distinguishes here between a distance training event and a distance training program. A distance training program is not a program of instruction, such as a curriculum of courses or modules. A distance training program refers to an organizational process, consisting of policies and procedures specific to departments' or divisions' functions and responsibilities. In contrast, a distance training event does represent an independent course or module. The distance training event is often an isolated and separate delivery exercise.

Introduction

A century of dramatic change and innovation in organizational and instructional hardware and software has resulted in telecommunications and satellite technologies that are poised to support significant improvement in the interactivity, collaboration, and real-time delivery of distance education and training. Yet even with such promise, not all organizations are successful. While some companies and agencies boast an anticipated 1200 percent increase in distance training over the next five years (Picard, 1996), others lament their distance learning experience with a been there, done that attitude (Green, 1997).

Green (1997) acknowledges that technology-laden distance learning is neither simple nor inexpensive. Whereas onsite classroom learning requires trained instructors, strong lesson plans, and ongoing feedback to students, distance and distributed education and training requires all this plus expert design and development for using instructional technology, critical-path planning, and an accurate timeline to ensure proper, coordinated, and effective implementation (Piskurich, 1997). Unsuccessful distance training events mercilessly reflect lack of preparation or unfocused or mis-directed instructional objectives.

To realize the full potential of distance learning, designers and developers must apply an analytical approach to the design, selection, and utilization of distance learning media and methodology (Pisel, 1995; Schreiber, 1996). The availability and utilization of information and communication technologies alone are not enough for distance learning and distance training to succeed (Visser, 1997). It is a clear understanding of the instructional needs of the training program that drives effective selection of instructional media, appropriately chosen instructional methodologies, and ultimately successful implementation of distance learning.

An organization that finds its initial distance learning efforts result in less than desired outcomes can determine areas for improvement by considering the following phenomena. Sometimes an instructional analysis has not occurred. Content information may have been presented in a disorganized fashion rather than selected, structured, and sequenced appropriately (Visser, 1997). If an instructional analysis has occurred, instructional methodologies may have been designed that are inconsistent with the capabilities of the selected delivery tool (Green, 1997). Further, trainers may have been reluctant (or unable) to use the new technologies (Picard, 1996).

Often times content applications have not been defined by an organization's business goals and objectives. This results in a distance learning event that may be effectively implemented (from a procedural perspective) but contributes minimally to an organization's strategic gains. Finally, organizational technology and instructional personnel may have been treated as marginal costs rather than core costs (Green, 1997). This results in front-end costs that may significantly exceed expectation (Picard, 1996) and produce less-than-desired overall return on investment. Whatever the specific causes, initial distance learning results can be dismal when critical components of the process are overlooked or misunderstood.

Application of Instructional Systems Development to Distance Training

Distance and distributed education and training represent a process composed of multiple and diverse elements. These elements or components are associated with several categories, including the learner, instructor, learning environment, instructional delivery technology, and the culture of the organization providing the training. To understand the instructional needs of a distance training event or program, it is necessary to understand the primary components of the distance learning process itself. Further, as an organization strives to design and implement distance training that contributes strategically to the institution or agency, it is necessary to define instructional needs relative to performance outcomes and achievement of business goals and objectives.

Instructional Systems Development (ISD)

Over the years, researchers have advocated the use of a systems processing approach to analyze and design instruction. Dick and Carey (1994), Gagne, Briggs and Wager (1992) and Patrick (1992) represent just a few. The Instructional Systems Development (ISD) approach provides a strategy for accounting for all the components of an instructional process, as well as explaining the role each component plays within a given instructional event or program (Dick and Carey, 1996).

Applying the systems processing approach of ISD to the development and delivery of distance and distributed education and training provides a strategy for understanding the roles of the student located at a remote site and the instructor designing materials to be delivered at a distance over some technical medium. A systems processing strategy enables investigation of the relationships among various elements of the process, including, in addition to the student and instructor, the learning environment (for example, site planning for a satellite broadcast, or desktop access), the instructional technology (compressed video or Internet), and culture of the institution or agency (including level of organizational technology capability for providing distance training). Employing a systems approach, identifying all the components, and determining the exact contribution of each to the outcome ensures a stronger, more effective distance training effort (Moore and Kearsley, 1996).

The application of ISD to distance and distributed learning strengthens the design and development of distance training because it enables the instructional designers and content specialists to (a) focus on what the learner at a distance is to learn, (b) become aware of and remain alert to the interactivity between students and instructor, as well as the hardware and software used for delivery, and (c) replicate effective distance training instructional events to meet business goals and objectives of the organization (Dick and Carey, 1996; Moore and Kearsley, 1996). The use of an ISD approach discourages the designer from trying to create instruction for a telecommunication or satellite technology delivery medium prior to completing an analysis of what it is to be taught and how. The designer who employs a systems approach sets up a checks-and-balances system that ensures that the instruction created is strengthened by the technology chosen to deliver it at a distance.

Instructional Systems Development represents a systems processing approach to the analysis, design, development, implementation and evaluation (ADDIE) of education and training. The ADDIE process is a reiterative phenomenon that when applied to distance and distributed education and training facilitates procedural review of design and delivery of instruction at a distance.

ADDIE and Distance Training

The application of ISD to distance training facilitates a customization of the ADDIE process. The activities and tasks associated with analysis, design, development, implementation, and evaluation of instruction are tailored to address the specific characteristics of distance and distributed learning. For example, as the ISD process is applied to business-driven distance and distributed learning, planning of distance training events includes not only instructional analysis but also organizational analysis and determination of business goals and objectives. Performance outcomes become identified by operational business needs, as well as instructional or procedural requirements.

The design and development phases of the ISD process applied to distance learning include preparation of appropriate instructional events and instructional methodologies consistent with the selected delivery tools. Instructional designers and content experts apply conceptual frameworks of learning at this stage to determine how content information and knowledge will be transmitted and transformed by the learner. Strengths and weaknesses of technology delivery tools are reviewed; availability and access to technology is determined; and accommodation is made to the organizational (or departmental function) technology plan.

As the processes of design and development progress, a *transitioning* occurs that moves the designer from instructional analysis and design of instructional events to development of instructional methodology and distance learning delivery strategies. Flowcharts are used to illustrate distance education and training teaching and learning activities. Instructional materials are then developed and incorporated to facilitate effective implementation of the distance training event or program.

The implementation process for delivering distance and distributed learning successfully relies on the contributions of an interdisciplinary team and organizational support for continuation and maintenance of the effort. The distance training team (or Core Steering Committee) can facilitate mutual respect and ownership among multiple experts within the organization for successful implementation. Delivery of the distance training event or program becomes stable and predictable but not inflexible. Organizational policies and procedures begin to develop, and recognition of distance learning by the institution or agency (as a whole) occurs. Strategic contributions result from the distance training events, and implementation efforts become institutionalized.

The evaluation process of distance and distributed learning includes both formative and summative assessments. Formative evaluations occur repeatedly and focus primarily on the learner, instructor, learning environment, delivery technology, and organizational culture. The inter-relatedness of these elements is constantly studied and the cause-and-effect accounted for. Summative evaluation determines the overall strengths and weaknesses of the distance training effort.

Employing a systems approach to design and deliver distance training ensures a stronger, more effective effort. For this reason an instructional design model has been created to guide planning and preparation of distance training that tailors the primary processes of analysis, design, development, implementation, and evaluation to providing successful business-driven distance and distributed learning.

Instructional Design Model for Distance Training (IDM-DT)

Figure 3.1 illustrates a model of instructional design for development and implementation of distance training. This model manifests a systems processing approach to distance and distributed learning. The purpose of this model is to identify the organization's business goals and objectives, identify performance outcomes that contribute to these goals, identify distance and distributed instructional events and instructional methodologies which facilitate performance change, select the most appropriate technological tool to deliver the distance training, and

FIGURE 3.1. INSTRUCTIONAL DESIGN MODEL FOR DISTANCE TRAINING [IDM-DT].

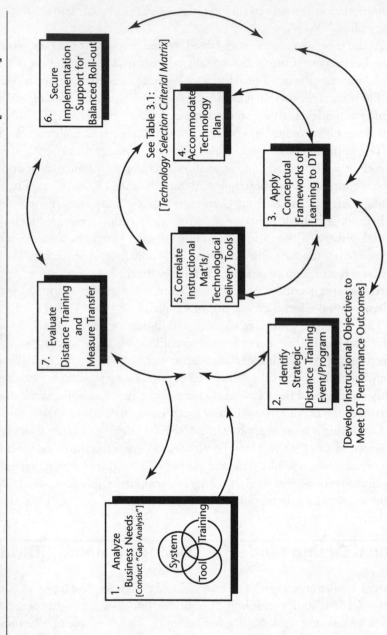

The goal of the proposed instructional design model for distance training is to maximize utilization of technology and institutionalize an organization's distance learning efforts. Instructional needs and performance outcomes of a distance learning event or program are defined by business goals and objectives. The impact of organizational culture, as well as internal corporate dynamics, are also considered within the model.

engage organizational support for ongoing maintenance and service. The ultimate outcomes of the instructional design model are maximum utilization of technology and institutionalization of an organization's distance training efforts.

The Instructional Design Model for Distance Training (IDM-DT) correlates instructional strategy, delivery technology, and desired performance outcomes. The model is driven by an initial "gap analysis" (to determine business needs), followed by identification of associated performance objectives that make strategic contributions to the organization. The IDM-DT provides a methodology for meeting the demands of distance training instructional event(s) through applying conceptual frameworks of learning, using selection criteria to identify effective technology delivery tools, and designing instructional materials consistent with the strengths of the delivery tools. The impact of organizational culture and internal corporate dynamics is also addressed.

Following is a discussion of the Instructional Design Model for Distance Training. It represents an eight-step reiterative process that provides a model for development and implementation of distance and distributed education and training. The eight steps or categories of tasks include (a) analyze business needs, (b) identify *strategic* distance training events and programs, (c) apply conceptual frameworks of learning to distance training, (d) develop and accommodate (organizational) *technology plan,* (e) correlate distance learning instructional materials to technology delivery tools, (f) secure implementation support, (g) implement a balanced rollout strategy, and (h) evaluate distance learning processes and measure transfer.

The potential of the IDM-DT to positively impact delivery of distance learning within an institution or agency is enhanced significantly with participation of an organizational team. This team, sometimes referred to as a Distance Learning Core Steering Committee, is comprised of education and performance experts, information systems engineers, communications professionals, and executive managers. Team dynamics and the internal corporate interface will be discussed further as part of the concepts associated with developing an organizational technology plan and securing implementation support for distance learning at an organizational level.

Analyze Business Needs

The first step of the instructional design model for effective design and development of distance training (see Figure 3.1) is an analysis of business goals and objectives of the organization. Successful distance training often is defined by the strategic contribution it makes to an organization. Such contributions are measured against specific business needs.

Accurate identification of a company or agency's business needs and determination of whether distance training can provide a solution requires several questions to be answered. First, is the initial crisis or organizational *alert!* for distance learning related to a systems problem, a problem with some organizational tool, or a specific training or performance need? Second, if the recognized problem is identified as a need for performance change, will the change occur through education and training for increased knowledge and skill, improved execution of a task, or attitudinal change? Finally, if education and training for enhanced performance is the answer to the organizational problem, it must be determined whether such activities can occur effectively at a distance.

In an attempt to identify business needs of an organization and the potential for distance training to address these needs, the following tasks are helpful: (a) conduct an organizational needs analysis, (b) determine if a gap exists between what is operationally and what should be (or what is desired) within the agency or institution, and upon completion of a gap analysis (c) confirm primary business goals and objectives of the organization relative to desired performance change.

The first analysis, an organizational needs analysis, integrates collection and evaluation of data to identify and confirm specific organizational traits and characteristics. A number of techniques and instruments are employed to collect organizational data. Live interviews may be conducted, or self-administered self-paced surveys may be distributed. Multiple levels of staff and managers are engaged in the data collection process. An intended outcome of organizational needs analysis is the identification and confirmation of documented processes and procedures within the agency or institution, as well as any unseen patterns of structure that influence individual and organizational behavior (Senge, 1994). This structure may be unofficial (undocumented) processes and procedures which represent "the *real way* things get done in the company."

The next process of analysis includes a gap-analysis. A *gap-analysis* employs live interviews and self-administered survey instruments to determine whether inconsistencies exist between what is operationally and what should be within the organization. An *operational* measure may include production levels, product reliability, fixed and variable costs, gross margins of ROI, and response to customer service. An ultimate objective of gap-analysis is to identify what performances actually occur throughout the organization and compare this to the performances necessary to meet specific business needs.

Robinson and Robinson (1996) describe the use of Performance Relation Maps to compare current staff behaviors and the related operational results to desired (although not yet attained) business goals and objectives. The business needs of an organization are defined by the gap between what currently is and what should be, as stated in the business goals and objectives. An organization's vision and mission statements may be used to identify a corporation's or agency's business goals and objectives.

The final stage of analysis in Step One of the IDM-DT is defined by confirmation of an organization's primary business goals and objectives. Once confirmed, this analysis focuses on the significance of business goals and objectives in identifying appropriate performance change to facilitate organizational improvement and growth. Effective resources for data to confirm an organization's business goals and objectives and to confirm the potential for performance change to facilitate improvement include (a) key individuals who work with clients and are directly responsible for attaining business goals (Robinson and Robinson, 1996) and (b) a variety of internal and external documents provided by the client organization or industry (for example an organization's Strategic Plan, customer demographics reports, an organization's operating statements, the information system's threeyear technology plan, an organization's past and current task force activities, and government and industry standards and economics projections) (Robinson and Robinson, 1996; Senge, 1994).

Identify Strategic Distance Training Events and Programs

Strategic contributions to an organization are those which engage a company to work smarter, innovate faster, and ultimately perform stronger than the competition. To ensure that distance training contributes strategically, distance learning performance outcomes must meet the business needs of the organization. At this stage in the systems processing model for designing and developing distance training, it is necessary to determine whether training is, in fact, an effective solution to improving performance and meeting the business needs of the organization, and whether such training can be delivered successfully at a distance to realize performance outcomes.

Step Two of the instructional design model for developing distance training includes two primary tasks: (a) identifying business-driven performance outcomes that may contribute strategically to an organization and (b) conducting a cost-benefit analysis to determine the potential return-on-investment (ROI) of distance training to attain the identified performance outcomes.

A performance outcome is a detailed description of what the learner will be able to do upon completion of a learning event (Dick and Carey, 1996). A learning (or instructional) event is the arrangement of external activities to engage and support the internal processes of learning (Gagne, 1975). An instructional event is manifested by a description of pre-instructional activities, one or more instructional methodologies employed to present information, what the students do with the content information received, and how performance is tested. (Note: Design and development of instructional events occurs in Step Three of the IDM-DT process.)

A cost-benefit analysis is recommended to determine the potential ROI of the distance training instructional event in attaining the identified performance outcomes. Costs include core costs, as well as marginal costs. Core costs are the costs associated with doing business and are identified and budgeted accordingly. Marginal costs represent non-documented overhead and are embedded informally in other budgets. Benefits may be avoidance of lost productivity, as well as strategic gains from just-in-time information. (See Step Four of the IDM-DT for further discussion of costs and organizational technology plans.)

Following are some recommended strategies for (a) identification and development of business-driven performance outcomes and (b) implementation of a related cost-benefit analysis. It is strongly suggested at this stage to engage a small group of organizational managers, training professionals, content experts, and end-users or members of the target audience to complete the following tasks. (The following discussion results from review of related research by Alessi and Trollop, 1991; Dick and Carey, 1996; Robinson and Robinson, 1996; Schreiber, 1996; and Senge, 1994).

Identification and Development of Business-Driven Performance Outcomes

1. Write down (on individual sheets of paper or one large poster-board) the business need(s) identified from previous organizational and gap analyses; define each business need in operational or measurable terms (such as productivity levels, product reliability, and gross ROI);
2. Discuss driving forces behind business needs;
3. List past and current training and non-training strategies used in an attempt to meet these needs;
4. Identify implications for performance improvement as envisioned by clients, instructional designers, content specialists, and performance consultants;
5. Brainstorm to identify the behaviors of staff and managers that would contribute to improving performance and fulfilling the identified business need(s); content specialists, subject matter experts and designers may need to conduct task analyses and analysis of processes and procedures within the organization to identify these behaviors; examine external forces (outside the immediate function or organization) that may influence behavioral change or performance improvement; do not eliminate any suggested behaviors at this stage;
6. Sort through the stated behaviors and select those that most efficiently and effectively contribute to fulfilling the stated business need(s);

7. Select indicators of these identified behaviors; *indicators* are demonstrated skills and knowledge or exhibited behaviors indicative of specific attitudes;
8. Incorporate each indicator into a statement of what the learner will do upon completion of the distance training event or program; and finally,
9. Evaluate the resulting statement(s) for clarity and their relationship to the initial business goal or objective and/or business need.

Conducting a Cost-Benefit Analysis for Distance Training. A cost-benefit analysis is recommended to determine the potential ROI of distance training in attaining the identified performance outcomes. Costs and benefits of both hard dollar savings and strategic benefits should be included in the analysis. The following tips have been developed (from field experiences) to aid in the justification of identified costs:

- Document the financial and business objectives of the project
- Develop, as appropriate, instructional and delivery strategies that address the objectives
- Analyze distance delivery systems (stand-alone, intranet/web-based, asynchronous, live interactive distance training, one-way video two-way audio distance training)
- Analyze current operational expenses
- Relate the financial results of the analysis to the business objectives
- Account for total travel costs
- Examine productivity savings
- Estimate strategic gains
- Do not over-analyze

Apply Conceptual Frameworks of Learning to Distance Training

To develop and execute instructional events that successfully facilitate attainment of distance learning performance objectives, a designer must plan an effective instructional strategy that reinforces an identified model of learning. An instructional strategy primarily describes how content information will be presented and what the learner will do with it. A teacher-led instructional methodology may be used, or an individual, self-paced methodology may be determined to be the stronger instructional strategy.

Essentially there are two frameworks from which to view education and training at a distance. Berge explains that in the first framework (see Chapter Two), content and knowledge determined by someone else is transmitted to the learner. In the second framework, a learner transforms information, generates hypotheses, and makes decisions about the knowledge he or she is constructing or socially constructing through interpersonal communication with others (Berge). Successful distance training occurs when instructional events are consistent with the characteristics of the selected learning model.

Step Three of the Instructional Design Model for Distance Training focuses on the design and development of instructional events that are effective in facilitating learning at a distance. To ensure that an instructional event is consistent with the characteristics of the selected learning model, however, an instructional analysis is recommended. An instructional analysis facilitates effective design and development of instructional events to facilitate mastery of identified performance outcomes. The following paragraphs describe the process of instructional analysis, followed by a description of the characteristics of effective instructional events for distance training.

Implementation of Instructional Analysis for Design of Strategic Distance Training Instructional Events. The goal of instructional analysis is to develop primary instructional objectives which facilitate mastery of the business-driven performance outcomes. Instructional objectives are statements of what the learner will do with some level of proficiency. Dick and Carey (1996) recognize three primary strategies for instructional analysis: hierarchical analysis, procedural analysis, and cluster analysis. Hierarchical analysis identifies primary intellectual goals and describes subordinate knowledge and skills accordingly. Procedural analysis identifies psychomotor goals and describes sequential, subordinate tasks. Cluster analysis identifies verbal information goals and categorizes the subordinate terms and vocabulary.

An instructional analysis of business-driven performance outcomes is similar to the type of instructional analysis conducted by educators to determine educational outcomes. This process examines the following traits of associated content information: (a) sequencing of concepts, (b) size of instructional module(s) or activities, (c) style or mode of presentation, and (d) types of examples used to illustrate ideas (Gagne, 1975; Patrick, 1992; Dick and Carey, 1996). The sequencing of concepts is determined by the type of reasoning intended; a learner who progresses in thinking from general to specific ideas experiences deductive reasoning. This is in contrast to inductive reasoning whereby the learner begins to construct generalizations from individual, specific examples. The size of the content modules depends on audience prerequisite skill levels, motivation, and experience with delivery technologies. The style or mode of presentation of content information may range from expository to discovery, including tutoring, drill and practice, games, role-play, problem-solving, or discovery labs (respectively). And examples and non-examples may be identified to reinforce learning.

Following is a set of activities that are helpful in implementing instructional analysis of business-driven distance training performance outcomes (this discussion results from review of related research by Alessi and Trollip, 1991; Berge, 1994; and Dick and Carey, 1996):

1. List on paper the business-driven performance outcome(s) identified previously;
2. Identify a primary instructional goal that facilitates mastery of the identified business-driven performance outcome; determine whether the instructional goal represents development of an intellectual or psychomotor skill, completion of procedural task, or categorization of verbal information;
3. Describe target audience; identify dominant learning style, prerequisite skill levels, motivation and experience with delivery technologies; describe size of audience, remote site locations, and access to hardware and software for distance delivery of instruction;
4. Apply appropriate instructional analysis techniques: hierarchical, procedural, or cluster analysis (or some combination); flowchart or map subordinate and coordinate relationships among knowledge, skills, and tasks associated with the primary instructional goal;
5. Discuss the following questions embedded in each type of instructional analysis:
   - Hierarchical analysis: what must the participant already know or be able to do in order to learn subordinate knowledge and develop subordinate skills to ultimately attain the intellectual skill and perform the intended outcome?
   - Procedural analysis: what would the learner have to do in this step in order to progress closer to completing the final intended task?
   - Cluster analysis: what verbal (or written) information is needed by the participant to learn the categories of knowledge necessary for performance of the intended outcome? What rules or discriminations are appropriate for categorizations?
6. Examine strengths and weaknesses of various instructional methodologies (such as lectures, role-play and discovery labs); discuss how to teach to facilitate learning and attainment of instructional goal(s); and finally,
7. Brainstorm to identify learning activities that facilitate student-student collaboration, student-student and student-instructor interaction, flexibility in communication (synchronous and asynchronous), and locus of control over content and pace of instruction.

An instructional analysis identifies the instructional methodologies most conducive to participant prerequisite skills, motivational level, and experience with technology. An instructional analysis is a procedure that, when driven by business goals and objectives, identifies and confirms the knowledge, skills, and attitudes required to master strategic distance learning performance objectives.

Characteristics of Instructional Events for Distance Training.

Prior to designing successful instructional events, the instructional analysis is conducted to determine how content information may be selected, structured, sequenced, and presented to the learner in a manner consistent with his or her dominant learning style (Visser, 1997). For example, an individual may learn more effectively through visual interaction rather than aural stimuli. Such information strengthens the subsequent design of instructional events and related instructional materials to meet the learning needs of the audience member. In this example, a teaching strategy would be employed which utilizes models and diagrams (rather than lectures or audiotapes) to teach the content.

Instructional events can be thought of as having three primary components: an introduction to the instruction, a body of activity, and a conclusion to the learning experience (Alessi and Trollip, 1991). The introduction describes pre-instructional activities and sets the frame-of-reference for learning. Pre-instructional activities may establish motivational level of participants or engage participants in prerequisite skill development. The frame of reference for learning may be established through the use of an advanced organizer or demonstration of performance outcomes. The introduction of the instructional event sets learner expectations and identifies protocol and procedures for participation in instructional activities.

The body of an instructional event can be thought of as containing five features: (a) presentation of content information, (b) guidance of the learner, (c) elicitation of learner input and response, (d) providing feedback, and (e) evaluation of mastery of business-driven performance objectives. The presentation of content information may be defined by instructional methodology or a specific instructional learning objective. For example, if the instructor is teaching a skill, he or she may model completion of the task. Respectively, if the instructor is facilitating learning verbal information, he or she may present rules and examples of discrimination or provide other nonverbal information (Alessi and Trollip, 1991; Dick and Carey, 1996).

Guiding the learner and eliciting learner input and response is often defined by instructor-led activities although guided discovery is also an effective instructional strategy. Once the participant in the distance learning event observes the presentation of information or experiences in some way transmission of content, he or she may respond. Depending on the instructional materials, learners may be engaged to answer questions about factual information, apply rules and principles to solve problems, or practice procedural tasks (Alessi and Trollip, 1991). Guiding the learner and eliciting learner response during a distance learning event include varying levels of student-student collaboration, student-instructor interaction, student-materials interaction, and access to or control of learning stimuli.

Finally, providing feedback to the distance learning participant facilitates instructor-student interaction, further engages the individual, and increases motivation for ongoing practice and long-term retention of skills and knowledge by the learner. It is also in this aspect of design of distance learning instructional events that evaluation is provided to the learner regarding his or her ongoing mastery of the business-driven performance objectives.

The conclusion of the distance training instructional event is designed similarly to the final stages of the body, such that feedback is provided to the learner and performance outcomes are evaluated. The significance of the conclusion of the instructional event is the inclusion of a statement reiterating intended learning objectives, a review of the more salient concepts and issues related to the learning event, and a summative evaluation of learner performance. This final assessment of performance enables future remediation or enhancement, depending on whether the participant exhibits the identified performance outcomes.

Upon review of the preceeding discussion, it becomes apparent that embedded within the design structure of instructional events lie three primary characteristics that influence effective development of distance education and training. These include (a) type and level of interaction, (b) synchronicity of the interaction and personal communication, and (c) locus of control over content and pace of instruction (Berge and Collins, 1995c; Mackin and Hoffman, 1997; Mantyla and Gividen, 1997; and Moore and Kearsley, 1996). There are four types of learner interaction: learner-learner, learner-instructor, learner-content, and learner-interface (Mackin and Hoffman, 1997; Moore and Kearsley, 1996); two modes of communication: synchronous and asynchronous (Berge and Collins, 1995c); and two primary loci of control: internal or student-maintained versus external or instructor-maintained (Berge and Collins, 1995c; Schreiber, 1996).

Instructional events for adult distance learners are strengthened by increased levels of learner-learner and learner-instructor interactions and maintaining learner-centered or learner control over content and pace of instruction. Both synchronous and asynchronous communication are appropriate, depending on the selection of instructional delivery technology and the design of instructional materials.

Learner-learner and learner-instructor interactions are increased when instructional events incorporate activities that encourage dialogue and engage learners with questions and discussions, role-play, and other collaborative efforts. The Interactivity Guide Pyramid (Mantyla and Gividen, 1997) describes a balanced mix of activities that may be integrated into the instructional design of the distance training event to enhance learning. These activities include case studies, storytelling, debates, and simulations.

Finally, learner-interface interaction is improved when an instructional event ensures limited distraction from side-effects of technology or from hardware or software demands. For example, when using live two-way interactive video transmissions, post a still image or picture on the monitor screen during off-line student activities. Or if the internet is being utilized to provide an online course, effectively plan and prepare uploading instructional materials and documents so software and hardware compatibility exists and student access is strong and downloading uneventful. The learner-interface interaction, described by Mackin and Hoffman (1997) as the learner's adjustment to the distance learning environment (defined by a particular technological learning platform), is strengthened by improved utilization of delivery technology.

Successful distance training occurs when instructional events complement or reinforce a selected model for learning. For example, if the goal of a distance training event is to improve information transformation, an instructional strategy must be developed that facilitates social interaction and constructivist learning. The technology used to deliver the information and aid instruction must provide strong interaction and socialization. In this example, the Internet may successfully deliver the distance training, as long as the instructional materials and instructional events are designed appropriately. However, if significant interpersonal skills development is needed (such as skills needed for team-building), live two-way video interaction with limited numbers of remote sites may more effectively deliver the distance training event and facilitate mastery of the performance objectives.

Accommodate (Organizational) Technology Plan

A new generation of technological advancements has resulted in the availability of an eclectic array of hardware and software that an organization may use to deliver distance training. These are the same technologies a corporation or agency uses to process data, manage personnel and human resource services, and communicate electronically. It is the front-end costs however and lack of design and implementation plans for facilitating learning at a distance that thwart an organization's procurement, practice, and utilization of technology for distance training.

Step Four of the IDM-DT provides a number of suggestions and tasks that aid in the procurement, use, and integration of organizational technology for delivering distance and distributed learning. Field experiences indicate that there are two over-riding influences that affect identification and selection of technology for specific distance training events and programs. One influence comes from the instructional design needs of distance learning; the other is generated from organizational characteristics and business needs of corporations and agencies.

The following discussion provides a two-prong approach to strengthening an organization's efforts to procure, utilize, and integrate technology for delivering distance and distributed learning. One approach is driven by instructional needs of distance learning. This strategy identifies and selects instructional technology based on a set of learning and usability criteria. The other approach is based on organizational and business needs. This strategy examines corporation and agency characteristics and how they affect identification, selection, and procurement of technology for distance training.

While companies strive for a seamless integration of organizational technology, corporate (executive and operations) officers scrutinize purchases and return on investment closely. Organizations are demanding clear justification for significant expenditures on hardware and software.

Business-Driven Procurement and Utilization of Organizational Technology for Distance Training.

Current organizational attempts at online and distance learning have resulted in less than desired outcomes (Picard, 1996; Green, 1997). There is an identified business need to deliver training faster, cheaper, and more effectively. Yet most organizational efforts to provide distance learning have been improvised with little institutional planning. Often organizations look to computing services to provide technical support services and instructional integration of content. Pedagogical applications and instructional personnel are considered marginal costs. And utilization of organizational technology for instructional purposes competes for existing resources along with all other technological applications within the corporation or agency (Green, 1997; Schreiber, 1996).

Research and personal field experiences suggest that solutions exist to help strengthen an organization's practices and procedures for procurement and utilization of technology for distance learning (Cronin, 1994; Green, 1997; Schreiber, 1996). Two of these solutions are (a) developing and implementing an organizational Technology Plan and (b) creating and recognizing an interdisciplinary Distance Learning Core Steering Committee.

An organization's technology plan guides decision-making regarding procurement and utilization of technology. It provides policies and procedures for analyzing cost-benefits, allocating resources, and controlling budgets. A well-developed technology plan is a component of an organization's mission and strategic statements, and is defined relative to the organization's business goals, initiatives and challenges for the near-future (Green, 1997).

A strong organizational technology plan is characterized by the following criteria (these traits were identified from review of related literature by Cronin, 1994; Green, 1997; Picard, 1996; Schreiber, 1996):

• A description of how technology will support, facilitate, and sustain the organization's business goals, initiatives, and challenges for the next three to five years;

- A statement of the options for what technologies will enable accomplishment of the how described previously;
- A statement recognizing distance and online education and training as a distinct identity with its special mix of pedagogy, customer and audience, and products;
- A statement of specific guiding principles for ongoing technological improvement in the organization to accommodate and propagate flexibility and changing business initiatives and challenges; this statement is less broad than the organization's mission and vision statements;
- A statement of strategic and tactical goals to engage benefits from cutting-edge and innovative advances in communication technologies supporting distance education and training;
- A clear description of associated core costs (*cost of doing business*) and marginal costs (*non-documented overhead* or *embedded costs*, costs bundled into an already existing core account); and
- A description of line item expenditures for the following core costs: distance training course design, materials development, distance delivery skills training, computing services' support of distance learning users and providers, and computing services' support of integration of instruction.

In addition to these characteristics, an organization's technology plan should include (a) an overall financial plan for routine amortization and replacement of computers, software, and other key hardware and software components, (b) a defined role for information technology and www resources in the distance learning effort, and (c) a strategic plan for the role of information technology in instruction and distance training, as well as dissemination of information that is content specific.

The extent to which the technology plan described here becomes implemented depends on an organization's structural and functional capability to support the effort. The probability that an organization's technology plan will be effectively implemented in support of distance training increases significantly with the presence of an interdisciplinary Distance Learning Core Steering Committee.

A Distance Learning Core Steering Committee (or simply, any interdisciplinary team charged with support and service of maximizing utilization of organizational technology) is often created by one of the following three procedures: (a) an executive appointment, (b) induction by an organizational task force, or (c) reactivation by organizational demand. This interdisciplinary team is made up of members from various functions within the organization, including executive management, information technology, network services, broadcasting and or communications, instructional design, training, and performance consulting areas.

In addition to the members permanently appointed to a Distance Learning Core Steering Committee (or similar team), there are floating members engaged for specific applications and implementation. Two categories of floating membership are subject matter experts and end-users or members of a specific target audience. The composition of a corporation or agency Distance Learning Core Steering Committee (or similar team) depends on an organization's size, resources, and organizational structure.

Technology plans evolve and take on unique characteristics as an organization's level of maturity grows regarding its technological capability to provide distance training. The supporting interdisciplinary distance learning team becomes more sophisticated in providing services and facilitating ongoing implementations of distance and distributed learning.

In less-evolved organizational environments, a technology plan is recognized only on a functional or departmental level, and often there are several of these plans circulating throughout the company or agency. A duplication of distance training efforts results, sometimes resulting in outcomes that are at cross-purposes with the organization's goals. Costs are covered by individual budgets; there is limited integration among efforts; and return-on-investment decreases.

The goal is to develop, implement, and sustain a technology plan at an organizational level and facilitate interdisciplinary contributions from the Distance Learning Core Steering Committee.

Instructional Design-Driven Identification and Selection of Technology for Distance Training. As an organization's technology plan becomes recognized and the interdisciplinary distance learning team coordinates development and implementation of distance training events, decisions must be made regarding which technology is most effective in delivering what type of distance instruction. A continuing debate among instructional designers ensues, however, regarding the appropriate time (during the process of design and development of distance training) to identify and select technology to deliver distance and distributed learning.

Some researchers proclaim that learner characteristics and the design of instructional events must be considered long before any delivery technology is selected (Reed, 1996; Fortenbaugh, 1997). Others argue that technological media are merely vehicles for delivering instruction and do not influence directly student achievement (Schlosser and Anderson, 1994; Portway and Lane, 1994). The answer not unexpectedly lies somewhere in between. All instructional technologies possess strengths and weaknesses and the most effectively implemented distance training events and programs maximize utilization of the chosen (or available) delivery medium. The guiding principle is to design instructional events that are consistent with and fully use the strengths of the delivery technology.

Maximizing utilization of technology for distance training is characterized by a clear concise understanding of instructional goals and performance outcomes and subsequently designed instructional events and instructional materials consistent with the chosen medium. The key is to work with rather than against the capabilities of the technology.

All technologies possess unique capabilities. For example, a primary strength of the Internet is its ability to deliver instruction and engage learner interaction in an environment that does not require students and instructor present together at a specific time or geographic location (Berge and Collins, 1995c). Teaching and learning activities are available upon request with minimum constraint to access. Optimizing utilization of the Internet is then represented by instructional events that facilitate social interaction and constructivist learning (Berge and Collins, 1995c), as long as instructional strategies include processes and procedures for participant meditation and reflection on content issues.

The strengths and weakness of technology for delivering distance education and training can be described through an assessment of the medium's usability characteristics. (A *usability characteristic* may be type and level of interactivity or user access.) In contrast to the preceeding example, the strengths of live interactive video communication include real-time visual interaction that fosters cultural indoctrination, common language-building, and immediately available feedback to and from the instructor and students (Berge and Collins, 1995c; Schreiber, 1995a). Consequently, if a performance need exists to build such interpersonal skills, then utilization of the delivery medium of live interactive two-way video is an appropriate selection. (Note however that interaction is maximized during live two-way video communication when the number of remote sites is limited to six [Schreiber, 1995a].)

For review of the strengths and weakness of multiple technology delivery tools, see Table 3.1: Technology Selection Criteria Matrix. This matrix correlates technology delivery tools to specific characteristics of distance training. Usability criteria drive the correlations.

The technologies examined in Table 3.1 include (a) the Internet (intranet/extranet), (b) satellites, (c) fiber optics, (d) CD-ROM and laser disks, (e) audiotapes and videotapes, and (f) printed materials. The associated instructional applications include (a) web-based computer-based training (CBT) and online courses, (b) electronic performance support systems, (c) high fidelity broadcasts and teleconferencing, (d) digital compressed video transmissions, as well as analog communications, (e) independent computer-based training, (f) audio-video recorded lectures, and (g) texts, handbooks, and manuals. And the usability criteria that determine the strengths and weaknesses of various organizational technologies for communication and training at a distance include (a) type and level of interactivity,

(b) costs of design and implementation, (c) user access to distance learning technology, (d) learner style, and (e) type of intended learning outcome (such as acquisition of knowledge, skill-building, or attitudinal change).

Correlate Distance Learning Instructional Materials to Technology Delivery Tools

Maximizing utilization of technology for distance training is characterized by a clear concise understanding of instructional goals and performance outcomes and subsequently designed instructional events and instructional materials consistent with the chosen medium. Instructional materials may be a variety of electronic and paper-based text and graphics, as well as three-dimensional models and other manipulatives. CBT materials may also be employed. The key is to design instructional materials that work with rather than against the capabilities of the technology.

Step Five of the Instructional Design Model for Distance Training describes effective design and integration of instructional materials with delivery technology. Maximizing the use of technology to implement distance learning relies on how consistent the instructional materials are with the strengths of the hardware and software employed to deliver the training. The following paragraphs describe the correlation of instructional materials and two primary distance training technologies: interactive television and the Internet.

Interactive Television Technology   Live interactive video conferencing permits two-way audio and one- or two-way video communication (see Table 3.1). The effectiveness of this technology to deliver distance training to both visual learners and verbal learners depends on how well the instructional materials are designed to utilize both the live video and audio capabilities of the technology.

Visual learners respond to pictures and graphics, while verbal learners respond to voice and text (Schaaf, 1997). Instructional materials used with live interactive video technology include presentation slides, charts and graphs, videotapes, and three-dimensional objects. Presentation slides, charts, and graphs may be presented on diskette or projected via a document camera. The design of these visuals should be as simple as possible. A learner is more fully engaged by the presentation of a limited amount of information (Alessi and Trollip, 1991). (Detailed information may be distributed in a handout.) As Ostendorf (1994) proclaims . . . when in doubt, leave it out . . . .

Presentation slides, charts, and graphics delivered via interactive television technology are most effective when designed within the following parameters (Alessiand Trollip, 1991; Ostendorf, 1994; Portway and Lane, 1994; Schreiber, 1995a):

TABLE 3.1.   TECHNOLOGY SELECTION CRITERIA MATRIX.

Implementation: Learning/Teaching Characteristic[1]	EPSS	Internet [Intranet/Extranet] Online Courses	Email	Satellite [wide band 1-way video]
Access (User)		information dial-up (hardware/software compatibility)		formal/ prescheduled
Audience (Size)		asynchronous: unlimited synchronous: ≤8 remote sites		
Cost: Communication[2]		----minimal----		high
Cost: Start-up		----organizational shared cost----		high
Fidelity: Audio		low-medium fidelity sound		high fidelity sound
Fidelity: Video		low-medium fidelity motion		full motion
Instructional Adaptability		can support learning style		can support learning style
Instructional Methodology		student-centered and instructor-led		instructor-led
Instructional Strategy		information dissemination, Q&A, interactive discussion		lecture, presentation of info on policy/ procedures
Interaction: Type/Level		significant student-student and student -instructor		low student-student and medium student-instructor
Learning Outcome (K, S, A)[3]		----K, S, and/or A ----		primarily knowledge-based
Scheduling: Synch/Asynch		--asynch/synchronous--		live or pre-recorded
Support Service Need:		----minimal----		extensive
Update Capability		----just-in-time----		just-in-time

1. Information compiled from contributing case studies and other field experiences.
2. See Chapter Two and related case studies for detailed discussion about cost-benefit analysis.
3. K = knowledge, S = skill and A = attitude

Land Lines/ Fiber Optics [compressed 2-way video]	CD-Rom/ Laser Disks [CBT]	Audiotape/ Videotape	Printed Material
informal dial-up	manual distribution (hardware/ software needed)	unconstrained (hardware needed)	unconstrained distribution
~ 6 remote sites (18–20 learners per site)	unlimited	unlimited	unlimited
low-medium	NA	NA	NA
medium	low-medium	low	low
high fidelity sound	high fidelity sound	high fidelity sound	NA
medium- full motion	high quality graphics	full motion	NA
can support learning style	supports remedial learning	minimal support of learning style	minimal support of learning style
student-centered and instructor-led	self-paced	self-paced	self-paced
role-play, Q&A, interactive discussion, demonstration	tutorial, drill & practice, simulations	presentation of information	presentation of information
slgnificant student-student and student-instructor	medium interaction student and mat'ls	NA	NA
K, S, and/or A	K, S, and/or A	K, A	K
live	NA	NA	NA
medium	minimal	minimal	NA
just-in-time	medium flexibility	inflexible	inflexible

- A maximum of five to eight lines per slide
- Approximately six words per line (36–48 words) per slide
- Type size of twenty–twenty-six points high
- Bold lettering
- One and a half to two times more space between lines
- No more than three types styles (fonts) per page
- No more than three colors per page

Delivering distance training via interactive television technology relies heavily on use of cameras to project instructional materials. These instructional materials may include 11-inch by 8 and 1y2-inch presentation overheads, or 14-inch by 17-inch flip charts. When a document camera is used, the lens should be set at an appropriate zoom angle; if the zoom is too wide, details will be lost. If the materials include presentation overheads, the visuals should be properly centered with text positioned horizontally across the screen. If the materials include flip charts (avoid blackboards and marlite boards), write with very thick markers (avoiding pale colors). Whatever the case, be sure the camera lens is positioned so the instructor's arm or body does not block the view (Ostendorf, 1994; Portway and Lane, 1994).

Distance learning instructional materials may include videotapes for use with interactive television technology. If this is the desire, sound may be the most important parameter of the technology that determines effective use of the instructional material. Be sure microphones are positioned appropriately throughout the room, either hung from the ceiling or stationed on tabletops. If microphones are grated or toned down, be sure the videotape sound is not obscured. Finally, decrease room echoes and increase quality for receiving sound via the audio/videotape by using acoustically absorbent rather than reflective surfaces. Use drapes over exposed glass.

Internet/Intranet Technology   Instructional materials consistent with the strengths of the Internet/intranet include a variety of electronic text and graphics, as well as computer-based training materials. In an online course, for example, a lecture may take the form of text posted to a bulletin board. The posting may contain complete articles, excerpts from articles or texts, and questions and answers prepared for follow-up discussion (Paulsen, 1995). Internet/intranet-based courses may provide access to online resources through a web page. Some of these resources may be bookmarked by the instructor; others can be provided as optional readings.

In addition to online lecture slides, research papers, instructors' notes, tutorials, and tests may be posted. Slides on demand may be available via electronic libraries (Elangovan, 1996). The use of a mailing list aids in distribution of materials, as well as serving as a vehicle for electronic announcements. Students may be guided through synchronous and asynchronous online "chats" with USENET and other associated discussion groups (Elangovan, 1996).

Computer-based training products may also be used as instructional materials for online courses. These products may be distributed in a self-contained CD-ROM format or accessed via the Internet/intranet. Regarding the integration of computer-based training instructional materials with internet/intranet technology, beware of incompatibilities. High-end multimedia CBT requires large amounts of computer memory, audio/video boards, and high-speed connectivity for transmission.

A final consideration to ensure successful correlation of instructional materials and technology tools for delivery of distance training is the human factor effect. Instructors and other distance learning facilitators who may be inexperienced with technology must learn and respect the unique requirements and parameters of hardware and software, as well as the learning environment that will be used to deliver instructional materials. For example, a distance learning event transmitted via television (one- or two-way video) can be viewed by a participant as something that may be "tuned-out" at any time (Ostendorf, 1994). If presentation slides used in this medium are not visually engaging or are designed inappropriately with conflicting text and color layouts, then the instructional materials fail to facilitate maximum use of the technology. Similarly, if presentation slides are posted for an Internet/intranet-based online course and the phrases are abridged or ambiguous or supplemental text resources are omitted, then again the instructional materials do not maximize utilization of the technology.

Secure Implementation Support For Balanced Roll-Out Strategy

Corporations and agencies that implement successful distance training that contributes strategically to the organization exhibit coordinated support from multiple functions within the institution. Education specialists, subject matter experts, information systems engineers, communications professionals, and executive managers interact collaboratively as corporate facilitators of distance and distributed learning. As indicated earlier in discussion of the IDM-DT (refer to Step Four), this collective behavior is ultimately facilitated by an organization's Distance Learning Core Steering Committee (or similar organizational team).

Step six of the IDM-DT examines the processes and procedures in which an organization must engage to secure implementation support for distance training at an institutional level. Change-management and transition-management theories are discussed. These theories provide a foundation upon which an organization can evolve the necessary sophisticated, interdisciplinary, and broad-based support behaviors needed for strategic application of business-driven distance and distributed learning.

(Note: The following discussion results from the application of change-management theory and transition-management theory to securing organizational support for implementation of distance and distributed learning. The initial research on organizations and management by Robinson and Robinson (1996) and Bridges (1988) provides a foundation for this application.)

Understanding transition-management theory aids in securing organizational support for implementation of strategic applications of distance training. However, prior to this discussion it is important to note that an organization's potential for success in delivering strategic distance training relies on attainment of certain sophisticated behaviors. These behaviors include (a) proactive institutional planning for design, development and delivery of distance events and programs; (b) organizational recognition of distance training as a unique entity with specific products and services and subsequently independent budgetary needs; (c) availability of organizational computing services and technical support services for implementation and evaluation; and (d) collaborative contributions by interdisciplinary groups, including subject matter experts, end-users (participants in the distance training events), and instructional designers.

Three additional organizational phenomena impact effectiveness with which institutional support is secured for implementation of distance training. These include (a) identification and recognition of business-driven distance learning goals and objectives, (b) presence of an organization interdisciplinary distance learning team, and (c) active maintenance of an organization technology plan.

It is ultimately the interdisciplinary distance learning team that takes responsibility for negotiating and securing organizational support for implementation of distance learning. And although the organizational state (as described in the previous paragraph) is the desired condition, most often the distance learning core team must move the organization to this state as implementation support is pursued. Securing support for strategic distance learning occurs by preparing, monitoring, and facilitating implementation of distance training events and programs.

Preparing the company or agency to support strategic application of distance training requires that the distance learning core team describe in the most fundamental terms the innovations occurring with implementation of the event(s). The core team should look ahead and identify those individuals and groups most affected by the implementation process and communicate evolving roles and responsibilities associated with this implementation.

In the case of distance learning, information systems staff and computing services personnel are key individuals to securing organizational support for distance training events and programs. The core team should assess the transition-readiness of this group and determine appropriate activities to engage them in support of the implementation process (Bridges, 1988). The readiness of the group to provide implementation support is a measure of the group's structural flexibility, procurement practices, and identity with the organization's technology plan. The more flexible the function's structure, the more decentralized its procurement practices, and the stronger its identity with the organization's technology plan, the more ready the group is to support the implementation of strategic distance training at an organizational level.

The next phase of securing organizational support for implementation of strategic distance and distributed learning is driven by what happens to individuals and the organization during the implementation period. These happenings may be foreseen or not, depending on the level of maturity of the implementation process and how predictable implementation procedures are. Such incidents may include unexpected disruption of standard practices and procedures and inadequate flow of information from management and the distance learning core team across functions of the organization, as well as up and down the hierarchical structure of the organization and perceived (or real) inconsistencies with (former) cultural orientation of the corporation or agency.

The second phase of activities that facilitate securing organization support of distance training falls into the category of monitoring the progress of the implementation. The responsibility of the distance learning core team at this stage is to observe the distance training activities, anticipate weaknesses in the implementation process, and head off unexpected incidents (such as previously described). For example, if the organization's standard budgetary practice for covering delivery costs associated with instructional technology traditionally resulted in independent function expenditures and now a strategic application of distance learning event requires group budgeting (perhaps involving computer services and technical support as well as training and performance enhancement departments), then the distance learning core team must recognize the new phenomenon, increase communication across associated functions, build awareness, negotiate collaboration, and remedy any confusion or disgruntlement regarding roles and responsibilities.

The final phase of securing organizational support for implementation of strategic distance and distributed learning requires a strong application of facilitation processes. *Facilitation processes* include activities that (a) increase the ease of transition, (b) lower the intensity of opposition or obstacles, and (c) provide ongoing stimulation of "a" and "b." At this stage, the distance learning core team may set a challenging but realistic pace for accomplishment of an identified distance training event or program. Securing implementation support for the time-line will be strengthened however if the necessary support functions in the organization have been engaged during the decision-making process.

Additional tasks for the distance learning core team during this phase of securing implementation support include creating incentives or rewards for both short-term and long-term involvement by related organizational functions (computer services and technical support, as well as training and performance enhancement departments), and reviewing, updating, and reinforcing the communication plan (implemented in earlier stages). The communication plan investigates communication resources within the agency or institution, identifies communication channels, communicates the timeline for roll-out, and ultimately engages interdepartmental support and organizational-level support for implementation of strategic distance and distributed learning.

The ultimate goal of this stage of the instructional design model for developing strategic distance training is to establish an implementation process that is stable and predictable but not inflexible. Once this process is in place, the organization can evolve to institutionalize its efforts. (See the Introduction and the related discussion of organizational technological capability maturity for implementing distance learning.)

Evaluate Distance Training Processes and Measure Transfer

Step Seven, the final step in the IDM-DT process, describes how to evaluate delivery of distance training instructional events and programs, as well as the instructional design model itself for developing distance and distributed learning. Measuring transfer of information and the knowledge and skills for successful attainment of business-driven performance outcomes is also discussed. Formative and summative assessments provide the primary vehicles for evaluation.

Both formative and summative assessments represent important operations of the overall distance learning model. Formative assessment maps the ongoing design and implementation of distance training and determines the impact of materials development and selection of instructional technology on one another and on the general process. Formative assessment also includes reiterative review of all components of the distance learning system with primary focus on the learner, instructor, learning environment, instructional delivery technology, and organizational culture. Formative evaluations provide continuous feedback to developers to improve design and implementation of the ultimate distance training event or program.

Summative assessment as a final evaluation determines the overall strengths and weaknesses of the distance training effort. Summative evaluations may be embedded within a distance training course or event to assess instructor capability, student or participant interaction, user-access to delivery technology, remote site characteristics, and final instructional materials used for the instructional event. Summative evaluation of a distance learning program integrates systematic collection of data over time. The goal of summative assessment of a distance training event or program is to evaluate overall instruction and learning at a distance.

Conclusion

Applying a systems processing approach to the development and delivery of distance and distributed education and training provides a strategy for understanding the roles of the student located at a remote site and the instructor designing materials to be delivered at a distance over some technical medium. The instructional design model developed in this chapter, IDM-DT, enables investigation of the relationships between and among various elements of the process, including in addition to the student and instructor the learning environment (for example, site planning for a satellite broadcast or desktop access), the instructional technology (compressed video or Internet), and culture of the institution or agency (including level of organizational technology capability for providing distance training).

The IDM-DT provides a strategy for accounting for all the components of a distance learning instructional process, as well as explaining the role each component plays within a given instructional event or program.

Employing a reiterative process of analysis and design to develop strategic distance learning also helps to maximize utilization of technology and institutionalize an organization's efforts. Instructional needs and performance outcomes of a distance training event or program become defined by business goals and objectives. The impact of organizational culture, as well as internal corporate dynamics, are understood, accounted for, and accommodated.

CASE STUDIES

CASE STUDIES

PART ONE

DISTRIBUTING INFORMATION AND INCREASING KNOWLEDGE

CHAPTER FOUR

BUILDING CUSTOMER RELATIONS: WEB-BASED TRAINING FOR THE HOME IMPROVEMENT INDUSTRY

Dennis Fukai, Kerry Kitchen, and David Aurelio

The Challenge of Distance Training in Home Improvement

The challenge of distance training for the home improvement industry is to find ways to provide customers detailed information about the products that it sells. In fact, the retailers involved in supplying tools, equipment, and materials to the do-it-yourself market are really in the business of providing construction information. The more a customer knows about their products, the more those customers will be willing to purchase and have the confidence to use them in projects in and around their homes. In this way, information and customer services are critical factors in the sales strategies of the companies working in this competitive industry.

As evidence of these motivations, consumer interest in home improvement can be seen in a variety of print and electronic media. However, almost all of these publications provide the information necessary for the homeowner to complete a particular project. In other words, information delivery focuses on specific and immediate solutions. A premise of this chapter is that this approach misses the opportunity to develop long-term relationships with customers that might lead to ongoing working partnerships. The cultivation of partnered relationships is the theme of customer service for many home improvement retailers. This concept is part of a larger goal to build customer confidence in the expertise of a particular company. It also recognizes the importance of the customer's self-confidence in the ability to handle a series of gradually more complex projects because they lead to progressively larger material purchases.

This chapter outlines a way to use the World Wide Web to establish a training environment that would set up these cultivated relationships. This would extend the reach of the company's interactions with its customers onto the desktops of a home computer. The idea is to capitalize on the web's graphical capability and focus on a training experience where learner-centered activities can nurture the customer's interest in home improvement projects. This suggests that home improvement retailers can use distance training to do more than provide customers with immediate answers. They can use the web to mediate their communications by establishing long-term relationships in the form of distance education and information resources.

This chapter suggests a construction trainer specially designed to provide this web-based learning experience. Every piece of this specially designed trainer is anatomically correct. This means that it can be viewed from any angle, sliced, deconstructed, and reconstructed to show various phases of its assembly. A computer program processes a model of this trainer by capturing images of it according to predetermined combinations of pieces and viewing angles. This limits the level of detail that must be absorbed at any one time and allows a set of framed web pages to juxtapose informational relationships according to interaction dictated by the learner. (See Figure 4.1.) Each view of the model has "hot spots" where a mouse click on one of the pieces of the model posts graphical information into an adjacent frame. These include plans, elevations, enlarged two-dimensional details, and specifications or assembly animations. These juxtaposed images show different phases of the construction process and can be further queried for detailed information. In this way, the model embodies a collection of types of materials used in a variety of applications and displays them as a distance training environment.

The goal is to furnish construction information about the trainer in order to demonstrate a variety of general project concepts. The idea is to stimulate creativity through the acquisition of broad construction knowledge and increase the sales of home improvement products by cultivating customer relationships through the learner-centered, web-based interactions. This mixes market presence with education and enhances the competitive position of the retailer through construction information. These are important potentials to keep in mind in a highly competitive industry because home improvement retailers must constantly find ways to maintain their edge in a dynamic and complex market.

FIGURE 4.1. FRAMED ENVIRONMENT OF PCIS TRAINER.

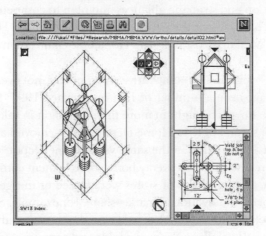

The Home Improvement Industry

Despite predictions of a slow-down and intense competition in the last few years as retailers vie for market share, the home improvement industry is continuing to slowly expand into one of the largest retail segments of the United States (Kalish, 1992; Geoff, 1995). According to American Demographics and the Joint Center for Housing Studies, renovations and repairs account for 40 percent of the total spending for residential construction (American Demographics, 1996; Joint Center for Housing Studies, 1996). Spending on home improvements includes major changes and additions to owner-occupied houses and the replacement or repair of electrical, plumbing, telecommunication, and heating and cooling systems. Because baby boomers, aged thirty-two to fifty, are in the prime years for home improvements, this market reached a record $69.5 billion in 1995 and has been on a fairly stable climb even as some homeowners outgrow their penchant for do-it-yourself projects (American Demographics, 1996; Joint Center for Housing Studies, 1996). Interestingly, this trend is not just in the United States and can be seen in a number of other rapidly industrializing countries. For example, Home Centers Ltd. of Bnei Brak is Israel's largest home improvement retailer. It sells home improvement materials to that nation's upwardly mobile middle class and is actively expanding to acquire control of new stores in Cyprus, Greece, and Jordan (*Chain Store Age*, 1997a). Some retailers based in the United States are establishing active regional partnerships to expand into foreign markets in Canada, Mexico, and South America (Tice, 1996). Other retailers are moving into these markets by acquisition and strategic alliances and plan to compete aggressively for market share. These include the new Sears Hardware Outlets, Kmart's Builders Square, Lowe's, Menan, Ernst, Waban's Homebase chain and many other conglomerates (Berner, 1997).

Of course in this competitive environment, not every store will succeed, and there have been a number of failures (Berner, 1997; McCormack, 1997). For example Lowe's brought in more than $7 billion in sales for a 15.8 percent gain in 1996, second only to Home Depot, which enjoyed a 17.4 percent increase in sales on $19.5 billion in the same year (Home Depot, 1996). At the same time, forty percent of the top twenty home improvement companies saw sales decrease in 1996, and hundreds of stores were closed or merged to position themselves to compete for a dwindling market share. For example, Seattle-based Ernst Hardware took a $120 million loss and closed nine stores after only a year of operation (Tice, 1996). Even the most visible and aggressive retail giant of this industry, Home Depot, can be seen to be experimenting with the market. It slowed expansion with its stalled Expo Stores and revamped its prototype Cross Roads stores to be more in line with its successful superstores. Nevertheless, Home Depot was the tenth largest retailer in 1995 with more than $15.5 billion dollars in retail sales. The trend continued with more than $938 million in earnings in 1996, up from $731.5 million in 1995 (Shulz, 1995). According to Home Depot's Annual Report, 1996 total sales were 14 percent of the total $135 billion home improvement industry. Important is that in the wake of its aggressive expansion, the company has left many casualties, and it continues to move aggressively to capture market share (McCormack, 1997). Though the potential of some cross shopping seems to be possible between these companies (Clement, 1996), the structure of the home improvement industry means that they are all competing for the same customer base. It seems clear therefore that the growth in this sector has been dominated by the expansion of relatively few retail companies all vying for the same consumer market sector. This competitive climate means retail costs, quality of goods, customer service, and advertising are important factors to ongoing success in this volatile and complex market.

Competitive Customer Orientation

Unlike sales to professional builders, direct sales to the consumer require convenient locations, expensive fixtures, customer service, and regular advertising. For example, in an analysis of the business strategies of Wickes Lumber, David Shulz discusses Wickes' orientation to the professional builder and how that orientation changes the corporation itself (Shulz, 1995). More than 80 percent of Wickes' sales are to the professional builder. And while it recognizes and serves the consumer market, it plans to continue to increase its focus on the professional builder because of the potential for larger transactions and minimized overhead. The key to the difference in market strategy in organizations like Wickes or Eighty-Four Lumber, the nation's largest professional builder-oriented chain, is their ability to operate out of what appear to be bare bones facilities. Most contractor sales are counter orders, telephone bids, and project-based materials subcontracts that allow a focused inventory and little need for elaborate retail floor fixtures, extensive advertising, or prolonged interaction with a lay customer. In fact, an ordinary do-it-yourselfer may feel a bit intimidated in such an environment because there is little emphasis on that level of customer service.

At the same time, customer service is one of the primary market strategies of the do-it-yourself home improvement industry. Knowledgeable people, short courses, sales material, well stocked and lighted shelves, and accurate information are part of the business of a consumer-based home improvement center. For example, at retail outlets like The Home Depot, experienced home decorators serve lay customers and subcontractors as sales representatives and an innovative and aggressive spirit pervades their employees. Established in 1978, the company is well known for its imagination and service orientation. In early 1997, it had more than 570 stores open with a goal of 111 more for the year (*Chain Store Age*, 1997a), all working independently to inform and educate their customers in the use of construction materials. As a result, Home Depot has recorded a 31 percent increase in dividends compared to a Standard and Poor's five-year index of 13 percent and continues to penetrate and capture market share wherever it sets up shop (Moreau, 1995). Nevertheless, Home Depot's competitors are not just stepping aside. They have mounted similar customer-oriented campaigns. For example, Lowe's moved early into the market with its own superstores wherever it saw niche markets that Home Depot was less likely to penetrate. They mix the same formula of information, service, and product, and compete directly in many communities, sometimes locating directly across the street or in the same neighborhood as established Home Depot outlets. In addition, regional chains like Ernst, HomeBase, Pay N Pak, and Hechinger have all developed informative services and educational displays in their superstores in order to reach out to the do-it-yourself consumer.

The Media of Consumer-Based Construction Information

These factors combine to create a dynamic and growing consumer-oriented industry, one that is both a model of customer service (Henderson, 1996) and a reflection of the relationship of culture and the communications media. In fact, the cultural ramifications of the media to the home improvement industry extend in all directions and are little understood. One author tracks the do-it-yourselfer into everything from outerwear to the proliferation of suburban four-wheel drive utility vehicles (Henkoff, 1995). One thing is clear, the emphasis on service in the home improvement industry focuses on information—perhaps stimulated by an underlying social motivation for that information—in relation to personal property and cultural control. For example, this motivation is clearly visible in the popular media, spawning both comedic and serious television programs, thousands of magazines and planning guides, and hundreds of how-to, the-way-it-works, and do-it-yourself books (Mullany, 1996). Whether these programs generate further interest in home improvement or home improvement generates interest in more media is difficult to determine; however, there is plenty of evidence that there is a strong need for information about construction that can serve the home improvement customer.

As such, construction information is available in print from publishers like Time-Life Books, Ortho, and Sunset and other magazines covering every conceivable kind of construction. Some of these books use home computers (Neibauer, 1995) or offer combinations of books and CDs that teach and train the do-it-yourselfer. These include CDs that are available for both home repair and improvement that have been reviewed quite favorably in comparison to traditional print media. For example, the Reader's Digest version of one of these CDs includes 400 megabytes of video clips—though a review of the CD recommends purchasing the book as a supplement. Home Depot also produces a book and CD; though considered dull and unimaginative, it is thought to have plenty of information for the do-it-yourselfer (Himowitz, 1996). A much more imaginative CD by the Software Toolworks uses a "navigable" house where the user wanders through rooms clicking on household tips linked to graphic images of different household projects. The user walks through clicking on different parts of the house to access information about various installations. In another example, a company called Books That Work mixes a book, CD, and the World Wide Web to give a total home improvement experience (Windstrom, 1996). This company was started with $750,000 in venture capital after one of its owners made four trips to the lumberyard in an effort to build a simple deck. In addition, a number of software products exist that can assist the home improvement customer in planning a project. These include two relatively simple design tools called 3D Home Architect and 3D Landscape. 3D Landscape even allows the customer to place the plants and watch them grow over preset times. Other producers, such as Parametric Technology Corporation's Pro/Engineer automation software, consider their software to be so easy a child can use it (Smith, 1995). And industry giant AutoDesk, with its dominant share of the professional CAD business, has a do-it-yourselfer's version of its product entitled Home Series for the homeowner and small contractor. Finally, a web-based example might include the Popular Mechanics HomeArts web site, which has been online since August of 1995 and contains information and ideas for virtually any home improvement project. All of these products are information resources that help consumers plan their projects, budget materials, and make purchase decisions.

A Networked Infrastructure for Customer Service

It is important to point out that the idea of a media of consumer information is closely related to existing inventory or price management database systems. However, these databases support sales tracking and planning guidelines and focus on a different need within the retail outlet. They are consumer enhancement and development tools that allow retailers to correlate customers' purchasing habits and compare them with regional trends or the sales activities at a particular store. Even though the home improvement industry is considered deficient in this regard (*Chain Store Age*, 1996), there is little doubt these information tools are important for business management and can indirectly serve the customer. They are strategic tools that have value for the administration of a number of business decisions and can be correlated with the needs of general customer information in a number of important ways.

This is possible because the network infrastructure of major home improvement retailers is more than capable of handling these managerial information technologies. Though they are not databases that one would want to make available to the customer on a sales floor, they are robust and quite powerful. For example, in late 1994, Home Depot abandoned a corporate wide X–25 and satellite net and installed a TCP/IP-based Ethernet Local Area Network (LAN) similar to the system that links most universities (Cooney, 1994). Though already somewhat antiquated, this effort is an indication of the company's recognition of the value of networked and computer mediated voice and data communications. Important is that the system is able to provide rapid expansion and reduce frame relay times necessary to support the information needs of its rapid expansion program. This means in-store processing systems and PBX voice lines located on sales floor terminals attach to the mainframe at the Home Depot headquarters where central and historical data is maintained. The idea is to keep floor terminals simple, centrally manage the remote systems, and fine tune the bandwidth and frame relay environments to deal with the specific data needs of inventory, flow, and management at the local level. These local terminals are tied to standardized servers at each store and handle tasks such as ordering, receiving, personnel management, and administrative functions but are fed by the mainframe and maintained by corporate information managers.

The installation of such a robust system has its costs in the support necessary to maintain user proficiency through retraining and error correction. For companies such as the Home Depot this has triggered a move toward even thinner-client technologies to reign in the variety of programs running on the platforms operating on its networks (*Chain Store Age*, 1997b). The corporation found that the cost necessary to support problems encountered by local users on aging computers was a factor that challenged the efficiency of its network. In contrast, a Java or HTML programmed web-based intranet suggests that system operators could standardize both programming and user support from their headquarters—or any other point on the company network. In June 1997, the company wrote a number of programs from scratch to meet this thin-client objective because of the ease of authoring specialized software to place on the web. This is important because it recognizes the underlying strength of web-based information systems.

What the Home Depot and other corporations recognize is that web-based intranets can fundamentally differ from early LAN networking in their ability to deliver easily developed programming, a standardized look and feel to their interfaces, localized resources, and streamlined support services (Marlow, 1997; Millikin, 1996). This means that even if content is distributed widely over an Intranet, it can be maintained from a central location where control and coherence can be monitored at a lower cost. This is because networks offer the potential to reduce hardware demands and allow a mix of platforms running the same browser. This standardizes data, client training, and programming. In addition, a gateway to the World Wide Web means access can be extended to outside suppliers, independent vendors, manufacturers, and most importantly, retail customers. The advantages are well documented in the popular and academic press (Millikin, 1996; Marlow, 1997; Graham, 1997). For example, the market value of the inclusion of a simple URL for customer reference suggests increased consumer awareness and reinforced confidence in the retail message (Marlow, 1997). This includes a fundamental advantage to both the retailer and the consumer because of the living nature of the data (Armstrong, 1997).

This means information can be easily and quickly updated interactively and leads to user-centered acquisition of the information. Probably most significantly, an alternate line of communications is created where customers can access the information a retailer can provide. The advantage of this might be especially clear with professional or semi-professional constructors. This is a market segment estimated by the observations of one of the authors of this chapter to be somewhere around 30 percent of counter sales at one of the Home Depot stores. However, for do-it-yourself consumers, the availability of an educational resource that can provide construction information on the sales floor and continue to be accessible from their homes may be critical to their purchase decisions. This may be especially true if the possibility for an ongoing dialogue with a sales representative also exists.

What this suggests is an information system that can demonstrate and teach the lay consumer how to use the materials he or she is being encouraged to purchase. In fact, systems similar to these have been shown to be effective in the sales of wholesale lighting products (Kempfer, 1995). These systems were also thought to be effective in increasing sales and credibility in the design of wood decks in a lumberyard's custom computer design center (*Chain Store Age*, 1995). They also share the customer education objectives of most of the home improvement print or electronic media. The primary differences between these information resources and a web-based application are the same as those developed in the thin-client technologies inherent in web-media. As outlined in the preceeding paragraphs, these include customized intranet programming and updates, reduced cost for user support, centralized maintenance of the database even with multiple content providers, an interactive graphical interface, and the ease of access on both the sales floor and the World Wide Web.

Construction Information on the Retail Sales Floor

A fundamental problem on the sales floor of retail outlets that specialize in home improvement is to provide construction information to customers in a way that instills confidence in the advice they are being given and their ability to do the project once they get started. This includes describing hardware and manufactured materials that are for sale, explaining the use of equipment and tools, and suggesting the best alternatives for each customer's project. In response to the challenge presented by the consumer in this market, home improvement retailers conduct do-it-yourself clinics on everything from dry wall finishing to installing a patio door. There are even videos running continuously on sales floors and a good deal of promotional literature available for customers to pick up and take with them. Some retailers also use computer programs to simulate construction or design projects, stretching their liability in the indirect sale of expert information. Unfortunately, this risks not only the reputation of the store but offers what may appear to be simple solutions to site, code, and construction problems that may not be apparent unless a design professional reviews the particular project requirements. If structural failure or injury occurs or a project violates local or national codes because of an error or omission, the home improvement retailer may be liable.

In the end, the most effective method of providing construction information to a customer is a knowledgeable sales representative. This is clearly the philosophy of many successful retail outlets but is especially true in the home improvement market. In a hardware department this means a patient and experienced sales person who can find one of the thousands of widgets a customer may need and only vaguely be able to describe. It also requires personnel who can carefully explain how those products should be used and what problems a customer might encounter in their application. Finally, this includes thinking through the entire project with a customer to make certain he or she has everything needed to complete the project.

In a similar way, construction information is a particular challenge in the sale of lumber and material departments of a home improvement center. In this part of the sales floor, construction materials are offered in basic shapes and sizes but must be cut, assembled, and finished by the customer. What this means is that customers need to understand how to calculate the quantities of a variety of material and connections for an abstract project that is usually no more than a vague idea in their minds. Even when a drawing or plan has been prepared, it is usually a very rough sketch of the finished project and does not include the underlying structure and details associated with the project's construction. The sales representatives must therefore extract and clarify the idea, assist in designing the project, help estimate the quantities that are involved, and then show the customer how to use the materials and put them together. This is a daunting task even for a licensed contractor or architect, but on a crowded sales floor, construction information like this becomes a particular challenge. This is especially true when customers find they have to return to purchase additional items that were missed by the original sales representative.

Some sales representatives use plan books and diagrams to explain the relatively difficult assemblies that will be required for even the simplest project. These are often a collection of two-dimensional plans and sections, joined with a variety of manufacturers' literature on specific products. But this construction information is fragmented and requires some skill at plan reading and understanding complex site conditions. These can be difficult or impossible for customers to interpret and even more difficult for some to implement once they get all of the literature and materials home to begin the actual work. Plan books and boilerplate construction diagrams are also inflexible and even when drawn in three dimensions, they are difficult for do-it-yourselfers to visualize. The result is all too often a lost sale as customers become intimidated by the effort or unable to transfer their understanding to the materials they need to purchase. This means a good deal of time spent explaining construction details without a resultant sale, the loss of potential customers during that time, cross shopping by the customer to get other opinions (and more instruction), incorrect use of materials, and dissatisfaction with the retail experience because of miscommunication.

In a wish list for an online construction information system that might address these needs, one can imagine a system where a sales representative might key in or select from a menu a number of construction options. For example, for a roofing project roof pitch, alternate materials, and sizes could be keyed in, and on "Enter" a materials list and perhaps even working drawings could be generated as computer output. Similarly a deck could be both specified and diagrammed using standard details and lumber sizes so that once a sales representative inputs the height of the deck, surface materials, and step or handrail options, the computer would print the materials list and drawings necessary for the construction. Some software programs attempt this feat, and a few are in use on some sales floors. Unlike an imaging program that may help in the selection of wallpaper or fabric for a piece of furniture, a retail construction information system has to avoid the inherent responsibilities of providing too much construction documentation. In other words, while integrating such a system into an intranet is possible, the effort would be substantial, and the results may appear to provide design services rather than sales support and product information.

Distance Training and Home Improvement

It is important that the support and information provided to a customer do more than document the construction of a project. The need for construction information by the do-it-yourselfer is an opportunity to begin a dialogue and stimulate interaction in an information environment that informs the customer and builds a sense of confidence and interdependence that leads to informed purchases. This is a continuing education opportunity, where consumers and retailers can participate in an integrated training process by selecting the kind of information necessary to successfully complete not only a single project but many others to follow.

Unlike professional or paraprofessional construction training ("Iron Age New Steel," 1997; Shepherd, 1996), this suggests a training program that can provide lay consumers with both the depth and breadth necessary for them to design and build a variety of projects. At the same time such a program might allow customers to feel they have gained some understanding of the construction process. This could include standard construction detailing, but the most important element of such a system would be to focus on education as an interactive training relationship (Carpenter, 1997; Salahaldin, 1991). The advantage of this is that a retail outlet can assume a mentoring role in an informational exchange with a customer thus increasing the skill level and confidence of the customer, while at the same time serving that customer with the tools and materials necessary to complete the project. Though there are owner-builder schools operating with some success (Ross, 1994; Hellmich, 1989), the impossibility of such a relationship is obviated by the lack of similar construction training in a retail environment. However, this owner-builder education can be made available to customers using the distance training potential of a home improvement retailer's intranet servers.

This means the existing network of major retail outlets can provide educational material that may build relationships in ways that improve consumer confidence and increase sales potential. This sets up a competitive advantage in a limited market, reduces the time necessary to explain construction information on the sales floor, standardizes sales information and quantifies it for purchase, and sets up the potential for long-term collaboration with do-it-yourselfers and builders for a series of progressively more complex projects.

Computer-Mediated Communications and Training

The idea of distance education and training in a home improvement retail environment builds on some fundamental changes in the way recent computer and network technologies can orient the customer to sales and product information. The first is the computer's ability to mediate exchanges in ways that are difficult to develop in face-to-face conversations. This is known as computer mediated communications (Santoro, 1995). Computer communications break down barriers and encourage uninhibited interaction (Jones, S. G., 1995). Edward Barret defines this as "sociomedia" and believes that this ability to eliminate social boundaries is an important aspect of computer technology (Barret, 1992). His thesis is that the ultimate value of these machines is as a mediator for "social" purposes. He points out that they "objectify, exchange and collaborate, invoke, comment upon, modify, and remember thoughts and ideas" as an extension of our social interactions (p. 1). This idea is at the core of the power of computers to transfer information because it builds relationships that reinforce the educational experience.

A second change brought about by distance learning technologies is a subtle shift in the way information is acquired. This shift suggests that information, as a practical knowledge, is the result of social construction. The general theme is that meaning, as information accepted and absorbed by users as fundamental to their knowledge of a subject, must be constructed through interaction. This interaction assigns meanings and values through inputs that evolve in the exchange; and the experience of these exchanges guide final acceptance of the information we acquire, constructing certain truths that are then maintained in further interactions (Jones and Maloy, 1996; Dewey, 1963). Important to the do-it-yourselfer is that interaction suggests improved retention and deeper understanding of the practical application of something that may at first appear abstract or of limited application. This means that a hidden potential of distance learning must also include its inherent interactive technologies.

The third change suggested by distance education is the asynchronous nature of computer-mediated communications. Asynchronous communication blends with the constructivist notion of interaction and the construction of knowledge. This is because once the information is in place and accessible, the customer defines the pace, quantity, and quality of the information transfer. Users therefore set the pace by their interactions with the learning material. This means that interaction is not a simultaneous one-on-one relationship with an instructor or sales representative but can occur at any time that customer has either the time or the interest to acquire the information. This allows a user-centered or what many educators call a learner-centered experience (Jones and Maloy, 1996; Johnson and Johnson, 1989; Harrison, 1996; Smith, 1995). In other words, users control the quantity of information they absorb and therefore regulate their understanding of the material according to their interests.

In summary, taking the constructivist's notion of context and activity, where learning (as new information) emerges from interaction and communication as social construction, the asynchronous nature of computer-mediated communications may offer an opportunity to literally define the learning process. These ideas set up the potential for social construction in a controlled interactive virtual environment. If we substitute the constructivist learner for the user (or do-it-yourselfer), and think of learning as the transfer of information within a controlled interactive activity, we may be able to satisfy customers' need for information by focusing on the way they acquire that information in the learning process. In other words, the design of the computer interface could actually control the quality and quantity of information transfer. If information can be controlled, directed, and represented according to a perceptual order of communication relationships, meaning (as understanding) might then be shaped by the computer-mediated environment. This means when we recognize that networked technologies are a sophisticated information environment that stimulate interaction and create meaning through that interaction, the power of distance learning as a forum for education seems clear.

An Anatomically-Correct Three-Dimensional Model

Given the inherent strength of computers to communicate ideas and provide the context for user interaction, the challenge is to turn these interactions into a training environment, not as a regulated formation of predetermined instructions but as a purposeful association of ideas that can expand consumers' understanding of the general principles of design and construction. The singular advantage web-based technologies can bring to these associations is their ability to present these interactions as a visually perceptive environment. The idea is that interaction within the virtual environment centers visual or graphically referential data-links that disclose an underlying data structure as user-centered segments of information. Users therefore remain in control of their movement within the data and build perceptive relationships with the information through their interactions. These perceptual references can therefore build on the referential structure of the brain and how it reinforces memory and learning through patterns and textures (Johnson, 1991).

The central thesis of these information relationships is therefore to provide a visual reference to the information to associate the mind's eye with an underlying data structure. The idea of associative visual relationships to orient the user to information is not new (Loftus, 1976; Bedard, 1989; Kojonen, 1989). The concept of graphic representation of information is also well documented (Smith, 1988; Tufte, 1993; Tufte, 1994; Turkle, 1990; Fluckiger, 1995; Hellman and James, 1995) and has been the subject of both science fiction and research on the manufacturing methods of major corporate projects (Sabbagh, 1996).

The goal is therefore to provide a construction training system using visual references that a user can remember within the information environment. To meet this goal, a piece-based construction information system called PCIS (pronounced "pieces") has been designed to catalogue the construction of a specially designed trainer. The three-dimensional computer model of this trainer is "anatomically correct." This means that instead of a simple diagrammatic representation of the building, every piece of the construction is visible in the context of its final assembly. The model is therefore central to the data relationships because its "anatomy" organizes the data structure. This means the virtual representation of the trainer can be sliced, elevated, and deconstructed into a set of hierarchical files. PCIS sorts these files into directories on a web server where they can be called into frames by mouse clicks on the graphic interface. In other words, these files are screen "shots" taken from preformatted camera positions and posted into the directories according to a designated graphic file format that can then be posted behind image maps. The user thereby accesses the information system with a browser connected to the intranet or World Wide Web using "hot-spots" on the pages to call the files into their designated frame. Important is that these frames and the images are juxtaposed in ways that give the information coherence and visually strengthen referential relationships in the data (Gloor, 1997; Andleigh and Thakrar, 1996). This means that the action of clicking on a piece of the model reinforces the learning experience by interactively referencing information in adjacent frames. This juxtaposition gives a sense of coherence from link to link as iconic references that reinforce the information relationship (Horton, 1994b). (See Figure 4.2.)

It is important to remember that the data in this visual relationship is piece-oriented. This means that the image of each piece of an assembly relates to a separate chunk of information in the database. These chunks are components of the database and set up the graphic simulations of the data environment. The construction model thereby defines the spatial relationships of the total assembly because it acts as a graphic index to the underlying information. This supporting data includes details of the construction, manufacturer information, and special instructions for the pieces themselves. Because the data is closely related to its graphical representation, the user can visually access information about the pieces. It also means one can search, sort, and even play with combinations of the data to simulate alternatives in the construction process. Most important, the data organizes the information as a virtual document, and the computer mediates user perception of the construction process. This means that the information is never visible as a whole. In fact, this is a "virtual" document because users may not know if they have ever seen the entire information system, only that they were able to get the material they needed when they needed it (Horton, 1994a). In this way, the training environment is not an abstract diagram of a building with labels and dimensions but a sortable graphic representation of its construction as an interactive representation of its construction.

FIGURE 4.2. JUXTAPOSITION OF THE FRAMES.

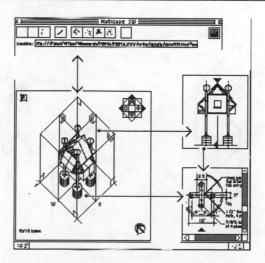

The Interactive Interface to the Datacentric Model

In general, there are two main elements of the model in PCIS. The first is a series of isometrics that represents graphically scaled information, and the second
is a set of perspectives that give a sense of the shape and form of the trainer. In
the first part, a mouse click leads to an introductory page that shows the trainer
rotating through four isometric angles. These isometrics are proportionally scaled
views of the same model. The user can interact to deconstruct the trainer from
any of these angles. This means that users can remove the roof, siding, or frame
of the trainer according to their interest. At any one of these levels of decon-
struction, the model can be rotated to one of the other isometric angles. From this
new viewing angle the user is free to reconstruct or deconstruct the model and
query the hypergraphic images for additional information. A data-theater sur-
rounds the orthographic index to capture projections of the pieces of the object.
This data-theater is visible in any one of these views. (See Figure 4.3.) Projections
therefore include elevations, plans, slices, and close ups of the trainer. For example, a click on one of the elevation-panels leads to a corresponding projection of

FIGURE 4.3. THE DATA-THEATER FOR THE TRAINER.

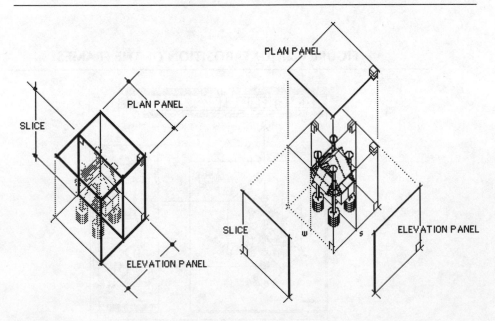

one side of the model. This projection can then be deconstructed by further mouse clicks to access information on finishes, framing, and construction of each face of the object. From above, the plan panel projects a plan view that can then be deconstructed in layers to show roofing, framing, floor plan, foundation layout, excavation, and even the underground utilities. The view can also be played as an animation of the construction sequence from that particular view. In addition, there are animated slices that cut through the object to give heights and materials. These slices allow the user to see the interior of the trainer and explore hidden portions of the construction. They differ from sections through the model in that the user can continue to deconstruct or construct the trainer by moving through the material layers of the slice.

A click on one of the pieces of the trainer leads to two-dimensional drawings and details of the actual construction. This means a mouse click on one of the pieces will bring up additional details in an adjacent frame. Animations of some of the more complex details allow them to be viewed sequentially to show the nuances of a particular construction process. It is important that these details can be called from any one of the various views that might be visible as a result of any of the combinations of mouse clicks in the framed environment. Again, the educational objective is to respond to the user's queries by juxtaposing the graphical data in a way that allows the user to understand the construction details and the assembly process.

The user can switch the orthographic index to a framed virtual environment. (See Figure 4.4.) In this part of the database, a different set of directories posts eye level images of the anatomic model so that it appears to be turned and viewed from various perspective angles. In other words, the user is free to move around the object by following a set of framed views of the trainer. Though a fully VRML or immersive information landscape is possible, early tests indicated that such a space is disorienting and frustrating to navigate (Fukai, 1997). Instead, a framed series of preset views allow greater control over the information transfer because it restricts the user to specific moves and directions (Turner, 1996). In this way, the trainer can be intentionally framed to deliver a particular view of the construction information. The strength of framing in cinematic research is fairly straightforward (Deleuze, 1986; Hayword, 1993). The idea is to sequence the images so that they present the object in the manner that transmits the information objectives of a particular scene. In this virtual environment, scale, solar patterns, and visual representations of the assembly of the pieces is most important. For this reason, viewing angles emphasize certain parts of the trainer to encourage interaction by the user. A mouse click on one of the pieces of the virtual model thereby leads to specifications and manufacturing information about the construction materials. Where available, links on these pages lead to resources and

FIGURE 4.4. THE VR INDEX.

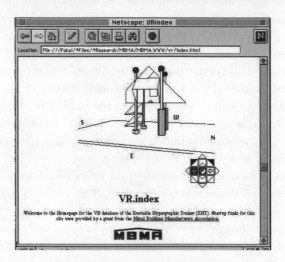

information on the Internet. A map of the viewing angles orients the user to the virtual model, including the ability of the user to move in closer to the model. The data theater used in the orthographic environment is visible as a reference to the position of the model; however, the user must return to the orthographic environment to access scaled elevations and slices of the trainer. (See Figure 4.5.)

Implementation of a Home Improvement Trainer

In this case study, the PCIS concept is implemented on a trainer with a combination of both wood and metal construction. The model of the trainer demonstrates a variety of generic construction information without being so simplistic as to appear obvious or sophomoric. It includes structural conditions such as simple and cantilevered beams and joists, tension and compression connectors, gables, and trusses. It also includes typical details for projects such as decks and stairs, as well as installations for doors and windows. To present this information in a visually referenced training environment, PCIS uses a hypergraphic interface to guide the customer through the information. The interface is hypergraphic because a mouse click on a graphic representation of a piece of the construction leads to detailed information about that piece. This could include banner advertising by the manufacturers of the materials in that piece. In this way, PCIS

FIGURE 4.5. THE FRAMES OF THE VR INDEX.

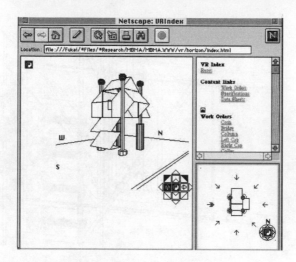

can index any number of project phases for various types of construction. For example, the trainer shows standard wood framing, while variations represent light-weight metal framing and standard metal building manufacturing techniques. The phases included for these framing types follow the construction process from layout to final finishes. The trainer therefore gives construction information for a variety of possible project applications without suggesting a specific solution for any particular project. The objective with this trainer is to educate and inform the customer's imagination in order to cultivate a long-term interest in applying a high level of construction knowledge to a succession of home improvement projects. (See Figure 4.6.)

The objective is to set up a learner-centered construction information environment where do-it-yourselfers are free to wander through an information database and inform themselves of various construction techniques. In this way, they will gain the confidence they need to purchase items for their projects, using sales representatives as resources to make final decisions about certain products. This means the training experience must work effectively in two ways. First it must allow multidirectional exploration so that users feels free to query the database by deconstructing, reconstructing, and inquiring about the pieces of the assembly. Second, the images must graphically enhance the information transfer. In other words, customers must be able to see the construction sequences as a consequence of their interactive motivation toward the information. The idea is to allow users to

FIGURE 4.6. DETAILS EMBODIED IN THE TRAINER.

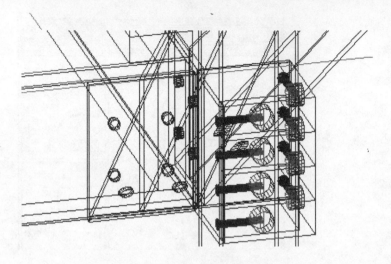

establish their own level of training by allowing them to acquire information according to their individual need to know.

It is important to remember that the images for both the orthographic and virtual parts of the PCIS environment come from the same anatomic model. PCIS processes the model to capture bitmapped images according to a set of predetermined views. As outlined in preceding paragraphs, these shots are converted to graphic files and posted to directories to be called into the web pages visible within the framed browser. The active hotspots of the image maps are therefore not affected by modifications to the model as long as the basic structure of the trainer remains the same. A key to the success of the PCIS system is that the trainer is modular and therefore supports a number of alternate configurations without the need to change the format of the web pages and their image maps. This means many types of construction can be interchanged as long as the location of the anatomic model is calibrated prior to processing into the PCIS directories.

Conclusions and Applications

This project differs from other distance training sites because it acts as an interface to a three-dimensional datacentric model. Important is that the construction information derived from interactions with this model are generic and therefore applicable to a number of different projects. The idea is to provide a hierarchy of information about construction, taking a broad all-inclusive view of the model as an initial level of inquiry and then penetrating its details according to the motivations of the user's interests. This leaves the learner in control of the educational process.

PCIS is important because it is learner-centered. It builds on the computer's capacity to mediate communications, sets the stage for interaction and the construction of meaning, and allows this interaction to occur asynchronously at the pace of the user. This makes it especially valuable as a sales tool in the home improvement industry, first because it provides a generic resource that allows the discussion of various construction details on the sales floor. This means that sales representatives can walk their customers through a construction condition on the web site and those same customers can then access that information from their home computers. Second, distance training continues the dialogue with the customer after initial contact. This expands the customers' understanding of not only the initial information but broadens their interest by providing a learning environment that can continue to be explored for a variety of new projects. This dialogue provides a point of contact for further sales within the virtual training environment.

In early testing, PCIS demonstrates the serendipitous potential of image mapped graphics in distance training. As such, it can be easily duplicated and used in a variety of other training applications. While its computer model and imaging can be fairly complex, its web construction is simple and straightforward. This is because PCIS avoids complex codes and proprietary plug-ins that are not widely available. As such, it uses images, animated files, and simple programming to create its learning environment. This means that any set of computer drawings or photographs can be loaded into directories and juxtaposed to create visual relationships that reinforce the learning experience. Applied to construction information, multi-framed datacentric modeling would enhance information transfer by enriching visual clues or strengthening the mind's associations with certain combinations of images. These visual multimedia relationships offer a variety of combinations of interactive experiences all governed by the learner's motivation and interests. This means a datacentric environment can rapidly transfer information according to visual patterns on a need-to-know basis. This limits the amount of information that must be mastered by prioritizing it into chunks of data that can be acquired as the application for that information emerges. This allows learning to occur through a hands-on experience in the context of its importance and orients the educational experience by placing it in the control of the learner. In this way, interactive users set the pace of their own self-discovery.

CHAPTER FIVE

INCREASING EMPLOYEE KNOWLEDGE AND UNDERSTANDING OF OPERATIONAL SYSTEMS: INTEGRATING MULTIPLE TECHNOLOGIES AT NYNEX

Barry Howard

What do you do when your corporate vision demands a higher degree of competence from its employees yet those same employees have no time to attend the training efforts that would bring them the knowledge and skills to achieve those competencies? What would you do when field organizations are more confident that their home-grown conference-room classes are superior to those of the centralized training organization? What happens when managers and employees are asking for courses in two-hour sections scheduled at the needs of the business or the individual not at the needs of the training school? For the NYNEX Corporation (now Bell Atlantic) the answer was large scale electronic education (using the computer and telecommunication to deliver education).

This chapter describes the need that drove NYNEX to make distance training a major portion of its educational program, the wide selection of tools that it used, and the planning and organizing processes that enabled the program to mature. It concludes with a review of the strengths and weaknesses of the overall program.

NYNEX'S Training Need

NYNEX, like most large multi-location organizations, was facing all of these challenges. With a growing Call Center operation at each of its major building sites and an increased requirement to keep employees close to the work location to satisfy customer requirements, locally delivered training was a must. Cost however was a principle concern in sending instructors out to each site, especially when the class size had to be reduced to keep employees on the line serving customers. In addition, there was a need for classes that were directly related to performance, short modules specifically focused on methods and procedures. Traditional instructor-led training would not have been cost-efficient for the short classes. The clients of the training, sensing the problems generated by their new requirements, were unhappy and considered creating their own form of training, which may have been fragmented, inefficient, and ineffective.

The NYNEX Solutions(s)

NYNEX had a number of alternatives to solve this increased remote, modularized training load that its clients demanded. Here are some of them:

Business As Usual

This approach was the easiest. It required no new organizations, no new infrastructure. It would have allowed the centralized training operation to continue with instructor-led courses, continuing the focus on primarily new employee training. It would have forced remote clients to develop and deliver continuation or ongoing training with their own instructors. While easy, this alternative was the least cost-efficient, allowing inconsistent instructor-led training to be delivered at each of its locations.

Rapid Cutover to Electronic Education

This approach, while successful in some companies, would not have fit the NYNEX environment. With its increased need for training and limited capital and expense funding, a successful mass cutover would have proved elusive. In addition a focus on a single tool (at that time) would probably have left NYNEX with touch screen or laser disk technology deployed in all of its locations, without the opportunity to explore the new technology tools being offered in the marketplace.

Incremental Cutover to an Electronic Education Spectrum of Tools

The incremental approach offered NYNEX a cautious alternative. It would require a constant battle for funding and support. It would require a constant touch with the changing electronic education tools market. On the positive side however it would allow a high degree of experimentation on a small scale. The results of the early pilots would provide leverage for the production effort that could be implemented for all the locations.

The author selected the last alternative to bring NYNEX into the electronic education world. Initial staffing was drawn from the Information Technology (IT) training staff, replaced by an even larger circle of outside suppliers. Eventually, the IT training process was completely outsourced to a strategic training vendor that freed all but a skeleton staff to concentrate on electronic education. The multiple tool strategy was fundamental, allowing NYNEX to bring computer, video, and network-based solutions simultaneously. It allowed the planning and marketing effort to reach a wide audience with widely diverse needs.

The NYNEX Electronic Education Toolbag

Using in-building learning centers (see later sections on the learning centers), NYNEX had the opportunity to exploit a wide variety of electronic education tools. As delivery to the desktop and home has become more feasible (network enabled training (Internet, and so on), the tools have expanded. Here is the current[1] list, in the approximate order that NYNEX brought them into production.

- Computer-based training (CBT) (text and graphics)
- CBT simulation training
- One-way video (using business-broadcast television)
- Multimedia (video and audio and CBT)
- Two-way video (using video teleconference)

---

[1]At the time of this writing, Fall 1997. With the growth of Internet and server-based tools, the list could be expected to grow at the rate of one to two new tools per year based on seven years of experience.

- One-way video interactive (using student response units and other non-video tools)
- Network-delivered computer based training
- Network-enabled training—synchronous training
- Network-enabled training—asynchronous training
- Electronic coaches (electronic performance support systems)
- Desktop Video Learning (planned)
- Transitional systems (video to CD-ROM)
- Electronic evaluation systems for distributed delivery

To assist the reader, I have supplied a series of tables that link most of the production tools to the key indicators and learning objective(s) that NYNEX employed.

TABLE 5.1. OPERATIONAL ISSUES FOR ELECTRONIC EDUCATION.

EE Tool	Audience Size	Cost/Student	Cost per Course	Time to Implement
Computer-based training generic	Entire organization	Low	Moderate	Weeks
Computer-based training custom	Organization	Moderate	High	Months
CBT simulation training	Department	Moderate	High	Months
One-way video	Hundreds	Low	High	Weeks
Multimedia	Organization	Low	Moderate	Weeks
Two-way video	40 'max.'	Low	Low	Weeks
One-way video—interactive	300 'max.'	Moderate	High	Months
Network-enabled training—Synchronous	Department	Low	Low	Weeks
Network-enabled training—asynchronous	Entire organization	Moderate	Moderate	Months
Electronic coaches	Department	Moderate	Moderate	Months

TABLE 5.2. ELECTRONIC EDUCATION TOOLS AND LEARNING OBJECTIVES.

EE Tool	Awareness	Knowledge Transfer	Skill Development	Expertise Building
Computer-based training	X			
CBT simulation training		X	X	
One-way video	X			
Multimedia		X	X	
Two-way video			X	X
One-way video—interactive	X	X		
Network-enabled training—synchronous		X	X	
Network-enabled training—asynchronous		X	X	X
Electronic coaches		X	X	X

Computer Based Training (Text and Graphics)[2]

The overall NYNEX strategy for most of its electronic education implementation was a proof of concept effort (a small pilot) followed by a leveraged implementation (a large scale cutover) using the proof-of-concept as the base.

[2]Both CBT as is described here and multimedia are different executions of computer-based training. Separating them based on video and audio capabilities allows me to describe different distribution strategies. In general, CBT with only text and graphic capability (especially with only sixteen colors) allows delivery on more basic computers. Multimedia requires a higher end computer workstation, generally with more elaborate video and audio capability.

Computer-Based Training in the early 1990s was a perfect tool for this strategy. By purchasing the CBT from quality vendors as off-the-shelf packages, NYNEX could be assured that the design had been tested across a wide group of users and that the cost of the first effort would be limited based on a wide market for the tools. The implementation process could be fast. This last characteristic was critical in the early stages, demonstrating that a change from instructor-led could bring early results. The early curricula chosen included CBT used for computer related subjects, allowing the displacement of outside vendors rather than full-time employees. It delayed the impact on internal forces until later tools were adopted.

Selecting good CBT from the maze of providers provided a model that was reused at many points in NYNEX electronic education history. A variety of evaluation tools were used to separate the real vendors from those who were just learning. They included

- Detailed vendor interviews (vendor strength)
- Subject matter expert review (for content)
- Instructional design review (for learning values)
- Operational reviews to be sure that the CBT would run on the many NYNEX computers
- Userability reviews to be sure that the students would be comfortable with the look and feel as well as the navigational tools
- Competitive bidding where possible (not frequently at that time)
- Industry reputation gathered from peers at conferences

Notice that production value was not one of the evaluation processes. The slick, demo-quality, upper management-focused product frequently fails the other tests listed here. For new players, high production quality in the opening portion of a salesperson's pitch can be a warning sign. One vendor was more anxious to demonstrate his production quality CD-ROM-based lingerie catalog than demonstrate his simplistic CBT.

NYNEX's early CBT was distributed by company mail. Later on, the corporate network provided a better tool. Early user acceptance was high, but a significant amount of attention needed to be focused on completion, measurement, and tracking to ensure that floppy disks and support material did not sit on the desk waiting for the right time for training. Penalties and rewards for returning the media helped, as well as certification programs. The requirement to attend a follow-up, instructor-led workshop had the highest potential of driving the student to complete the CBT (at the desk or home) and then return the media, the evaluation sheet, and the collateral material.

By selecting CBT that could run on simple computers (at that time a 386) user problems were minimized. Still, NYNEX had to invest in staffing a CBT help desk to handle the wide variety of computers on which this tool was run. Fortunately the personal computer with all its variations was the prime delivery platform.

As will be seen later, CBT delivery strategy parallels many of the same characteristics of multimedia, differing in the degree of interaction and distribution. (See footnote on page 96.) One very clear parallel is the changing expectation of the student after a CBT experience.

Because of the high quality of the purchased CBT, students quickly learn, adapt, and then enjoy the self paced, engaged user controlled experience. Within a few courses, the students begin to demand the same learning experience for their job-specific training. This enthusiasm pushes the demand for custom CBT for corporate-specific subjects. At NYNEX, custom CBT development followed purchased CBT by about one year, accelerating afterwards. Some of the most aggressive acceleration came from client (not trainer) stimulation. One type of customized training was simulation.

CBT Simulation Training

NYNEX's early attempts to bring CBT to the desktop were the direct result of client satisfaction with the purchased CBT. The first custom desktop applications that were requested were for training on NYNEX's own operational systems (systems that performed processes associated with NYNEX's core business-telecommunications, including order entry, maintenance scheduling, accounts inquiry, and hundreds of others).

CBT simulation training required training modules linked to specific portions of operational screens. Snapshots (bit mapped pictures of operational screens) were the way that the operational systems were captured to be brought into a training environment. Adding text and edits for each of the fields provided the equivalent of an on-screen tutor. NYNEX purchased a special-purpose minicomputer to assemble the text, edits, and images together in a learning flow. While moderately successful, each of these systems required significant startup time, significant investment in training technicians to operate the software and field support in supplying subject matter experts to insure that the training matched the working environment. In addition, the system was DOS-based at a time that the world was moving to more graphic windows systems. As a result, CBT simulation using a dedicated minicomputer for course creation was used for a few courses and then dropped in favor of the electronic coach (covered later). The training through simulation for operational systems that was completed found its way to desktop training and as a classroom enhancement.

One-Way Video (Business Television)

NYNEX had developed its business television facility for a variety of applications including corporate leaders' announcements and a newscast operation. Using this facility for training was reasonably easy. With little investment a number of classes were delivered, reaching large audiences with courses that needed knowledge transfer objectives. What limited interaction was needed (mostly question and answer) came from students who called in. While successful, the medium had many limitations, namely cost per broadcast and the very limited engagement of the student. The video studio was controlled by expert practitioners who were more focused on high production values rather than learning objectives. These cultural conflicts frequently required a compromise in the quality or efficiency of the training classes. They did however demonstrate that learning could be carried on the medium. A number of years later, training turned to this one-way network for a more interactive effort.

Multimedia (CBT with Text, Audio and Video)

The powerhouse of NYNEX's electronic education strategy is the learning center (discussed in detail later in this chapter). Initially built with low end PCs, some VCRs and videodisks (even some touchscreen technology), they have grown into a modern training factory using state-of-the-art multimedia workstations and a growing video local area network capability.

NYNEX's initial experience with multimedia focused on purchased courses. Inexpensive, well tested and implemented with high production values, these packages were perfect for the early trials. Initially installed in small groups, they appealed to the improvising learner who matched learning with business needs. The video and audio was a welcome addition to the simple text and graphics of CBT.

As the number of titles grew, a number of things occurred.

- NYNEX needed to build an evaluation process for the ever-growing number of tools.
- NYNEX also had to develop a set of standards that fed this growth process. They included
- Technical standards (would they work on NYNEX's computers?)
- Instructional design standards (would students really learn?)
- Userability standards (would the users be able to handle the navigation, lessons and testing?)

NYNEX developed a number of panels, processes, and tracking systems to develop these tools.

Two-Way Video Using Videoconferencing

Of all the electronic education tools that NYNEX has used, video distance learning using video conferencing is closest to a standard classroom. The resemblance
is deceptive however, as the classes look very little like the 'old' NYNEX classroom.
With over 10,000 students affected each year, and a course variety that includes
virtually any type of class, this medium is second only to multimedia in its impact
on the NYNEX student.

An experience in two-way video is very different than one-way. Not only are
both sides of the network seen but the atmosphere is relaxed, similar to the on-
site classroom and a marked contrast to the broadcast-like one-way, high production
value classroom. Errors are okay, and experimentation is fine. The student-focused
nature of the class forces it into a very relaxed mode. When observing one early effort, when a craftsman had put his feet on a desk in the middle of a class exercise,
a vice president said, "Look at him, he is really enjoying this." When a laughter-
filled segment in the middle of a class focused on the accents of the Boston team
versus the Brooklyn team, another vice president noted, "There is more culture
sharing going on across the network than I get at all of my meetings."

Adapting the videoconferencing for distance learning was easy. Some additional microphones for the larger rooms, a personal computer for instructor's slides
at each site, and some extra chairs and tables for the ten-plus student rooms
were all that were really needed. The rest was garden-variety videoconferencing.

Adapting the course delivery was another matter. While early attempts may
have looked like one-way classes, experienced trainers soon recognized that this
was the perfect medium for a new kind of learning. Student-focused learning
became more common. With its ability to originate anywhere, students quickly
became the "instructors," reporting on team projects, participating in games, and
helping classmates at other locations. Students easily learn the controls for the
cameras and can easily be motivated to move the camera to highlight other students. As a result the instructor truly can be become the facilitator.

Adapting the course development process was another challenge. The designer needs to think in terms of computer tools for visuals. He or she needs to
design student interaction at 50 percent or greater, a NYNEX goal. A video transition is also planned every ten minutes, changing the setting or the focus of a
lesson.

Adapting students to this medium was easy. The novelty of sharing the classroom with students from across the organization overcomes any concerns about
transmission quality. The motivation generated by not having to leave home to take
a course pays great dividends even when the student is asked to take the lead in the
classroom. The ability to use the medium for short courses (such as "lunch and

learn" training at mid-day) brings managers into supporting roles when they realize how much work time can be retained while still having the training active. When senior managers can calculate return on investment from work time saved, they will pay for all the equipment and staffing that the training department could require.

Adapting existing instructors may turn out to be the most difficult part. Concerned about job elimination, loss of classroom privacy, and new technologies, the instructors may resist the change in their classrooms to the new distance learning format. Special management incentives or rewards will be required to motivate the old team. Some organizations may elect to staff the function with new blood. At NYNEX, the creation of the producer's position was an effective catalyst to make the change happen. The producer was really a combination project manager, salesperson, instructor, and developer who when trained could ease others through the distance learning change.

Over the years, the great success of the video broadcasts masked the administrative, operational, and developmental systems that keep the program going. These methods have survived two total changes in staffing (due to voluntary retirements and some downsizing adjustments) with the program continuing to function.

With the merger to Bell Atlantic, the distance learning program can only see expansion to a much larger geographic footprint, a much larger scope of courseware, and a much larger student and manager base. Expansion however should be easier, with a proven base of experience and operational procedures to support the larger delivery system. With the larger base, the cost of development per student of new courses will drop even lower.

One-Way Video Interactive

With the success of the two-way video program, NYNEX found its video conferencing straining with the new volume of classes competing with conferences. (The Training and Education department became the largest single user of the videoconference network.) NYNEX had to turn back to its one-way facilities for the capacity to handle the growing number of courses. With its experience in limited interaction one-way video, NYNEX turned to a consultant from another corporation who had used a one-way network to create two-way-like interaction. The secret was in the preparation of site-identity exercises and strong collateral material.

Site-identity exercises in this medium translate into competitive exercises in which the on-camera instructor advises each of the locations to complete some form of project off line. Each site then works on its own, usually competing against the clock or the other sites. When completed, the sites then call or fax their results to the teacher at the expiration of the time allotment. The teacher then calls each site in turn at random ("Hot Potato"), or with a variety of other protocols. Prizes, a facilitator at each site, and a supplementary communication system (call-in phones) are necessary to make this work, along with a well-paced delivery. The producer has to limit the number of sites (three to four) to keep this interaction going.

The results have been very satisfying. The one-way interactive broadcast has been able to reach a large number of students (300–400) in a limited number of sites, with a short knowledge transfer lesson. One such effort was so successful that it grew into a bi-weekly update for Call Center personnel on Saturday mornings.

One-way interactive serves a totally different training objective from its sister formats and requires a great deal of planning to make it work. Some organizations have used student response systems (a keypad, microphone, and polling system that runs parallel with the video broadcast) to accomplish similar goals with a more technical flavor. It is a valuable adjunct to the other mediums and allows clients and developers to select the optimum medium for learning, time, and cost efficiency.

Network Delivered Computer-Based Training

When NYNEX purchased a groupware system (Lotus Notes) for its e-mail and database systems, Training and Education found it a perfect tool for delivering CBT directly to employees' desktops. Once at the desktop the employee could take the course, download it to his or her hard drive, or download to a floppy disk(s) to take at home. Purchasing libraries from a variety of vendors and adapting them to this new delivery engine, students could order and receive courseware without the heavy overhead of disk mailing and tracking systems.

The value of this new delivery system was seen in early months of operation where 500 or more courses were ordered. When the operational systems were improved to provide one-click access to the courses, the volumes grew even more. Of even greater value were surveys that showed the courses were being taken at home, on the employee's own time, creating enormous benefit for the individual and the organization.

To reduce network and disk download overload, the courses were kept to small sizes (less than five megabytes). This also ensured that the average home PC could handle the course, usually text, graphics, and some limited audio.

CBT, in this new delivery format, continues to attract a large volunteer student population. Tracking continues to be an issue as students complete their courses off the network. As the CBT moves onto the Internet, this missing link is expected to close.

Once developed, the employee support for this delivery system is minimal, with automated software and large server storage drives picking up the workload.

Network-Enabled Training—Synchronous

After NYNEX completed the delivery of CBT via the network, its attention switched to the more advanced use of the Internet for training using a synchronous strategy (students and teachers working together in the same time slot, using a separate medium for a talking path and the shared display as a common graphics screen). While NYNEX has not brought this tool into full production status, it appears to have great promise because

- The vendor tools are more mature.
- Synchronous training imposes a discipline that requires that students are at least present for the class.
- The Internet continues to gather extensive interest for classroom-like delivery.

Network-Enabled Training—Asynchronous

Asynchronous network-enabled training (Internet, and so on) has the potential to reproduce most of the interactions found in the classroom without requiring that students and instructor being engaged at the same time. With network-enabled-based tools, teacher-to-student communication can be maintained. With simple e-mail student-teacher communication can be accomplished. With chat rooms, shared documents, and multithreaded discussions, student-to-student communication and learning can take place.

With all this communication and graphics capability, asynchronous learning should be easy, allowing a true educational process to occur in a "your-time, your-place" mode. NYNEX's early experience with this tool revealed the following concerns:

- Student commitment issues need to be addressed in advance. Students need to be aware that "your time" does not mean anytime, and the student must stay up with the class. A significant student drop-out rate was attributed to students who had not allocated sufficient time for the course.

- Navigation issues, knowing where you are and where to go next, need to be simple. Any complexity will result in a student's loss of interest. New asynchronous engines (learning shells) may hold great promise by creating a simple, universal navigation process.

- Body language. The instructor must be able to read the body language through the network and determine when a student is slipping back, having trouble with the material, or falling asleep. The new shells may solve that problem by providing graphical representations of a student's activity and contributions by examining other indicators for this information (number of accesses over time, number of bulletin board entries, and so on.)

NYNEX's experiments with asynchronous web-based training ceased after its initial two pilots (team building courses) produced by an outside supplier, waiting for a good commercial shell to be produced that would automate the navigation and body language processes. At the time of this writing a number of the new software programs were just reaching the marketplace. As with most obvious but difficult market winners there are a wealth of marginal vendors in the market. Let the buyer beware.

Electronic Coaches (Electronic Performance Support Systems)

True electronic performance support systems, where learning is built within the operational system, available while the system user is trying to complete a transaction, are not simple to create. They require that the information technology (IT) organization make a commitment to building learning into its system while it is building the computer code that will operate the system. Too often the IT department is faced with cutover pressures, bug-free code pressures, and client anxiety pressures that make the embedded training effort a burden. In addition, those who have tried to make this work have found that the trainers waste significant time while the system designers change and modify their system to meet user demands, destroying much of the training in the process. We tend not to measure our IT whiz kids on the true cost of implementing their computerized systems, so the cost of training is something that the user or the training department must bear. Any illogical non-intuitive process that the user must learn now becomes a training process, separate from the system itself. Electronic performance support systems, while absolutely needed, are just beginning to be implemented.

An alternative is the "almost" electronic performance support systems, the electronic coaches (as NYNEX named them). These very new server-based systems allow the training department to build a shell around the operational system (main frame or server based) and add an icon for the user to call for electronic support. The beauty of the system is the fact that, except for knowing that the electronic coach is present on the network, the IT department is not involved at all. Lessons made of text, graphics, audio, or even video can be called by the educator to respond to a user's questions. The questions can be at the system, screen, or even field level.

NYNEX's early pilot of an electronic coach demonstrated this freedom from IT restrictions and had immediate benefit to the user. The system being used by NYNEX also allows these lessons to be called from other courses, creating a learning repository. In addition, student notes and comments made during the lessons (for example, "I don't understand the lesson"; "this lesson was great") can be fed back to the developer to close the loop on instructional design.

The promise of these electronic coaches is to provide true desktop support for the enormous population of legacy computer systems, while true electronic performance support systems are built for the new ones. This training on older computer systems is so vast that electronic coaches could be active for decades.

The benefits of electronic coaches include

- Reduced initial training time for line employees (only the frequently required learning is necessary, the "Just In Case" can be embedded within the coach)
- Improved customer perception of employees (reduced requirements to transfer the call to an expert or supervisor)
- Reduced documentation required (methods and procedures can be placed within the coach)
- A living, constantly changing training environment (system changes, data content changes, and student suggestions can be changed with the system operational)

Transitional Systems (Video to CD-ROM)

When an organization invests in video distance learning *and* multimedia learning centers, there is a great opportunity to reuse the products of one medium within another. With the help of a number of service bureaus, transitions from video to CD-ROM based multimedia can now be done easily, quickly, and cheaply.

NYNEX's experience went like this. After a particularly successful one-way video production, many individuals would ask for a videotape to use for absentees, refreshers, and meeting support. The linear videotape however had limited learning value to the viewer, even though it contained interactions of peers captured during the broadcast.

With the help of the service bureau, the broadcast was converted to CD-ROM within weeks. But instead of a simple conversion, the service bureau enhances a basically linear process to create a user-controlled learning experience.

First the original video is broken into learning segments so that students can select the major section of the broadcast that was relevant to them. The multimedia screen divided into many segments can show the instructor, the slides or graphics, the navigation buttons, and the actual narrative in a text form. This last box also provides a powerful learning tool, a lecture text search engine. This allows the student to select only those words that are important and then allows the computer to display only that portion of the course. Although the student may ultimately watch the entire broadcast, he or she has total control of the learning environment and feels the control needed to match learning styles. A graphical look of the screen is shown in Figure 5.1. New versions of this transition software are being produced to allow Internet-based links between the student and other students and the instructor, further enhancing the learning experience.

Electronic Evaluation Systems for Distributed Delivery

With all of NYNEX's activity in electronic education, moving education close to or at the desk or at home, many of the administrative support systems had to be modified to maintain the quality and efficiency of the educational product. The reader might well picture the change from well equipped, carefully planned classrooms in a centralized facility to a widely dispersed, more improvisational virtual classroom with characteristics that vary from geography to geography and culture to culture. Materials distribution (texts and exhibits) and materials collection (exams and assignments) all require a new look. Fortunately, the same electronic medium that enables learning technology can also be used to support these administrative activities.

One specific area that NYNEX implemented replaces a paper-based evaluation process. Evaluation has always been an issue in corporate learning, with the well known four levels starting with the end-of-class smile sheets we all recognize with all their bias and time weaknesses.

Some highlights of the system include

FIGURE 5.1. MULTIMEDIA SCREEN

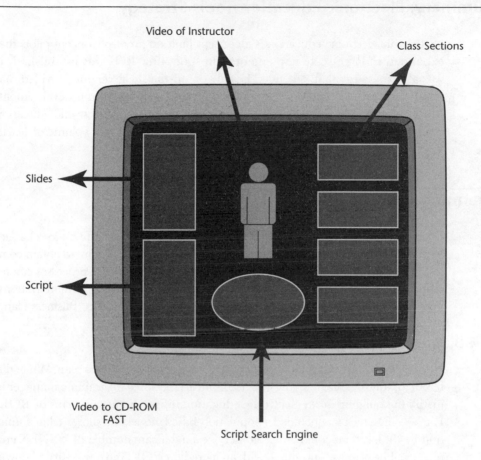

Video of Instructor

Class Sections

Slides

Script

Video to CD-ROM
FAST

Script Search Engine

- A thirty-day interval for improved student reflections on job impact
- An easy to use interface making student entry easy
- A facility to capture numeric data ("On a scale of one to nine rate the . . ."), for subsequent analysis using PC tools
- A facility to capture narrative data that allows the student to provide rich details. By capturing the student's own voice, the emotions associated with that information are also captured
- A facility that allows the information to be reviewed by higher management and then forwarded back to the manager responsible, closing the loop
- A system built on a low-cost voice mail system with minimum technical requirements

Summary: Electronic Education Tools Strategy

Large-scale electronic education is a concept built on proof-of-concept pilots that expanded to large-scale implementation soon after ROI was established. It was also a strategy that depended heavily on off-the-shelf, vendor provided materials (especially in multimedia and CBT), followed by custom development. Most important, it involves the use of a wide spectrum of electronic education tools rather than relying on any one tool to satisfy the expansive volume of learning needs.

Planning Processes for Electronic Education

Every organization has some form of structured process to create major changes in its infrastructure. Electronic education has to fit into that structure to obtain commitment at a variety of levels within the organization. While the processes can include organization strategy, technology infrastructure, measurement systems, briefings, vendor negotiations, and so on, it usually begins with the "Business Plan."

The Business Plan

The basic building block for any corporate change is the business plan. While different for any organization, business plans invariably force the training manager to justify the building of an electronic education infrastructure in terms of ROI.[3] For NYNEX, the plan included a population-based model that showed that a small number of locations could be used to service a significant number of NYNEX employees. The plan was submitted with an incredible ROI. And it was turned down.

When The Plan Is Turned Down

While a good plan, it failed to link with the major forces that were changing NYNEX at that time—process reengineering. As it turned out, process reengineering was a perfect partner for the training plan. Breaking down departmental isolation and moving employees together to serve the customer both helped to make electronic education feasible, especially in building-based learning centers.

[3]Return on Investment calculated by a number of different accounting packages that combine capital and expense based costs as well as variety of cost savings. These analyses rarely include the soft values of electronic education, including improved employee retention and the value of using a familiar work tool (personal computer) as a teaching tool.

Best of all, linking the electronic education plan to an existing change process made the effort so much easier. Later on, after the initial installations, new locations would vie to get the same level of facilities as their peers.

Key to the business plan was the ROI calculation. Driven by the population of potential students and the annual training requirement, calculating the reduced cost was simple. Key to that effort however was including the saved time off the job for the potential student. It's the multiplier that demonstrates the real value of electronic education:

- The ability to deliver training locally
- The ability to deliver courses in hourly increments, matching business volume shifts with training opportunities
- The ability to use tools that reduced the time needed to learn specific educational goals
- The ability to deliver "Just In Case" training

One Development Process: The In-Building Learning Center

A major element of the NYNEX plan was the concept of an in-building facilitated learning center. It included five major elements:

1. A multimedia room with fifteen or more learning stations using high end MPEG CD-ROM workstations
2. A video conference room adapted for video distance learning
3. An instructor-led technical classroom with LAN-linked workstations
4. A full time (outsourced) facilitator to run the complex and the multimedia center
5. A quick start-up supply of off-the-shelf multimedia

The learning center provided a place for electronic education to happen by being at the center of a remote corporate location. The place allows the centralized training organization to have a presence within the client's space. The creative value of the outsourced facilitator has gone beyond loading CD-ROMs and turning on video equipment to include things such as the following:

- Marketing
- Scheduling
- Guidance counseling

- New media evaluation for individual students
- Building newsletters
- Local curriculum design
- Video distance learning support for locally originated curses

NYNEX now operates sixteen locations and is expected to expand to Bell Atlantic and new locations.

A sample learning center could look like Figure 5.2. The multimedia learning centers have been built in every major population center within NYNEX. Using population studies, they can reach over 90 percent of the employees who

- Work in the building that houses the learning center
- Live near the building that houses the learning center
- Work in a satellite location near the learning centers

FIGURE 5.2. FULL SERVICE FACILITATED LEARNING CENTERS.

Facilitated MultiMedia Room

Instructor-Led Technical Classroom

Video Distance Learning Room

The multimedia learning center usually includes fifteen workstations equipped with earphones for private listening. Driven by a video LAN learning centers will receive both courseware and course video from a LAN server located on site. The primary courseware is bought off the shelf from a variety of suppliers, with a large concentration of courses in the computer field. The key ingredient of the success of the learning center is the facilitator.

The learning center facilitator is a full-time support individual who markets, schedules, operates, and tracks the learning center activity. In addition, the facilitator supports the video distance learning center, usually located in an adjacent classroom. The skills of the individuals vary but usually include computer literacy, marketing, and curriculum assembly (assembling modules of multimedia courses to fit individual requirements). Outsourced from a variety of sources (usually PC training companies) they have proven their value and versatility in providing standard courses to match custom requirements at each of the individual locations. As with CBT, the success of the off-the-shelf products has driven the demand for custom multimedia after students have their early experiences.

What cannot be seen in visiting the multimedia learning center is the administrative infrastructure that ensures the smooth operation of each of the learning centers. The scheduling, tracking, marketing, new course evaluation, and client information systems keep working occupancy close to 60 percent, even when each student visit is measured in fragments of a day. The ability of a student to use a lunch hour for training, of a manager to allocate a slow period for training, and to shift hours to the evening to reach after-hours students on their own time all contribute to expanded use of the facilities. A single NYNEX (now Bell Atlantic) manager telecommuting from her home manages the entire operation.

Strengths and Weaknesses of Electronic Education

After almost ten years of implementing the electronic education tools mentioned earlier, NYNEX can look back to a perspective that includes a high degree of electronic training, successes, and failures. Early projects (purchased CBT for instance) have led to more elaborate technology (multimedia), more involved distribution (network delivery), and more involved development projects (custom CBT for NYNEX-specific subjects, simple video broadcast that has led to two-way video, one-way interactive and so on.) With each step NYNEX became more committed to the electronic education delivery concept.

Building electronic education requires an organizational investment in people, both insourced and outsourced. The evolutionary plan requires an organizational continuity to learn from one production operation and turn it to the next technology step. As each technology step improves student engagement, the continuity ensures that lessons learned are leveraged and disasters avoided. While combinations of employees, contractors (who function as occasional employees), vendors (suppliers), and custom development houses will work better for some organizations than others, someone with more than just today's focus must maintain the long-term view to ensure that projects come to fruition. NYNEX created a small permanent staff, supported by the "outsiders" listed previously and some key insiders drawn from other training disciplines or clients.

The bottom line includes the following contributions from electronic education:

- Less time off the job for commuting for training
- More use of shortened, modular courses
- Improved employee performance
- Increased employee satisfaction with training
- Reduced cost per student
- Improved distribution of time critical training materials
- Reduced centralized classroom need
- Reduced centralized instructors

And the potential in the future of

- Reduced initial training days
- Improved employee confidence
- Faster implementation time for new courses

Some of the weaknesses include

- An initial requirement to market both concept and courses
- The building of an electronic education staff or infrastructure within the existing staff
- A risk that senior management will view electronic education as a substitute for all educational efforts
- A risk that local management will see electronic education as a replacement for corporately funded training (providing the time for training)

- Some false starts in early custom development projects
- A resistance from existing instructors and managers in implementing electronic education

Utilization[4]

NYNEX's aggressive program using the wide spectrum of electronic education tools has resulted in over 10 percent of its courses being delivered in some form of electronic education. This figure is probably understated, failing to count CBT courses delivered to one person but taken by many, fractional students who just take a portion of a course in multimedia, or one-way video students who are difficult to track. Of even greater significance is the fact that more than 60 percent of NYNEX's training effort is directed at new employees, leaving electronic education as the delivery agent for one in three classes for existing employees.

More specifically, NYNEX delivered

- Over 20,000 student days of multimedia training (custom or purchased) in facilitated multimedia learning centers. Note that many of these days consisted of fragmented sessions over a number of days. The result is far more training events, matching business peaks and valleys.
- Over 10,000 students in two-way video distance learning.
- Over 500 students per month ordering CBT delivered via Lotus NOTES.
- Bi-monthly broadcasts using one-way interactive video distance learning in a news program format.
- Many one-way video broadcasts using business television.
- A number of trials of asynchronous learning using a notes delivery system.
- Multiple custom developments of CBT and multimedia running simultaneously using a pool of external vendors.
- A video-to-LAN implementation for linking facilitated multimedia learning centers.
- A pilot of audio graphic training in preparation for Internet-delivered synchronous training.
- Multiple CD-ROM-based transition courses, using video distance learning as the source for multimedia courses delivered in the learning centers.

[4]As this article was completed after the author left NYNEX, the data reflects 1996 full-year data.

Putting It All Together

NYNEX's experience with electronic education tools spans almost ten years of business planning, trial implementation, and expansion into production for a wide variety of tools. NYNEX's strategy was to embrace each tool for its specific advantages, maximizing its contribution on a wide scale. NYNEX rarely was an "Early Adopter," preferring to learn from the experiences of others and then apply them on a macro scale. The process required creative vision, driving management, and a team of enthusiastic managers to keep all of the systems operational. As NYNEX approaches the year 2000, it is well positioned to absorb the next revolution of electronic education tools.

CHAPTER SIX

DISSEMINATING TIME-SENSITIVE INFORMATION: USING INTERACTIVE DISTANCE LEARNING (IDL) TO DELIVER TRAINING AND EDUCATION WITHIN THE AMERICAN RED CROSS BIOMEDICAL SERVICES

Lissa C. Klueter and Elizabeth C. Kalweit

The mission of the American Red Cross Biomedical Services (ARCBS) is to fulfill the needs of the American people for the safest, most reliable, and most cost-effective blood, plasma, and tissue through voluntary donations. Nearly six million volunteer blood donations are made to the Red Cross each year, making it the nation's largest blood supplier. The Red Cross also provides tissue for nearly one quarter of transplant surgeries. Additionally, the Red Cross develops, tests, and implements training programs in areas such as the operation of sophisticated blood testing laboratories and the selection of donors (ARCBS, 1997).

Ensuring that each staff member is competently trained to perform the regulated procedures that meet the Food and Drug Administration's (FDA) federal regulations in the areas of collection, manufacturing, and distribution of blood components is the responsibility of the ARCBS training department, the Charles Drew Biomedical Institute (Drew Institute). Regulated training requires certification that each employee is competent to perform his or her job function. It requires a series of critical control points throughout the training process and an annual competency assessment.

In addition to regulated training, the Drew Institute provided education in three curriculum areas: biomedical technology, management development, and total quality management. To support regulated training requirements to provide education in the four curriculum areas and to meet the needs of a geographically dispersed audience, the Drew Institute investigated various distance learning technologies in 1995. Challenged with the task of providing standardized, timely, and cost-effective instruction and continuing education for thousands of ARCBS staff and volunteers who are geographically dispersed throughout the United States, the Drew Institute selected an IDL system to augment its business television (BTV) network. The Red Cross had successfully used BTV since 1989, and adding IDL[1] seemed to be the logical next step.

The IDL system, as with any investment in technology, was purchased with the expectation that it would reduce training costs and improve the organization's efficiency in delivering training. The strategy was to use only the best instructors to deliver courses to larger audiences. This would reduce course material distribution costs and reduce travel costs for trainers and participants. It was also hoped that the IDL system would enhance standardization efforts. It is believed that each trainer's style and interpretation of the material leads to variability in the delivery. In a regulated environment it is important that each staff member hears the same message and performs the same procedure exactly the same way. Using one instructor to address larger audiences reduces the delivery variability and provides greater standardization.

Implementation Strategy

The ARCBS faced many challenges in implementing the IDL technology. This section describes those challenges in each of the following areas: acquisition announcement, development of a support infrastructure including remote site preparation, IDL staff training, and installation.

Acquisition Announcement

Once the distance learning technology was selected and approved, the next step was to announce the acquisition of the technology and to present an imple-

---

[1]The acronym IDL is used throughout the chapter to refer to a satellite-based, one-way video, two-way audio system with participants using keypads in remote classrooms. These systems are also called viewer response or keypad systems. Sometimes the term interactive video teletraining is used as an umbrella term for this type of system. It also includes two-way video and audio and desktop video conferencing systems. Please see the technical section for a more complete description of the IDL system used in the ARCBS.)

mentation plan to all ARCBS facilities. The vehicle selected to accomplish this was the Principal Officer Letter (POL). The POL was sent by the chief operating officer to all senior principal officers and principal officers of all blood services facilities (internal communication, POL 95-150, 1995). The POL described the rationale for supporting distance learning through the acquisition of the IDL system. It also provided a technical description of the IDL system, an implementation strategy, a list of critical activities and considerations, an implementation checklist, and a resource checklist.

The POL stated that implementation would be centrally coordinated by staff in the Drew Institute and the business television unit in the Red Cross Corporate Communication department. The POL identified the contractors supporting the installation, selected through a competitive bidding process. The contractors included a value-added distributor of the IDL system selected by the ARCBS and the Drew Institute's implementation partner who provided IDL training. The POL provided comprehensive information on implementation, such as equipment distribution, installation, training, and ongoing support.

In addition to providing comprehensive information on the Drew Institute and corporate communication responsibilities in the deployment and implementation of the new technology, the POL also detailed the responsibilities of staff at each site. Critical activities that were defined included designating lead staff in each facility, selecting appropriate rooms for the IDL equipment, installing phone lines, training lead staff in technical operations and skills necessary to facilitate distance learning broadcasts, meeting key implementation dates, and understanding ongoing costs. Planning checklists, a list of contact names and information, and a list of sites initially receiving the IDL system were attached to the POL.

Finally, the POL included a checklist of technical requirements for implementing distance learning, regarding TV screen size, the type of telephone line to be installed, and the type of audio and video outputs on the TV and VCR. The POL asked each facility to return a Readiness Verification Form once all requirements had been met. The acquisition announcement and local staff activity generated as a result of the announcement also served to lay the groundwork for the development of a support infrastructure.

Developing a Support Infrastructure

Developing a support infrastructure for each of the sixty-six remote classrooms implementing IDL posed several preparation challenges. This section discusses these challenges in the areas of remote site preparation and IDL staff training.

Remote Site Preparation

The initial challenge was to solicit the help of existing BTV local site coordinators. BTV local coordinators did not have an official reporting responsibility to the Drew Institute. Taking on the additional responsibility to coordinate IDL programs was considered "other duties as assigned."

The additional responsibilities were not insignificant. IDL broadcasts required that the site coordinator monitor the broadcast schedule and schedule an IDL-compatible room as soon as possible to ensure its availability. ARCBS IDL sites co-located with Red Cross chapters had difficulty with scheduling rooms; many times a CPR or first aid class might be scheduled in the conference room equipped for IDL broadcasts. This also meant that the IDL equipment had to be stored after each broadcast.

On the day of the broadcast, the site coordinator performed setup procedures and participated in the roll call before the broadcast. Roll call is a period immediately prior to every broadcast when each remote site's visual signal and audio levels are checked. After roll call, the site coordinator acts as the facilitator of the broadcast. The facilitator is responsible for creating a welcoming environment and does this by distributing course materials, greeting training participants, and assisting them with log on procedures. The facilitator must remain available throughout the broadcast to provide additional assistance as required during the broadcast and during the evaluation period immediately following the broadcast. After the broadcast, the site coordinator dismantles and stores the equipment until the next broadcast. These activities require more time and effort on the part of site coordinators—time they may not have, given their regular duties. The Drew Institute addressed these problems by providing a strong support system for site coordinators that included equipment configuring job aids, administration guides which provided details of each upcoming program, and technical support before, during, and after each IDL broadcast. In addition, the Drew Institute made an extra effort to include site coordinators as a part of the delivery team and used their input to improve the implementation process.

IDL Staff Training

Several groups of staff required training to support IDL programs including site coordinators, program development and production staff, and instructors.

Site Coordinators. Local technical support on site coordinators must be chosen carefully. Site coordinators and their backups need a degree of comfort with technology. Including site coordinator responsibilities in the employee's job description will help to ensure that the training participant's exposure to IDL will be a consistently effective pleasant experience.

To prepare the site coordinators in the field to assume the duties of coordinating a broadcast at the remote classroom, the Drew Institute hosted a training broadcast. The purpose of the broadcast was three-fold: to provide instructions to install the local site controllers, to provide technical troubleshooting guidelines, and to review the various materials and job aids developed to support site coordinators during IDL broadcasts. Support materials included an introductory video that instructed first-time participants in the use of the keypad, an evaluation video used at the end of the broadcast, job aides to configure the site controller, and help-line phone numbers. Additional support materials developed for the training participants included table tents describing the use of the keypad and a short IDL participant guide.

Program Development and Production Staff. In addition to site coordinators, additional categories of staff members including instructional designers, curriculum managers, studio personnel, instructors, and technical support staff required training before the first IDL broadcast could be produced. This was accomplished in a phased approach which is described below:

Phase I: Core IDL Team. Roles and responsibilities were clearly defined for the personnel responsible for designing, developing, and delivering programs. It takes exceptional coordination to have a successful program. Clearly defined roles help eliminate duplication of effort or missed opportunities. Members of the core IDL team included a cross section of the various support staff categories including a program director, two instructional designers, a technical support manager, a studio manager, and a studio technical director. This group received training in all technical aspects of the IDL system from the staff of the Drew Institute's implementation partner. The implementation partner had been successfully using the IDL system for several years. This provided a unique opportunity for the core support team to interact with more experienced producers of IDL programs who could share their "lessons learned." This proved to be a very successful strategy and contributed to the rapid implementation of the IDL system.

Phase II: Instructional Designers and Curriculum Manager Training. Once the core IDL team was trained, all of the instructional designers and curriculum managers were given instruction in planning, designing, developing, implementing, and evaluating training delivered via an IDL broadcast. During this training, an instructional designer and curriculum manager were paired to develop a mini-lesson to be delivered during the course. At the end of the two-day course, each pair had acquired the skills necessary to develop training delivered via IDL.

Instructors. Training delivery using the IDL system requires special on-camera presentation skills. Choose, cultivate, and develop your presenters carefully. A presenter who is comfortable with live on-camera training delivery is not necessarily best suited for it. A droning "talking head" will be less effective than an enthusiastic trainer who is new to IDL training delivery because the former will not hold the training participant's attention as well as the latter. Fortunately, the ARCBS has many excellent instructors who easily adapted to teaching using this medium after receiving training. Although the ARCBS has an instructor practice studio, it does not currently have a formal IDL instructor training program. When instructors need to learn to deliver instruction using the IDL system, they are sent offsite to a special third-party training program. This program specializes in preparing instructors to teach using this medium. As the demand for IDL programs increases within the ARCBS, an internal train-the-trainer program will be more cost effective.

ARCBS has also used IDL to deliver programs that do not use a traditional instructor-led model. These programs include panel discussions with recognized industry expert guest speakers. Typically, these programs are delivered once and taped for repeated use. For these programs, it is not cost effective to send an instructor to a week-long external training program. In these instances, an informal competency analysis is used to determine what level of skill the presenter will need in order to present using the IDL system. Three competency levels have been established: guided, assisted, and solo. The guided level is used when a presenter will be doing several broadcasts, such as a series of programs. Presenters working at the guided level use a few of the IDL controls such as issuing questions and taking calls but require assistance from the technical staff for the more complex interactions such as issuing quizzes or switching screens. The assisted level is used for programs that will be offered only once or when the presenter is a recognized industry guest expert speaker who has volunteered to deliver a program. Presenters operating at the assisted level do little with the IDL system. Instead, all of the interaction controls, including question issuing and receiving participant calls, are handled by the technical staff in the control room. The solo level is used when instructors will be giving courses routinely. Instructors who are accomplished at the solo level control most of the interaction functions used in the IDL system.

Installation

Once remote sites were prepared and the IDL staff training completed, the Drew Institute coordinated the final activities for the first IDL program—a proof of concept broadcast to demonstrate the technology's feasibility as well as its potential for broader application. These activities included equipment installation, visual signature development, pilot broadcasts, and a demonstration broader application. Each will be described in this section.

Equipment Installation. The Drew Institute coordinated IDL equipment installation with the equipment vendor. The Drew Institute requested that each site have all members of its distance learning team present during this initial installation. A facility training broadcast was scheduled after the IDL equipment had been installed at each site.

The facility training broadcast was designed to provide education officers, site coordinators, and backup personnel with the training to develop proficiency with setup, operation, and maintenance of the IDL equipment. As stated in the program guide developed by the Drew Institute, the broadcast objectives included verification that the telephone lines and the IDL equipment were installed properly at each facility, demonstration of setup and operations of the IDL equipment, troubleshooting problems that can occur with IDL equipment, maintenance and technical support protocols, demonstration of site controller basic programming, and demonstration of basic keypad operations. Five broadcasts were scheduled over a three-day period to maximize scheduling flexibility for each site, in order to ensure higher attendance and a greater amount of participation.

Visual Signature Development. A visual signature comprises all the components that give a television program its look and feel, including video roll-ins, logos, music, and the stage set. The Drew Institute developed a unique visual signature that honored the contribution the ARCBS has made to the blood banking field, while conveying that the organization was moving into a new direction with the establishment of the Drew Institute.

Pilot Broadcasts. The facility training broadcasts were delivered via the Red Cross business television network and were designed to be highly interactive. The broadcasts were facilitated by a team of staff from the implementation partner, the manufacturers of the IDL system, and the Drew Institute. The agenda for each two-and-a-half hour broadcast included introductions and climate setting, session objectives review, an IDL video presentation, equipment inventory review, site controller equipment set up (which included wiring connections and configurations and equipment labeling), room configuration and keypad wiring, programming (keypads, site controller, audio), log in procedures (facility log in, roll call, audio quality, problem solving, error messages or codes, technical support protocol), the IDL system demonstration, and conclusion.

The facility training broadcasts concluded with education officers and site coordinators having a better understanding of how the IDL system worked, not just technically but of its application as a training delivery tool. A future proof-of-concept broadcast was planned to introduce the key personnel who are stakeholders in training and development to distance learning.

Proof of Concept Broadcast. The target audience for the demonstration broadcast was much broader than it was for the implementation broadcast. In addition to the designated lead staff in each facility who participated in the initial broadcasts (education officers, site coordinators and designated backup personnel), key personnel such as leaders in human resources, public relations, fiscal management, and other stakeholders in training and development were asked to participate in this broadcast. Instructors who may in the future be selected to facilitate interactive training were also invited to participate.

Because of the considerable financial investment in the IDL system, immediate "buy-in" was obviously necessary. That is why senior management staff at ARCBS headquarters showed support of and commitment to the investment by participating in this live broadcast. The agenda for the demonstration broadcast consisted of welcoming remarks from the Senior Vice President of ARCBS, followed by an introduction to the IDL system by the Vice President of Training for ARCBS. An IDL orientation was conducted by the Director of Training Delivery, followed by a highly interactive demonstration by a national representative of Hewlett-Packard. The Senior Director of Curriculum Development discussed future programming plans. After a question-and-answer period, participants evaluated the program anonymously using their keypads. Responses were enthusiastic. Interestingly, while it was not possible to assign each participant a keypad, observers in the room reported afterward that they benefited from exposure to the broadcast by watching others in the classroom participate via their keypads. The successful proof-of-concept broadcast paved the way for interactive training delivery as well as broader application of the technology.

Broader Application. Before the end of the fiscal year, in June 1996, the IDL system was recognized by ARCBS leaders for its versatility as a communication tool. The first telemeeting of a CEO and his paid- and volunteer-leadership staff throughout the New York-Penn Jersey region was successfully conducted using the IDL system.

In December 1996, the Senior Vice President and the Chief Operating Officer of ARCBS held their first management round-table telemeeting using the IDL system. They presented summary information on results and accomplishments associated with the FY 1996 management agenda to senior management across the country. CEOs interacted with the presenters using the voice feature of the IDL system, used the keypads to answer questions regarding biomedical issues, and completed an evaluation of the broadcast via keypads.

These telemeetings were noteworthy for several reasons. During previous BTV broadcasts, in which the IDL system was not used, staff participation was virtually nonexistent. The convenience of the microphone built into the interactive response keypad prompted a significantly higher level of participation. During broadcasts in which the IDL system was not used, the presenters were typically unable to fill the time allotted for question-and-answer periods. This caused long awkward silences during live broadcasts. Participants were simply unwilling to leave their seats, locate a telephone, call the number on the screen, wait to be patched through, ask their question, and try to return to their seats in time to hear their question answered. During the telemeetings in which the IDL system was used, the presenters tended to run out of time because audience participation was so high.

Organizational and Cultural Issues

Organizational and cultural issues greatly impact design and delivery of distance education and training. Following is a discussion of two organizational characteristics which must be considered to ensure effective implementation of distance learning: financial expectations and learning paradigm.

Managing Financial Expectations

The commitment by the organization to invest in IDL technology required senior management's support and a commitment of financial resources. Once the decision was made to go forward, management was eager to see a return on its investment.

While it is true IDL can provide significant cost savings, the travel savings should not be overemphasized (Defense Technical Information Center 1988). Reduced travel is an obvious benefit to an organization implementing IDL, but it is not the only reason to use it. Frequently, it allows organizations to do things that are otherwise impossible due to scheduling constraints or staff availability. It also allows delivery of a standardized message.

In organizations with tight budgets, programs that do not directly support business needs will usually not be funded. When considering IDL for training, use a cost-benefit model that accurately compares how your organization currently conducts training (for example, classroom, on-the-job training, preceptor, and so on) to using a distance learning system. If your organization uses desk-side training as opposed to classroom training to teach new employees their duties, develop a cost benefit model that compares distance learning system costs to desk-side training not classroom training. Careful planning and practical cost-benefit analyses ensure that management expectations remain realistic.

Expectations were also managed by providing periodic status briefings on the implementation process and program development plans. Once program delivery began, the IDL technology could provide instantaneous statistics on the number of audience participants and the number of participating sites. That information, with the final costs of training delivery via IDL, was used to determine that per-student costs were significantly lower with IDL. Participant satisfaction-program evaluations revealed that the initial IDL offerings gained higher ratings than any program previously delivered using the BTV network. This reinforced management belief that it had made the right decision to invest in IDL.

Learning Culture Paradigm Shift

The primary barrier to designing and implementing IDL programs was the ARCBS's learning culture. This culture relies heavily on a traditional, instructor-led delivery approach. Shifting this cultural norm to IDL programs was challenging. Naturally, highly trained instructors feared that this technology might one day replace them, and this fear triggered resistance to the new IDL design and delivery approaches. While distance training can more effectively train larger numbers of audiences if applied appropriately, care must be taken to avoid over comparison to classroom training (Defense Technical Information Center 1988).

In addition, the cultural shift from learning in a BTV format to an IDL format posed challenges. This is primarily because television is a passive medium. IDL requires participants to interact. At the local level, it demanded that people participate in the broadcast while it was airing. With BTV, it was customary at the local level to tape the broadcast for viewing later. It also required new instructional design and development skills and required new thinking for business television personnel. It required staff to modify studio production standards that are appropriate for good business television to standards that support the delivery of well-designed instructional programs. Well designed IDL programs create a informal classroom atmosphere rather than a formal polished scripted program.

Program Development Process

Having training or telemeetings already "in the pipeline" before deployment of an interactive distance learning system keeps interest high and prevents the development of programs for the sake of using the technology. This section describes how the ARCBS develops IDL programs. The various stages are described, including the program identification, planning, design, development, delivery, and evaluation processes. The order of the stages suggests a linear process; however many of the steps in each stage are done concurrently. This section will also provide a description of some of the programs that have been delivered. Although the ARCBS uses the IDL system to support telemeetings, focus groups, and panel discussions, this section will focus on describing how training programs are developed.

Program Identification

New program ideas are identified in a variety of ways. Sometimes the Drew Institute initiates new training and education courses. Other times a non-training department such as Quality Assurance will suggest a program. Regardless of how the program is initiated, the goals of the program are reviewed to determine if it supports the organization's goals, if sufficient funding and sponsorship are available, and whether a large enough audience exists. Audiences for the IDL-delivered training range from technical and nontechnical paid employees and volunteers to educators, management personnel, customers, and invited guests. Technical staff members performing regulated activities include nurses, laboratory technicians, medical technologists, and collection specialists. Educators include staff and supervisors who ensure staff competency in the use of the latest regulatory and procedural information. Management and nontechnical staff include staff who do not routinely perform regulated tasks but may benefit from an education program. In addition, the ARCBS frequently invites external participants such as hospital customers, FDA regulators, and local physicians to attend broadcasts. After a potential program has been identified, all available training mechanisms are considered when determining whether or not IDL technology is appropriate to accomplish the learning goals.

In some cases classroom training is perfectly appropriate and should not be adapted to distance learning. In other cases, a self-study course (CBT, CD-ROM) may be the best vehicle. Ensure that there is a link between the organization's business needs, the IDL systems' capabilities, and the programs planned.

Planning

If a training program meets all of these criteria, the planning process begins. The first task in the planning process is to assemble the development team and perform logistical activities. The IDL development team comprises department sponsors, a program manager or curriculum manager, an instructional designer, a desktop publisher, technical support, instructors or moderators, subject matter or guest experts, a studio director, field representatives, and a financial manager. Initially the program manager, instructional designer, financial manager, and department sponsor meet to identify the program's goals and develop a project plan and budget.

During the planning phase, logistical activities are also conducted. Logistical activities include checking the training calendar, reserving satellite time, reserving the studio, identifying presenters or moderators, and notifying the field.

As soon as the logistical activities are completed, goals and objectives of the program are developed, and an administration guide is sent to the field. The administration guide provides local education staff and site coordinators with details on the future program. Education managers and site coordinators use the administration guide to schedule remote classrooms and to advertise the program at the local level.

Design

During the design phase an instructional designer will make several decisions that are documented in a design document. Specifically, the designer refines the instructional objectives, determines the instructional strategy, and develops the program treatment. The treatment is a description of how the program will flow and its look and feel (for example, game show format, panel discussion, lecture). During this phase the designer also determines the various elements to be included, such as videos, slides, visual aids, props, questions, and quizzes. In addition, the designer must identify strategies for interaction. A rule of thumb for this type of media is to plan an interaction at least every ten to twelve minutes. Interaction can include group discussion, activities, question-and-answer sessions, and formatted questions—multiple choice, true or false, pop questions, and quizzes. While planning the interactions, the designer must be sensitive to changing the stimulus frequently. This can be accomplished by planning short instructor-led segments, followed by a video clip, a group activity, a question-and-answer session, or a series of formatted questions. Variety keeps participants alert and encourages their participation. Don't be afraid to use humor and have fun. During a broadcast delivered on Halloween, the studio crew used ghosts, goblins, and other scary distractions to maintain participant interest. The designer must also decide what other instructional strategies are required to support the broadcast as a learning intervention. Examples of instructional strategies are pre-broadcast or post-broadcast learning activities such as a case study, remote classroom discussion, or follow-up self assessment study questions. These materials combined with the broadcast itself help to ensure that the program achieves the overall intervention goal.

While every program should strive for high quality in terms of accomplishing learning and communication goals, it is important to maintain flexibility. The temptation is to script out every word and action because our television culture has high expectations for polished productions. But overproduction adds unnecessary costs, increases the development time and length of the broadcast, and frequently does not improve results. Remember, this is training or a meeting, not the nightly news.

Development

Based upon the requirements specified in the design document, the development team begins working together to organize the various program elements and develop a rundown. Table 6.1 provides a sample rundown. The rundown provides a sequential listing of broadcast events and program elements, such as slides, questions, and quizzes. It is used in a paper rehearsal while various program elements

TABLE 6.1. SAMPLE RUNDOWN.

Instructor Rundown Project Title			QA IDL Teleconference: QA/RA: Milestones, Expectations, and Plans
Production Rundown	Time Seg/Total [150 min]	Instructor Action	Instructor Rundown
Opening Credits		none	
Introduction to IDL		none	
Welcome to broadcast	3/3	Presentation	Welcome to the QA Teleconference. Our focus for this session is our QA strategic plan and specific activities that are underway to further that plan.
		Slide 1	Review agenda
		Presentation	Let's start off by finding out how well you feel we have done with implementing the QA Program. Here's an IDL question:
IDL Question	2/5	Read IDL Question #1	How do you rate the progress ARCBS has made in implementing the Quality Assurance Program to date?

are still being developed. The studio director relies on this document in studio rehearsals and on the day of the broadcast.

Delivery

At some point prior to the broadcast, the program will be rehearsed in the studio. The rehearsal provides an opportunity for on-camera presenters and studio personnel to practice the timing of the program and to work out any last minute changes in the program elements. The participants in the rehearsal usually include the on-camera moderator or presenter, an invited guest speaker, the director, the camera crew, the TelePrompTer operator, a floor director, IDL technical support staff, an instructional designer, and a very nervous program manager.

In the writers' experience, regardless of the amount of preparation done before a broadcast, there are always last-minute changes to program elements. Anticipate and accommodate these circumstances to the extent possible, since they can frequently add value to the training.

On the day of the broadcast, a final rehearsal is usually held, and visual and audio checks are conducted (such as roll call) with the participating sites to test the equipment prior to the live broadcast.

Evaluation

In addition to the BTV evaluation form used to collect level-one participant reaction data the IDL system is used to collect anonymous feedback. This evaluation is conducted immediately following the program using the participant keypads. The advantage to this method is the rapid collection of reaction information. Within minutes of the program, data can be summarized for an initial assessment of the program's success. Custom reports can also be generated shortly after the program using a response analysis software program developed specifically for the IDL system. Exhibit 6.1 provides a sample evaluation form used for IDL programs.

Examples of Programs

Using IDL, the ARCBS has delivered a variety of training programs, continuing education programs, and telemeetings. Examples include a series of programs designed to provide up-to-the-minute information on advances in transfusion

EXHIBIT 6.1. SAMPLE PROGRAM EVALUATION.

Purpose: Your responses to this evaluation will assist us in assessing the program format, presentation, and interactivity; and enhancing future programs.

Directions: Complete this evaluation by pressing the gray function key on your keypad located directly beneath the answer option in the display window. Press **Next Quest** to advance to the next question. Upon completion of the evaluation, the keypad will display the question "Are you finished?" Select **YES** to complete the evaluation or **NO** to return to the questions. At any time before entering **YES,** you may review or change your answers by pressing **PREV Quest** to move to the previous question and **NEXT** to move to the next question. Once you have selected **YES,** your results will be transferred to the broadcast site for tabulation. You will have 10 minutes to complete this evaluation.

Overall Rating

Question	Excellent	Good	Fair	Poor	
1. My overall assessment of this training is:	A	B	C	D	

Program Materials

	Strongly Agree	Agree	Neutral	Disagree	Strongly Disagree
2. The class materials (participant materials, program guide, etc.) were well-organized and easy to follow.	A	B	C	D	E

Program Assessment

	Much too difficult	A little too difficult	Appropriate	A little too easy	Much too easy
3. The information was at the appropriate level of difficulty:	A	B	C	D	E

	Much too fast	A little too fast	Appropriate	A little too slow	Much too slow
4. The pace of the class was:	A	B	C	D	E

(continued)

EXHIBIT 6.1. (CONTINUED).

Question	Strongly Agree	Agree	Neutral	Disagree	Strongly Disagree
5. The pre-class activity added value to my understanding of the material presented.	A	B	C	D	E
8. The class met the stated objectives.	A	B	C	D	E
9. Group activities and/or case studies used during the class facilitated learning the course content.	A	B	C	D	E
11. The presenter(s) adequately answered the questions that were called in.	A	B	C	D	E
12. The presenter(s) provided clear explanations and directions.	A	B	C	D	E
13. Overall, the presenter(s) were effective.	A	B	C	D	E
15. The number of times where I had the opportunity to participate was sufficient.	A	B	C	D	E
16. The number of opportunities for participants to call in with questions was appropriate.	A	B	C	D	E
17. The use of graphics/visuals improved the explanation of the content.	A	B	C	D	E
20. The use of One Touch technology enhanced the value of the class.	A	B	C	D	E
21. The instructions on how to use the One Touch keypad were adequate (e.g., video clip, supporting materials).	A	B	C	D	E
22. I feel comfortable using the One Touch keypad.	A	B	C	D	E

Please send additional comments or suggestions to
username@companyname.org, or fax them to (000) 000-0000. Thank you.

medicine delivered by topnotch experts, instruction on the implementation of a new master training system, skills training for conducting root cause analysis, and a program designed to help staff prepare for significant organizational change. In addition, IDL has been used for several organizational telemeetings that helped forge positive working relations between ARCBS staff and external partners at the local level. Detailed program descriptions are provided in the following paragraphs.

Advances in Transfusion and Transplantation Medicine (ATTM) Series

The ATTM series provided nurses, physicians, collection staff, and laboratory staff with technically advanced information on transfusion medicine. This information was delivered by recognized industry experts. Viewers were taught how to recognize and identify clinical symptoms of transfusion complications and donor reactions. The ATTM programs also provided techniques for preventing and managing complication and reaction situations. Throughout the program learners were provided with numerous opportunities to interact with the experts. Periodically, formatted questions were issued to viewers to test their knowledge and understanding of the complex information being provided and to promote the transference of their new knowledge to their work settings. In addition, materials were provided to the broadcast participants one month after the broadcast to reinforce the learning they experienced during the original broadcast. The materials contained instructional objectives, program slides, and study questions. Using a taped version of the programs, participants could use the instructional guide to refresh and reinforce their new skills and knowledge.

Master Training System

The Master Training System provided two teleclasses and a telemeeting that introduced a new training documentation system for regulated training. The first teleclass provided education managers and regional quality assurance staff with an overview of the intent and direction of the new system and how it would be implemented in the organization. The second teleclass was delivered two weeks later. It provided follow-up from the first teleclass and a chance for participants to ask questions and resolve issues during the implementation process. The final program, a telemeeting, was delivered three months later, after completion of the implementation process. FDA investigators, FDA national and district staff, local senior management, and ARCBS education and QA staff discussed the new training system.

Advanced Deviations Management

This program was designed for any person involved with the manufacturing process who is responsible for leading investigations. The primary focus was to provide staff with skills in the area of root cause analysis. The training methodology asked participants to work through a pre-class case study one hour prior to the broadcast. The case study prepared participants for the instruction delivered during the broadcast. This strategy reduces the amount of satellite time required and therefore reduces costs.

Change: How to Prepare Your Organization

This four-hour program targeted key leaders throughout Biomedical Services to help them successfully implement complex change initiatives. The presenter for this program was the recognized expert in the area of complex change implementation.

Quality Assurance Staff Telemeeting

The national headquarters QA staff used IDL to hold the department's staff meeting. This meeting included 300 staff members located throughout the country and was intended to foster better communication between national headquarters staff and field staff. It provided the entire QA staff with an opportunity to gain greater insight into the direction and goals of the department for the coming year and to exchange information on various projects.

Management Round Table

Senior executives presented a year-end summary of accomplishments. Information was shared on various project initiatives and the organization's current market position. Viewers were invited to directly address their questions to the executive presenters using the IDL system.

Successes

Implementation of the IDL system from the acquisition announcement to the pilot broadcasts took two months, which is an extremely short time frame for an organization the size of the ARCBS. This was largely due to strong change-implementation leadership and a well-executed plan that was built upon the existing corporate experience with BTV. The organization has trained as many as

750 participants simultaneously delivering standardized training information. The training programs used the organization's best instructors, moderators, and recognized industry experts cost effectively. The average length of each broadcast is approximately two hours and fifteen minutes with an average of 368 participants per training session. The average cost per student is $27.17.

Other advantages the ARCBS has experienced using IDL technology are as follows:

- Reduced time away from job duties
- Greater local participation
- Reduced travel costs for presenters and participants
- The ability to leverage the involvement of the organization's leaders, exceptional trainers, and subject matter experts to communicate directly and broadly to the field
- Delivered standardized messages and instruction
- Shared information across the organization—organizational learning (versus localized delivery of training)
- Improved data gathering efforts by recording and analyzing data collected from participants at all sites (responses to questions, quizzes, and anonymous evaluations)

Challenges for the Future

At the present time the organization is seeking to further maximize its use of the IDL system. The Drew Institute is analyzing how programs are identified, funded, planned, developed, and implemented in an effort to increase efficiency, reduce program development costs, and use the IDL system as a strategic organizational learning tool. This analysis has identified several barriers to using the IDL system for education, training, and communication activities, including the lack of a champion to promote the use of the IDL system within the organization; a cumbersome, lengthy, and costly development process; misconceptions of the IDL system's capabilities; a need to increase awareness of training decision makers on what type of training programs are appropriate for IDL, a lack of procedures for routinely considering the IDL system for delivering new procedure-based training programs; and insufficient coordination between various departments for promoting and handling requests for IDL services.

While it is clear that the ARCBS had a winning strategy, the success has been limited largely because it focused upon installing equipment and training the support personnel to deliver programs and focused less attention upon educating potential users and promoting the system's capabilities through an ongoing internal marketing plan. This has led to a lack of awareness on the part of department managers of how the IDL system can help them meet their department's communication, education, and training needs. A marketing plan must be developed that continuously provides information to potential users of the IDL system to educate them as to how the system can support the strategic goals of the organization.

Conclusion

The Red Cross recognizes that these are challenges that can be overcome and that there is great potential for the IDL system to be a powerful organizational communication and learning tool. This recognition is based upon its documented earlier successes using the technology. Also, the IDL system's versatility as an information-gathering tool has recently caught the attention of leaders in the community-services side of the Red Cross. In May 1997, the Drew Institute collaborated with the marketing department to conduct focus groups at the Red Cross National Convention in Louisville, Kentucky. Marketing presented possible advertising campaigns to Red Cross paid and volunteer staff and received immediate feedback from participants using the IDL keypads. Participants also had the opportunity to explain their opinions to the presenters because the forum was designed to mimic a talk-show style format—a host with a wireless microphone solicited additional feedback regarding the data collected, which in turn further engaged the audience and increased their involvement. Of the four major forums presented at the convention, Marketing's "Motivating the Customer" IDL session received the highest ratings, both for the highest number of participants and the highest level of participant satisfaction.

It is partly due to the collaboration between Drew Institute staff and the community services marketing staff involved in delivering this forum that senior management has recognized that IDL technology can add value to a wide range of events. Implementation of IDL in the community services side of the Red Cross is currently underway. The Red Cross has decided to expand its IDL network to include sixty new sites. The expanded network will allow the Red Cross to use IDL to support other lines of services, including Health and Safety, Armed Forces Emergency Services, and Disaster Services. In addition to delivering training, the organization is planning to expand its use of IDL technology to conduct other communications and training activities, such as needs assessment focus groups. Plans are underway to develop a distance learning unit that uses a blend of distance learning technologies—IDL, Internet—to support the organization's training and educational needs. An internal marketing plan is being developed to continually promote and educate potential users on the business need for IDL, its potential applications, and its cost-benefits. Ideally, this information would be available on-demand (intranet-based training, network-based training, and so on), so that potential users such as department managers could immediately access the information when they are deciding to use the IDL system to meet a specific communication, education, or training need in their departments.

The Red Cross is looking to distance learning technology to significantly reduce training costs as well as improve quality and efficiency in the next few years. Although it has made tremendous strides since it first began using IDL to support training and education activities, the Red Cross must now face the challenge of overcoming the existing organizational barriers to sustain and integrate this technology into its learning culture.

Technical Section

The IDL system provides one-way video with two-way audio. The presenter's image (video) and voice (audio) are sent via an uplink located at the Red Cross studios in suburban Virginia to a satellite. The satellite relays the signal (video and audio) to sixty-six fixed downlink sites (such as remote classrooms) located throughout the United States. In remote classrooms, participants view the presenter on a television set that is tuned to a specific receiving channel. They use keypads equipped with microphones (audio) to ask questions and interact with the instructor and other participants. The interactive response keypad system also allows the instructor to issue formatted questions (multiple choice, true or false, yes or no) and quizzes. Student responses are transmitted via telephone lines to the IDL host computer located at the studio. Figure 6.1 illustrates how the IDL system transmits video, audio, and data simultaneously using satellite and telephone lines. Student responses or data are recorded in a database for further analysis.

Prior to installing the IDL system the Red Cross used a business television network (BTV) for communications and educational purposes. The network consisted of a studio, uplink and 125 downlink facilities located throughout the United States. Interaction with on-camera presenters was accomplished via a toll free number.

FIGURE 6.1. IDL SYSTEM.

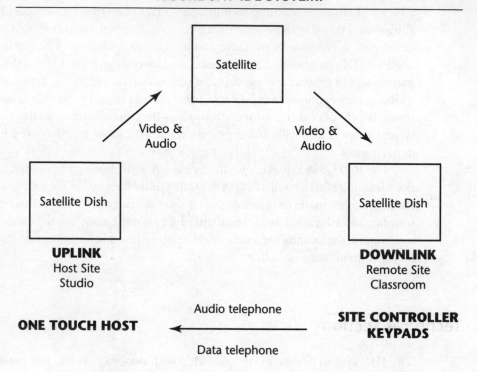

CHAPTER SEVEN

DISSEMINATING TIME- AND REGULATION-SENSITIVE INFORMATION: ONLINE TRAINING SEMINARS AT MORTGAGE BANKERS ASSOCIATION OF AMERICA

Therese Monahan

The Mortgage Bankers Association of America (MBAA) is a non-profit trade association for real estate finance professionals. The MBAA has approximately 2,500 member companies representing 200,000 to 250,000 employees. These member firms range from large companies with more than 10,000 employees in offices located throughout the country to small, "mom and pop" shops with one office and a handful of employees. Providing educational and training programs for the employees of these companies is one of the numerous member benefits offered by the association.

The MBAA's Education Department provides both traditional classroom-based training and distance education programs. The Education Department began in 1948 with the School of Mortgage Banking. During the past fifty years the MBAA's School of Mortgage Banking has developed into a program that is highly regarded throughout the mortgage banking industry. The school consists of three one-week classes that are held on college campuses throughout the country. In addition to the school, the MBAA also offers a few other traditional classroom-based seminars geared to commercial real estate finance professionals.

Since the mid-1960s, the MBAA has provided distance education in the form of correspondence courses. In the 1990s, these courses remain popular and are a major revenue source for the association with over 6,000 courses delivered annually. In the mid-1990s, the MBAA began experimenting with using various technologies to deliver training including interactive videoconferencing via satellite broadcasts and online training via computer conferencing utilizing an independent network.

The cost of providing training via interactive videoconferencing proved to be too expensive for the MBAA. Because the MBAA is a nonprofit association, the Education Department must be able to provide low-cost training solutions to its members and still deliver educational programs that at least break even. To break even on videoconferencing programs, the MBAA would have to charge too high a registration fee to reach the break-even point on course offerings. The MBAA's initial experience with online training via computer conferencing proved to be more successful in providing a low-cost, interactive, and collaborative approach to training.

The Problem

The MBAA had three traditional classroom-based seminars that were requirements for two of the association's designation programs (Accredited Residential Underwriter and Accredited Residential Originator). Typically, these seminars were held at least once a year in a hotel or conference center in a major metropolitan area. Over the past few years, enrollments in these three seminars declined significantly due to fewer companies with training budgets that would allow for tuition, airfare, and other expenses. In addition, one of these seminars was geared specifically to mortgage loan originators. As originators are typically paid on a per loan basis, time away from the office means fewer dollars in their personal bank accounts.

Although the MBAA already had a series of correspondence courses, a solution to create new correspondence courses to replace these seminars was not deemed viable. The biggest reason is that while enrollments in these seminars may be based on course content from the employer's perspective, students see networking as a major factor in their decision to attend one of these seminars. The correspondence courses do not currently offer any interaction with other students and thus do not provide the needed networking component.

The MBAA needed a low-cost distance learning delivery method that would allow interaction among students and allow them to concentrate on the skills they need to do their job in a more efficient and effective manner. Videoconferencing was determined to be not only too expensive but also not the best delivery method for the types of interaction required for the seminar format. A web-based solution was considered as a strong possibility but ultimately was regarded as not feasible at the time due to limited access to the Internet by most of the employees of the MBAA's membership.

The Solution

Computer conferencing was chosen as the delivery method for the seminars. Computer conferencing allows for rapid feedback and encourages "lively discussions and a degree of involvement not often seen in the classroom" (Waggoner, 1992, p. 196). The MBAA contracted with a private network provider to distribute these seminars via computer conferencing (using FirstClass by SoftArc). This outside contractor provided a "virtual campus" that was structured in such a way as to provide an organized format for class discussions and group activities. This virtual campus was accessible either via the Internet or directly via a toll-free number.

Instead of one three and a half day traditional classroom-based seminar, an online seminar would consist of a series of two-week modules that cover the same content as the original seminar. The seminar instructors now serve as online experts and are available as a reference or guide to the students. The students work on skills-based exercises in a collaborative setting. A course facilitator is used to ensure that the students actively participate in course discussions and do not experience difficulties in getting through the course materials. Of the original three seminars, two were converted to online training seminars, one for loan originators and the other for underwriters. The curriculum for the third seminar, appraisal review, was reassessed and combined into an existing correspondence course and one of the two-week modules of the online seminar for underwriters.

As the MBAA had offered an online workshop that utilized computer conferencing software in the previous year, the decision to convert the existing seminars was less of an issue for management. However, the decision did require a thorough review of the delivery method and the viability of the online seminar format. Part of this review focused on how to market the online training programs, as this was a new delivery method for the mortgage banking industry.

The online seminars were developed by MBAA staff and employed a skills-based approach to learning. Each two-week module and corresponding assessment included real-life experiences. As an example, a two-week module on sales techniques for loan originators included a lesson on how to handle telephone rate requests. The final assessment for this segment was an actual telephone call from the online expert. The expert called the student at the student's office and asked him or her for the mortgage company's current rate for a fixed-rate mortgage. The student was expected to handle the phone call using the skills learned during the seminar module. During the entire two-week period of the course module, the student is able to interact with an expert, in this case a nationally known expert in sales training, as well as fifteen to thirty other students from different mortgage companies around the country.

The result was a training solution that allowed the MBAA to continue to offer its seminars for loan originators and underwriters, thus providing the necessary curriculum for the association's accreditation programs and the needed skills for industry professionals. The students ended up with a program that was less expensive than the original seminar while still allowing a way to meet and work with other originators and underwriters at different companies across the country.

Program Development

As clear as the training problem and solution may be after the fact, the process of creating any new program is fraught with various issues and concerns that must be resolved before a quality program is developed.

Selling the Program to Management

A key point in producing a successful program is having the full backing of management. It is one thing for management to agree to a program and quite another for management to fully back the development of a program with a feeling of excitement and energy. It was anticipated early in the development of the online training programs that senior management needed to be included in and supportive of these new programs.

Although the MBAA had successfully produced distance education programs for years with its well-established line of correspondence courses, staff recognized that this delivery method was much different and warranted a special approach.

Fortunately, a substantial sponsorship from an associate member for one of the online training seminars was obtained early on. This sponsorship included both money and content materials that would serve both as an economical and psychological buffer against any hesitation on the part of senior management. The economics were that in the current format, the seminars had dwindling enrollments, and in light of declining revenues an alternative delivery method was worth exploring with the sponsorship money providing a cushion in terms of instructional design costs. The psychological aspect was that the new delivery format had the financial backing as well as the instructional backing of an associate member. This made the change from a traditional classroom-based program to a distance education program a bit easier to accept.

Also, as staff was proposing to contract with an outside vendor that would supply the infrastructure of the virtual campus, management was more willing to accept this new delivery format. Without the initial start up costs of developing the means to deliver the programs, management was willing to take on the project, knowing that a long-term investment in hardware or software was not at risk.

The MBAA has an annual review of all of its educational programs. This event, Program and Education Review, allows a select group of the association's officers and members to assess carefully all courses, seminars, conferences, and workshops that were offered the previous year. The main purpose of the review is to ensure that the educational/training offerings are appropriate given the current needs of the industry and that the programs do not overlap in terms of content. This annual review also focuses on the participant evaluations and the number of enrollments in each of the programs.

MBAA staff directly responsible for any course, conference, seminar, workshop, and so on must appear before this panel and provide detailed information, written and oral, on the program content, enrollment figures, and evaluations received. In addition, this report must include an overall assessment of the current program along with any recommendation for changes to the program for the coming year. Although the review is a somewhat intimidating process, it also allows for programs to be showcased before influential individuals within the association, including future MBAA presidents.

It was with this thought in mind that staff set out to include a demonstration of the association's first attempt at delivering a course via computer conferencing, a three-week online training workshop for quality assurance professionals. The concepts behind computer conferencing are not easy to describe but when seen can produce excellent results in getting across the power of the medium. A demonstration also eliminates some confusion and miscommunications that can occur when the audience does not have a good sense of how a computer conferencing system works. This demonstration would provide the panelists with a sense of how these traditional seminars would be converted and delivered using this new format.

As expected, the demonstration of the previous workshop was a success. Not only did the review committee like what it saw, committee members also envisioned applications for computer conferencing well beyond its ability to deliver training. The ability to see beyond training applications made it clear that the committee members not only understood how computer conferencing works but how it could change how the association could communicate with its members on many different levels. This single demonstration to the Program and Education Committee had a significant effect on the backing that the program would receive as it went forward.

In addition to backing this new distance learning delivery method, it was clear that distance learning was gaining respectability within the association as senior management and its officers approved the department's request to apply for accreditation from the Distance Education and Training Council (DETC), the nationally recognized accrediting body for distance training programs. The Program and Education Review Committee supported this initiative, which consisted of obtaining accreditation for all of the association's distance education programs, both the correspondence courses and the online training programs. The application process was a chance for the Education Department to strengthen its existing programs and formalize written policies and procedures for the development of distance learning programs. The MBAA was approved by the DETC in January 1997.

Creation and Delivery of Online Training Seminars

The conversion of the classroom-based seminars to an online training format was helped significantly by the association's prior experience in producing a three-week online training workshop. By starting slowly and creating a new training workshop for quality assurance professionals via computer conferencing, the MBAA gained the needed experience and confidence to do more of this type of training.

Selection of the Provider

While the MBAA had prior experience in this delivery method, it was not a foregone conclusion that the contractor used in the first online training workshop would be selected as the provider for these online training seminars. Geared with the previous experience in offering a course via computer conferencing, MBAA staff felt that a wider search of companies offering similar services should be evaluated. However, after reviewing several different options and providers (including some using FirstClass) the decision was reached to remain with the original contractor. The initial experience with this particular contractor was, overall, a very positive one, but the choice to remain with that contractor centered around the ease of use of the campus interface that the contractor had developed. As will be discussed, the ability for the learner and online experts to get up to speed quickly in understanding how to use the technology was a critical point in providing the service. In addition, in the time between the initial course offering and the conversion of the seminars, the contractor had upgraded the computer conferencing software to allow access via the Internet. Internet access was viewed as a strong positive given the comments received by students who had taken the original workshop.

Internet vs. Private Network

While it might seem a foregone conclusion that Internet access would be preferable, this was not the case. The MBAA is extremely sensitive to its members' need for privacy. As with most companies, firewalls are created to limit access to the Internet. Understandably, this is especially true for companies in the financial services industry. Also, staff had to consider that the majority of MBAA member companies did not have access to the Internet. Although the association was seeing rapid growth in companies that were gaining Internet access, staff could not develop training programs that left the bulk of association members without the ability to access those programs. Realistically, it was also understood that the likelihood of a company obtaining Internet access solely for the purpose of gaining access to training programs was a long shot. Fortunately, the provider selected was able to offer two options: a) connection to the server via the Internet and b) direct dial to the server.

The MBAA worked with the provider to establish a toll-free number that would allow students to access the campus without incurring additional costs. However, the cost of the toll-free number had to be taken into consideration when establishing the cost of tuition. When trying to estimate toll charge expenses, it was expected that one-half of the students would access the training program via the Internet. This assumption was made because it was anticipated that not only would some students have the ability to access the online training programs at work using the Internet but also some would access after work (those who had an Internet connection at their homes). During the initial launch of the program, is was discovered that the use of the Internet was more like one-quarter of the students. Company firewalls made access to the private server via the Internet impossible, and the number of students working at home was not as high as had been expected. However, staff noticed that a few participants were able to request from their companies (and receive) a stand-alone PC with modem for Internet access. Although initial projections were not valid for the toll charge expenses, it is anticipated that the association should reach those anticipated numbers within the next year of the program.

Curriculum Assessment

As mentioned previously, the MBAA was converting two existing traditional classroom-based seminars to an online training format. These existing seminars were three and a half day seminars that were held at a hotel or conference center. These seminars were a vital part of the curriculum for the association's Accredited Residential Underwriter and Accredited Residential Originator programs. Although the seminar content was well established as the programs were typically offered at least once a year, the content was assessed continually. Prior to each time the seminars were offered, an assessment was made to ensure that the topics were appropriate given industry needs and that the content was current.

However, for this assessment, the curriculum was assessed using a slightly different approach. Each seminar was divided into its corresponding topics. Typically, over the course of the three and a half days, six to seven topics were covered in the classroom, each consisting of approximately four hours of classroom work. This work consisted of lecture, case work, and group study activities. In addition to the six to seven topics, a final examination was given on the last day of the seminar. The final exam format was usually a combination of multiple choice and short answer essay questions.

Harisim and others (1995) contend that an online seminar is similar in many ways to a traditional classroom-based seminar. Students prepare by reading or listening to the assigned text or lecture, then discuss the materials. "Online they do this by logging on to a designated network space. A virtual seminar is an electronic equivalent of walking into a physical seminar room; students log on to the designated conference to type in comments and to read and respond to their peers and instructor. An online seminar series may begin with the instructor acting as the seminar leader and modeling how to moderate a discussion, but it should soon move on to student-led discussions on topics" (p. 128).

Originally, the seminar was to be a six-week online course with each topic covering one week (six total topics). However, based on the experience of the first online workshop, it was anticipated that most individuals would not be able to commit to such a long time span for a course. During the course of six weeks there could possibly be conflicts with travel, vacations, and so on. To counter this anticipated problem, the decision was made to break up the topics with each topic covered over the course of two weeks. Due to the need to build start-up times into the curriculum, additional time was given to each topic. The start-up time is necessary as new students need to get used to the campus and to learn the basics, such as downloading assignments and sending responses to class discussions.

While not originally planned, an additional benefit for students resulted by breaking the topics into discrete course modules: a student could take one or more topics of interest. Instead of taking all six (or seven) topics, a student could choose to take only those courses that were of interest. Since the seminar would still be a requirement for the MBAA's accreditation programs, required and elective course modules were determined that would allow students the flexibility to create a more individualized program of study.

Conversion of Materials

As the seminars already existed in a classroom format, the conversion process readied the materials for an online format. The computer conferencing software is mainly a text-based delivery system; however, the file transfer capabilities allow for downloading of additional materials. In order to keep downloading times to a minimum (most students use 28.8 modems), file size is a major consideration, and large files are avoided.

The majority of the lecture and accompanying training materials were converted to text format (using Adobe Acrobat) and accompanying PowerPoint presentations. At the beginning of the course, students download Adobe Acrobat Reader and PowerPoint viewers as needed. Lecture materials are supplemented with additional published articles on the specific topic. These articles from MBAA publications are sent to the student prior to the course start date along with the communication software and the installation and user guide for the online "virtual campus." In addition to text materials, PowerPoint presentations and small computer-based training modules (developed using ToolBook II) aided in developing course materials that created a visual stimulus for the learner. Adobe Acrobat also allowed for the creation of forms and student work materials necessary for group discussions and class activities.

A survey of MBAA members was completed prior to beginning development of the program, which helped the MBAA determine the hardware and software capabilities of potential students. Based on the information received, it was determined that the majority of the students would not be equipped for multimedia. As the conferencing software is text-based, this did not present a problem. However, there were some of the seminar topics where multimedia (audio and video) was important in the delivery of the instruction. In those cases, video and audio tapes were used to supplement the instruction. These supplemental materials were sent out prior to the class start date along with the start-up materials.

Eye to the Future—Web-Based Delivery

In the conversion of the program from a classroom-based to a computer conferencing format, an important consideration was that the initial conversion of the program was only a short-term goal, as the long-term goal was to develop the program for web-based delivery. MBAA surveys of its members indicated that while there was a significant and steady increase in members with Internet access, the majority of members had not provided Internet connections to staff. This is an important distinction as even for companies with Internet access, often that access was not available to staff members who would most likely be the target for these online training seminars. As such, the conversion process had to take into consideration that the ultimate delivery would be web-based. The creation of course materials using products such as Microsoft's Word97 and PowerPoint97, Asymetrix ToolBook II, and Adobe Acrobat assisted in creating course materials that would provide an easier transition to the web.

Instructional Approaches

Instructional approaches which are useful for web delivery include providing an asynchronous environment, collaborative learning, online experts, skills-based instruction, assessment methods, the ability to tailor courses to individual need, and use of subject matter experts.

An Asynchronous Environment

Computer conferencing software allows for a rich text-based format. Although there is a lack of face-to-face interaction, students are able to interact (via text) with each other as well as with an expert. The format used for the MBAA's online seminars was an asynchronous environment. Students were asked to log on to the campus at least once a day to download any assignment materials and to interact with other students by joining in class discussions and activities.

The asynchronous learning environment was chosen due to the expected class make-up. (A synchronous chat feature is available on the virtual campus; however, it is not required for class activities.) MBAA membership reaches across all fifty states, and time zone differences are reason enough to drive the need for a totally asynchronous environment. However, although it was anticipated that the majority of the students would be logging on exclusively from work, other students would prefer to do their studying from home. It was determined early that having a set time for students to log on was not the best use of the medium, nor was it the best way to attract and retain students. It was never anticipated how beneficial the asynchronous environment was until a student from Australia enrolled in one of the seminars. The first international student truly tested the power of the delivery method.

Collaborative Learning

This new type of classroom environment not only allowed students to use their own experiences as a link to their new learning venture, it required it. The collaborative learning environment encouraged students to share their experiences with one another and build on them as part of the learning endeavor. Students were required to respond to each posting and were encouraged to ask questions of one another.

Online Experts

The online expert was expected to log on at least twice a day to check for any questions from students. Students who asked a question directly of the expert were answered within twenty-four hours. However, if a student asked a question in the classroom, the expert was told to wait it out, as a way of encouraging classroom discussion rather than stifling discussion by just giving the answer. Experts were also used to step in to get the discussion back on track when incorrect information by a student was not challenged or corrected by any of the other students. The facilitator or the expert was also responsible for wrapping up class discussions when it was time to end that particular discussion. While the majority of class discussions had a set time frame of two to three days, some class discussions were extended due to the involvement of the students and interest shown in the discussion topic.

As Katz and Lesgold (1993) suggest, regardless of whether in a classroom or electronic learning environment, the instructor's role when students are engaged in collaborative learning is to provide advice on demand, provide quality control over peer review and other collaborative activities, and manage collaborative activities. The online seminars were structured in such a way as to allow the online expert and the course facilitator to share these roles.

Skills-Based

The seminars in their traditional form had always been skills-based in that the topics covered job-specific skills that were either new to the mortgage banking industry or skills that were changing due to changes in technology or other environmental influences. The new online training seminar format allowed for topics to be explored in greater depth and challenged students both individually and collectively to find new ways to do their jobs more effectively. A topic such as credit scoring for underwriters not only presented the basic information on how credit scores are developed and used in underwriting but also presented scenario-based activities that students worked through that allowed them to use the new skill in a work-related situation.

Assessment Methods

While it was important to retain the skills-based structure of the seminars, the final exam that concluded each three and a half day classroom-based seminar was discarded in favor of creating a series of project- and problem-oriented assessment tools that allowed for a more useful approach to measuring the skills acquired. Instead of multiple-choice questions, the new online format allowed for open-ended activities that required students to respond to real-life situations. To the extent possible, the assessments were given in a format that closely resembled what the learner would be expected to do on the job. As Cunningham (1992) argues, "assessment arises naturally. The 'test' of whether someone can complete a task is the task completion itself" (p. 40). In most cases, the final assessment required the learner to complete a job-related task. The online experts were used to provide immediate feedback for students and to guide when corrections were needed.

Given the short duration of the class and trying to keep the workload to a minimum, leveraging upon the work of each student was employed. In the collaborative environment, students share experiences with one another, but in the case of leveraging, students would directly share answers with one another as well. For example, in a course on appraisal review there was an activity that involved a series of six mini-assignments. Each assignment would take approximately thirty minutes to complete. Rather than ask each student to complete all six assignments, each student was asked to complete only one. However, students had to post answers and accompanying work to the classroom. When all assignments were posted, all answers and work were given, and the student only had to do the work of one—but gained from having all six completed. It is an excellent way of covering more material in greater depth in a limited amount of time.

In every case in which students had to post their answers to the classroom, the students were selected to complete an assignment based on their level of experience. In an online environment, it is rather difficult for a student to hide, and it becomes evident quite quickly which students are stronger than others. This difference in student abilities is used advantageously in situations when assignments are to be posted to the classroom. In these situations, all assignments are paired so that for each assignment given to a weaker student, at least one strong student is given the same assignment. This ensures that when the answers are posted to the classroom, all students have a good solid foundation of knowledge based on the experiences of their peers. The weaker student is assisted by the stronger student, and the stronger students also gain from the answers given by the other more experienced students.

Tailoring Courses

The online training course materials are structured in such a way as to enable the course facilitator and the online expert to tailor courses based on the specific student population. Much like a classroom situation, an online environment allows for that "teachable moment" when a topic such as reverse mortgages might be making big news during the span of the two-week module on reverse mortgages. The MBAA's weekly electronic newspaper *Real Estate Finance Today* can be downloaded to students, and a class discussion can ensue. And similar to real classrooms, "virtual" classrooms allow the course facilitator to generate new discussions and make assignments based on information revealed during classroom discussions and activities.

Use of Subject Matter Experts

Of course, as the trade association of real estate finance, the MBAA is fortunate that through its membership base, the association can utilize (volunteer) experts in the field of mortgage banking as online experts and as Subject Matter Experts (SMEs) in the development of course materials. The use of industry experts was especially important as these seminars although already existing in the form of a traditional seminar need to be continually revised to ensure that the content is current and relevant to the industry. It was determined early that in order to keep expenses to a minimum, volunteer SMEs would be used to both validate the materials and provide assistance as online experts for the course modules.

Marketing the Program

While developing a new program may provide challenges and tax the imagination when trying to create a new learning environment, marketing the new program requires not only a unique approach but also a concerted effort. MBAA markets its training programs to both members and nonmembers. And although the MBAA determines prior to developing training programs that a market exists for the program, the association must find the market and fill the classes.

The marketing of the online training seminars created a unique opportunity for the MBAA because not only did the program need to be heavily marketed to ensure a successful program but the marketing materials needed to explain the online training programs in a way that would be easily understood by potential students who most likely did not understand the underlying concepts of computer conferencing.

Network MBA: The Distance Learning Center for Real Estate Finance

In an effort to create a distinction for distance learning programs offered by the association, the MBAA wanted a distinct umbrella name that would ultimately be recognized immediately by potential students while capturing the essence of the distance learning program. Network MBA is now used for all MBAA distance learning programs accredited by the Distance Education and Training Council.

Catalogs and Brochures

The MBAA produces high quality catalogs and markets to all member firms as well as nonmembers who have purchased the association's training products or who have attended MBAA conferences, seminars, and so on.

The MBAA publishes an annual planning guide that contains a schedule of all MBAA conferences, seminars, and training programs, as well as all books and periodicals offered by the association. However, since this annual planning guide is published only once a year and covers a twelve-month period, it is difficult to use it to market new programs that will not be developed until well into the year. So, in addition to the annual planning guide, the MBAA publishes twice a year a catalog of all the education department's publications and training programs.

In addition to catalogs brochures are sent on almost all MBAA training programs. These brochures include registration information and detailed information on the specific program. Due to the change in seminar format and the new delivery method used, the association determined that it would be best to find a new marketing company to promote this new product line. After completing an extensive search, two companies were interviewed, and a small company with an innovative approach to design and marketing was selected.

The resulting marketing brochure had the different look that the association wanted to achieve. However, due to time constraints the marketing materials were mailed only weeks prior to the start of the program. Typically, brochures are mailed at least eight weeks prior to the start of the program. Even though 15,000 brochures were mailed, the short turn-around time hurt registrations. Each two-week module was budgeted for thirty students, but only one-quarter of that number materialized. The marketing materials however drew substantial interest with many individuals requesting information on future programs.

Trainers' Symposium and Sneak Peeks for Trainers

In an effort to get widespread acceptance of the online training concept, an online program specifically for trainers was developed. Another two-week program, the idea was get trainers accustomed to the delivery method while providing them with a training program on topics such as instructional design and technology. The importance of seeking acceptance from trainers cannot be minimized. Many trainers within a mortgage banking company are responsible for placing employees in proper training programs throughout the year. By providing trainers with a program where they have used this online training concept, they will be more likely to encourage their company's employees to take one or more of the online training seminar modules.

Because the concept of computer conferencing is not easy for everyone to grasp, being able to see the program in action is important. Not only is this provided to trainers during the Trainers' Symposium, but the association also gives "sneak peeks" to certain trainers as a way to promote the program. These "sneak peeks" allow trainers to see firsthand how the online training programs work and how the students work together on and through the course materials. Trainers are given one- or two-day access to the virtual campus for a quick tour and to see how the courses progress.

While these two methods are valuable, another method has been used by companies that was not pre-planned by the MBAA. Companies have selected one or two employees to take an online seminar as a "guinea pig" for their company. These individuals take the seminar and make recommendations to their employers as to which staff members would benefit from the training. And while not planned this method of exploration has provided a big boost to the MBAA, as the power of word of mouth in this case has been an effective way to market the program.

Outcomes—Student Reactions

The design of the programs had input from the subject matter experts and the online experts used in each of the training modules. In addition, each training module concluded with a student evaluation form. Because each online training seminar consisted of a series of two-week modules, input from the first modules was received prior to the start dates of the later modules. A distinct advantage of online training is the ability to make changes on the fly; basic program changes could be made based on student input from the first courses. This was extremely helpful as changes could be made to the course format based on input from the students.

Overall reaction to the online training format was extremely positive. However, there were initial problems that had to be overcome. The majority of the problems centered on connecting to the server and downloading and installing the required software (Adobe Acrobat Reader and PowerPoint Viewers). The difference in computer expertise varied widely among the students: some students had never downloaded files before. The contractor handled the system support side of problems, so the bulk of students dealt exclusively with the contractor on the initial start-up problems. For the majority of the students who experienced problems, the problems were resolved within the first two days of class. As most of the students enrolled in the complete seminar (five two-week modules), the initial set-up was an investment in time for the entire seminar.

While the students enjoyed the ability to interact with each other, several students suggested that interaction with the online expert should be increased. While it was planned that students would use the expert as a resource and the bulk of all discussions would be between students, reliance on an expert who could tell the students "what to think" was a difficult concept for some students to get used to. This was resolved in later course modules in which the facilitator modeled for the students the proper use of the expert. Once the behavior was modeled a few times, the students felt more comfortable approaching the experts when necessary.

Other students who had experience with the MBAA's line of correspondence courses reacted to the online training in a similar manner and had some difficulty in adapting to the interactivity of the online seminars. After seeing this several times in the first course modules offered, the modules were changed in such a way as to mandate more interaction. Mandating that the students interact with one another forced students to change the way they approached the course materials. It was anticipated that by mandating more interaction, students might be turned off to the learning experience when forced into an uncomfortable situation. However, for the majority of the students the increased interaction only helped to spawn more interaction.

The feedback from the course evaluations was invaluable and helped in making changes to the program as it progressed. While course evaluations were given to students at the completion of each module, a summative evaluation is planned to evaluate the entire seminar as well as to provide more detailed information on the individual course modules.

Lessons Learned—What Comes Next for the MBAA?

The conversion of seminars from classroom-based to an online training format was a measured success during the first offering. The students were able to cover at least the same amount of material as they did in the classroom but in greater depth with more time spent on the materials and longer access to the expert. The next step for the MBAA is to offer the seminars again and attempt to increase enrollments.

Each of the two seminars will be offered twice during the next year, and a new seminar will be added to the online training series: a seminar for commercial real estate finance professionals. This seminar will be structured like the current seminars and will be developed using experts in commercial lending.

Marketing, definitely a weak link in the seminar series, will be more effective as the MBAA's catalogs and annual planning guide will have the programs listed and thus will reach a greater number of potential students. In addition the seminar brochures will reinforce the catalog material and will be sent in a more timely manner. Also, the online programs will be marketed on the association's web site and will provide more detail on each course module and provide sample screens. Sample screens are another way to allow a "sneak peek" into the classroom and give potential students a better understanding of how the instruction is delivered.

During the next year, greater emphasis will be placed on training for the online experts. Faculty training is an important part of a successful program, and proper training for the online experts will contribute to a richer learning environment. Training for the online experts will be developed that will formalize the process for online experts without jeopardizing the flexibility and spontaneity of the expert's role in the virtual classroom.

While the primary goal of the MBAA is to expand this program of online training, a secondary goal has been the conversion to a web-based solution. The current computer conferencing software used for the online training seminars is not web-based. However, it is anticipated that a shift to a web-based conferencing system will occur during the next year. While the lack of a web-based solution has been appropriate thus far given the access to the Internet within the potential learner base, the rapid increase in Internet access will make a web-based solution more appropriate for MBAA members. It is expected that a such a solution will provide greater capabilities for the delivery of instruction. The program design allows for a fairly easy shift to a web-based format.

Currently the conferencing system is owned by an independent contractor, but ultimately the MBAA would like to purchase the delivery mechanism that is used to provide these online training programs. Depending upon how quickly enrollments increase and the popularity of the programs rise, the purchase may happen when the association shifts to a web-based solution. Investing in technology is a tremendous step and must occur only when the support from the member base is evident.

As Porter (1997) suggests, distance learning programs "require a great deal of support: financial, technical, educational and professional. If any type of support is lacking, the program suffers" (p. 197).

The next few years should prove to be a turning point for the MBAA in distance education. With the association's newly accredited programs and dedication to the use of technology in finding effective, low-cost training solutions for the mortgage banking industry, the MBAA's online training programs have the potential to become more accepted and evolve to be a major force in delivering training.

CHAPTER EIGHT

GRADUATE PROGRAMS AT A DISTANCE: A PARTNERSHIP BETWEEN THE CALIFORNIA DEPARTMENT OF REHABILITATION AND SAN DIEGO UNIVERSITY

Michelle M. Warn, Charles Compton, Susan Levine, Sandra Whitteker

In the last twenty-five years, the government has turned its attention to the protection of civil rights for individuals with disabilities. The Rehabilitation Act of 1973, the Reauthorization of the Rehabilitation Act in 1992, and the 1990 Americans with Disabilities Act provide powerful legislation prohibiting discrimination against Americans with disabilities and approving funding to provide rehabilitation services to such individuals.

To realize the vision of these laws, organizations and services emerged intending to help this population "achieve valued social outcomes, including employment and integration into the communities of their choice" (Bellini, 1997, p. 155). The California Department of Rehabilitation (CaDR) provides vocational rehabilitation services that assist individuals with disabilities to obtain competitive employment in integrated settings and maximize their independent functioning at home and in the community. To achieve this mission, CaDR employs some two thousand staff, many of whom are rehabilitation counselors. At the state level, these counselors are the direct, hands-on providers of vocational rehabilitation services to people with disabilities and offer evaluation, counseling, training, placement, and rehabilitation technology assistance to qualified individuals.

Rehabilitation counseling is a multidisciplinary profession, requiring proficiency in a variety of areas including psychology, history, sociology, and law (Bellini, 1997). Acknowledging that counselors must possess sophisticated skills and knowledge in order to properly serve their clients, amendments to the Rehabilitation Act mandated that states establish a system to ensure that rehabilitation counselors were certified and licensed according to the highest standards. Title I, Section 101(a)(7) of the Reauthorization of the Rehabilitation Act states:

"The State Plan shall include . . . (7)(A) a description (consistent with the purposes of this Act) of a comprehensive system of personnel development, which shall include—

(B) policies and procedures relating to the establishment and maintenance of standards to ensure that personnel, including professionals and paraprofessionals, needed within the State agency to carry out this part are appropriately and adequately prepared and trained, including
  (i) the establishment and maintenance of standards that are consistent with any national or State approved or recognized certification, licensing, registration, or other comparable requirements that apply to the area in which such personnel are providing vocational rehabilitation services; and
  (ii) to the extent such standards are not based on the highest requirements in the State applicable to a specific profession or discipline, the steps the State is taking to require the retraining or hiring of personnel within the designated State unit that meet appropriate professional requirements in the State . . ."

(Reauthorization of the Rehabilitation Act, 1992).

In California, this law was interpreted to mean that newly hired rehabilitation counselors should hold a master's degree, while current counselors who did not possess such a degree were eligible to receive state assistance in obtaining one (Federal Register, 1997).

In an attempt to fulfill the federal mandate of bringing the educational level of its staff up to the minimum requirements set forth by the Rehabilitation Act, CaDR announced that it would pay tuition for counselors pursuing a master's degree in Rehabilitation. While some counselors did pursue a degree, most uncredentialled counselors have yet to embrace the offer. This lack of action among counselors may be partly due to the fact that few universities offer a degree in rehabilitation counseling, and most of these are geographically inaccessible to them. Also, the work and family schedules of many counselors are such that seeking a degree in a traditional educational setting is not feasible.

It became clear that if CaDR was going to fulfill its obligation under the Act, a new means for educating its employees would have to be found. Could a distance education program be the answer? It would resolve the problem of geographic inaccessibility and would provide greater flexibility in terms of scheduling. Further, San Diego State University would be willing to collaborate with the department to offer its Rehabilitation Counselor program in a distance format.

The goal of the Rehabilitation Counselor Master's of Science Degree at San Diego State University is to advance students' skills, knowledge, and professionalism in the field of rehabilitation. Coursework is designed to help students gain an awareness of issues and thought processes that influence current thinking, policy, and social outcomes. The program provides an in-depth understanding of the profession and the support systems that are available to individuals with a disability. It also develops important skills and knowledge in a multitude of domains including medicine, vocational counseling and placement, individual and group counseling, case management, multicultural issues, and more.

Measuring the Need

To determine whether CaDR counselors were interested and eligible to pursue a master's degree, a team from CaDR developed and distributed a survey to all of the counselors throughout the state. The survey measured counselors' current educational levels, their interest in obtaining a master's degree by traditional and distance formats, and their willingness to commit time and money toward this goal. A total of 545 surveys were returned for a 63 percent response rate.

A counselor was eligible for a master's program if he or she had an undergraduate degree but had yet to acquire the graduate degree. The survey revealed that 54 percent of the respondents already possessed a master's degree in Rehabilitation Counseling or a related field and therefore satisfied the new educational standards. However, 41 percent of the counselors possessed a bachelor's degree with no post-baccalaureate degree. Of these, 87 percent were interested in pursuing a master's degree in Rehabilitation Counseling via a distance format. Consequently, almost 200 of the survey respondents were potential candidates of a distance program if it were implemented.

To measure the counselors' level of motivation, the survey asked respondents what kind of financial commitment they would be willing to make toward their education. Over half of those who were eligible for participation in a distance master's program affirmed that they would be willing to pay some or all of the costs of tuition. This information confirmed that the cost factor was not the major issue that kept people from pursuing their graduate degrees.

A Collaborative Endeavor

The survey results were complied, and the data indicated that many of CaDR's rehabilitation counselors were ready and willing to participate in a distance program. The need, interest, and commitment were established. The survey team presented its conclusions to the Director and her executive staff, who then requested a videoconference with San Diego State University's (SDSU) Rehabilitation Counseling Program's distance learning team. All agreed that we would go forward in seeking the mutual support of the university and CaDR to offer a pilot master's program over distance.

Gaining CaDR Approval

To increase a new program's likelihood for success, it should be sponsored by individuals who rank fairly high in the organizational hierarchy (Hammer and Champy, 1993). Fortunately, CaDR had the enthusiastic support of its highest officials. The Director, the Deputy Director of Field Operations, and the Assistant Deputy Director all believed in the viability of this program and that it would benefit the department in the long run. Consequently, although many barriers seemed to defy implementation of the program along the way, these individuals along with other proponents within the department had the foresight and the authority to carry the idea through to its fruition.

CaDR agreed to begin the distance master's program by introducing a group of rehabilitation counselors from across the state to participate as students in what would essentially be a distance education pilot program. The agency also agreed to assume the tuition costs of every student. Finally, CaDR allowed students a small amount of time off work per week to be used toward activities related to their education. The costs of books and materials as well as necessary travel would be borne by the student.

Gaining SDSU Approval

As the distance education spokesperson for the pilot program, our Department Chair met formally and informally with university stakeholders including faculty, the Dean, and the Vice President. These groups voiced their concerns that the program's excellence would suffer if it were offered over distance. Our Chair suggested instead that although location and delivery strategies may vary when distance is involved, the key to rigor in any course is in retaining the same content and grading standards as those applied to the university's on-campus courses. This dialogue became an invaluable part of the development process of our distance program and led to a mutual understanding among the stakeholders. Certain issues of concern began to emerge during these discussions:

Evaluating Participation and Competency. The SDSU distance team recognized that maintaining academic standards was a crucial element in the acceptance of the program by the university's accrediting bodies. Consequently, measurements used in the traditional educational setting were translated into the distance format as closely as possible. For assessment of knowledge and skills competencies, each class retained its instruments and grading standards. To maintain professor-to-student interaction requirements (forty-five hours per three-unit course), the distance program replaced on-campus class time with instructional lectures delivered by audiotape, videotape, email, and via the web. We also determined that professor participation in electronic discussions should serve as part of this interaction time. In addition to the professor-student interaction time, students were expected to spend time outside of class reflecting and studying. We determined that readings, assignments, and electronic discussions were considered appropriate indicators for time spent outside of class. Using all of these measurements, we ascertained that our professors spent far more time interacting with distance students and that our distance students spent far more time per week academically compared to their on-campus counterparts.

The Western Governors' Association is developing a distance learning model in which traditional evaluation standards are being reanalyzed. Measures such as "seat time" and face-to-face activities are being replaced with measures of competence more appropriate to the distance arena (Barnard, 1997). In the future, we hope to integrate new more explicit evaluation criteria as indicators of the satisfactory completion of coursework.

Instructor Qualification. In keeping with the recommendation that distance instructors should hold the same credentials as our on-campus professors, we retained our existing faculty for the distance program. This proved to be quite a burden on already busy professors, who approached this added responsibility with trepidation. However, they have proved willing to meet the challenge of this pilot program and feel they have gained valuable rewards as a result (see Redesigning the Coursework for Distance later in this chapter).

Access to University Resources. On-campus students have access to a full range of resources within close geographical proximity. Libraries, bookstores, financial aid centers, and administrative offices are all within walking distance. Partial distance learning programs that we had offered in previous years required that students attend certain semesters on campus in order to use the library to conduct research. We also provided these students with graduate assistants who would obtain articles and books to be faxed or mailed to the distant student.

Today, our distance program students can log in to the newly developed SDSU on-line library, with limited access to research databases and abstracts of articles and books. Once they've identified their research material, however, students still have to physically visit a university campus near them to obtain relevant material. Fortunately, the California State University system is addressing access of materials for distance programs. At many campuses, students are able to check out materials as long as they are within the State University system.

As of yet, SDSU does not provide on-line registration and payment. To help our distance students with necessary academic paperwork and administrative needs, such as student IDs, we have an administrative assistant who manages the collection of registration fees and paperwork and handles all interactions with admissions and records offices.

Encroaching Territory. Universities are recognizing that distance education programs afford new opportunities and are beginning to offer courses nationally and internationally. When a student's choice of schools is no longer constrained by geography, he or she may pursue a degree at a university in another town, even though the same degree is offered locally. Factors that once affected the marketability of a university, such as convenience to home or beauty of the campus, are beginning to diminish in importance. The question of "to what institution do students belong" is a political and emotionally charged one that will probably take precedence within educational circles over the next few years. Fortunately, because the Rehabilitation Counseling Master's Degree is so specialized, we did not encounter this problem with our program. However, as our department investigates delivering other courses and programs via distance, we do expect this issue to resurface.

Throughout our discussions with both the Department of Rehabilitation and the university, we stressed the experimental nature of our distance venture. There were many unknowns, and we expected to make mistakes. New systems and processes needed to be developed to accommodate this program and others. We asked for flexibility and the willingness on the part of all stakeholders as we launched this unprecedented new effort.

The Participants

Once a decision was made by the department and the university to establish a distance program, the SDSU Distance Learning team was given just four months to interview and enroll students, bring them up to speed technologically, and begin delivery of the first course. The department provided a list of students throughout the state whom we interviewed for academic and technological eligibility. We selected a cohort of thirty-six students to go through the two and a half year program.

The Students

During the interview process, we emphasized to candidates that the distance learning student must develop self management skills that may not be necessary in more traditional learning settings. While distance learning allows great flexibility as to when and where learning occurs, success is dependent on the student's ability to develop an academic routine. Distance learners must also take more initiative in communication and interaction than they might in the classroom. Without the benefit of the full range of communication resources available in face to face interactions, the onus is on the distance student to maintain an open communication link, request clarification, and direct interaction in a way that will serve to increase the learner's personal understanding. The presence of these qualities in candidates factored greatly in the selection process.

Candidates were also screened for technology skills and access to computer systems. Because CaDR didn't want students to conduct educational activities at work, they would need access to equipment and Internet services from home or somewhere outside of the office. In the way of hardware, the students needed a personal computer with a modem that could run a World Wide Web browser and an email package. Basic skill requirements included use of word processing software and rudimentary use of email and the World Wide Web.

The resultant student body consisted of a wonderfully diverse group of individuals who would be logging into us across the state, from Los Angeles to as far north as Humboldt County. For many of them, hailing from Asia, Mexico, and South America, English was a second language. About 15 percent of the class were individuals with a disability. These disabilities varied from limited motion impairments to sight impairments to deafness.

The Distance Education Team

During the evolution of the distance program, roles emerged that required distinct skill sets from various members of the distance team. In some cases, one team member wore two hats, however, a larger distance organization might find it necessary to dedicate personnel to each of the following areas: Distance Education Champion, Project Manager, Instructional Designer, Administrative Support, and Technical Support.

Distance Education Champion. Distance Education is still a novelty in both academia and business. New methods, practices, and technologies come into the picture on a daily basis, constantly shifting the boundaries of this field. Implementation of a distance program can be expensive, and there are many choices. As such, organizations and institutions are hesitant to adopt a program without extensive deliberation. The distance education champion must be an influential leader who is willing to educate stakeholders and decision makers frequently throughout the acceptance and establishment of a distance program (Duncan and Powers, 1992). This individual must be willing to take a high profile and to disseminate the direction, needs, and goals of the program to a wide range of individuals and groups to ensure its funding and support. The champion "articulates a vision and persuades people that they want to become part of it so that they willingly, even enthusiastically, accept the distress that accompanies its realization" (Hammer and Champy, 1993, p. 71).

Managing the Program. The program manager is directly responsible for the tasks and processes that create a successful product. The manager maintains the goals and vision of the overall program and keeps the distance team's efforts focused. Some important duties include ensuring a consistent and high quality learning environment that serves both instructor and student, coordinating resources and events, and monitoring the success of the program by soliciting feedback and implementing formative and summative evaluations. Because the program manager monitors and directs all functional aspects of the program, it is helpful to have a good understanding of technology as well as instructional design.

Instructional Designer. It is unfair to expect an instructor to be an expert in distance learning technology as well as in his or her field of instruction. Designing a course for distance is incredibly time consuming and intensive. Course materials, delivery methods, and even coursework often take great departure from the on-campus counterpart. Finally, delivery of information and materials along with support and tracking of the students can become time consuming and more complex over distance. Our instructional designers are invaluable to the instructor as they assist with these tasks in the development and implementation of courses.

It is our policy that the curriculum should direct the methods and media used in a course rather than vice versa. Therefore, before we determine a distance format, we ask the professor to describe usually on a week by week basis how the course is taught presently. We analyze the goals, objectives, and teaching strategies presently used in the class. We then look for ways to complement the professor's teaching style with our own pedagogical approach: learner-centered, context oriented instruction, use of cooperative learning activities, and establishment of an over-arching conceptual framework. From this point, we begin to decide what methods and materials to implement in the curriculum.

One of the most important roles of the instructional designer is that of briefing the professor about distance education. Even for the professor with previous experience in distance education, appropriate distance tools and format vary significantly among distance programs and even among classes within the same program. Once the designer has an idea of what distance strategies might be optimum for the class, the next phase usually entails a mock-up of each week, which is then presented for consideration and rework. All final decisions in course delivery, format, and materials rest on the instructor, and are subject to his or her approval.

Without the luxury of rich communication environments that exist in face-to-face interactions, confusion and miscommunication during class time may be more difficult to arrest and can quickly lead to frustration and loss of student interest. Therefore, once the course is up and running, it is imperative that the instructional designer and the professor take an active role in keeping the students on track through regular communications, class activities updates, and frequent online participation. Often, the designers will also work with the professor during the session to keep wayward discussions in check and to help monitor the receipt and completion of assignments.

Administrative Support. Distance students do not have the resources readily available to them that on-campus students do. Access to registration, admissions, libraries, textbook, and materials packets must be provided by the distance program itself. Administrative support staff are an invaluable part of a distance team. They act as liaisons between the student and campus, assist with duplication of materials and mailings, manage records of students and classes, track costs, and help coordinate program activities.

Technical Support. The Information Systems (IS) team implements the electronic communication tools that make a distance program viable: websites, email discussion lists, message boards, chat rooms, teleconferencing systems, and more.

In our program, the IS group also provides basic technology support for students. While it is up to the students to purchase equipment and software and acquire the skills necessary to maintain and use their systems, there are technology skills specific to the program that the distance program must teach. Also, because it is important in distance environments that students keep up with the classwork, we try to serve as a first line of contact to students with system problems or who are unsure about how to use the technology.

Pedagogical Rationale

The opportunity to develop a master's degree over distance allowed us to rethink the instructional pedagogy of the Rehabilitation Counseling Program. For on-campus courses, faculty met regularly to keep the program current, both in information content and in teaching strategies. However, some professors still had the desire but not the time to update their own course materials and methods. The faculty also wanted to more closely integrate all courses throughout the program in order to facilitate students' organization of knowledge and to build a holistic understanding of the field of rehabilitation. Here was an opportunity as we reworked each course to tie short-term topics and assignments into the Rehabilitation Program's macro-context.

On campus, our professors anchored much of their instruction to real settings by bringing in guests from the field and by requiring that students apply course material to their lives through case studies and personal story. With our distance student population, all rehabilitation counselors, we had a wellspring of experience from which to develop discussions and illustrate the theories and principles taught in the courses. We decided that while didactic instruction was important for relaying important facts, concepts, and principles, it would mainly serve as fodder for dialogue among students and faculty as they brought the information alive through personal interaction. By implementing a cooperative learning environment, students were encouraged to verbalize and elaborate the material to each other, gain from each other's insights and special interests, and become sources of information for the course. Thus, the students contributed as much to the learning environment as the professor, whose role became colleague and facilitator rather than that of director and sole source of knowledge. As a result, the professor experienced the class in a fresh and exciting new way.

Redesigning Coursework for Distance

The faculty was apprehensive about the new program and with good reason. With already full schedules, they perceived that the translation of their current course into a distance format would demand a large investment of time. They were also uneasy about using new distance technologies and wondered how they would actually teach a course in this unfamiliar environment. Finally, they voiced valid concerns about sacrificing course quality for delivery over distance.

Indeed, the time involved in redesigning their courses was extensive, even longer some said than it might take to develop a brand new course. A significant part of the redevelopment went toward reevaluating methods of instruction and coursework delivery. The instructional designers worked with the professors to analyze goals, objectives, pedagogy, content, and activities and suggested ways to incorporate learner-centered and context situated teaching strategies. As one professor put it, "I had to change the entire way I conceptualized the learning experience. I had to break old mindsets . . . I'm a content expert, I've developed a teaching style idiosyncratic to my personality. This (experience) has forced me to look at content from a pedagogical perspective."

Although the experience was personally challenging and time consuming (professors joked about barely making minimum wage), so far they have found it to be rewarding. "I don't think I've ever worked so hard on a course and had as much support and help . . . from (the instructional) designers. It's been exhausting . . . but it's also been rewarding . . . The success of this venture hinges on the support we get, not just for the technology—email, etc.—but for the instructional design, even more so." On-campus courses also benefited from the effort as professors brought new materials and teaching strategies to the classroom. "In my (previous) on-campus courses, the competencies and objectives emerged as the course went along. Here, they had to be determined from the start."

Adjusting to the Distance Environment

As mentioned earlier, not all individuals are suited for a distance learning program. In addition to developing independent study skills and an assertive communication style, students and faculty both have had to adapt to the lack of face to face contact.

> "It has to do with the style of learning. Students need to adjust to a whole new way of learning and relating to others. It can be exciting to log on and find lots of email and messages on the (message board) to read. However, it can be a lonely experience too. I am a very social person and get a lot of energy from discussion with others. This is very different from a classroom setting, and sometimes it has been a hard adjustment. The flip side is that we have access to (each other's) thoughts and comments twenty-four hours a day to read or reread as we like. Humor has been a great way of connecting with each other. There are times I really feel close to my classmates even across the miles and there are times when I really miss having them to interact with in person" (Harner, K. Personel communication, 1998).

We are attempting to respond to this human need by offering more opportunities for richer communication exchanges (see Richness of the Transaction later in this chapter). The desktop videoconference meetings enable students within a region to meet face-to-face and to interact with others by videoconference across the distance. Increasing the size of the presently small videoconference monitor will dramatically improve the sense of interaction with remote sites. We are also beginning to experiment with telephone conferencing and have had wonderful success with group communication in that context. Finally, CaDR has generously funded travel for the entire group to occasionally meet in a single location for one or two days. All of these have contributed to increased bonding and genuine friendship among all members of the group.

Increasing Accessibility

As service providers in the field of rehabilitation and as educators of a diverse student population, much of our attention is on making our coursework accessible for all individuals. So too we found as we take steps to make our materials accessible for a few individuals that the entire group benefits. As is the case so often when a product is modified to accommodate a certain population, the product is easier to use by everyone (Vanderhieden, 1994).

Access for Persons who are Deaf or Hard of Hearing. We have transcribed all audiotapes and some videotapes in their entirety and made the transcripts available on the web. Again, the transcripts turned out to be useful to the other students by furnishing them with a hard copy of the materials, which they could download, highlight, and study.

For one class in which the subject matter was highly visual, we realized that transcripts would not properly convey the content of the videos. Therefore, we added open captioning (in which a transcript of the speech shows up at the bottom of the screen). This process seems to work for our deaf student, and we are pleased to add open captioning to our distance materials repertoire.

Access for Persons with Visual Impairments. Computer mediated technology has been a boon to our visually impaired students, who are able to configure their software to increase the size of the text on their screens to aid in reading. They also use screen readers that speak the words on a screen and that will accept spoken input. We also send lessons and resource materials in fourteen point font whenever possible.

Access for Persons with Limited Motion Impairments. By far, the biggest challenge has been adapting materials for those with a limited range of motion or with a repetitive motion injury (such as carpal tunnel syndrome). It would be difficult to reduce the amount of typing and computer work that is required in this distance program. Many of our students are in a quandary, unable to use the mouse or keyboard much yet needing to participate in electronic discussions and to write project papers.

This is a very real concern for us, and so far we have been only marginally successful in helping these students. It seems there is no single solution that minimizes keyboard strokes. Some students use voice command software that accepts voice input in place of typing. Others are using software that replaces or reduces mouse and keyboard usage by substituting arrow keys. Proper ergonomics also helps. We are continuing in our quest to find better solutions that can be easily and inexpensively implemented by our students.

English as a Second Language (ESL). For some of our students, English is not the primary language, yet most of the distance coursework involves intensive reading and writing, "In this program, we really get to know our classmates by how well or how poorly they express themselves in writing." Interestingly, literature shows that electronic communication allows students time to compose their thoughts, type their message, and to edit their written work. (Barnard, 1997; Petrovic and Krikl, 1994). Through this form of communication, ESL students, as well as those who are slower typists (such as those with a limited range of motion) are given a chance to participate as fully as other students (Roth, 1992). Professors observed, "In class, students with poor verbal skills usually can't respond to spontaneous conversation, [however,] on-line they can be thoughtful, and you get a better idea of who these people are as individuals."

The Reticent Student. Literature suggests that those who usually don't contribute in face-to-face conversational settings seem more willing to share in an electronic venue (Kiesler, Siegel, and McGuire, 1984; Petrovic and Krikl, 1994; Roth, 1992; Sproull and Kiesler, 1995). Our professors were impressed with how powerfully the electronic discussions elicited the participation of the majority of the students rather than just the few vocal ones. They therefore felt the quality of the learning experience was better than in the on-campus course due to the expansion of perspectives shared among the class members. Electronic discussions allowed students to have access to a multitude of ideas, increasing the richness of their experience. Also, because of their willingness to contribute on-line, the professors could get to know even the shyer students. "I knew at least a bit about each of them, (whereas) on campus, usually only ten or so are active contributors to the discussion."

Varied Media. Because all individuals have different cognitive strengths and styles of learning, we used a wide variety of tools, media, and techniques. These learning methods were designed to be flexible, providing resources to students in a way that would allow them to glean information in the way most suited to them (Gardner, 1993). For example, the website held much of the course information that was also available by email. Video and audiotapes elaborated the text and hard copy materials. Video and audiotapes were also available in transcript form. We provided web links to elaborate and illuminate the readings and lectures. Electronic discussions rephrased content in personal less formal terms. All materials worked in concert to reiterate and extend the students' experience of the course content.

Development of Electronic Courses

Six months into the program, we have delivered five distance courses with two more in progress. The pace has been staggering as the distance team and faculty find themselves redesigning entire classes while still meeting deadlines imposed by the start of each session. We have chosen four courses to outline in this chapter due to their variation in content and approaches to delivery over distance.

Class One: Introduction to Distance Technologies

The interview process revealed that many of the students were beginners in the use of a computer. We decided that we would need to first provide a one-unit course that would improve students' technology skills and increase their ability to access course information. This course covered the basics of email and the World Wide Web. Lessons were designed for the lowest common denominator in student skill level.

The class was conducted entirely by email. Over the next six weeks, the instructor emailed lessons to the class every three or four days. Lessons explained how to use the in and out boxes, how to send and receive email, how to manage messages, how to reply to messages, and so on. These were presented in a step-by-step manner much like a software instruction manual.

The instructor gauged the delivery of new lessons by students' feedback and their success in executing exercises and assignments. As a result of these exercises, the goals for the course were pared down considerably, and the focus became acquisition and refinement of basic skills. However, for students to be able to participate in their first rehabilitation course, it was imperative that they develop the ability to hold electronic discussions and work in groups. Consequently, even though many students were not yet ready, the instructor pushed students to learn electronic discussion procedures and protocols, to establish group addresses, and to begin exchanges with their own group members with whom they would be working in the next session.

Remarks

Without the benefit of face-to-face instruction, teaching and learning technology over distance can be a frustrating experience. In the first month, the instructor spent over four hours a day working individually with many of the thirty-six students by email and telephone. On campus, such support is provided by well equipped and well staffed computer labs. Without access to university technology resources, we found and still find technology support and services to be a significant part of our distance learning expense.

The instructor also found that teaching technology on-line necessitated the following:

- Keep lessons short, break them into multiple messages if necessary,
- Present lessons in instruction manual format, step one, step two, and so on,
- Be ready and willing to say the same thing more than once!
- Be willing to work with individuals on a one-to-one basis,
- Realize that many students require support throughout the first few months as they acclimate to their systems and software.

Class Two: Introduction to Rehabilitation

This course offers an overview of the field of rehabilitation and a brief introduction to upcoming coursework in the rest of the master's program. It affords the opportunity to reflect upon the foundations of the rehabilitation profession and gain an awareness of policies and social influences that drive current thinking.

The design of this course as with all courses for this distance program was in keeping with our desire to create a learner-centered environment. In all but the most ideal learner-centered environments, however, it is still necessary to develop a foundational springboard from which the student can depart in his or her learning adventure. Therefore, in this course the professor delivered basic concepts and principles to the students through lecture, readings, and resources, which guided the learning process. He then asked students to personalize and reformulate the lectures and materials in their own words and stories via electronic discussion.

Activities and Media for Distance Delivery

Aiming to create an interesting stimulating environment and foster a sense of community and collegiality, we carefully considered all the components of our courses. Media and activities were investigated from a dual perspective: 1) what role do they play in the distance relationship between the professor and student? and 2) how can we use them to address the varied learning styles of our students?

We also realized that distance can increase confusion if there is inconsistency or too much complexity in any part of the program delivery. Therefore, we chose to utilize the different forms of media in very specific and consistent ways. Likewise, we maintained a predictable schedule of activities, and updates were regularly sent by the instructional designer. In this way students would receive the updates, even in the absence of the professor (the Department Head in this case, who sometimes conducted class from Japan, Europe, and Guam!).

Weekly Discussions. Discussions were designed and implemented in a way to create a safe and amicable space where the students could effectively interact with their professor, guest lecturers, and fellow students. These discussions usually involved all students, the professor, and guests. However, in some weeks we experimented with breaking the students into groups to discuss a topic among themselves. The groups then summarized their discussions to the entire class at the end of the week.

Discussions were based on weekly reading assignments, audiotapes, and videotapes. Before commencement of the weekly discussion, the professor would review and expand on the week's topic with a paragraph or two. He would then offer three or four discussion questions to kick off the weekly discussion, which began on Wednesday and carried through noon Saturday. After that, students could (and frequently did) continue with the discussion but were encouraged to take a break. Termination of the previous week's discussion the following Wednesday kept everyone "on the same page."

Small Group Projects. The group project was designed to increase the sense of community among students and to utilize pedagogical strategies such as cooperative learning and shared meaning. Students worked together on a scholarly report, which was then presented through the World Wide Web to the entire class. Email facilitated communication among the group members. Suggested strategies for participating in a group over distance were provided to students in a "How To" web page.

Individual Projects. Each student was also required to produce a scholarly report independently. Students were asked to select a topic of special interest to them and investigate the subject in depth. The result of their efforts would be realized in a paper to the professor and in summaries published to the class, thus becoming in themselves a source of information for the entire group.

Hard Copy Materials. Fundamental information was delivered mostly through textbook and handout materials.

Videotape. We decided that videotapes could be used to compensate for the perceived isolation from the professor. Through videotape students could come to know the professor's personality and communication style. For this first course we used videotapes to provide module overviews, allowing the professor an opportunity to offer students a big picture of the field of Rehabilitation.

Audiotape. We felt that audiotapes would offer another means of rich communication between student and professor. We used audiotapes as the primary means of delivering weekly topic content. Surprisingly, these turned out to be an ideal medium for this group of students, whose duties frequently take them out of their offices and into the field. They could now make good use of otherwise lost driving hours and frequently expressed their gratitude for the opportunity to do so ("I love my audiotapes!").

Audiotapes also accommodated the professor's teaching style. Discovering that it was much faster to deliver a lesson spontaneously in the studio than it was to compose and write an electronic lecture of equivalent content, the professor opted for time in the studio as much as possible.

We discovered another powerful use for audiotapes—the professor could invite distinguished guest lecturers from all over the world via audiotaped telephone interviews. Using this medium, our distance students enjoyed the "virtual presence" of knowledgeable experts who would rarely be available in a face-to-face, on campus setting.

Desktop Videoconferencing. Students came together approximately once a month for a videoconference. Four sites were established throughout the state with desktop videoconferencing systems installed by the Department of Rehabilitation. San Diego State University housed the fifth site. These systems consist of a personal computer equipped with a camera, microphone and speakers, allowing live audio and video interactions with remote sites. These particular systems also allow software sharing between sites, including the World Wide Web and electronic chalkboard. This feature was useful for demonstrating new web sites and electronic resources.

Desktop videoconferencing sessions were used to further a sense of community among students and faculty through dialogue and exchange of ideas. We also used these sessions to solicit regular feedback from the students concerning the progress of the course. At the site meetings, facilitators would conduct exercises preparing students for the video conference itself. At the end of the conference, if appropriate, facilitators then held a final discussion to summarize the meeting.

The World Wide Web. The website evolved as it came to be used to communicate a variety of information. By the end of the course it contained:

- The course syllabus,
- A weekly schedule of activities outlining in detail each week's resources, materials, and assignments (similar to guidebooks used in correspondence courses),
- A "How To" page offering explanations of how to use the media, how to participate in a group discussion, and other instructions pertinent to taking the course,
- Web lectures—when it was not possible to produce an audiotape,
- A "Resources Page," providing additional electronic resources relevant to the content areas,
- A student roster with pictures and short bios of each student. This web page became invaluable to the students and instructors as they sought to familiarize themselves with those whom they came to know so well online,
- An in-depth explanation of the assignments to minimize the flood of email questions which ensued about assignments, and
- Student projects to showcase the students' efforts and provide them with further motivation towards excellence.

Remarks

As we evaluated the progress of this initial course, we realized we would need to modify our use of media for certain activities in subsequent courses. Following is a discussion of various instructional strategies relative to specific media used for delivery.

Use of Email for Discussions. Asynchronous communication such as email offered students and instructors the opportunity to operate within their own schedules. Both the late nighters and the early risers could be accommodated in this way. We had students communicating with us as early as 5:00 A.M. and as late as 2:00 A.M.

All participants were taken aback however by the amount of information thirty-six students could generate. In the first few weekly discussions, the students and faculty were receiving sixty to eighty email messages a day! This overwhelmed students and staff alike. Soon students began to economize their communications. Email became more succinct and focused on the topic. Students also began to prioritize their message reading according to whom and what was really worth reading.

Still, we knew email was not the best solution for this volume of discussion and that it was difficult to manage the influx. It was then that we began investigating alternative forms of electronic communication such as message boards and chat rooms (implemented in the next course).

Group Projects. Group work presented challenges, some of which have yet to be completely resolved. Group dynamics issues and barriers were similar to those experienced in group work on campus but were compounded by the real distance between students. Logistics such as who would take on what tasks were difficult to resolve asynchronously. Sometimes three or four days or more would pass without a group member responding to an emailed question by the group leader. One group demonstrated initiative and ingenuity by holding a group video conference between Sacramento and Santa Barbara. They were so successful that we encouraged the rest of the class to follow suit if they wished.

In the next course we were able to resolve some of the difficulties afforded by asynchronous constraints by introducing chat rooms so that students could hold real-time meetings online.

Desktop Video Conferencing. At the onset, we believed video conferencing would be the one component of our program that would provide that vital link between the professor and the students. However, there have been some issues concerning the technology that have inhibited its use. While the standard sized video window on the computer screen works well for a few individuals grouped around the computer, it is not feasible for a class of ten to twelve in a conference room. We are purchasing equipment that will transfer the image onto a large monitor, which will improve participants' ability to see each other. However, email communication has been so successful, we have not needed to depend on this medium as much as we had expected.

Course Three: Applications of Rehabilitation Technology

This course describes the use of technology for people with a disability and teaches how to identify and develop assistive technology for an individual's needs. On campus, the professor uses visual presentations augmented by lecture. In the first third of the course the professor introduces a wide variety of assistive technology and numerous examples of previous class projects using slides, videotapes, and guest speakers.

The second part of the on-campus course uses a hands-on and cooperative approach. An equal number of students from three academic disciplines—rehabilitation, special education and engineering—form into project design teams. The assignment is to find and solve an assistive technology problem for a real client—an individual with a disability—who is also a member of the team. Students are responsible for problem analysis, product design, and production of one piece of assistive technology for their client.

Activities and Media for Distance Delivery

In transitioning this course to distance, we wanted to retain both the hands-on and cooperative learning aspects of the course. We decided to focus on the analysis and design aspects, using actual clients within the Department of Rehabilitation as partners for the students. Our students then applied the skills learned in the class sessions to analyze and identify assistive technology solutions for their partners. Conveniently, as actual rehabilitation counselors, some students were then able to implement the solutions they had devised in class. Thus, the student experience was still highly contextual and team oriented.

Transition of Discussions from Email to Message Board. Email discussions were still a vital part of the course for the first three weeks. At that point, we initiated the use of a message board in place of email. The message board was a central area that students would log onto from the web. Here they could post a message that the entire class could see and respond to. Because of the way the message board organized postings by topic, we felt it would prove much more fruitful for tracking and participating in electronic discussion as readers could follow a thread of conversation chronologically.

We were concerned about introducing the message board in the middle of class session but felt the benefits outweighed the learning curve we knew students would have to undergo. However, the resultant revolt was beyond our expectations. Strangely, students had become more attached to the use of email than we realized, as they had come to love that method of conversing in spite of being initially overwhelmed. When we requested that students move discussions to the message board, they complained of feeling restricted by the board and of experiencing a sense of loss of freedom and creativity in using it. Many threatened not to use the message board at all. Eventually, with coaxing and reasoning and the elimination of one of the assignments by the professor to allow for time spent learning the new technology, students began to understand and accept its benefits over email.

Ultimately, the message board has proven extremely valuable in providing structure and focus to the discussion. Some more notable advantages over email include

- The ease of following a thread of discussion.
- Use of the message board as a permanent resource. (One student described being away on vacation for a week and being able to return to the message board and read the exchanges like a novel.)
- Increased ease for professors and guests to participate, manage, and track the progress of discussions.
- The ability for the distance team to remove unwanted or inappropriate messages, such as personal messages to the professor.

Guest Experts. We were fortunate to have the electronic participation of both authors of the required texts for the course. After students read the texts, the professor solicited students' questions for the authors. Each author then developed an electronic lecture responding to these questions. The authors were also available to the students for direct interaction via the message board.

The authors and students alike found the experience rewarding. The authors were impressed with the quality of questions and contributions, and students gained valuable insight into the rehabilitation profession. It also presented a unique opportunity for both authors to evaluate the efficacy of their books from the perspective of an experienced and knowledgeable group of counselors.

Videotapes. The visual hands-on nature of assistive technology forced us to use videotapes far more than we had in the previous class. Audiotapes were eliminated entirely as a means of content delivery, and videotapes became the mainstay. Along with videotapes of our own creation, we created lessons around commercial tapes many of which were provided free by vendors serving the disability community.

Class Four: Practicum

The goal of the beginning level practicum course is for students to develop basic counseling skills in an apprenticeship environment. Throughout the course students learn to facilitate relationships, acquire empathic communication and listening skills, demonstrate the ability to give and receive constructive feedback, and learn to use self-reflection to guide their continuing development.

In the on-campus course, students meet weekly in small groups with a professor to review and discuss basic counseling skills and text materials. They practice counseling by role playing and by audio and videotaping their own counseling sessions with clients, which they present to members of the class. They then receive feedback from the instructor and other students in their group, who use an assessment instrument to guide their observations and feedback. In addition to practice with feedback, instructors place a high value on "modeling." Using this technique, instructors counsel in simulated or actual situations, demonstrating communication and relationship skills as they interact with the counseled.

Factors Contributing to Pedagogical Strategies

The novelty of delivering this type of course over distance was evidenced by the paucity of reference material. Other university distance programs offering coursework of this kind require that students attend these classes on campus, even if the rest of the program is provided in a distance environment. For example, Utah State University offers a distance Master's in Rehabilitation Counseling. However, courses offering the skills included in the SDSU practicum are taught face to face (Gerard, G. Personal communication, 1997). We were able to find only one reference which discussed a class offered via distance learning which even approximated our beginning practicum course (Kincaid, 1997). Here, an undergraduate counseling skills class was provided in both traditional and distance formats. The author reports no difference between the mastery levels of students in the distance and traditional classes. However, as she notes this paper does not describe a controlled research study.

Besides the strong reliance on face-to-face communication and instructor responsiveness, one other factor contributes to the difficulty of teaching this course over distance. Often, students may feel vulnerable about their participation in these courses, where the learner is observed in potentially self-revealing behaviors by the instructor and fellow classmates. Part of the professor's role then is to facilitate this process in such a way that learners feel safe. Professors are accustomed to picking up non-verbal and paraverbal cues to aid them in this process.

For all of these reasons, SDSU professors were extremely concerned about teaching this class without students' physical presence. Because of the heavy emphasis on interpersonal and intrapersonal processing and a lack of precedents for distance learning models to teach counseling skills, professors decided early in the analysis phase that the class *must* include some in-person, face-to-face communication. However, since learners are currently employed full-time, they are unable to take much time away from the office. We are meeting these contrasting requirements (geographical dispersion, minimized time away from work, and in-person face-to-face instruction) by

- holding three face-to-face seminars to allow interpersonal interaction with the instructor such as role play, practice, and feedback,
- personalizing exercises and evaluations by assigning partners (dyads) who work together as peers throughout the course,
- using rich forms of instructional media such as audio and videotape (see Richness of the Transaction later in the chapter),
- breaking the class into three smaller sections, each run by a credentialled instructor. This allows the professors to spend more time with each student and attend to individualized needs.

Richness of the Transaction. The very nature of counseling, which consists of face-to-face interaction with its many subtleties and nuances, seems to dictate a similar setting for instruction. One of the challenges in designing this course was to find ways to compensate for the absence of weekly face-to-face contact and to capitalize on the capabilities afforded by asynchronous communications for deeper processing and increased learner-learner contact (albeit not in person).

According to the Information Richness Theory (Markus, 1994), elements that contribute to the richness of a message include timely feedback, the ability to convey multiple cues, the tailoring of messages to personal circumstances, and language variety. Using these criteria the richest way to communicate is through face-to-face interaction. In face-to-face exchanges multiple cues are delivered via body language and tone of voice. Also, the message can be modified according to reactions from the communication partner. Communications technologies diminish the sensory aspects of a message in one way or another. For example, communication by telephone eliminates visual cues; electronic text eliminates visual and audio cues; and each reduces the message's richness and aptness in its own way. Based on the Information Richness Theory then, face-to-face communication is the most expressive; however, audio and videotaped communications are richer than text-based interchange such as email because they involve using more of the senses.

Activities and Media for Distance Delivery

Pedagogical, logistical, and instructional considerations informed the choice of learning strategies and media for this course. As noted previously, the course will include some face-to-face meetings though far fewer than in the on-campus course.

- *Audio- and Videotapes.* Students will prepare audiotaped and videotaped counseling sessions. We selected audiotaping as the primary medium because we felt it would be easier for distance learners to manage the logistics of audiotaping without sacrificing too much communication richness.

- *Expert videotape.* Students will individually view and evaluate a videotape of a counseling session conducted by an expert. The tape will be time stamped to allow students and instructor to synchronize their observations, even as they view the tape asynchronously and in different locations. After students submit their individual evaluations, the instructor will provide his or her comments, which they can compare with their own observations.

- *Practicum observation and analysis scale.* The instructor and instructional designers have devised an assessment instrument which students use to measure personal skills and the skills of their peers. With items measuring competencies in all the areas students are expected to develop, such as listening, providing feedback, probing, and so on, the scale was developed from and represents the course objectives. As students apply the analysis scale to exercises several times throughout the class, they will gain awareness into the process of counseling and be able to describe and implement these methods and techniques in professional settings.

- *Electronic discussion.* These will be used to provide a group forum for in-depth discussion of most of the course content and process. Discussion activities will be student- and instructor-moderated.

- *Dyadic interactions.* Learner-learner and learner-instructor teams will replace some of the group interaction that occurs in the current practicum class. Student audio tapes will be peer reviewed and discussed online and in face-to-face seminars. Dyadic interactions are far easier than groups to arrange and schedule.

- *Text materials.* Text and hard copy materials will be used more extensively than in the classes so far. Textbook and other materials developed by the instructional designers and course instructor are introduced in order to enable more expert input without requiring the instructor to be physically present.

- *Workbook exercises.* Exercises will provide additional practice by requiring students to respond to counseling scenarios and self-reflective activities.

- *A study guide.* This guide will focus on administrative procedures (with some course content as well) and will provide the additional structure required to minimize potential confusion due to distance. The study guide will be available in hard copy and on the course web site.

- *Self-reflective writing.* These activities will be used more extensively than in the on-campus practicum course.

We feel this sequence of instruction will lay the foundation for a powerful practicum course without the need for extensive face-to-face contact. Modeling and counseling is provided through videotape and face-to-face practice. Audio and videotapes provide the basis for self- and peer-analysis, guided by a counseling skills analysis scale. Guidance and continued processing of observations and experiences are provided by instructors and peers through electronic discussions.

Impact on the Department of Rehabilitation

Students comment to us about how their learning has positively impacted how they do their jobs. Although the Rehabilitation Counseling Master's program is designed to increase students' understanding of the Rehabilitation field at a macro level, they find they are able to apply their newfound knowledge at the office daily.

The Merging of Education and Training

Often there is an inherent dichotomy between organizational training and academic education with each addressing different learning needs. Training responds to organizational processes and job functions. Organizations implement training programs to address specific skills and knowledge that enable employees to improve job performance. Education on the other hand aims at enriching and expanding the role of an individual within a profession and in society. Ideally, it empowers that individual to develop self-directed learning skills for continued personal growth in that field. "Training teaches the how of a job; education increases insight and understanding . . . it teaches the why of a job" (Hammer and Champy, 1993, p. 71).

In the information age, rehabilitation organizations are reexamining models of business, service, and health against a backdrop of sociological and technological change. In response to economic pressures, these agencies are streamlining procedural and administrative red tape and flattening organizational hierarchies (Hill and Schroeder, 1996). As this process continues, roles in rehabilitation become more demanding and diverse. The organization must fully utilize each employee as a rational decisive being. As roles shift from those of controlled laborers to empowered decision makers (Hammer and Champy, 1993), managers become more like coaches, and staff collaborate with others internally and externally to extend and share resources (Drubach, Kelly, Peralta, and Perez, 1996).

Organizational intelligence has been defined by Peter Drucker as the "obtaining, digesting, and utilizing of knowledge by which to increase the effectiveness of decision making" (cited in Johnson, 1988, p. 19). By developing an intelligence network, organizations apply human knowledge to maximize information and decision making. The skills that enable rehabilitation personnel to gather and refine information, find creative alternatives to existing processes, and network with others are becoming vital to the success of the rehabilitation organization. Consequently, training and educational goals must merge, expanding the purpose and direction of employees. In this way, they will receive broader knowledge and tools to best serve clients and the organization.

A Seminar to Evaluate the Program

Recently, the CaDR executive staff requested a two-day seminar with the students and the SDSU distance learning team. The executives were interested in knowing more about the students' experience so far and also wanted to explore how recently acquired ideas and knowledge may benefit the organization as a whole. During the seminar, students met in small and large groups to discuss how the program affected them personally and at work and to discuss how their learning might be used to advance the goals of the department. As they met, similar experiences began to emerge:

Understanding the Big Picture. As we had hoped, students were beginning to understand the Rehabilitation field from a holistic perspective. They realized how social and political events directly affected their profession. "We have a sense of the history of our program and the philosophies that have shaped it. It helps us to make sense of our jobs when sometimes policies or practices (seem confusing)." More importantly, they began to see things from the client's viewpoint. Rather than "being on the other side of the desk, we're in the trenches alongside the client." In this insightful role, they became more responsive. "We're looking at the whole being rather than just a work plan and moving from case processor to clinician." Additionally, by becoming aware of the system surrounding the client, students found they could increase the involvement of the community in their search for solutions and were able to guide other organizations in providing services not previously offered.

Personal Growth and Introspection. The coursework challenged students to reflect on their own practices and beliefs. Indeed, students reported feeling emotionally "stretched" and were stimulated to personal growth. They experienced a surge in self-esteem as they began to apply new knowledge and resources at the office, "All in all, my attitude is improving; I'm feeling good about my work, and it's reflected everywhere. I think the Department will have an improved RC (rehabilitation counselor) for their money . . . ."

They also reported feeling more confident in their interactions with clients, in how they assessed their own work, and in the way they felt they could approach administration. As a result of this sense of empowerment, they were better able to argue their case to administration and justify their recommendations for clients.

The strong electronic community also served to increase confidence and reduce anxiety. Through the sharing of experiences and feelings both academically and professionally, students were able to build an invaluable support network. Even more importantly, they had a safe environment that they could come to for feedback. "We have a sounding board in each other."

Understanding Technology. Our distance education program is based on the philosophy that the materials and media support not dictate the curriculum. Therefore, we forget that the students' gain in technology skills can be an important by-product of distance learning. Our students stressed the value of their growing technology skills on multiple levels. They were now able to comfortably search the web and use electronic resources to find solutions for clients. They also could make informed choices when clients' requested computer systems.

Changing Roles. Students voiced a growing awareness that their role as employee in the department was metamorphosing. Rather than the two-dimensional employee-employer relationship they had become so familiar with, they began to understand the perspective of the administrators and to see the organization as a complex holistic system. From this vantage point, they became cognizant of ways to improve the organization. They now wanted more access to the decision-making mechanism in order to influence change within the agency.

Taking It Back to the Office. Students indicated that they could now see the difference between education and training. "It's not about training; it's about empowering. How do you empower people to become initiators in their area of specialty?" Through the program, they found they had discovered new resources within themselves to meet the challenges of the job. They also wanted to adapt many of the tools and content of their coursework for use in their profession:

- They considered ways that they might ask the training department to bring in more experts from the field, so they could continue to stay abreast of current events.
- They also felt strongly that some of the issues presented in class such as ethics be developed into a course offering for the entire department.

- During the seminar, students came up with creative new ways to use email and the web to share information and ideas to improve inter- and intra-organizational communications.
- From the practicum class, students appreciated the growth in their counseling skills through constructive criticism in a peer setting. "I think all program supervisors should receive training on how to critique counselor's interviews." They were also inspired by the idea of videotaping counseling sessions and wanted to see this tool used throughout the department.
- After a dynamic and enthusiastic electronic discussion about peer mentoring in class, students felt strongly about creating a similar support system within the department. A focus group met in person and worked online to develop a proposal to present to the executive staff. As a result of this enterprising team, the implementation of a peer mentoring system is now under serious consideration by the department.

The Distance Education Environment

In just the few short months that this distance program has existed, we have witnessed certain phenomena that have not been evident in the on-campus program. We think these developments are probably a result of the combination of pedagogy and media used in the distance environment. Instructional strategies that were more conducive to the distance environment, such as cooperative learning and learner-centeredness, encouraged group cohesiveness that would be more difficult to achieve in a traditional didactic instructional environment. These instructional strategies work better online than didactic or behaviorist methodologies (Barnard, 1997; Willis, 1993). Although the media or the pedagogies alone might influence the outcomes below, we believe it is through their use together that we have experienced such powerful results.

Strong Student Community

Without doubt, the fact that our students are members of the same organizational culture contributed to the rapid development of the electronic community. These shared experiences along with commonality in the job significantly enhanced mutuality among the group. However, this powerful network would have remained untapped had there not been the opportunity for discussion and cooperative learning. While the delivery of content has been crucial to learning, we believe it is the synergistic effect of the electronic interactions that has led to the incredible growth in the relationships among students in this program and the accelerated development of a strong networked community.

"This program has helped open my eyes to what my colleagues are doing. So much of this job is done individually . . . Occasionally we will staff a case to get others' ideas on how to solve a problem. But this program provides a vehicle for RCs (rehabilitation counselors) to share ideas, practices, dreams, success, and not-success stories as a learning tool. I have connections now that I didn't have before, and I have resources in those connections. We have a network of committed counselors to tap into if needed" (Harner, K. Personal communication, 1998).

Even the professors discovered a wealth of expertise: "(I asked the students about) services for persons who are HIV positive and got wonderful information back which I will now be sharing . . . at an AIDS seminar next week. If I didn't have access to this group of professionals, I wouldn't have gotten this state-of-the-art information."

Professor as Coach

Another unexpected result of this highly interactive learning environment was its effect on the professors. In taking on the role of coach and facilitator, they gained new insights and awareness from the students. Class became as exciting for the professors as it was for the students. In fact, as a result of this and other paradigm shifts in their instructional methods, they modified their on-campus courses to reflect pedagogy used in the distance program.

Marked Writing Improvement

Finally, our professors have noticed that students' writing skills have improved significantly in just a few months. Although we will be developing an evaluation to measure this, we believe that this is probably due to several factors, such as the students' ability to regularly read the work of peers who write well, the knowledge that peers will be reading their work, and extensive practice due to the amount of writing that is required in the program itself.

Conclusion

All participants have shown great flexibility, patience, and commitment throughout this pilot program, despite the technological, administrative, and academic obstacles. Even more, students and faculty alike have enthusiastically declared how rewarding this experience has been for them. Although just recently implemented, this program exhibits a dynamic and thriving learning environment in which students and faculty grow and build networks.

The partnership between San Diego State University and the State Department of Rehabilitation has been rewarding for both sides. The SDSU rehabilitation counseling classes are undergoing fundamental reanalysis and modifications that can inspire on-campus as well as distance classes. CaDR has set in motion a process to develop its workforce into leaders and decision makers. As these students discover and begin to draw upon their potential, they will make significant contributions to the organizational intelligence and success of the agency. "Overall, this program has given me the opportunity to continue my commitment to work with people with disabilities and to promote independence and respect (for them.)"

There are still obstacles to the continuation of the program, obstacles which are common to many distance learning programs. Debates about competency standards, administrative procedures, access to library and other campus resources, uses of technologies, and rigor of the coursework will continue until resolutions are found. Distance courses require great amounts of resources and time, and it can be difficult to find adequate funding and a competent and knowledgeable team.

Distance programs must be flexible enough to attend to the needs of their students. Culture, physical disability, language skills, and learning preferences should be considered early in the development phase of any program. Fortunately, one of the strengths of distance education lies in the fact that students have more power to direct when and how they access and interact with the materials and instruction. Learner centered instructional strategies enable a more flexible approach. Cooperative learning techniques and context-based instruction were implemented extensively through electronic discussions and shared personal stories to bring the instruction to life. As a result of these discussions, students have discovered a safe environment in which to share ideas, request feedback and advice, and enjoy fellowship.

We look forward to another year and a half with this bright group as we continue the pilot program. Because the program so far has had such a positive impact on them, students have expressed their interest and commitment in seeing this program being made available to their co-workers. We too believe the program so far has met with great success and hope to expand its availability to CaDR and other rehabilitation agencies in the near future.

Special thanks to the efforts and enthusiasm of the students, professors, and administrators within the California Department of Rehabilitation, the Interwork Institute, and SDSU's Department of Administration, Rehabilitation and Postsecondary Education (ARPE). We would like to extend special appreciation to Brenda Premo, Director of the California Department of Rehabilitation, Margaret Lamb, Deputy Director, Field Operations Division, Manuel Enriquez, Assistant Deputy Director, Southern Region, and Fred McFarlane, Director of the Interwork Institute and ARPE Department Chair.

PART TWO

BUILDING SKILLS (TECHNICAL AND CRITICAL THINKING)

CHAPTER NINE

RESKILLING EMPLOYEES FOR COMPETITIVE ADVANTAGE: REINVENTING LEARNING AT UNISYS CORPORATION

Mick Mortlock and Edward Dobrowolski

In the late 1980s a number of business and technological forces converged to dramatically alter the landscape of the computer industry. To remain competitive in this changing market, technology companies had to rethink and restructure traditional business methods. Faced with the challenge of reskilling a workforce with limited resources, Unisys Corporation was among the first in the industry to implement distance learning techniques.

This chapter describes the forces that revolutionized the computer industry and how they interacted to advance distance learning at a major technology company. It also details how individuals involved in this environment responded to these forces.

In 1998, Unisys Corporation felt energized for success. In less than one year as CEO, Lawrence Weinbach had quadrupled the value of the company, tripled the value of the company stock, and reduced corporate debt by almost one billion dollars. These gains came from focusing on customers, the corporate image, and employees.

The head of human resources, Senior Vice President Dave Aker, spearheaded a drive to become an "employer of choice" that caught the imagination of employees. A new corporate university was put in place to capitalize on the energy and catapult Unisys into the next millenium.

The picture has not always been this rosy. In 1986 Unisys was fresh from a merger between two computer giants—Sperry Corporation and Burroughs. With 120,000 employees worldwide before the planned 1986-1987 divestiture of its noncomputer businesses, the new company had high expectations that increased size would drive success in computers. Largely unrecognized by Unisys or its rivals at that time was a fledgling revolution that was quickly changing the computer industry. With an added burden of high debt from the merger transaction, Unisys had to quickly redefine itself just to survive.

When James A. Unruh became CEO in 1990, he evaluated the company's position in an industry where technology was drastically reducing profit margins on computer hardware. Proprietary mainframe systems were also being challenged by increasingly powerful desktop computers that shared applications software, regardless of brand. In addition, customers were demanding support in applying technology.

That assessment led to a new services-led and technology-based Unisys. The company was first among computer industry pioneers, including IBM, NCR, and Digital Equipment, to restructure to meet unprecedented change. These companies reduced employment levels by some 40 to 50 percent in the 1990s. Unisys also divested its large defense business in 1994. The company entered 1998 with approximately thirty-two thousand employees and an expectation to grow over time.

One Company, Three Businesses

To meet the new needs of business and government, Unisys reorganized over several years into three major business units. A new services organization called Information Services would work with Unisys clients in solving business problems with information technology-based solutions. Services would encompass consulting, systems integration, applications, and outsourcing. The business had great potential for high revenue growth.

A second unit, Computer Systems, would continue to manufacture and market computer technology, capitalizing on the company's expertise in mission-critical high-volume transaction systems. As over 1,500 worldwide government agencies, most of the major airlines and banks, and many retail operations were powered by Unisys systems, Computer Systems was a critical but lower growth part of the computer business. As a full-service technology company, Unisys would continue to invest in its strengths and outsource what it chose not to build.

To meet the blossoming need for network-related computer support, Unisys would transform the Global Customer Services unit to offer state-of-the-art network integration and management services, from the desktop to the data center. This third "leg" would grow as it replaced important but declining traditional mainframe maintenance revenue with high growth network integration and management services revenue.

Armed with a full-service strategy, Unisys now needed to develop a workforce that could launch and develop these businesses. This was a formidable task as the company had to reskill its employees, while trimming staff to a size that revenues could sustain.

Reskilling the Mainframe Veterans

Prior to the reorganization, Unisys employed thousands of highly skilled engineers and scientists who were expert at designing, building, and repairing mainframe computer systems. But with market demand increasing for newer desktop computer systems based on the latest technology and with that technology also making proprietary systems simpler and more reliable, there was less work for these competent people. How could a shrinking company with a new strategy capitalize on its human assets in a changing world?

To quickly and efficiently reskill its people to better compete in the changing computer industry and to achieve maximum efficiency within its training function, Unisys merged its disparate training groups to create a Worldwide Training and Development organization. By placing this organization under the leadership of a former member of the Unisys sales force, high-level executives rather than mid-level managers now discussed training issues.

Under new leadership, the vision of distance learning soon became the cornerstone of employee development at Unisys.

Dr. David Owens was recruited to lead the development of this new training approach. Owens had developed models for distance education long before computer-based training (CBT) was established in the education market. He had a strong background in educational television and intimately knew its strengths and weaknesses. From his experience, Owens had concluded that the future of training demanded more than television, as television had no interactive component.

In the past Owens had developed new and sophisticated applications of interactive video, audio, and computer-based training. But even with this expertise, Owens faced some formidable challenges at Unisys. Luckily, he viewed these complex obstacles as opportunities.

Under Owens Unisys began reducing its reliance on traditional classroom training and opened fully equipped computer learning centers stocked with custom computer-based training and other courseware. The company also analyzed the use of satellite communications for remote training.

Reduced Need for Classroom-Based Technical Training

Unisys training had typically been held in three major centers located in Lisle, Illinois; Princeton, New Jersey; and Milton Keynes, England. These training centers were used primarily to teach field engineers from around the world how to install and service the Unisys product line. Equipped with the company's latest multimillion-dollar mainframe systems, these facilities provided field engineers with hands-on experience in maintenance and repair.

State-of-the-art mainframe systems with longer "mean time to repair" intervals reduced the need for this type of technical training, however. Fewer service calls meant fewer field engineers were required on staff.

Contemporary systems also were incorporating more sophisticated, self-diagnostic software and hardware that automatically determined when a circuit board needed to be replaced with 90 percent accuracy. With these new systems, an engineer could just locate and replace the faulty board. By embedding intelligence in systems diagnostics, Unisys didn't need to train as many engineers to do costly complex circuit analysis.

Budget cutbacks and reduced training travel also contributed to the end of the training centers. A smaller workforce also meant field managers could no longer afford to have employees away from their work for multi-week courses, common in Unisys training.

In addition, Unisys no longer needed to develop most of its coursework, as much of the training curriculum was available off the shelf, thanks to industry standardization. Systems were also easier to repair, which cut the length of time required for training. All of these factors put pressure on the internal training systems and organizations to devise alternative strategies to classroom-based training.

If Not In The Classroom, Where?

As a global enterprise, Unisys operated in most of the world's countries. Its workforce was not only spread out, it was very diverse and functioned in the language and culture of its host location.

Educating trainees in centralized centers for training and acculturation was relatively easy though expensive. When instruction moved out of the classroom, the task was even harder as new methods had to replace former programs. One potential solution was interactive distance learning.

The Unisys Business Television System provided a vehicle for distance learning by linking Unisys offices around the world via satellite. Using satellite technology, Unisys could dynamically exchange information with employees in remote locations. Through the use of touch pad interactivity linked with telephony, it offered enhanced communications over standard linear television by enabling instant question-and-answer sessions between presenters and worldwide participants.

Seeing the possibilities of satellite technology, Owens partnered with Information Services to use this methodology to train employees in the use of the new Microsoft™ Office Suite of products. Ninety sites and nine thousand employees later, Owens realized it did not do enough. Unisys needed a system that provided education on demand at exactly the time an employee needed training. Working with a small group of technologists who recently moved to corporate headquarters in Blue Bell, Pennsylvania, Owens began to systematically attack the distance learning issues.

Technology-Based Learning Development Group

Headed by Ed Dobrowolski, an instructional designer with ten years of experience in technology-based learning, the group had previously launched a pilot project using interactive videodisc technology (IVD) to replace instructor-led training on the repair of computer peripherals such as printers.

The course contained various question modules, enhanced by a touch screen monitor. Students could identify printer components while they were still installed in the printer or among a number of removed components. They could select a correctly adjusted assembly from a series of assembly images and view the results of an incorrect installation through a video sequence in which a door would not close or an error message would appear after the assembly was complete.

The course ended with a troubleshooting exercise that required students to explore a malfunctioning printer, using a series of touch screens to determine the cause of its problem. Once a diagnosis was made, students could remove and replace the faulty components simply by touching the appropriate screws and assemblies. The program continued even if the component was not the actual cause of the printer problem. At the end of the exercise, students would run a full systems test to determine if the problem was solved. If not, they started again. If successful, a student would receive an "online diploma."

The classroom version of the large-scale printer course took five days. Using enhanced instructional design techniques and new courseware development tools, Dobrowolski and his team reduced it to five hours. A comprehensive evaluation, including a test in which students repaired an actual printer with a series of problems, showed that IVD students performed as well as classroom students even though they had never seen the printer except in video prior to the test. When the IVD students were allowed fifteen minutes of self-orientation with the printer, they performed better than the classroom students did.

Financial constraints prevented the team from producing additional IVD programs. Instead, the team went on to develop computer-based training (CBT) programs without video or sound for two major Unisys proprietary mainframes. Used by employees and customers alike, the courseware reduced training time to one quarter of instructor-led training. It also enhanced learning by using the same elaborate troubleshooting scenarios proven effective in IVD training to ensure students were fully prepared for the real world.

With these successes in place, Owens decided to launch a major effort in distance learning. His target was to deliver 70 percent of the company's education offerings using distance learning technology by the year 2000.

Multimedia Learning Centers

Owens acknowledged that the classroom was critical for some types of training although not all. He had successfully led the development of technology-based training for pilots and engineers who operated and serviced Boeing aircraft. If this type of training was effective with operations as complex and missions as critical as those at Boeing, he reasoned it could be equally successful at Unisys.

With the financial picture at Unisys improved, Owens attempted to move a significant portion of Unisys training out of the classroom into multimedia learning centers around the world. In 1994 Unisys opened over 150 learning centers, each equipped with leading-edge multimedia systems including sound and CD-ROM drives. Business units provided the physical space and staff to operate the centers, which ranged from elaborate dedicated facilities with numerous carrels and a full-time staff to a PC in a supply cubicle with a stack of courseware.

The Intranet Emerges

During the deployment of the multimedia learning centers, Jim Roth, a Unisys veteran, determined that the "Unisys Backbone" (the LANs and WANs) could connect the different Unisys sites in courseware distribution. Student records could also be retrieved from this network. The "Unisys Backbone" essentially became the Unisys intranet, with the distribution of courseware as the first task of that fledgling network.

Initially, only a few courses were loaded onto a server in Roth's cubicle. Eventually, the intranet enabled multimedia learning center administrators around the world to download upgrades to existing courseware.

The Power of Collaboration

Roth advocated the principle of training—anytime, anywhere. To help bring this concept to fruition, he assembled a team that would look beyond the distribution issues and focus on CBT courseware. When organizing the group, he realized it needed to be cross-functional to be truly global and gain acceptance from the individual training and business units. In addition, Roth realized that a major investment in courseware should affect the company as a whole and not just the major industrial countries.

The CBT team ultimately consisted of individuals from the company's three major business units as well as its Federal Systems Division. They came from sites throughout the world, including South America, Africa, Australia, Europe, North America, and Asia. The team's wide-ranging expertise included network architecture, information technology, and instructional systems design. Its primary mission was to evaluate different brands of courseware and identify those that would support the world-class business that Unisys planned to build from its three strategic business units.

As a model of collaboration, members of the CBT team were encouraged to voice their many competing and legitimate differences. They disagreed respectfully and ensured that everyone was given the opportunity to express ideas and opinions. The team approach was fundamental: raise the issues, prioritize them, and resolve them one at a time. When an issue couldn't be resolved, it was put on a list and revisited until consensus was reached. This model of teamwork served Unisys well.

Building Partnerships

After investing numerous hours in courseware evaluation, the Unisys CBT team selected CBT Systems as its preferred vendor. Initiated as a small company in Ireland, CBT Systems developed hundreds of world-class courses in just a few years. The company pursued Unisys not as a customer but as a partner. By working jointly with CBT Systems, the Unisys CBT team determined that it would be possible to combine the best of the two companies and further the objective of providing training—anytime, anywhere.

The team also believed that CBT Systems offered the best products on the market. Courseware incorporated an effective interactive instructional approach that was motivating both cognitively and affectively. The student was always an active participant in the learning environment, acquiring new skills by applying and adapting prior knowledge and experience to new situations. Feedback applied in the instruction was positive, timely, and individualized.

Courseware also included discovery and simulation training. Discovery questions kept students continually involved during the training process. Many courses included simulations in which the courseware responded like actual software. The simulations allowed students to complete the same task through any number of different paths.

In addition, CBT Systems could be used on legacy as well as state-of-the-art computer platforms.

Satisfying Company-Wide Training Needs

To meet the immediate training needs of the company, the CBT team proposed a deal with CBT Systems in which it would buy the rights for unlimited use of courseware by Unisys employees. The CBT Systems contract would allow Unisys to select about two hundred CBT courses, which could be alternated every six months. This way, the ever-changing and diversified training needs of the corporation could be met.

Courseware would be made instantly available to employees on CD-ROM or by downloads off the Unisys intranet to meet immediate training needs. For instance, if an employee needed to manage IPX traffic on a cisco router to function on the job, that employee could wait until a class was offered somewhere or immediately take a CBT course and begin using the skills.

After meeting with training and development managers in each of the business units, the CBT team began examining the feasibility of a company-wide contract that would make the cost of investment more reasonable when divided among the units. This cross-company collaboration brought the business units together but introduced a new complexity.

Even though Unisys operates as one company providing information services and technology solutions, each of its business units is significantly different. A manufacturing function has very disparate retraining needs than a consulting company. Subsequently, there were some discrepancies among the business units as to which two hundred courses should be purchased from CBT Systems. Each of the primary businesses wanted a significant number of courses that were not desired by the others. For example, Computer Systems was the only organization desiring "C++ Programming," while Global Customer Services wanted "Windows NT: Performance Tuning and Optimization." Eventually, an agreement was reached.

The Intranet Extends Its Reach

To get CBT courseware into the hands of as many Unisys employees as possible, the Unisys Worldwide Professional Development organization became one of the first users of the company intranet. Using web technology, CBT courses were distributed to the learning centers and downloaded by Unisys employees who had web browsers installed on their computers. The World Wide Web enabled Unisys employees to access any of the two hundred CBT courses anywhere in the company at any time.

In the first week, hundreds of hours of CBT courses were downloaded to employees' desks. Once the web site was publicized, one thousand course downloads occurred per week on average.

Greater use of the company intranet produced new technological complications. With the limited capacity of the network, some courses took several hours to download. Users persevered and set their computers to download overnight. As the intranet grew, pioneer web users were outnumbered by typical users, who required a more efficient means to access courseware. To supplement the intranet, the CBT team produced CD-ROM versions of the courses. Owens and his team began to see the concept of just-in-time-training become a reality.

Building the Intranet Capacity

Today, Unisys has an extensive communications "backbone" that is used throughout the company. However, its original communication lines were intended for traffic of a different order of magnitude.

The legendary Univac computer and its progeny were designed for transaction processing for airlines, banking institutions, and governments. They could issue airline tickets or welfare checks with ease. A high-grade communication infrastructure was not needed to tie them all together. When these systems ruled the earth, multimedia and the World Wide Web were still fantasies in the minds of science fiction writers.

Formerly, only telephone service tied together many worldwide Unisys sites and field locations. Today, almost all of the company's thirty-two thousand employees are linked together by an array of communications technologies. In addition, Unisys is upgrading its communications infrastructure to fiber optics and more advanced technologies. Its world-class Intel® Pentium-based servers and line of computers have more than enough processing power to move the volumes of data required to process full-screen digital video with fully orchestrated stereo sound.

The Shifting Business Climate

By June 1997 the company's financial situation had substantially improved. Information Services had aggressively addressed revenue problems caused by rapid growth and was poised to grow profitably. Computer Systems had successfully introduced a very successful mainframe-class enterprise server that bridged the gap between proprietary mainframes and open systems. And it was positioning itself to be a major player in enterprise-class Windows NT systems that many consider to be the "mainframe system" of the future.

Global Customer Services had launched NetWORKS™, a service that enables Unisys technicians to predict, diagnose, and in some cases repair faults in customer computer systems without traveling to the customer site. It operates from a newly opened remote network management center.

With the company stabilized, Unruh announced it was the right time for him to step down and for the board to select a new CEO to grow Unisys. In September 1997 Unisys elected Lawrence A. Weinbach as Chairman, President, and Chief Executive Officer. Recently retired as CEO at Andersen Worldwide, Weinbach had quadrupled the size of the company in eight years.

Unisys employees and management then began a task that was new to many—growing the company. While employees had become skilled at conserving cash, Weinbach joined Unisys because of its growth potential.

Evaluating the Need for Computer-Based Training at Unisys

As the popularity of CBT courses grew so did the demand for more than the allotted two hundred CBT programs that Unisys offered its employees. It became clear that the company would have to expand its program offerings to meet increasing demand.

To justify the need for an expanded contract with CBT Systems, the CBT team conducted a comprehensive evaluation that identified who had actually taken these courses. As courses were distributed in a number of ways and could be run from a CD-ROM or downloaded from the intranet, it was difficult to know who was actually taking the courses. The universal license also allowed multiple users to access multiple copies of specific courseware, which muddled the picture even more.

To find all potential students of CBT, the team first surveyed a sample of about ten thousand Unisys employees by using Lotus Notes and the World Wide Web. Questions were created that allowed employees to respond simply by clicking on the screen. Completed surveys were directed to a team database that automatically tabulated returns. With more than two thousand responses, the automated system made it easy to process information.

How Unisys Employees Like to Learn

The CBT team's survey revealed that there was still a preference for instructor-led learning in a classroom setting. Although this was not surprising, what was unexpected was the preference for CBT as a very close second. The survey had asked, "Which way do you prefer to learn?" and listed six instructional methods that were to be rated on a scale of one to five by order of preference. Results revealed that employees preferred classroom learning first, followed in order by CBT, self-study text, videotape, satellite broadcast, and audiotape.

When asked whether they had taken classroom or CBT courses in 1996, 64 percent of respondents noted that they had taken classroom training, while 46 percent said that they had taken CBT Systems courses. This showed that the CBT courses were clearly meeting a need within Unisys. In fact, the lowest CBT course usage at any business unit in the world was 30 percent. These were very encouraging and surprising numbers—information that became the foundation for recommending the acquisition of a much larger range of CBT courseware.

Employees who reported never having taken a CBT course were asked why. The overwhelming response was "We did not know the courses were available." The CBT team used this information to demonstrate the need for a marketing plan that increased employee awareness of the course offerings. Other obstacles to CBT usage were issues such as "too busy," "insufficient management support," "the courses are irrelevant," and "I don't have the right equipment to take the course."

When CBT users were asked if they would recommend CBT Systems courses to others, an astounding 84 percent said that they would.

This was powerful data that the CBT team used to convince Unisys to purchase CBT Systems' entire library, which in 1998 includes 600 courses.

The Future Is the Web!

With the web and intranet growing rapidly, Aker directed Owens to create The Employee Network, an intranet-based information site that contained information from Human Resources as well as data on corporate travel, facilities, and other resources. This was information that Unisys employees could use to make their jobs easier.

Ed Dobrowolski's team of CBT developers was tapped to develop this web site. With the success of that initial effort, the teams moved on to other web projects, including the creation of a career development web site.

Under the direction of Mr. Aker the Career Fitness Centre was launched as a World Wide Web site on the Unisys intranet. Mr. Aker felt passionately committed to providing employees with a set of tolls to take responsibility for their career. He appointed Senior Project Manager Virginia Clark who envisioned a design that would help managers and employees better manage their careers to fulfill individual career aspirations and company goals.

Distance Learning and Career Development

In a complete reversal of company downsizing rampant in the early 1990s, corporations in 1998 are desperately trying to attract and retain employees with the necessary skills and abilities to successfully compete in the computer industry. The market for specialized skills in network integration, e-commerce, and other technical skills is especially competitive. In addition, the perception of lifetime employment no longer exists. Unisys needs to attract, retain, train, and deploy the right person with the right skills at the right time.

Using the Career Fitness Centre, employees can hone their skills to remain marketable, while Unisys is more likely to have the right person with the right skills on staff at the right time. By providing career development support, Unisys expects to retain its highly trained talent while reducing recruitment costs. The solution marries employee and employer needs into a new working relationship that encourages career development.

Career Fitness Centre

Through the Career Fitness Centre, employees can explore the latest hot career trends in each of the Unisys business units. Qualifications needed to succeed in specific positions are detailed, along with links to training that can help employees learn required skills.

The Career Fitness Centre provides access to job postings, job profiles, skills assessment tools, resume builders, development tips, feedback and coaching techniques, and many other tools to help employees with career development. The web site links directly into the downloadable courseware intranet site, which provides a context to lists of courses while helping employees plan their training and their careers online. The Career Fitness Centre also integrates the human resources information management system and other software tools. The phone numbers of career coaches who have volunteered their time to assist employees in career development planning are also listed.

Now Unisys has a truly integrated distance learning solution: online career development support and just-in-time training, both of which are available on the World Wide Web. Unisys is taking this integrated model one step further with the introduction of Unisys University. Personally spearheaded by Mr. Aker and CEO Weinbach the university will drive Unisys's effort to enculturate its workforce with a new culture as well as provide a strategic umbrella for its entire education function.

The Future

The past ten years have been quite a journey for Unisys and its employees. The story gives proof that the future of the computer industry cannot be precisely predicted. However, there is much speculation on the future of training at this information services and technology company.

The web is the most powerful distance-learning and education medium ever invented. It enables communication via telephone, television, and audio. The web can assess learning styles, deliver instruction to that style in a selection of rich media, assess the effectiveness of that instruction, and if satisfactory charge the learners' credit card.

As Forrester Research (1997) predicts, the total Internet economy will skyrocket from $8 billion in 1996 to $327 billion in 2002. In addition to developing business supporting Internet commerce and web sites, the company plans to use the web to build its internal development capability while increasing the effectiveness of its training and development.

More and more training will become web-based, eliminating the need to download courseware. Over the next several years, employees will use the intranet to coach and give one another advice. The web will link Unisys to outside vendors for courseware and university training. The company also will move toward just-in-time-training for discrete tasks. For example, workers needing to provide feedback to other employees will be able to go on the Web and access a short training segment on giving feedback. A database will be developed on these discrete learning objects for quick access by all employees.

In addition, Unisys will continue to develop industry-leading classroom-based education systems with the goal of empowering employees to manage their own career growth, while ensuring the company has the skilled employees it needs to become a major competitor in the marketplace.

Partnerships

Building strong partnerships with vendors is also an important venue for the future. While CBT Systems upgrades its course offerings, Unisys will continue to provide greater skill sets and opportunities to its workforce.

Unisys will explore other new partnerships that can improve the skills of its workforce, while developing and strengthening the resources and business of both parties.

Conclusion

Unisys has overcome one of the most traumatic periods that faced corporations since World War II. The fundamental change in the computer industry and the company's response to it required massive retraining, which in turn triggered dramatic changes in the way training was delivered at Unisys.

The company rose to the challenge by making hundreds of hours of computer-based training available to its employees through the intranet, learning centers, and CD-ROM. Distance learning is now an integral part of the new Unisys. To cope with continually changing market and business forces, Unisys plans to keep pace with changing technology, capitalize on the skills of current staff, and frequently consult with each business unit to ensure it meets the needs of its employees. As CEO, Lawrence Weinbach said in a recent report to Unisys shareholders, "I firmly believe that our greatest differentiate in the marketplace is the technical excellence, the tenacity, the creativity, and the 'can-do' attitude of our people. Investing in these competencies and encouraging these qualities will make us an employer of choice; applying these competencies to serve our customers will make us a winner in the marketplace."

CHAPTER TEN

DELIVERING TECHNICAL TRAINING TO ADVANCE TECHNICAL SKILLS: INTERACTIVE VIDEO TELETRAINING IN THE FEDERAL AVIATION ADMINISTRATION

Lynn W. Payne and Henry E. Payne

The Federal Aviation Administration (FAA) is the federal agency charged with providing a safe, secure, and efficient global aerospace system that contributes to national security and promotes the U.S. aerospace. The agency has more than 48,000 employees who work twenty-four hours a day to accomplish this mission. Training in the FAA is vital for providing employees with the skills and knowledge they need to function properly on the job and to safely operate and maintain the world's busiest aerospace system.

The FAA provided technical training to more than 22,000 of its employees, primarily at its technical training facility located in Oklahoma City, Oklahoma, in fiscal year 1997 (Federal Aviation Administration, 1997). The FAA paid over $85 million dollars to provide this required training to its employees. In general, 25 percent of the FAA's technical training budget goes to pay for travel and other expenses associated with providing this training. As impressive as these numbers may be, the FAA remains deficient in meeting all of the training requirements its employees need to fulfill the agency's mission.

Problem Statement

The FAA's technical training budget was cut by Congress from over $135 million in 1992 to just over $77 million in 1996, a 43 percent decline (Federal Aviation Administration, 1997). This dramatic reduction in the training budget resulted in the number of FAA students receiving technical training declining from over 28,000 to just over 16,000, a corresponding drop of 41 percent (Federal Aviation Administration, 1997). A congressional mandate during this same period caused the FAA to go through a downsizing activity that reduced the size of the agency by 11 percent. This downsizing asked fewer FAA employees to do more during an era of a severely constrained and continually declining training budget while the mission of the agency did not change. The problem the FAA faced was finding ways to reduce the overall cost of providing training while increasing the training opportunities for employees. The FAA needed to solve this problem in a manner that was not prohibitively expensive in its start-up costs and that could begin to show a return on the investment almost immediately.

FAA management determined in 1995 that it wanted to convert 40 percent of its resident-based training for delivery by some form of distance education technology by the year 2000 to reduce overall training costs to the agency. The initial plan had the agency converting 8 percent of its existing resident-based training for delivery by print-based technology or correspondence courses, converting 16 percent of its existing resident-based training for delivery by computer-based multimedia technology, and converting 16 percent of its existing resident-based training for delivery by compressed digital satellite technology the FAA calls Interactive Video Teletraining (IVT). As the FAA already had a correspondence course program and a multimedia computer-based training program, it needed to develop an IVT program to provide high quality highly interactive training to geographically dispersed learners and thus reduce the agency's dependency on expensive centralized training facilities.

Population

The population targeted for the IVT Program was all FAA employees and first-line managers and supervisors. The FAA is organized along ten lines of business, such as Air Traffic, Airway Facilities, Flight Standards, and Civil Aviation Security, each performing specific activities that contribute to the overall accomplishment of the FAA mission. In addition to the ten lines of business, the FAA also has a number of administrative support activities that assist the lines of business in the accomplishment of their respective missions. Of the FAA's 48,000 employees, just under 18 percent are minorities, while over 23 percent are female.

FAA employees vary widely in age, from their early 20s to over 60. The FAA has a large portion of its employees who are or will be retirement eligible in the next few years. As the older employees retire, they will have to be replaced, and those replacements will have to be trained.

FAA employees also vary widely in formal education, from high school graduates through doctoral degrees. However, the majority of FAA employees while having some college do not have bachelor or associate degrees.

These wide ranges in education and age also provide for a wide range in acceptance of the use of training technologies by FAA employees. The younger employees tend to embrace and use training technologies while the older employees tend to be somewhat skeptical and shy away from their use if at all possible.

Desired Outcomes

The FAA wanted to convert a little over 2,000 hours of resident training for delivery by IVT by the year 2000, beginning in 1995 (Federal Aviation Administration, 1995a). To accomplish this large transition from traditional classroom training to telecourse delivery, the FAA planned to install a multi-channel compressed digital satellite uplink, six studios, and 392 receive sites. The initial goal was to have a receive site within a fifty-mile radius of every FAA employee in the continental U.S., Alaska, Hawaii, and Puerto Rico.

A second required outcome was a lower overall cost of training. It was clear that the FAA could not meet all of its training requirements using its predominantly resident-based training system. The solutions to this training problem such as IVT had to be less costly than the current resident-based training program.

A third required outcome was related to the quality of the instruction as measured by learning outcomes. The FAA is and has been very satisfied with the quality of its existing resident-based training program. In fact, the FAA is the training provider of choice for virtually all aviation training for international students requiring these types of training courses. The quality of the telecourses delivered by IVT could not have significant and noticeable reductions in quality as compared to existing resident courses. That is, learning outcomes for IVT classes as measured primarily by within course and end-of-course exams had to be similar to learning outcomes for traditional resident-based classes.

Description of Process

To help solve part of its training problem, the FAA looked to a form of distance learning called IVT. IVT is a one-way video and two-way audio training system. The training is provided by satellite delivered compressed digital video and audio transmitted to remote receive sites located across the continental U.S., Alaska, Hawaii, and Puerto Rico. Learners returning audio and data use terrestrial telephone lines to provide a high level of interaction between the instructor and the learners and between learners at different sites.

The FAA's lines of business identified resident-based courses, some existing courses, and some new courses they wanted to deliver by IVT. These courses were converted either by the use of contractor support or by in-house training developers for delivery via IVT and included the addition of interaction opportunities for learners. These courses were then delivered by either FAA or contract instructors using the FAA's IVT broadcast facility.

Outcomes

The FAA has collected a rather impressive number of outcomes and lessons learned. Some of these will be looked at as successes; some will be looked at as failures, while still others will be simply looked at as something learned. Regardless of whether they are considered a success or failure, these outcomes and related lessons learned are what accurately describe the FAA's IVT Program.

First, the FAA's progress towards achieving its three major desired outcomes will be reviewed. These three major desired outcomes are the number of hours converted for delivery by IVT, the cost of IVT training as compared to resident-based training, and the quality of IVT training as compared to resident-based training. After looking at the three major desired outcomes, lessons learned and words of advice will be provided.

Number of Hours Converted

The first major desired outcome was the conversion of 16 percent or a little over 2,000 hours of the FAA's resident-based training program for delivery by IVT. At the end of fiscal year 1997, the halfway point, the FAA had converted only about 183 hours or approximately 1.46 percent for delivery by IVT, substantially less than should have been converted. There are several reasons for this lack of progress. First, the lines of business decided to put many of their IVT course conversion plans on hold pending the final outcome of a Department of Transportation Office of Inspector General (OIG) program audit. Second, the agency froze IVT course conversion funds pending the outcomes of the OIG audit and subsequent Congressional review. Many of the lines of business also decided that they did not have the personnel to convert and deliver planned courses due to deeper than expected budget cuts. The FAA has developed an additional 107 hours of new courses for delivery by IVT. In terms of the number and percentage of students actually trained, just over 22,000 total FAA students were trained in fiscal year 1997, with about 1600 or approximately 6.96 percent of those being trained by IVT.

To meet this goal, the FAA had to install the infrastructure to support the delivery of the IVT courses. The revised Program Master Plan (Federal Aviation Administration, 1995a) that was converted into the revised Integrated Program Plan (Federal Aviation Administration, 1996a) called for the IVT program to install a multi-channel compressed digital satellite uplink, 60 receive sites, and initially one automated studio. This was a significant reduction from initial program goals of 392 receive sites and six channels. This decrease was caused by budget reductions that resulted from eroding management support for the program directly related to the resistance to change to IVT on the part of the training program managers in a number of the lines of business.

To date, the multi-channel uplink, 31 receive sites, and one automated studio have been installed. Due to additional program budget cuts resulting from Congressional oversight based upon an audit from the Department of Transportation's OIG, the IVT Program's expenditure of funds to meet program goals has been put on hold. The OIG's audit is discussed in more detail later in this chapter. Clearly the FAA is lagging behind its revised objectives for its IVT program.

Cost of the IVT Program

Cost was the second desired outcome area with which the FAA was concerned. Any training solution the FAA implemented had to be less expensive than its existing resident-based training, or there simply was no advantage to implementing that solution. IVT is clearly less costly. The FAA has conducted two major cost benefit analyses, and both have shown the IVT program to be cost effective. The benefit-to-cost ratios for these analyses ranged from 2.19:1 to over 11:1, depending upon the number of courses converted for delivery by IVT, the cost of course conversion, and the rate of course compression (Federal Aviation Administration, 1996b). FAA management is convinced of the cost effectiveness of IVT.

Quality of IVT Courses

The last major desired outcome of the FAA's IVT program was in the area of quality. Any solution implemented by the FAA could not result in the lowering of learning outcomes. The FAA is very satisfied with the quality of its resident-based training program. In order to demonstrate that IVT did not lower the quality of learning outcomes, the IVT Program conducted a number of evaluations that compared the learning results of an IVT course to its resident-based version, or where such a comparison was not possible, such as with a new course, pretest to post-test comparisons were conducted.

The first IVT course to resident-based course comparison was conducted with the Cockpit En Route Inspection course. The resident course was thirty-six hours long, while the IVT version of the course was only twenty-four hours long. Due to unforeseen difficulties, the design for this comparison was a post-test control group design, in which the resident class was used as the control group (Borg and Gall, 1989). Also, intact classes were used as it was not possible to randomly assign learners to groups. The mean post-test score for the resident class was slightly higher (M 5 89) than the mean post-test score for the IVT version (M 5 87) (Ward and Warm, 1994). There was no statistically significant difference in learning outcomes, which was consistent with media comparison studies in general (Clark, 1994; Morrison, 1994) and with learning by television studies in particular (Moore and others, 1990; Payne, 1997; Hunter, Renckly, Smith, and Tussey 1995; Russell, 1992).

The second comparison was made between the pretest and post-test results for four modules of the Staff Work course. This training was four separate modules from the Staff Work course, which included problem solving strategies, gathering and organizing information, communicating with others, and presenting information to others, with each module averaging around 100 students. The mean pretest scores for the four modules was 59.5 percent. The mean post-test score for the four modules was 70.0 percent. While the gain in post-test scores was statistically significant at the $p < .05$ level of significance, it was much lower than expected (Ward and Warm, 1995a). Later analysis of attendees revealed that the course manager did not restrict enrollment to staff level employees. As a result, the modules had students ranging from entry level clerical workers through upper level executive managers. This range of students many of whom were not the intended audience for the course accounted for the relatively low learning gain scores.

Another pretest to post-test comparison was conducted with the Alcohol Testing course. As this was a new course, there was no resident-based version for comparison. This was a six-hour course broadcast to 591 supervisors and managers across the FAA. The mean pretest score was 54 percent, while the mean post-test score was 80 percent, for a 26 percent learning gain. This gain was statistically significant, at the $p < .05$ level of significance (Ward and Warm, 1995b).

Since none of the comparisons included pretesting and post-testing both a resident-based class and an IVT class, FAA management asked the IVT Program to conduct an evaluation with a pretest and post-test design. A Quality Assurance course was selected for this comparison (Lennon and Payne, 1997). Since random assignment of learners to groups was not possible and small class sizes required the use of intact classes as groups, a quasi-experimental nonequivalent control group design was used (Borg and Gall, 1989). The two key features of this type of design are the lack of random assignment of learners to groups and the administration of both a pretest and a post-test to both groups (Borg and Gall, 1989). Two resident classes were used to form the control group of thirty-one students while the IVT class consisted of eighteen students. The resident class version was sixty hours long while the IVT version was forty-six hours long. The resident classes (M 5 28.08) scored slightly higher than the IVT class (M 5 27.50) on the pretest, not statistically significant. However, on the post-test, the IVT class (M 5 48.83) had a higher mean score than did the resident classes (M 5 48.54). As with the pretest, there was no statistically significant difference (F [1, 46] 5 1.6, p, 0.05) between the two groups on the post-test (Lennon and Payne, 1997). FAA management has accepted these results along with the results of hundreds of other published studies comparing teletraining to classroom training as proof that there is essentially no difference in the quality of training between IVT versions and resident versions of the same course, as measured by within course and end-of-course examinations (Payne, 1997; Russell, 1992). That is, they believe learners learn as much in IVT versions of courses as they do in traditional resident-based versions of those courses.

Lessons Learned

While the FAA has made progress in varying degrees towards the accomplishment of its desired outcomes, a simple reporting of status does not tell the entire story of the FAA's IVT program. The FAA has accumulated a number of lessons learned, some positive and some negative. In fact, it is the activities that led to learning these lessons that more clearly explain the history that has led to the current status of the FAA's IVT Program.

IVT Program Costs

The first lesson learned dealt with costs and how to control them in the area of broadcasting training courses. Letting go of the traditional broadcast television paradigm frees designers to automate television broadcasting to a degree seldom seen. The result of such thinking for the FAA was a broadcast capability that had the uplink requirements, receive site requirements, and studio requirements automated to the maximum extent possible. The compressed digital satellite capability selected by the FAA was provided through the General Services Administration's Federal Telecommunications Services 2000 contract. The uplink and selected receive sites are remotely activated through a Network Operations Center located at the service provider's offices in Atlanta, Georgia. This meant the FAA did not have to hire an engineer to operate and maintain the satellite uplink or technicians to operate and maintain the receive sites. This network management service is provided through the contract at an annual cost of less than one-fourth of the salary of an uplink engineer alone. Receive site equipment operation is simple. A site administrator simply turns on a power strip and with two simple button pushes has the site up and running. Being an IVT receive site administrator is a part-time extra duty assigned to an existing employee and thus does not directly add to the cost of conducting training with IVT.

The FAA designed and developed an Automated Instructor Presentation System (AIPS) to reduce the cost of delivering the instruction and to increase the level of control for the instructors. A large recurring operating cost for most other satellite broadcasts is the cost of the personnel supporting the broadcast. Many traditional broadcasts include a producer, a director, a floor manager, camera operators, a video technician, an audio technician, a graphics person, and a video tape technician, just to name a few. The FAA realized that if it was to meet the requirement that IVT be less costly than traditional resident-based training, it could not afford to broadcast its IVT courses in the traditional broadcast television model. Another model had to be found. The AIPS was that model.

The AIPS is a highly automated control room and studio that reduces the support personnel from the eight to fifteen used in traditional television broadcasts down to one technical director. By using control computers, touch screen monitors, and automated broadcast equipment, the FAA has developed a relatively low capital cost, low operational cost, easy-to-operate broadcast capability that provides all of the quality the FAA requires for its IVT broadcasts.

The AIPS also helped meet one of the concerns expressed by instructors in telecourse environments. Traditional television broadcasts treat instructors as talent. That is, the instructors are told where to sit, where to look, what to say and how long they have to say it. Also, the use of support materials, such as graphics and video tapes are displayed and changed at the will of the director. In other words, in the traditional television broadcast, instructors have little or no control. In their traditional resident-based classrooms however the instructors have total control. They control the rate and pace of the course. They control where they sit, stand, or walk. They control what they say and the time they take to say it. They control the use of support material such as graphics and video tapes, along with when and how long they are displayed. In short, instructors are used to being in control in their classrooms. FAA instructors do not differ greatly from other instructors when it comes to classroom control and their desire to maintain it. Recognizing this, the FAA wanted to provide its instructors with as close to the same level of control in IVT classes that they have in their traditional resident-based classes. The AIPS with its touch screen monitors in the studio provides instructors with much the same level of control as they have in their traditional resident-based classrooms. A touch screen monitor allows instructors to select a variety of preproduced media and to operate the media at the pace they choose. A second touch screen monitor also allows for interaction between instructors and learners and between learners located at different sites. While the technical director is available to assist with as much of the technical presentation as the instructors desire, the decision on the technical director's level of involvement is up to the instructors. The AIPS is not only cost effective it also helps provide instructors with the level of control they need to be comfortable as well as successful in IVT classes.

Cost containment through automation has been a huge success. The use of an automated uplink and automated receive sites is not new and is used by a number of distance education programs across the country. The use of the AIPS has also proven to have been a wise decision. The FAA's AIPS was installed in March 1995. It is conservatively estimated that the AIPS performs the functions of at least eight technical support personnel. Based upon the salary and benefits that eight technical support personnel would have been paid, the AIPS has already paid for itself. Industry has also recognized the AIPS as a major technological achievement. Numerous business, academic, and government organizations have benchmarked against the FAA and particularly the AIPS. General Motors, Federal Express, General Electric, Veterans Benefits Administration, Federal Judicial Center, and the Canadian Postal Service are but a few of the organizations that have visited the FAA's studio in Oklahoma City, Oklahoma.

The cost of course conversion is potentially the largest expense to a telecourse program. IVT Program management recognized that managing the cost of course conversion would be key to containing the overall cost of the program. To this end, two separate notices were run in the *Commerce Business Daily* for potential sources sought for IVT course conversion. The FAA asked industry to respond to what it would cost to convert existing traditional resident-based courses for delivery by IVT.

Industry responded to both notices. The first notice was posted in 1994 and had twenty-eight responses. The projected costs for converting existing traditional resident-based courses for delivery by IVT ranged from $15 per hour for low complexity conversions to $41,400 per hour for high complexity conversions

(Federal Aviation Administration, 1994). A detailed review of each proposal revealed that several of the responses did not meet the requirements of the FAA's IVT program and were eliminated. In the final analysis, the mean costs for course conversion based upon industry responses was $1,400 per hour for low complexity course conversions and $2,619 per hour for high complexity course conversions.

The second notice was placed in 1995 and resulted in thirty-one responses. Due to the wide range of responses to the first notice, the second notice provided very detailed guidance for the responses. Respondents were asked to provide three costs based upon low, medium, and high levels of complexity of the conversion. As with the first notice, the range of responses to the second notice was very wide, ranging from $78 per hour for low complexity to $66,000 per hour for high complexity. After eliminating those responses that did not meet the published requirements or that were statistical outliers, the mean cost for high volume-low complexity course conversions was $1,404 per hour; the mean cost for high volume-medium complexity course conversions was $2,500 per hour; and the mean cost for high volume-high complexity course conversions was $5,098 per hour (Federal Aviation Administration, 1995b).

The IVT program also has actual cost data from course conversions conducted since 1995. Three existing traditional resident-based courses were converted and delivered by IVT during the demonstration and validation phase of the FAA's acquisition process. The primary purpose of this phase was to demonstrate the technological feasibility of a selected solution to a mission area deficiency. The FAA had identified and documented a deficiency in training, and IVT was a partial solution to resolving this deficiency. The cost for converting these three courses ranged from $1,981 per hour to $3,115 per hour, with a mean cost for all three course of $2,485 per hour (Federal Aviation Administration, 1996b). All three of these courses were contracted out and converted by contractors as the FAA did not feel it had the in-house expertise to do such conversions. Also, during this phase, contractors were asked to try different techniques and methodologies for delivering these courses via IVT and for increasing interactivity. No attempt was made to control costs during this phase as the objective was to demonstrate and validate that the selected technical solution in this case IVT could help solve the identified problem of training deficiencies.

Since completion of the demonstration and validation phase, cost data has been collected on three additional existing traditional resident-based courses that have been converted and delivered by IVT. The per hour cost of converting courses for delivery by IVT ranged from $311 to $2,514. Two of the these courses were converted in-house by FAA employees. The costs of these two courses were $311 per hour and $729 per hour, with a mean cost of $400 per hour (Federal Aviation Administration, 1996b). One course was converted using contract developers at a cost of $2,514 per hour. The mean cost per hour for all three course conversions was $1,066. The IVT Program budgets $3,300 per hour as the average cost for converting existing traditional resident-based courses for delivery by IVT.

By working with the lines of business, the IVT Program has demonstrated that the costs for converting existing traditional resident-based courses can be controlled. Since course conversion costs are potentially the largest cost of a telecourse program and that includes the capital costs of the satellite uplink and receive sites, it was crucial that these costs be managed (Payne, 1996). In managing these costs, it was discovered that FAA employees could convert courses as well as contract developers, and at a much reduced cost.

Costs of the IVT Program are clearly a major concern to the FAA for several reasons. First, as stated previously as a solution to the FAA's training problem, IVT class delivery had to be less costly than its traditional resident-based counterpart. Second, as stewards of taxpayer money, the FAA has a moral obligation to the citizens of this country to use tax dollars in the best manner possible. Last but certainly not least, costs are important to the FAA because of Congressional scrutiny of the IVT Program that resulted from a program audit conducted by the Department of Transportation Office of the Inspector General (OIG).

The OIG decided to conduct an audit of the IVT program starting in April 1995, based upon a letter of concern received from a course manager of one of the courses converted and delivered in the demonstration and validation phase. This course manager expressed concern that delivering the course by IVT was not cost effective and that IVT training was inferior to his traditional resident-based classes. The OIG published its findings in December 1995 (U.S. Department of Transportation, 1995). One of the main findings in the report was that the OIG doubted the cost effectiveness of the IVT program and questioned whether IVT was an effective way to deliver FAA training. The more than two and one-half year involvement with the OIG by the IVT Program has resulted in a number of lessons learned.

A footnote is required here. While the initial complaint listed cost effectiveness and training effectiveness as the issues, the course manager who wrote the letter later stated his real concern to IVT Program personnel. His real concern was that if his course was delivered by IVT, he and the instructors for his course would lose their jobs. However, since the instructors involved have had the opportunity to become more familiar with IVT they not only do not oppose teaching by IVT they have actually recommended other courses they instruct as candidates for IVT conversion.

Program Documentation

The first and foremost lesson learned from the IVT program's involvement with OIG was the need for detailed program documentation. While resident-based programs are not required to demonstrate their cost effectiveness or their training effectiveness, programs that propose to replace traditional resident-based classroom training with technology delivered training are required to do so. In order to demonstrate both cost and training effectiveness, detailed cost and effectiveness documentation is required.

One example of this detailed documentation is the data required to prove training effectiveness or equal quality between IVT and traditional resident-based versions of courses. The post-test only control group design would have been satisfactory to demonstrate training effectiveness had the OIG not audited the IVT Program. Due to the OIG's questioning the results of the two IVT to traditional resident-based course comparisons, FAA management directed the IVT Program to design and conduct the more formal evaluation with pretest and post-test data for both groups (Lennon and Payne, 1997). This additional evaluation cost the program valuable time, money, and personnel resources and did not provide any additional information that was not available through previously conducted studies and related literature reviews.

Another example of the level of detailed documentation required pertains to costs. The latest IVT program cost benefit analysis has more detailed cost data than any other program in the FAA (Middleton, personal communication, March 6, 1996). Even with all of the data contained in the latest cost benefit analysis, the OIG continued to question the cost effectiveness of IVT delivered training. One major point of contention directly relates to the level of detail in the cost data collected during the demonstration and validation phase. Three of the courses converted for delivery by IVT required updating prior to conversion. Exact cost data for course conversion and non-course conversion activities, such as revising courses, updating required course documentation, and calculating travel expenses, were not collected. As a result, since the OIG has not been able to discern between course conversion and non-course conversion activities, it counts all of the costs as course conversion costs, significantly driving up the OIG's estimate of the cost to convert traditional resident-based courses for delivery by IVT.

A second major lesson learned from the OIG audit of the IVT program relates to the inclusion of instructors in the program planning of training technology interventions. IVT program management talked considerably about including instructors and how to include them in the program planning for IVT but did not follow through and actually include instructors. This was partly due to the considerable turnover in the position of Program Manager (four in two years) and by fear from some of these four program managers that including instructors would slow down program implementation. The result has been reluctance on the part of many instructors to embrace IVT. Many instructors saw IVT as a management intervention designed to eliminate their jobs, and they hoped that if they resisted long enough that IVT would go away. Plus, those instructors who converted and taught their courses by IVT were initially considered outcasts by their fellow instructors. The concern mentioned most often by instructors was a fear for their jobs. Instructors feared that if they converted their traditional resident-based course for delivery by IVT that they would lose their jobs.

Fortunately, over the past two years, many instructors have come to accept IVT as a viable alternative for certain traditional resident-based courses. There are two main reasons for this increased acceptance. First, they have seen traditional resident-based courses converted and taught by IVT, and those instructors who have taught these IVT classes did not lose their jobs. By observing other instructors teaching by IVT, instructors have come to understand that IVT requires an instructor just as do their traditional resident-based courses. Second, the instructors have had numerous opportunities to see IVT in action and to actually go into the studio and try out the technology in a non-threatening environment. Instructors are frequently invited to tour the studio to actually interact with the touch screen monitors similar to what they might do if they were to instruct from the studio. Familiarity has helped to reduce the resistance by many instructors.

Another major lesson learned was related to interaction in IVT courses. Instructors repeatedly told the IVT Program that one reason and for some the main reason they opposed IVT was they feared they would lose the interaction they had with the students in their traditional resident-based courses. Instructors consistently told the IVT Program that interaction was one of the keys to the success of their courses. Instructors voiced concern that not being able to see their students as they do in their resident-based classes would limit interaction and degrade the instruction. Even though interviews with instructors and students revealed that most of the FAA's traditional resident-based courses had about the same low level of interaction as other adult level courses, their perception had to be addressed.

A viewer response system was designed into the AIPS to provide instructors with a technology that would provide increased opportunities for interaction during IVT classes. Viewer response systems provide for both voice and data interaction (Portway and Ostendorf, 1997). Each learner has a simple keypad in front of him or her that allows the learner to talk with the instructor and with learners at other sites. Viewer response systems provide instructors with control over learner talk. A learner can only talk over the system when an instructor opens the learner's microphone. Up to two learners at one time can have their microphones open, allowing for manageable discussions while eliminating verbal free-for-alls that can happen in traditional resident-based classes and in telecourses that use simple audio conferencing systems. Instructors can also terminate learner conversations at any time by closing learner microphones, allowing instructors to control the pace of instruction and to eliminate unrelated "side trips" on which students occasionally try to take their classes.

Viewer response systems also provide instructors with the ability to ask every learner questions using the data capability. Yes-no, true-false, multiple choice and numeric questions can be prepared ahead of time and stored in the response system's control computer. Instructors can visually display each question during the broadcast, and ask learners to respond using the keypad. The control computer automatically tabulates the responses as the learners respond and displays them to the instructors in a bar graph format. This bar graph can also be shown to the learners if so desired by the instructors to allow learners to evaluate their responses and to determine how they are doing in relation to the rest of the class. After the broadcast, this data can be downloaded and analyzed by either question or student, providing instructors data they can use to help learners or to improve their instruction. This is data they cannot get in their traditional resident-based classes.

While the FAA's IVT program was comfortable with its selection of a viewer response system over a simple audio conferencing system, debate in the government distance learning community continues over which is best. Unfortunately, no research existed that directly compared these two systems for providing interaction. The IVT program decided to conduct a controlled study to see if there was a "best" technology for providing interaction in IVT classes.

This controlled study was conducted with upperclassmen enrolled in a marketing principles course at a historically Black university in the southwest (Payne and Payne, 1997). This population was selected because the IVT program was unable to secure permission of the labor unions representing the various segments of the FAA population initially selected for the study. The design for the study was a quasi-experimental nonequivalent control group design. Two intact marketing principles classes were used due to their small size, which made random assignment of learners impossible. One class had a unit of instruction converted for and delivered using an audio conferencing system, while the other class had the same unit of instruction converted for and delivered using a student response system. The same instructor taught both classes.

In contrast to most media comparison studies and studies comparing instructional television to traditional instruction (Clark, 1994; Hunter, Renckly, Smith, and Tussey, 1995; Lennon and Payne, 1997; Moore and others, 1990; Morrison, 1994), the marketing principles class using the viewer response system had a statistically significant higher mean post-test score (F [1, 53] 5 6.60, p, 0.05). There were no statistically significant differences between classes on learner satisfaction or on learners' perceived level of interaction. However, learners using the audio conferencing system had a significantly higher level of verbal interaction $(F [1, 53] 5 54.83, p , 0.05)$ while learners using the viewer response system had a significantly higher level of overall interaction $(F [1, 53] 5 4.32, p , 0.05)$. Based on this study and feedback from other FAA IVT instructors and students, the FAA's IVT program is comfortable with its selection of a viewer response system for use in its IVT classes. The answer to the question of which technology is "best" however, is most appropriately answered by the application of the technology and not the technology's capabilities.

Instructor Training

The last lesson learned to be included concerns instructor training for IVT. As the IVT Program began to think about transitioning instructors trained and experienced in instructing in traditional resident-base courses, it became very clear very quickly that this transition would need to be formalized. That is, FAA instructors would need formal training on how to instruct over IVT. Since the FAA has a division at its technical training academy in Oklahoma City charged with providing both basic and advanced instructor training for traditional resident-based courses, it was logical that this same group provide the transition training to IVT. However, before the FAA's instructor training cadre could begin training instructors on how to instruct in an IVT environment, they had to learn how themselves.

Two individuals were selected to be the developers and the initial instructors of the FAA's IVT Skills Course. They benchmarked with a number of organizations who trained instructors in IVT skills and brought in a number of distance learning consultants who specialized in IVT instructor training. These two individuals developed an IVT instructor training course that has become the envy of many government agencies. Almost every offering of the class has attendees from other government agencies.

The FAA wanted to provide instructors with training on the skills and knowledge that they need to be successful instructors in IVT classes. Benchmarking with organizations that were already conducting telecourses convinced the IVT program that instructors needed to be trained to be successful in IVT class presentations. FAA instructors continually express a desire to receive this training before they deliver their first class over IVT. The knowledge they gain and the skills they acquire and practice have proven successful in preparing instructors to do well in IVT class presentations. Occasionally, one of the lines of business will use a contract instructor who for a variety of reasons is not able to take the IVT Skills Course. The quality of that instruction over IVT is consistently not as good as that of those instructors who do complete the course.

A spin-off benefit of the IVT Skills Course has come in the area of course conversion. As discussed earlier, the FAA initially used contract support to convert traditional resident-based courses, and these conversions were expensive and time consuming. The IVT Skills Course contains training in course conversion techniques, as learners in the course are required to convert and present a segment of instruction. Over time, this segment of the course has evolved to the point that instructors are able to convert their traditional resident-based courses for delivery by IVT themselves with minimal assistance from IVT program personnel. In fact, the Quality Assurance course the IVT program used to do its head to head comparison evaluation was converted by the course instructor with assistance of an IVT program person. The cost to convert that sixty-hour resident course was $311 per hour (Lennon and Payne, 1997).

Clearly, the FAA's instructor training course for IVT skills has been one of the IVT program's outstanding successes. There is however one aspect of the course that could have been done better. The course came online during fiscal year 1995. As a part of the course, a closed circuit IVT teaching lab was developed and installed. This lab allows the instructors to practice their presentations and is used to present their course segment for evaluation and feedback from both the instructor and other class participants. The problem with the IVT teaching lab was its timing. It was installed before the design of the AIPS, the automated studio the IVT program uses to deliver its IVT instruction, was finalized. The IVT teaching lab is neither identical nor very similar to the AIPS. The lab meets the needs for the IVT Skills Course, but course graduates do require additional training and practice on the AIPS before they can actually deliver their IVT courses. This is a problem that a little patience could have avoided.

Discussion

Lessons learned provide those who are doing IVT course delivery or who are thinking about doing IVT course delivery the opportunity to capitalize on the successes and to avoid the failures of those who have gone before them. A simple description of lessons learned is often not enough for others to understand and apply the lesson. This section will provide discussion on how the lessons learned may be used to improve other IVT programs.

Program Documentation

The need for adequate documentation was mentioned as a lesson learned. When choosing a method, process, or technology, the most important factor is to define and document the requirement. Without this information and its related parameters, no justification for any selected technology can be made. Understanding and documenting the needs of a program and what restrictions apply will enable the planners to make the most informed decisions about their programs.

It is strongly recommended that program planners develop a data collection system based upon the assumption that their program will be audited. Planners should assume that every decision should be documented with the data upon which it is based. It is much easier to collect data and document decisions as they are made than it is to go back and recreate and recapture data a year or even several months later.

Data on program results should be collected from the beginning and should be an ongoing process. Clearly, results data, usually the most desirable by management, needs to be planned thoroughly for its timely and complete collection. The FAA initially did not think it would be using receive sites from other agencies very often so did not initially collect the data. As it turned out, the FAA has used a large number of receive sites from other agencies due to its inability to add additional sites pending the resolution of the Congressional review. The FAA went back and collected the data on non-FAA receive sites and used the data in building the case for program expansion with Congress. Documentation is one of the activities on which most programs spend the least amount of time but is potentially as important as the decisions and results they record.

Conducting Literature Reviews

Reviewing related literature can also assist the documentation process. By examining the test results of others and considering the purposes and needs of those tests, planners can sidestep certain mistakes and the costly effort of "reinventing the wheel." For example, the literature is replete with media comparison studies in which telecourse results are compared to traditional classroom results (Payne, 1997; Russell, 1992). There is overwhelming evidence from these studies that appears to say that there is *no significant difference* in achievement results between the two. It may be possible to avoid costly comparison studies and use the money in more productive ways. Literature reviews should become a part of documentation. As one member leaves the team and another joins, there is continuity in the program as the documentation provides a history of what has been considered and why and on what facts certain decisions were based.

Including Instructors in Program Planning

Similar to strategic planning, total quality management, and other organizational processes, inclusion of the various levels of personnel in the process is essential for success. Including instructors in the program planning for IVT can reduce the threat of trying something new. Change is a scary thing for many people, particularly for people who fear the change may eliminate their job, and the immediate response to this type of change is often resistance.

A defensive posture by instructors or any other group can be at least partially avoided by including them in all stages of the planning process. Listen to their concerns, attempt to explain the realities of the program in non-threatening terms, help them to feel a part of the program, and encourage them to take ownership of the process. Organizations are able to achieve more by involving those who are affected by the change and perhaps gaining new perspective on the issue rather than strictly making a management decision based on cost or some other empirical data.

Instruction is often considered a performance activity by instructors. As such, it is expected that in order to perform the instructor must have a face-to-face audience. Many performers and instructors *feed* off the responses from, or their interactions with the audience. Many instructors fear that without seeing their audience, there will be no interaction. Even though IVT has the ability to track interaction and it has been shown that the level of interaction between traditional resident-based courses and IVT delivery can be similar, instructor fears pertaining to interaction are real and must be addressed (Payne and Payne, 1997).

Interaction with the learners is the instructor's responsibility. Just as they encourage participation in the traditional classroom, instructors must do the same in their IVT classrooms. The difference in IVT is using technology instead of eye contact. Skilled instructors will make the same eye contact with the camera as they do with their students in traditional classrooms, will ask questions as they do in their traditional classrooms, and will encourage interaction from the learners as they do in the traditional classroom, both through audio and data responses. Instructor training can help an instructor become more comfortable with this variation of traditional methods.

Instructor Training

Instructor training clearly has an impact on the effectiveness of instruction. As with any course material, the comfort level of the instructor with the material and the environment can have an affect on the performance of the instructor. Instructor familiarity with both the equipment and the concept and practice of not seeing students' faces is critical for the effective delivery of IVT.

Although learning a new method of delivering instruction is not difficult, it is a necessary step that should not be ignored. Ignoring instructor training will almost certainly have a negative impact upon IVT instruction. The questions then become what is the best method for instructor training, what needs to be included in this training, and how much time should be allocated for this process. Assuming the instructor is already familiar with the course material, an adequate comfort level with the equipment can be developed in as little as a few intense hours.

Obviously the best method of instructor training should include time in the studio or with an identical studio simulator. As instructors go through the motions and learn how much control they can choose to maintain over the process, they will at the same time get used to delivering the material without a face-to-face audience. This hands-on training is also effective for those who are a little less anxious to "push the buttons." This individual in working directly with studio support personnel will become comfortable with knowing that the support staff will do exactly what they are instructed to do, (changing graphics on the screen, queuing video footage, connecting callers, and so on) and will not let the instructor appear to falter with the use of the technology.

The learning curve of the instructor must be figured into the training time allocated. Along with familiarity with the equipment, training must include the nuances of delivery by camera in order to produce the most effective learning environment. Items such as what colors are not appropriate for television broadcast, where to attach the microphone for maximum effectiveness, how to ensure that the microphone follows when the instructor's head turns away, how to avoid becoming a "talking head" on the screen, and how to properly use a pointer or one's finger when indicating material on the screen need to be stressed and practiced.

Whoever develops and delivers this training to instructors must be competent in broadcast delivery. Whether or not this is in-house training or contracted out depends on the expertise available and time and cost considerations. The FAA experience has convinced the FAA that instructor training is essential to the success of IVT courses.

Program Costs

Cost will be the last lesson learned discussed. Program costs are important regardless of the organization. In this day of downsizing and constrained training budgets, programs will continually have to prove that they are cost beneficial. That is, they must clearly demonstrate that the benefits of delivering instruction using IVT outweigh those of delivering instruction using traditional resident-based methods.

It is strongly recommended that non-broadcast professionals be included on the IVT team early in program planning. These individuals can provide the program with the continuous questioning of why things must be done the way broadcast professionals think they must be done. These individuals will help the planning team with identifying existing programs against which they can benchmark or identify and document new and innovative approaches to doing IVT. The FAA has demonstrated that this type of thinking and benchmarking can save literally millions of dollars in program costs over the program's life cycle. In this day and age of automation, hard decisions will have to be made by program planners and sold to upper management on acceptable trade offs between automating and using live people. Similar decisions will have to be made about using in-house personnel or contracting out services associated with the program. These two cost considerations are clearly quality and capability issues that will have to be worked out and negotiated among all concerned.

Lastly, program planners must fight for the acknowledgment and inclusion of intangible benefits as considerations in making decisions around IVT. Intangible benefits are those benefits that are not easily quantified but show a benefit for the program. Such benefits can include having trained versus untrained employees, training more employees faster by reducing the training cycle time, training more employees from more different locations, and increasing time at work. Other less recognized tangible benefits include the ability to get training to employees faster, using the technology for town-hall type information meetings, reaching employees who would not get the training any other way, disseminating a standardized training message through the use of the same expert instructor for all employees, and being able to share experts with all employees, just to name a few. While these intangible benefits are admittedly difficult to quantify in terms of dollars saved, they nonetheless must be considered in the decision making. Programs that are on the border line for being cost beneficial using tangible benefits can often be pushed over the top using intangible benefits that demonstrate the ability to meet a pressing organizational need.

Conclusion

The progress of the FAA's IVT program can be likened to a roller coaster ride. It has had its ups and downs, hard unforeseen turns, and changes in speed. Despite the roller coaster-like ride, the program continues to grow through the persistence of program personnel and management who believe in the need and the ability of IVT to meet that need. In closing, the last recommendation is if you decide to pursue an IVT type distance learning program, you must commit yourself and your organization to the long haul. Many will be drawn by the light only to be burned by the flame (Green, 1997). Be persistent, consistent, and patient. Major organizational changes such as converting traditional resident-based training to IVT take time, patience, and a continuous focus on the reason why the technology was selected and the potential results.

Technical Description of the FAA Interactive Video Teletraining System

The FAA Interactive Video Teletraining (IVT) System is a satellite delivered training system. Instructor audio and video are broadcast to students at geographically dispersed receive sites using digital compressed satellite signals. Broadcasts are at 3.3 mbps, which is considered near full motion video. This is about the same quality as Super VHS video tape recordings.

The instructor's broadcast originates from the FAA IVT studio in Oklahoma City, Oklahoma. The satellite uplink, high power amplifier, and encoding equipment is located at the studio. The FAA IVT satellite system uses Compression Labs, Inc. spectrum saver equipment for digitizing and undigitizing, and compressing and decompressing the satellite signals. The studio is a state-of-the-art, highly automated presentation system designed for training types of broadcasts. Through the use of automation, only the instructor and the studio technical director are needed for a broadcast. The instructor has the ability to control the sequence, pace, and flow of the instruction in the studio much as in his or her traditional classroom. Using two touch screen monitors, instructors can display videotapes, 35 mm slides, computer generated graphics using Power Point, audio tape recordings, compact disc audio recordings, and images of themselves. Chroma key is also available to the instructor for highlighting on or interacting with their video tapes and computer generated graphics. With the help of the technical director, names can be superimposed on the screen identifying presenters. Using a video toaster, the technical director has virtually unlimited special effects that he or she can use to enhance the instructor's presentation.

Students are located at geographically dispersed receive sites, which have an earth station or satellite dish and an integrate receive decoder (IRD). The IRD receives the compressed digital satellite signal and decodes it for display over the monitor. Each receive site is set up for five students. Each site has a twenty-nine inch color monitor, a four-head stereo videotape recorder, a student response system site controller, and five student response system keypads. Students are able to communicate with the instructor and with students and other receive sites using the keypads. Students log in to the student response system by entering the last four digits of their social security number. This data is captured by the student response system host computer in the studio and allows for electronic roll calling. A fax machine is located at each receive site to allow for small group work responses to be sent to the instructor in the studio.

Student audio is sent to the instructor using telephone lines and then broadcast over satellite. The instructor gets an indicator on one of the touch screen monitors that displays the student's name and location. When the instructor is ready to call on the student, she or he touches the indicator that opens the student's microphone built in to the keypad. Upon completion of the conversation, the instructor touches the indicator a second time which terminates the call and closes the student's microphone. The instructor is able to have two students talking at one time.

The instructor can display previously prepared multiple choice, yes-no, true-false, and numeric value questions using the video component of the satellite broadcast. All students see the question and have the opportunity to answer it using the keypad, which sends the students' response over telephone lines to the student response system host computer. Student responses are compiled by the host computer and displayed in a bar chart with percentages that can be shown to the students. The host computer also records every response made by every student to each question. After the broadcast, the data can be downloaded and sorted by question or by student, as the instructor desires.

The student response system provides a "flag" function that can be used for several functions. During instruction, it can be used for electronic confused looks. Students are instructed to press the flag key on their keypad anytime they are lost and are not willing or able to ask a clarifying question. The instructor presets the flag response so that when he or she receives a certain percentage of flags, a red flag flashes. This is the indication that he or she needs to stop and try to find out where students are confused so the instruction can be clarified.

Each geographically dispersed receive site has a site administrator responsible for security and set-up of the receive site prior to each broadcast. Once the site is set up and the equipment is functioning properly, the site administrator leaves. There is no facilitator or instructor in the receive site with students during broadcasts. A test monitor will be present when testing, but during instruction students are on their own. They do have a telephone in the receive site for calling the studio Help Line should their site experience technical difficulties during the broadcast.

Disclaimer: The views and opinions expressed in this chapter are those of the authors and do not necessarily represent those of the Federal Aviation Administration, the U.S. Department of Transportation or the U.S. Government.

CHAPTER ELEVEN

DELIVERING CLINICAL-BASED TRAINING IN A PUBLIC HEALTH SETTING

Janet L. Place, Tim Stephens, Patricia O'Leary Cunningham

Nurses are the largest group of health care professionals in North Carolina. There are approximately 3,500 public health nurses providing the majority of care to clients at the state's 100 county health departments. Many of these clients are uninsured, underinsured, or insured under Medicaid with limited access to care. This case outlines a collaboration between the North Carolina Department of Health and Human Services (DHHS) and the School of Public Health at the University of North Carolina at Chapel Hill (UNC) to deliver state-wide clinical training via interactive two way audio-two way video real time to public health nurses over the state's Public Health Training and Information Network (PHTIN). Specifically, this training provides public health nurses employed by North Carolina's county health departments with the skills necessary for taking detailed health histories and performing physical examinations.

The training program itself is not new. What is new is delivery using a distance learning format. This is significant for several reasons. Delivery of the training via distance learning increases access and decreases cost to health departments, while maintaining the quality of the training. In fact, there is early evidence to suggest that quality may be enhanced. Also significant is that while the PHTIN has provided hundreds of interactive video courses for North Carolina's public health workforce, this case represents the first effort to use the network to provide proficiency-based clinical training at a distance.

Need

The health care delivery system in the United States is undergoing large-scale change, with cost-containment providing a large measure of the driving energy. This shift requires a reengineering of the health care professional education system. Prudent use of scarce resources mixed with the need for measurable quality outcome objectives is imperative. These needs occur in an era of rapid technological change with digital networks linking the workforce together as never before.

Fifty-nine of North Carolina's 100 counties experience high poverty rates (over 10 percent below poverty line), while twenty others experience medium poverty 7.5 percent–9.9 percent below poverty line). Thirteen percent of the total state population and 20 percent of North Carolina citizens over sixty-five live below the poverty line. (North Carolina State Center for Health Statistics, 1996).

The state is consistently rated near the bottom in national health status rankings. Yet North Carolina is a center for medical and pharmaceutical research. According to *Healthy Carolinians* (Governor's Task Force on Health Objectives for the Year 2000, 1992), "40 North Carolinians die prematurely each day; many more become disabled, exacting enormous economic, social and personal tolls on our society. Tragically, most of the deaths and disabilities can be prevented by changes in lifestyle" (p. ii, Executive Summary).

The majority of health department clients are poor with no regular source of health care. These clients are at particularly high risk for preventable death or illness. According to the North Carolina Center for Health Statistics

- Approximately 17 percent of the state's working-age adults are uninsured.
- Those on Medicaid are almost three times as likely to be hospitalized for preventable diseases than those with insurance.
- 19 percent of minorities versus 5 percent of Whites report neighborhood or government clinics as their source of routine care. (North Carolina State Center for Health Statistics, 1996).

With the current focus on primary care settings as the point of entry into the health care system within the managed care environment, the role of registered nurses is expanding. This includes screening and referral, case management, and health education. Many public health clients come to health departments for specific needs. An experienced professional can use this opportunity to identify other potential or existing health problems. This assessment would identify those at risk of mortality or morbidity due to family history or age or preventable risk factors such as smoking, high fat diet, sedentary lifestyle, unsafe sex, or substance abuse. Moreover, with rural and underserved populations there is an increase in the type and amount of undetected chronic disease.

At present, many registered nurses are the *only* providers of screening and referral in certain health departments especially in rural areas. Therefore, it is important to ensure that these primary care professionals have strong analytical and technical skills necessary for identifying potential health risks and problems at early stages and for providing appropriate referral for treatment.

A shortage of upper- and mid-level practitioners, such as physicians, nurse practitioners, and physician assistants, in many county health departments means that fewer clients are served. The performance of physical assessments for screening purposes is within the nursing scope of practice. In North Carolina, the Board of Nursing requires additional competency-based training for nurses performing in this enhanced role.

Unlike advanced practice clinicians, nurses may not diagnose or prescribe; however, by screening and referring potential health problems and providing health education, nurses perform a vital role by making it possible to expand clinical services to under and uninsured clients. This is particularly important in view of the rates of hospitalization for preventable diseases for Medicaid clients. The most common services performed by these nurses are complete physical assessments with special emphasis on breast exams, Pap tests, and prostate exams.

State Commitment to Quality Training

The DHHS has made a commitment to increasing the skills of public health nurses in screening and referral through statewide training in adult physical assessment. Over the past several years the state and local public health nurse leaders have worked to standardize the adult physical assessment curricula in order to ensure consistent quality. In an effort to increase access the state subsidizes the training, making it possible to provide the training to professionals in all 100 counties.

Since 1989 564 nurses have received this enhanced role training. Of these 347 are currently performing physical examinations at county health departments, and 102 are working on their clinical practicums. The remaining ninety-five have either left their health departments, moved into management positions, or did not complete the clinical practicum requirement.

Course Description

The Adult Physical Assessment course provides competency-based training for public health nurses. Heavy emphasis is placed on building the critical thinking skills whereby nurses detect potential problems, ask the appropriate follow-up questions, and make appropriate referrals when necessary. Upon successful completion of this course, the participant is prepared to

- Elicit and document an age-appropriate health history; assess signs, symptoms, and risk factors for disease;
- Perform a physical assessment;
- Distinguish between normal, possibly normal, and abnormal conditions;
- Describe and record the assessment findings in explicit terms;
- Refer clients with possible abnormal or abnormal findings to appropriate medical care;
- Plan for appropriate medical care and follow-up; and
- Provide clinical management, utilizing the nursing process and principles of health promotion and disease prevention for individuals and populations at risk.

The course is comprehensive and covers physical assessment of:

1. Skin
2. Head, ears, eyes, nose, and throat (HEENT)
3. Abdomen
4. Breast
5. Male and female reproductive system
6. Prostate
7. Heart
8. Lung
9. Mental status
10. Neurological system
11. Musculoskeletal system

The goal is to provide quality training statewide to a greater number of nurses at a reduced cost to the local health departments without compromising quality. This is done by using state-of-the-art two way audio and video.

Target Population

The program serves both a direct and an indirect population. Clearly, the primary focus of the program is to enhance knowledge transfer and experiential learning for public health nurses in order to improve their physical assessment skills. The indirect population served is health department clients.

Background

Before describing the course as a distance education project, it is first necessary to look at the history of the course as offered in a traditional format. This historical perspective includes information on the supportive organizational structures already in place. These support structures predict the possibility of success for a decentralized training model. These include a history of distance learning collaboration between DHHS and the UNC School of Public Health and the regionalized management structure within the DHHS.

History of Adult Physical Assessment Training

Until mid-1996 adult physical assessment was offered in a traditional format—an eight-day course at various sites around the state, each followed by a six-month health department-based clinical practicum. The clinical practicum has not changed in the new distance learning design. The eight-day courses consisted of didactic instruction and clinical practice. In clinical training "didactic" refers to the period of systematic instruction, as opposed to the "hands-on" clinical experience. There were generally two instructors per day who were nurse practitioners (RNs with advanced medical training who are able to diagnose and prescribe). To enable the instructors to supervise the clinical practice, class sizes ranged from eleven to thirteen. Clinical practice took place in the same classroom as the didactic instruction. Participants practiced on one another or on models.

During the intensive clinical practicum, participants performed a series of examinations under the supervision of an approved clinical advisor. In 1996 the state implemented an additional quality assurance measure—an independent assessment of the participant's skills by an outside evaluator.

Since the inception of the training program there has been a clear indication that it has affected the quality of care for health department clients. An independent study of nursing knowledge and practice among public health nurses in North Carolina found that nurses who had completed the training have a higher level of confidence. According to the researchers, "The nurses who completed the physical assessment course were most likely to rate their skills as 'excellent' or 'very good' in educating about the need for mammograms (90.3 percent of nurses surveyed), teaching breast self exams (90.4 percent), performing Pap tests (87.4 percent) and taking a cervical cancer history (86.1 percent)." (Herman and others, 1998).

A 1997 assessment of training needs for public health nurses conducted by the program director reinforced the value of the training. When health department nursing directors were asked about how health departments were using the enhanced nursing role, responses such as the following were common:

"We are located in a rural area with limited MD services. The enhanced-role nurses are able to provide services in-house under the direction of the medical director. This has especially saved time for patients needing to travel more than thirty minutes out of the county for care for simple rather than acute situations."

"Enhanced nurses function at a higher level and reduce waiting time until an appointment can be made."

The Challenge of Meeting Demand

Through the years, as health departments became more aware of the value of enhanced role nurses, demand for this training greatly increased. When it became possible for health departments to receive Medicaid reimbursement for the services of enhanced nurses, the incentive for the training increased further. Yet, the clinical nature of the course necessitated keeping the class size to between eleven to fourteen participants per class. Every class in late 1995 and early 1996 had long waiting lists, often fifteen to twenty nurses. By 1996 due to pressure to provide training for more nurses, some classes had twenty participants, which exceeded the optimal number for clinical supervision.

At the same time health departments were concerned about the cost of sending staff away to be trained and the loss of staff time. Agency cost for travel and accommodations ranged from $300 to $1,500 per nurse. Analysis of the cost of lost staff time during training estimated the cost to be approximately $200 per day. This means that every nurse who went for eight days of training resulted in an indirect cost of $1,600. Many nurses themselves had personal limitations. Family obligations often limited the opportunity for participants to travel long distances for extended periods.

Something needed to be done to meet the demand while considering the resource and personnel constraints of the state and local health departments and the personal constraints of participants. Most importantly, cost-effective training and increased access could *not* sacrifice quality.

The state had a good track record in providing basic public health nursing information using a videoconferencing network but had never used it for clinical courses. Could a model be developed that would increase the number of participants trained without compromising the quality of clinical practice? In the past participants were able to practice their clinical skills under the direct supervision of clinical faculty at the class site. With videoconferencing, the faculty would not be physically present at all sites. Placing clinical faculty at all sites would be cost prohibitive.

State/University Collaboration for Distance Learning

The state DHHS and UNC School of Public Health (SPH) have a long history of collaboration for providing practical training for the public health workforce. The SPH was founded in 1936 as a training program for local health officers. DHHS and the SPH have remained committed to training public health practitioners. The SPH has the largest most comprehensive training and continuing education program of all schools of public health in the United States. The partnership with the state health department and local health departments is the basis for many of these continuing education programs.

The partnership began to offer training programs via videoconference networks in 1989. At the outset the public health partners used facilities located at universities across the state but owned and operated none of the infrastructure. In the subsequent eight years public health use of the statewide networks has grown significantly. In the first year there were four programs attended by just over four hundred health professionals. In 1997 more than twelve thousand people attended 273 programs.

This growth was spurred by two specific developments: in 1993 the SPH opened its own telecommunications facility, and in 1995 the state asked the SPH to provide the network hub site and services for a network of five local health department videoconference centers—the PHTIN. The first step allowed for control to be established over the development of programs, and the second completed the picture by providing a training system that exists specifically for the purposes of public health training. The PHTIN links the DHHS with five local health departments and the UNC School of Public Health through an advanced telecommunication infrastructure. Each site has a fully equipped video communications classroom for live, two-way interactive training.

Program Management Infrastructure

The solid structure of Adult Physical Assessment Program management is owed to the management structure within the DHHS. The state health department is located in Raleigh, but it has several regional offices with nursing consultants each working directly with the health departments in that region. There are five regional nurse consultants responsible for adult health promotion. These consultants have played a critical role in adult physical assessment training for several years. They work with course participants and health department leadership. Through a local precourse planning process, they ensure that the health department has an adequate system in place for quality assurance and clinical supervision.

In addition to the state's supporting infrastructure, in 1996 the Adult Physical Assessment training program hired a full-time director, who is employed by the university. The growth in numbers, complexity in planning, and school, state and local planning dictated the need for a manager to lead this course. This made it possible to work more directly with participants and to identify and address potential obstacles to completion. Collaboration between the director and the regional nurse consultants enhanced participant support at the local level. This meant better quality assurance and participant support.

One quality assurance component of the course structure is the Adult Physical Assessment Advisory Committee. This committee includes representatives from health department leadership, nurse consultants, faculty, the program director, and the State Director of Public Health Nursing. The role of this committee is to review formative and summative evaluation data and make recommendations for modifications. The committee also supports ongoing dialogue between the key players.

Development of Model

The formal communications links at the state and local level were essential in the development of physical assessment training via distance education. In collaboration with the Program Director and the state and local public health nursing leaders, a training model was developed. The course was taught in a series of four two-week modules over eight weeks at six PHTIN teleconferencing sites throughout the state. Each module was a full day of on-air didactic instruction. Participants would then return to their own health departments and perform prescribed clinical practice under the supervision of clinical advisors.

The eight-week course was followed by the traditional health department-based clinical practicum. Independent evaluation of the participant's skills followed the practicum. While directed by the state OPHN, the course was centrally managed at the School of Public Health. Serving as the pilot, the first course was limited to approximately six participants per site. Subsequent courses were increased to ten participants per site. Ten participants per site are the maximum number of participants that can be effectively and efficiently supported through the successive stages of training.

Course Components

The course has four basic components:

- Four-day didactic
- Clinical practice with a clinical advisor
- Extended clinical practicum
- Final clinical evaluation

Didactic. The interactive videoclass occurs one day every other week over an eight-week period and is taught by experienced nurse practitioners. Each two-week period covers one of the four modules. On the first day, participants complete a pretest that provides baseline data. Participants are given a posttest at the end of each module. Each day contains 6.5 hours of instruction covering a number of body systems. The modules are as follows:

Module I	History-taking, skin, eyes, nose, and throat
Module II	Breast and the male and female reproductive system
Module III	Heart and lungs
Module IV	Neurological and musculoskeletal systems

The instructors are based at the PHTIN hub site at UNC in Chapel Hill. All participants see, hear, and interact with each other and the faculty. Moreover, each videoclass site has a facilitator whose role is to enhance the local learning environment. They provide materials, proctor exams, and facilitate group activities. Regional nurse consultants serve as site facilitators. Each site also has a technical coordinator.

Guided-Clinical Practice. Following each on-air day, participants return to their health departments where they are required to perform two actual client exams on the body systems they have just covered. A clinical advisor who may be a physician, nurse practitioner, physician's assistant, or a nurse who has completed the training and practiced for at least one year supervises these exams. Clinical advisors are required to submit a clinical checklist to the program director verifying that the participant has successfully completed all required components of the examinations. The advisors are also encouraged to submit comments on each participant's skills and progress. The participants also submit their written physical findings and assessments, which are reviewed by the faculty and the program director for demonstration of the participant's progress.

Clinical Practicum. Following successful completion of the eight-week didactic course, participants perform a six-month clinical practicum. This is a critical part of the training. It is during this period that the participant hones his or her clinical skills through rigorous practice, again under the supervision of the clinical advisor. Participants are required to perform a minimum of seventeen exams, which must include at least two males. These are performed with the clinical advisor present who registers the completion of each exam on a clinical log. It is the responsibility of the clinical advisor to determine if the participant needs additional practice beyond the minimum number of required exams. When the log is complete it is submitted to the program director.

The clinical advisor is also required to periodically assess the participant's progress on the basis of a series of criteria. These include

- Patient rapport
- Preparedness
- Organization and thoroughness
- Technical proficiency

When the participant scores a three or four (out of a possible four) in each of these areas, the evaluation form is also submitted to the program director.

Final Clinical Evaluation. When the participant has completed the practicum, an evaluator from outside the health department performs an assessment of the participant's skills. The evaluator observes the participant taking a history and performing a complete exam. The participant must then write up the findings and submit the report to the evaluator. The participant must score 80 percent on this evaluation in order to pass. In addition to evaluating organizational and technical ability, special emphasis is placed in assessing the participant's critical thinking skills. Participants must clearly demonstrate that they are able to recognize potential problems and follow up appropriately with referral or counseling regardless of the purpose of the patient's visit. For example, a patient might come into the clinic for family planning services yet might have a suspicious looking mole, which needs to be referred to determine if there is a cancer risk. While it has never happened, a participant who scored under 80 percent (out 100 points) would have to repeat the entire course.

This final evaluation requirement was implemented at the beginning of 1996. It is a key quality control measure. Moreover, it helps to provide program management staff with data by which to compare the skills of those who were trained under the traditional and videoclass formats. Following the successful completion of the final evaluation, the nurse may perform unsupervised physical assessments within certain parameters.

Staffing

While videoclass instruction reduces the need for faculty to instruct, the increased number of participants and the decentralized nature of the model increased the need for central coordination and support. Each course has a lead faculty member. The program director continually monitors participant progress through the training process and works with the regional nurse consultants, individual health departments, and the state OPHN to overcome any obstacles.

Materials

Faculty members, the program director, and an instructional designer developed the curriculum. The instructional designer played a crucial role in assisting the planning team to develop materials that both enhance the lectures and help the participants to organize the lecture material. Key materials include the *Student Manual, Clinical Advisor Manual* and *Site Facilitator Manual.* Each course also includes both a formative and summative evaluation, which is used for continually modifying course materials.

Student Manual. Each module in the *Student Manual* includes

- Behavioral objectives
- Lecture outlines
- Key words
- Case studies
- Self-study assignments
- Clinical practice requirements
- Readings and additional resources

The self-study assignments are particularly important. While developed initially to provide the participants with self study that could be completed in the event of the technical failure of the telecommunications network, participants found the self study to be a very useful aspect of the course and recommended that it be used all the time. Self-study material includes questions and labeling exercises and short quizzes to assess the learner's level of comprehension. While these exercises are optional, the majority of participants do complete them.

Another modification to the *Student Manual* after the pilot course was the inclusion of lecture outlines. One of the most common concerns voiced by participants is that there was too much information to study. The outlines enable participants to follow lectures and fill in the most relevant information.

The process of clinical practice is clearly identified in each *Student Manual.* The clinical check lists spell out the steps of a physical examination that need to be covered during the required exams. Clinical advisors check off each step as it is completed and make comments where necessary. Participants then write up their findings, assessment, and plan for appropriate follow-up.

Clinical Advisor Manual. Clinical advisors have always played a key role in the training process. The *Clinical Advisor Manual* (Trester and Place, 1996) enhances the quality of the training. The manual includes the course curriculum, clinical assignments, and the forms and requirements for the clinical practicum. This manual provides clinical advisors with information about supervising and providing feedback.

Site Facilitator's Manual. A manual was developed for site facilitators that provides information on the course curriculum, directions on in-class independent and group assignments, contact information, and procedures for dealing with technical difficulties.

Supportive Components. There are several supportive components of the course that enhance course presentation and process. They include multimedia, clinical advisor training, guest speakers, and formative and summative evaluation.

Multimedia. While high quality visuals are always important in any training situation, they are critical to distance learning. A considerable amount of time is required for either creating or locating high-quality supporting visuals for the videoclass. Experience shows that the old paradigm of "talking heads" should be kept to a minimum. Videoclasses are enhanced through use of slides, full color overheads, and videos. In the future, new multimedia will be incorporated into the training, such as telemedicine. With telemedicine, a client can be examined using special versions of common diagnostic tools such as a stethoscope, otoscope, or opthalmoscope. The instructor would be able to look into the eyes or ears of a volunteer patient, and the results would be projected on the screen. Distance learning makes this type of multimedia possible. Although technically telemedicine could be used in a regular classroom, chances are that most classrooms would not be equipped for this.

Clinical Advisor Training. Clinical advisors are expected to be involved from the beginning. It was clear from early consultations that it was necessary to provide clinical advisors with training in order to explain the new requirements. The first clinical advisor training, also presented over the PHTIN, occurred just prior to the first offering. Clinical advisors were presented with the course requirements, the curriculum, and training in clinical supervision. In addition, all clinical advisors received the clinical advisor manual.

Clinical advisor training takes place annually and provides for ongoing feedback from these important stakeholders. In addition to providing clinical advisors with information, these sessions have also provided an opportunity for dialogue between course staff and clinical advisors. Common questions and concerns that are raised during these trainings have now been added to the *Clinical Advisor Manual* in a section on "Frequently Asked Questions." This has been received positively.

Guest Speakers: A particular advantage to distance learning is the ability to include guest speakers and master faculty who would not be able to travel to individual sites. This is an important element of adult physical assessment training. We are able to utilize the resources of the university faculty and the DHHS, and the participants get direct access to experts with whom they might not normally come in contact.

Evaluation

Ongoing monitoring and evaluation is a critical component of the course process. Every course includes a formative and summative evaluation. Regional nurse consultants also provide feedback on a regular basis. The fact that many of them serve as site facilitators means that they can regularly report on the experiences of participants at the remote sites. The program director is always assessing the course process on and off air. This enables a continuous dynamic in the feedback process. In fact, it is the informal mechanisms for evaluation that provide some of the most important data for modifying the course, strengthening process components, and identifying participants who need greater monitoring and follow up.

Formative Evaluation. Each two-week module is evaluated separately. Participants rate the following on a four point Likert scale, with 4 5 Excellent, 3 5 Good, 2 5 Fair and 1 5 Poor:

- How well each module's objectives are met
- Relevance of content
- Effectiveness of instruction
- Effectiveness of the faculty
- Multimedia
- Materials
- Training environment

There are also qualitative questions on how the participant expects to utilize the information and a section for general comments.

Summative Evaluation. The summative evaluation has many components, which are both quantitative and qualitative. There is a comprehensive didactic evaluation that follows the same format as the module evaluations but evaluates the overall course objectives and cumulative participant experience. The data is analyzed by the program director, and the information is used to modify future courses. In addition, the program director analyzes pretest and post-test changes for the didactic and clinical advisor comments in order to determine if certain areas need to be strengthened in the curriculum.

Baseline Informational Survey. Another part of the course evaluation is a participant survey, which is distributed on the first day. This survey helps the faculty to understand the overall make up of the class, their main work areas within their health departments, expectations from the class, motivation for being there, and perception of level of support.

All three evaluations are critical. The formative evaluation provides information on specific components of the course or specific faculty, which are not as clear in the summative evaluation. The summative evaluation measures overall satisfaction and reflects the learning curve. As is common among adult learners, the participants expect that they should be able to readily perform these new skills. Early module evaluations reflect participant frustration more than the latter module evaluations. As their skills and confidence increase, so does their satisfaction with the course. Both the formative and summative evaluations help the staff to understand how well modifications have worked and provide input for future modifications.

The participant survey provides descriptive data about each participant, as well as data for long-term analysis. Previous evaluations of the program have correlated perception of support to course completion rates and found that those who perceive little support or are attending because they have been sent are less likely to complete the clinical practicum on time. Some of these participants never finish. This survey data also helps staff to anticipate problems at certain health departments so that they may be addressed early. Finally, the survey provides faculty and staff with an assessment of the overall level of motivation.

Outcomes

Ongoing evaluation identified a number of successes and limitations to the model. Successes include increased access, reduced cost, higher quality of skills development, higher completion rates and the creation of a service learning component. Limitations fall into two categories: distance learning related and systemic. The former includes the challenge of making the course interactive and the threat of technical problems while on air. Systemic limitations relate to the decentralized management of the program. It is often difficult to ensure consistency of training at the health department level.

Successes

The first videoclass in 1996 trained thirty-nine public health nurses. In 1997 there were two courses training a total of 107 nurses. While the first course had some challenges, it was generally a success. Initial fear of "practicing" on real health department clients was overcome, and many participants expressed enthusiasm about the experience. Lessons learned were incorporated into the planning of successive courses.

Access. The video class clearly met the goal of providing greater access to the course. Table 11.1 shows the difference in the numbers trained using the traditional and video class formats. The video class made it possible to train nearly as many participants in two courses as were trained in nine courses in 1995. Since we began offering Adult Physical Assessment via distance learning, two additional sites have been added to the PHTIN that can be included in future offerings, thus further increasing access.

Cost. When analyzing cost within distance education, it is not always easy to calculate the value in a real dollar sense. The most tangible cost savings in delivering adult physical assessment training via distance learning is found at the health department level. Because the training is delivered regionally, there is less need for

TABLE 11.1. NUMBER OF NURSES TRAINED PER YEAR BY DELIVERY FORMAT 1993–1997.

Calendar Year	Medium	Number of Classes	Average Per Class	Total Number Trained
1993	Single-site	7	14	99
1994	Single-site	12	11	136
1995	Single-site	4	11	101
1996	Single-site	4	19	76
	Videoconference	1	38	38
1997	Videoconference	2	48	96
1998	Videoconference	2	60	120

participants to travel, thus eliminating the cost of reimbursement for travel and hotel expenses, which previously ranged from $300–$1,500 per participant. This, however, is a cost shifting because the program provider bears a greater cost for staffing the videoconferencing facilities, maintaining the equipment, and the telecommunications. The provider does see savings in the reduced number of teaching days. In 1996 for example, there were thirty-two teaching days for the four on-site classes versus four teaching days for one video class.

To understand the true nature of cost savings, it is necessary to look at the entire distance learning system and the PHTIN in particular. At the request of the North Carolina legislature prior to the establishment of the PHTIN, a comprehensive cost analysis was conducted on the PHTIN as a training system. The analysis concluded the system was not likely to result in dramatic direct cost savings but that based upon the successful design and implementation of training programs, it had the potential to provide dramatic indirect savings. This includes reducing staff turnover due to the lack of necessary skills, reducing use of substitute staff, and ensuring timely training in required areas.

The analysis took a look at the system in its entirety—analyzing the costs for all the partners (the training providers, the consumer, and the various agencies involved). This is necessary to provide an analysis that will discover the shifts in the allocation of costs, as well as any potential savings. For instance, travel savings that accrue to local health departments come as the result of an increase in the costs of the videoconference system provider. The savings to local staff were calculated to be slightly more than $7 million over seven years. Meanwhile the costs of building, maintaining, and operating the network were estimated to be slightly less than $7 million over the same time period. The network has to be justified on the basis of the central provision of services. Much of the cost of the infrastructure is a one-time investment. Thus the more it can be used, the more cost effective it becomes. Moreover, there is no way to put a dollar value on the cost of not training public health nurses. Without increasing access, nurses would not get the training that makes their services reimbursable under Medicaid and allows them to provide crucial services to underserved clients. They would also not be able to take upper level clinical courses that would enable them to perform in even more specialized roles within health departments.

Quality. Clearly no amount of local cost-effectiveness and increased access would matter if quality were compromised. In all courses to date there were 25–30 point increases in the pre-and post testing knowledge scores. (100-point tests) The clinical practice appears to significantly reinforce the material covered during the video class.

While it is too early to definitely state that videoclass participants have better clinical skills, it is clear that the quality of clinical practice has not been diminished. There does appear to be a real advantage to the continuous nature of the training and the ability of the participants to work with health department clients earlier in the process. Under the old format participants practiced clinical skills on each other in less than ideal environments. The first physically assessed actual clients were encountered during the clinical practicum. The busy nature of health departments meant that there was sometimes a lapse in time between the completion of the didactic and the commencement of the practicum. In many cases, participants did not even know whom their clinical advisor would be when the didactic training began.

Under the video class format, participants begin working with their clinical advisors from the start, thereby developing a closer working relationship. This carried through to the clinical practicum. In short, the videoclass places the course on a continuum. The clinical practice is a critical link in this process. Under the traditional site-based format, the didactic part of the course and the clinical practicum were two discrete parts of a training process. The faculty had little or no involvement with the health department. Thus participants often left the didactic portion of the course without a clear understanding of what was expected during the practicum. This increased the likelihood that the practicum would be delayed. Now the faculty, staff, and health departments all work together throughout the process, and the clinical practicum is an extension of the clinical practice. Course materials are also designed to clarify the clinical practicum requirements. Qualitative data from those who perform final clinical evaluations indicates that the video class participants exhibit a high level of confidence and motivation.

Clinical Training: Another important aspect of this training model is that it shows that it is possible to utilize the resource of the PHTIN to provide clinical training. This opens the door to offering other clinical courses in this manner. Already it is being used for upper level training in family planning nursing, maternal health nursing, and training in sexually transmitted diseases prevention and treatment.

Unforeseen Outcomes

There are several unforeseen outcomes to the video class model.

Completion. While this practicum is designed to be completed within six months, through the years participants have taken anywhere from six months to two years to complete the practicum. Now since participants are beginning their clinical practicums sooner, more are completing on time.

Service Learning. One of the most difficult challenges is convincing participants that they are not simply practicing on clients. By putting the hands-on training into the health department, the training experience becomes service learning. The clients are receiving a level of screening that they would not normally receive. A qualified clinical advisor is supervising the participant so the client is never at risk. Participants are being trained to use their critical thinking abilities and not simply check boxes on a form. The goal is train nurses so that they look at the client as a whole person. This is difficult to simulate in the classroom.

In each class to date there have been cases of previously undetected and potentially dangerous conditions identified during the clinical practice. The most dramatic case occurred during the first course offering. A client had come to the clinic for a routine visit. Normally, she would not have had a breast exam as part of her examination, but since a participant needed to practice the skills, the client agreed to have the procedure performed. A lump was found, and the client was immediately sent for follow up. It turned out that the lump was malignant, but it was still in an early stage. Had this lump been found later, it could have meant death for the client.

While other examples were not so dramatic, they clearly had an impact on class members. In the case of the breast cancer example, there seemed to be an immediate change in the attitude of the participants toward the clinical practice.

The clinical practice experiences of the participants have become a valuable part of class discussion. Participant experiences make for natural case studies and encourage critical thinking. An objective of the course is for participants to be able to differentiate normal from abnormal situations. When participants practiced on each other, all they encountered were normal situations. Commercially available videotapes on physical examination generally focus on normal situations as well. Therefore, providing participants with the potential of seeing and hearing unusual cases enhances the training and improves analytical skills.

Another advantage to participants practicing within their own health departments is that they are getting experience that is reflective of the actual situation in which they work. There is considerable variation between regions with regard to health concerns. The didactic portion of the course provides basic clinical information. How it is applied depends on the priorities and client demographics of each health department. By applying their assessment skills early to the real health department clientele, the participants are gaining experience that will help them to build their analytical skills sooner. Participants from urban areas see a larger number of refugees and immigrants. There are two parts of the state with large Native American populations. Thus from the start of the course participants have to adapt their skills to the needs and risk factors of the special populations they serve.

Limitations

The videoclass format has improved the quality of the Adult Physical Assessment course. There are limitations. Strong opinions exist pro and con throughout the state about the value of training using video conferencing. Many have become convinced that it is possible to deliver quality competency-based training in distance learning format. There are inherent challenges in aspects of the Adult Physical Assessment course, whether taught on air or in a traditional format.

Limitations fall into two categories: limitations of distance learning and systemic limitations. Distance learning limitations include those associated with the delivery system such as learner responsiveness and technical problems. Systemic limitations involve the conditions at health departments that influence participant support and motivation.

Didactic. A common misconception is that the didactic component of the course has been reduced thus jeopardizing course quality. In fact, the didactic component has not been reduced, but the delivery of the content has been redistributed. In the past, one or two body systems were covered in the morning of each class day. Clinical practice occurred in the afternoon. Now eight days of didactic material must be delivered in four days. This means that each 6.5 hour video class day covers three or four body systems. This is a lot of material to cover in one day, and it is often difficult for participants to retain it all. This is when self-paced independent study material and lecture outlines become meaningful.

Another issue is the lack of on-site practice. Although the previous method of on-site practice had many limitations, there was some advantage to practicing immediately. The new curriculum includes some on-site practice, where it is feasible. For example, participants can practice as the instructor demonstrates the use of an otoscope, opthalmoscope and the reflex hammer. However, as with all elements of the course, skill must come with a great deal of practice.

Interactivity. While the system is designed for interactivity, it is often reduced. Efforts have been made to include off air group activities, yet group work does not always prove successful. Due to the large amount of material to be covered in the didactic, some participants have indicated that they feel that group work is a waste of their time and that they prefer straight lecture. Some faculty are better than others in getting participants involved. In the future, more live demonstration is planned when possible that elicits return demonstrations so that participants may be more involved and ask questions about real situations.

Another issue with interactivity is access to faculty. Participants may ask questions during the day. After the class, they only have access to the faculty by phone.

While many distance learning courses enhance interactivity by way of e-mail and listservs, health departments have limited access to this technology. Thus efforts to utilize this medium to increase interactivity are limited at this time.

Technical Problems. Though rare, a telecommunications problem can cause considerable disruption to a video class. Sometimes the problem may be isolated to one site or may be within the whole network. During a recent class, an interesting technological glitch occurred. After lunch we were waiting for all the sites to come on air. Instead of one of the PHTIN sites, we were connected to a high school math class in another county. This made it rather awkward and humorous, as the subject that we were discussing was sexually transmitted diseases. It took a half hour to correct the problem. This disrupted the momentum and made it difficult to get back on track; however, the participants spent the time talking to each other at each site about their health departments' experiences. So what started as a disruptive technical problem turned into some needed interactivity.

Clinical Practice. Health departments are busy and understaffed institutions. While the health departments support the videoclass design as a cost-effective solution, there continues to be inconsistency in the level of support that the health departments can provide to participants. This is nothing new to the program. The varying rates in the time it takes different participants to complete the clinical practicum is indicative of the varying levels of institutional capacity for supporting health department-based clinical training.

While it is continually reinforced that the course is an eight-week course rather than a four-day course many health departments do not significantly alter the schedule of employee participants to allow performance of necessary clinical practice. This is an ongoing challenge that must be addressed systemically outside of the medium of instruction. The fact remains that understaffed health departments must prioritize between serving clients and providing supervised training. The irony is that making a commitment to quality training will speed up the training process and provide the health department with staff who are able to expand the services provided.

Unlike university hospitals health departments are not primarily teaching institutions. A flu outbreak or other public health emergency frequently pre-empts the best intentions of providing participants with dedicated tutoring. This means that while many health departments provide the participants with excellent instruction and assistance, others may only provide the minimum. This was often seen with the clinical practicum. The videoclass places additional demand on the health department to utilize their limited clinical staff for teaching. However, as more participants complete the training and begin to practice, they will be able to serve as clinical advisors. In addition, this training model is a trade off.

By accepting health department-based practice they are eliminating the need to send participants away for training for another four days.

While some participants are concerned that they are sometimes rushed to complete their clinical assignments, they are frequently reminded that the hands-on clinical practice that takes place during the eight-week didactic is still superior to the old method in which participants practiced on each other. Clinical practice at this stage is simply meant to give participants a chance to walk through the mechanical steps of the exam in a more realistic setting. Expertise is obtained through the clinical practicum. Some health departments are overcoming this limitation by assigning the participant with more than one clinical advisor. Others are arranging for participants to get experience outside the health department.

Participants seek additional recognition and compensation for their efforts. In the current system, this is a weakness. Training does not guarantee advancement, and this sometimes affects participant motivation. The State Director of Public Health Nursing and local public health nursing leaders are working with state personnel to improve this situation.

Technology Limitations. Some distance learning programs combine interactive video with web-based components. There are clearly some aspects of adult physical assessment that would lend themselves to web-based instruction. For example, this could be used to review anatomy and physiology so that it would not need to be covered during the video class. This would reduce the length of the video class day or provide more time for interactive activities.

Many health departments are new to e-mail and Internet environments, with upper management having first access to these tools. This limits the ability of the staff to diversify distance learning formats.

Lessons Learned

Each successive course has garnered useful information for improvement. Here are some overall guidelines for video conferencing, which come from our own experience:

> *Be prepared and flexible:* When an investment is made in a training design, it is critical that it not be allowed to fail. We have had to make some changes mid-stream, such as changing faculty, in order to ensure that the learners receive an optimal learning experience.
>
> *Staffing:* Staffing should involve instructional designers and those with experience in distance education.

Faculty: Not all instructors come across well on screen. There are several ways to prepare for this:

• Try to hire instructors with videoconferencing experience
• Provide faculty with videoconferencing training
• Include guest speakers

Be prepared for technical difficulties: Every so often something goes wrong with the telecommunications system. This should not be lost time. Provide self-study materials or group activities that may be performed while the system is down. Provide clear instructions to site facilitators on what to do and how to alert the central site about a problem that may be site-specific. It is useful to schedule a make-up day to be used in the event of a technical problem in which too much class time is lost. This is also important if the course is scheduled at the time of year when bad weather in one area might result in having to cancel all sites. It is also always important to videotape the sessions in case a problem is limited to one site. Participants can be provided with a videotape of the portions of the class they have missed.

Clear instructions and enhanced self-study: In a model such as this, the majority of learning takes place outside of the classroom. Therefore, participants and their advisors need to have clear instructions as to what is expected. This should be outlined in course materials.

Vary activities: In addition to varying instructors, it is useful to vary activities. Long periods of staring at the screen should be avoided if possible. This can be broken up with group activities.

Multimedia: Visuals are critical. Quality color graphics are essential. Black and white overheads are difficult to see at remote sites and hold very little visual interest. Create or utilize commercially available multimedia to illustrate important points. All materials should be created in landscape and all words should be in thirty point type or above.

Evaluation: Ongoing evaluation is extremely important for making process modifications and providing data to support the value of the training program. This is especially true in situations in which distance training is controversial as a method of teaching.

Conclusion

Although adult physical assessment training is still a work in progress, much has been learned to date, and the course has been improved. Not all of these improvements can be attributed to distance learning alone. However, the process of transforming the course allowed for modifications that strengthened several process components that were not new, such as the clinical practicum. For example, there would always have been value in providing clinical advisor training; however, this did not occur until it was implemented in the distance learning model. Other positive changes *can* be attributed to distance learning, such as centralized monitoring of course content. In the past there were different faculty at different sites, and the program director was not always present. Therefore, there was no guarantee of consistency between courses. Now there is more consistency in the information that is delivered, and the necessary process details have been worked into all aspects of the curriculum.

Clearly interactive video conferencing has many advantages. While this course is clinical in nature, this model could be adapted to any kind of competency-based training in which there is an element of experiential training. Advantages include:

- Increased access
- Decreased cost in staff time lost
- Reduced travel costs
- Less personal hardship on participants
- Decentralized experiential training that takes into account regional differences in clientele
- Decreased cost of instructors and the ability to use experts
- Better prepared workforce with less staff turnover due to lack of skills

Before such a distance education project can be implemented there are several elements to be considered that require time and resources. Key structural elements must be in place. These include

- Access to technology infrastructure or investment in one
- Mechanisms for local accountability
- Centralized management with decentralized feedback mechanisms.

Beyond developing an infrastructure, it is necessary to analyze the strengths and weaknesses of teaching with interactive video when developing the instructional design. Efforts made in anticipating and addressing limitations and taking advantage of strengths up front will result in enhanced experience for the learner.

CHAPTER TWELVE

SKILLS-BASED DISTANCE TRAINING FOR A GLOBAL ENVIRONMENT: MALAYSIA'S VIRTUAL UNIVERSITY

Manon Ress and Patrice Sonberg

The authors of this case study worked as educational consultants on the Virtual University project for eighteen months. They were subcontracted by the U.S. research and engineering company that was hired by the Malaysian corporation to manage the Virtual University project. The authors, based in Virginia, worked closely with the Project Team in Malaysia and the U.S.

The names of the corporations and academic partners involved in this project have not been used because of the instability and complex nature of the relationships between these parties over the last six months. This case study is written from the perspective of the authors and does not necessarily reflect the view of the corporations or academic institutions involved in the project.

The Training Ground of a Rapidly Developing Nation

In this case study the authors will describe the development of a distance education institution in Malaysia. This independent institution referred to as the "Virtual University" (VU) is supported by a private corporation with close ties to the government. The needs of the corporation developing the VU reflect those of the nation. The staff is young and somewhat educated but lack the computer literacy and technical knowledge necessary for the vision of upper management.

The middle management is composed of young professionals, mostly educated in the U.S. or Australia, while the upper management is composed of more mature individuals often educated in Britain or British schools. A microcosm that reflects the Malay society, the Malaysian corporation's culture is in the process of evaluating different education systems and their merits. The introduction of a foreign system—American, computer-based, at a distance—is not without a struggle, but the vision of the chairman and the needs of the nation are driving forces propelling this movement ahead.

In the initial plan, the VU mirrored a traditional American university in terms of degrees and curriculum but with computer-mediated courses. However, as the concept evolved, it became evident that the needs of the target population are strictly skill-based. The American ideal of a broad liberal education is far from what Malaysian businesses and even students can envision.

The VU although a degree-granting university is actually closer to the American concept of a training program. In developing nations and other nonwestern cultures, creating a university program at a distance is the only way to create a credible and market-oriented training program. The corporation determined that the major skills needed—both internally and throughout the nation—are computer literacy and English. In step with the country's mission to become a leader in information technology and the global economy, the corporation chose business and science as areas of study.

While the VU was originally scheduled to open in June of 1997, today, more than two years after its inception, the currency crisis in Asia has put the project indefinitely on hold, and the VU project team members have been reassigned to other projects. Since there are no measures of the successes or failures of the VU, this case study will simply outline the process of development thus far and highlight issues that demonstrate some of the gaps between theory and reality.

The first section reviews the Malaysian context: the historical, political, economic, and educational issues that have had an impact on the VU. The second section presents the players involved in the VU project and describes the stages of the development process thus far. The third section presents an overview of the VU and a description of the target student population. The fourth section focuses on courseware providers and the instructional process, using the English curriculum as an example. The fifth section is a discussion of the major issues encountered while following today's American principles of distance learning when developing a distance training program abroad. The final section reviews key issues and lessons learned during the VU developmental process.

Malaysia

In a country slightly larger than New Mexico, bordering Thailand, Brunei, and Indonesia, the tallest building in the world has become the emblem of a new era. With about twenty million inhabitants, Malaysia is a dynamic southeast Asian country embarked on a cyber future. From a rural economy to the development of the Multimedia Super Corridor (MSC), Malaysia is taking as its leaders like to say a "quantum leap." At present the MSC is a ten-mile by thirty-mile corridor stretching south of Kuala Lumpur, the country's capital. The hills are still covered with rain forests and palm oil plantations, but in ten years, the MSC may be the Silicon Valley of the East. Planned as a futuristic city it will host a new government center, Putrajaya, a multimedia university, and foreign research laboratories.

The MSC is the brainchild of Prime Minister Mahathir Mohamad, the leader of the young nation that gained independence from the British Empire in 1957. The country's constitution is modeled on British democracy but with clear limitations on political freedom. A democracy in a rapidly developing country, Malaysia has known years of ethnic conflict often linked to modernization. An example if not a model of a pluralistic society, the country's ethnic divisions—there are Malaysian Indians, Malaysian Chinese, Malaysian Malays, and indigenous people on Sabah and Sarawak—are reinforced by linguistic, cultural, religious, and economic divisions.

The Malay Agenda

Early in the colonization process, the British regarded the Malays as the only legitimate owners of land. They created an administrative class from the Malays elite who were English educated and in control of the bureaucracy, police, and army. While the Malays led the fight for independence and enjoyed significant political power, they lagged behind economically. Unlike their Chinese and Indian counterparts, they had remained a rural population not in contact with key components of modernization. The Malays lacked an educated working class.

Political developments in Malaysia in the context of steady economic growth show concern over this economic imbalance between ethnic groups. In the early 1970s the government initiated its New Economic Policy (NEP) which had two major goals: a) to reduce and eventually eradicate poverty for all Malaysians and b) to accelerate the restructuration of Malaysian society to correct economic imbalance between different ethnic groups. Benefits designed exclusively for Malays aimed to create a Malay entrepreneurial and shareholding class, as well as expand the Malay middle class. The implementation of the NEP involved measures that strongly discriminated in favor of Malays.

Today the Malays are the largest homogenous group in the country. They speak Malay and are Muslim. The Chinese community is divided along religious, cultural, and linguistic lines, while the Indians speak mostly Tamil and are divided into castes.

Education

Malaysia has recently seen a shift in the field of education. To go from a rural to a service-oriented economy, this country with a British legacy and strong Islamic values has to be creative in its national policies. From changes in the language of instruction to the forthcoming privatization of national institutions to the emerging information superhighway, the education system—as well as many aspects of society—are being redefined.

The Malaysians are proud that for the last 30 years education has been a key government priority and the percentage of the total GNP spent on education has been increasing. Government and businesses' concerns over the shortage of skilled workers have been reflected in the increasing budget for education. At the same time, the low median age of the Malaysian population—about twenty-six—has put enormous pressure on the existing educational system. Changes in the content, form and emphasis of education have accompanied the rapid expansion. After years of negotiating with the British legacy (until the 1970s the Malaysian students were still evaluated by British institutions), a new educational system is now emerging within the Malaysian framework.

Instruction in Malaysia follows strict national syllabi which have aided the new emerging emphasis on science, math, and technology. In addition, values and norms in line with the principles of the national ideology (Rukun Negara), the teaching of Islam in general has become a national requirement, even for non-public schools. To get a license to operate, an institution must prove that national values will be taught or are prerequirements. As the education system opens its door to private and foreign schools, the need to promote national values is made clear by the government.

In the 1970s, the national language, Bahasa Malaysia, became the official language of instruction. Chinese and Tamil are also used, especially at the elementary and secondary level. The decision to impose the national language as the main language of instruction has had mixed consequences: on the one hand it has certainly helped the Malays get access to education. On the other hand the need to know English to compete in the international marketplace is becoming more and more important.

An Insufficient Tertiary System

The enormous expansion in elementary and secondary education since the 1970s created pressures to expand opportunities for tertiary education. From one university in 1965—University of Malaya—to seven universities and dozens of colleges awarding certificates and diplomas in the early 1990s, the tertiary system remains insufficient. Thousands of students are enrolled in overseas institutions and receive government scholarships, while even more have no hope to access a national or private university. In 1996, there were near riots by offices where young Malaysians were trying to access the application forms for national teacher education programs. The lack of opportunity and the need of the nation put pressure on the government to open its doors to not only private universities but also to English as a main language of instruction.

As the needs for higher education and training are steadily growing, public universities are now on the brink of privatization, and the for-profit sector has gotten involved. While some Malaysians are critical of this privatization, to many the government is not abdicating its responsibility and role in education but simply cannot shoulder the burden of education on its own.

Education is a hot topic for everyone from the Prime Minister to the average Malaysian. Special reports on education issues are sold in popular bookstores, and most newspapers have weekly special issues on education. The power of the Minister of Education is well known. Decisions on policies are made by the centralized Ministry, and reforms are imposed from the top down without much discussion.

An Ambitious Corporation Answers the Need of a Nation

In the spirit of the "Malay Agenda," which supports the creation of a Malay business class, one of the country's largest commercial cooperatives embarked on the development of the country's first "Virtual University" in the Spring of 1996. With support from the national leadership, the corporation believed the VU could help it meet the goal of increasing the participation of the Bumiputras (indigenous Malay ethnic group) in commerce and industry.

This corporation, formed in 1977 by members of the country's ruling coalition, has wide and varied investments in property development, electronics and telecommunications, information technology, travel, plantation, education, and other fields. One of the first interests listed in the company's corporate profile is education, specifically privately supported education. Prior to the VU concept, the corporation had created an institute to provide commercial and technical training for students who don't have access to formal education. Many of these students have gone on to work for the corporation.

The Chair of the corporation, renowned for his innovation, independent spirit, and conservative politics, conceived the idea of the VU. Since his company was active in the field of telecommunication, a network-based educational institution made sense. According to the country's mainstream press, by the year 2000, Malaysia will need 100,000 IT workers—a nearly impossible goal given the current education infrastructure. The VU may not be able to produce the best IT education, but the Chair believes it will produce what is needed. Students of the VU—future employees and the new Malay business class—will have greater access to education at a lower cost and at the same time refine their skills in technology and English.

While the company recently became privatized, it retains close ties to the government. The company president's political power, an appointed member to the Supreme Council with relatively easy access to the Prime Minister, is undoubtedly an asset to this project. In addition, several members of Parliament sit on the corporation's Board of Directors. The need of the Malaysian economy coupled with the ambitions of a growing company has placed the VU project in a prestigious and perilous political position.

The corporation in Malaysia (sometimes referred to as "the client" in this case study) is working closely with an American research and engineering firm on the management of the VU project. Together these two firms created a Project Team now composed of system engineers (software and hardware) and business, marketing, and education specialists based in both the U.S. and Malaysia. The decision to work with an American firm was somewhat circumstantial. It so happened that the U.S. firm was working with the Malaysian corporation on a networking project when the VU concept was conceived. The two firms decided it would be mutually beneficial to join forces.

The Project Team and VU Development

The project team's initial assignment was to come up with a strategic plan which included the VU's mission, goals, and objectives. It also conducted an analysis of available resources and options for distance education in the U.S. and Malaysia. One of the most complex tasks facing the project team was to assess the demands of the society and business community, as well as the specific needs of Malaysian students and teachers. The tracking and evaluation of emerging communication technology and educational materials was facilitated (and complicated) by the World Wide Web. As the members of the team researched the web and received communications from vendors around the world, managing expectations became a central task. Meeting with potential vendors, the project team had to re-evaluate estimated costs, time frames, and what was actually for sale.

After the high-level VU concept plan was approved by the upper management of the U.S. and Malaysian partners (Spring 1996), a group of Malaysian businessmen came to the United States to visit campuses and meet with the U.S.-based members of the project team. The goals were to see distance education institutions and traditional university campuses involved in the integration of technology in the teaching and learning process. The American corporation and the Malaysian corporation discussed other projects during the visit, but the prestigious VU project was an important part of the trip.

In the second phase the U.S.-based members of the project team—education specialists, information systems engineers, and executive managers—went to Malaysia to meet their counterparts and discuss the technical, financial, and educational requirements. Meetings with the Minister of Education, visits to Malaysian campuses, and interviews with teachers and students helped frame the VU concept in the Malaysian context. A more detailed concept of operation was conceived as the team prepared for a formal presentation to the Prime Minister.

At the Multimedia Expo '96 in Kuala Lumpur, the project team presented the VU concept to the government, media, educators, and students, and the VU became a well-known project in Malaysia. With publicity came the support and also criticism that the design of any new education system would bring. The project certainly benefited from the exposure, but with exposure came scrutiny.

The day of the Expo when students and parents were invited was a difficult day for the team: large groups of young Malaysians, most of them Chinese or Indian, were asking for schedules of opening dates and application forms. Most were quite open about their worries of not being able to study their subject of choice (very often computer science). Repetitively, the team was told that Chinese and Indians have even less opportunity for higher education since a quota of qualified Malays must be filled before they are admitted. This measure of affirmative action has certainly helped work toward the creation of a young educated Malay business class, but it is also the source of clear dissatisfaction among the Malaysian minorities.

In the Fall of 1996 team-building efforts were important as the project team prepared for a design review in Malaysia for the corporations' upper management. Difficulties arose when the education and technology requirements were changed at the last minute and many face-to-face meetings were necessary. Unrealistic expectations became a major problem when, for example, some members of the team thought creating an education degree program for the VU would please the Minister of Education and therefore help the project. In another case, some members of the team wanted to create five different types of engineering degree programs in the already limited time frame. Despite these last-minute calls for changes, the design review was relatively successful, and the functions of the team and its members were redefined.

Two Steps Forward and One Step Backward

In early 1997 the project team was asked to support the writing of the application to the Minister of Education for a university license. Information is not shared freely in Malaysia, and obtaining guidelines for the application was a major endeavor. In the end, an outside Malaysian consulting firm was asked to write the document with the project team's input.

In February of 1997 a Malaysian delegation, a project manager, and an education specialist arrived for a month-long visit to the U.S. and Canada. The trip, labeled a "fact-finding mission," consisted of meetings with potential administrative software vendors and courseware providers. Meetings with North American educators focused on distance education, the integration of technology, and the impact of technology in the field of education and subsequently opened discussions within the team about expectations. The many sites on the World Wide Web announcing immediate access to courseware or even the availability of full-degree programs were put to the test and for the most part failed.

After the delegation returned to Malaysia, it was decided that the project team should provide a final version of the "master plan" for the VU, including a concept of operation (hardware and software systems, academics, and marketing), a quality assurance plan, and the baseline technology requirements. Assembling and organizing all the research and reports were major undertakings that lasted about six weeks.

It appears as if the client is now ready to discuss the final master plan. Educational and technical requirements are to be baselined, and the providers formally selected. The issues of where, when, and how the courses will be developed are still controversial. The Malaysians want to produce their own courses, not only to learn how to design and develop courseware but also because it is necessary to control the content of educational materials. The U.S. courseware providers assure the Malaysians everything will be customized, but the tight schedule makes it difficult to develop it in Malaysia.

The Virtual University

Distance education while certainly not new in Malaysia has evolved rapidly. From correspondence studies to virtual universities, the theory of learning and teaching at a distance has been radically changed by the introduction and adoption of the world of multimedia.

As a distance education institution, the VU will use the latest technologies available, integrating a variety of media with traditional course content. It will also create a new curricula emerging from the current evolution in Malaysian society, which is now placing greater emphasis on independent learning skills, critical thinking skills, and collaborative learning—all enhanced by distance learning.

While the specifics of the VU change on a somewhat frequent basis, the core of the institution has not strayed from the initial concept. The VU's mission is to expand quality and affordable higher education to the Malaysian people, increase the skilled workforce, make Malaysia an exporter of education, and enable Malaysians to compete in the world economy.

Early in the development process, it was decided that the VU was not going to be a distributed classroom system in which a classroom-based course from one location is extended to a remote group of students. Nor is the VU an open learning model in which mostly adult students can study at their own pace. The VU will be an independent institution providing undergraduate education to mostly full-time students. Close to the independent learning model, the VU has extremely ambitious goals. Among them is the integration of technology into international curricula customized for Malaysian students through a collaboration between government, corporations, educators, and engineers.

Computer-Mediated Learning

The specifics will vary, but generally all coursework—syllabus, readings, student-teacher and student-student communication, testing, and so on—will be computer mediated. Via a mixture of online study, email discussions with faculty and classmates, practical and case-based problem-solving, group projects and activities, and interaction with other students, the VU will address the academic and social needs of students. These web-based courses, called "courseware," will also provide access to stored texts, web sites, and other network-based data such as listservs and chat rooms. Students may periodically use textbooks and study guides for assigned readings and attend interactive video lectures and presentations.

Initially, regional study centers will be open to students on a twenty-four hour basis, and tutors offering academic and technical assistance will be on hand. Students will eventually be able to access all courseware from remote locations using a modem.

The various delivery mechanisms available at the VU and the option to choose the preferred mechanism is aimed to encourage students to find the mode of information delivery most suited to them. In doing so, they may discover their learning styles and preferences, while learning how and where to access information, how to apply the information they obtain, and when to seek more information. Educators hope students will take an active role in and responsibility for their own learning.

While many of those involved in the VU may already possess the technical skills that will allow them to succeed in a virtual environment, training for faculty, staff, and students is a crucial aspect of this project. Distance education can be a disappointing experience for both the instructor and students if the technology is not properly managed and understood. Courseware providers with expertise in training distance educators and students will work closely with the client to ensure a comprehensive and sufficient training period. The results of a needs assessment (surveys, interviews, research, and so on) will guide training design and delivery, and requirements will be reviewed and adjusted on an ongoing basis.

Curriculum. The VU will include a Foundation Year (FY) program (the most developed portion of the curriculum thus far) that aims to prepare Malaysian students to enter a national or international university degree program. The year-long trimester program contains a business stream and science stream, options which allow students to learn the latest in information technology and gain a basic understanding of the respective field. Business stream courses include business mathematics, accounting, and economics, while science stream courses include mathematics, physics, and programming.

The VU plans to eventually offer BS degree programs in Business and Computer Science, as well as a teacher education program, non-degree programs, and corporate training.

To prepare students for English as the language of instruction, the FY includes English as a Foreign Language (EFL) courses that integrate the latest in computer-assisted language learning (CALL) and a National Studies course covering Malaysian History, Islam, and Bahasa Malaysia. The FY also contains a learning skills (LS) course to prepare students for their role as distance learners and help them develop the appropriate study habits and critical thinking skills necessary in a technology-rich environment. Following completion of the FY program, students will most likely either enter a VU degree program or the workforce.

The principal admission criteria for the FY program is passage of the Sijiil Pelajaran Malaysia (SPM) or Malaysian Certificate of Education. This applies to both recent and older graduates. All incoming students will be expected to take an assessment examination so that VU academic counselors can provide individual guidance concerning diploma, degree, and career choices. (After the last two years of high school, Malaysian pupils sit for the SPM and can either enter the labor market or continue their education. Apart from pursuing their education in a university—and only the best are admitted—students can also apply at colleges, such as teacher training colleges, polytechnics, and other private colleges where professional courses are offered at both certificate and diploma levels.)

Testing in a distance education setting presents some special challenges with respect to security. If students take an exam or quiz at a remote location or in the study center with no supervision, the integrity of the tests could be compromised. Consequently, as in most distance education programs, VU students will complete their final exams in a proctored center. Another possibility is to use computer-based tests in which each student receives a different subset of questions randomly selected by the computer. In many learning courses, students complete a project or report based on a research study instead of a final exam. While these alternative forms of testing and evaluation do not eliminate the possibility of cheating, they reduce it significantly.

Student Population

The VU student—his or her characteristics, what he or she will be studying, and how—has been a subject of discussion at every level of the project. As early as the first VU concept plan, students have been described as eighteen to twenty-six year olds who have completed their upper secondary education, plus two years of pre-university education, and passed the SPM. The fact that the target population will be mainly undergraduate is unique for a distance education institution.

The market for the VU is clear: students who cannot access the few national universities nor afford foreign universities and students who have already entered the workforce but want a diploma. The VU has to answer the needs of the market and the nation. Young Malaysians want to be computer literate, English proficient, and have a "diploma paper" in hand. Malaysia needs skilled workers who can work with the latest technology, use English, and apply their diplomas practically.

The students want well-focused and market-oriented curricula; they want to be able to work, study and, maybe more than anything, access information. Choice regarding the course of study or even the courses themselves is not self-evident. Therefore, the VU curricula, limited to required courses in business or science, is very appealing to the Malaysians.

For many would-be critics of distance education, the potential open-enrollment policy will compensate for the new mode of instruction. In fact, bankers are even more confident than educators that the VU will attract students. Educators are most concerned with what and how students will learn, but the needs and the pressure to produce technologically literate employees are such that the VU has been welcomed by the society as a whole.

Career Opportunities. The Malaysian corporation is also looking for alliances with other businesses, local and international. In order to increase the pool of qualified and skilled professionals, the idea to train and educate people in service is the only acceptable solution for many businesses. In addition, the Malaysians are quite used to the idea of specialization at a very young age (their "major" is chosen for them at the beginning of their university years in accordance with their performance in the subjects and the needs). Businesses are comfortable with the specialized and limited areas of study offered by the VU.

The future of VU students should be promising: between Malaysia's full-employment policy (if you have a degree you have a job) and built in sponsorships, students are almost guaranteed a place in the workforce. Those familiar with business in Malaysia know any employer would be thrilled to have an employee who can speak and write English correctly, use a computer, and understand Western culture while maintaining his own identity. The future graduate of the VU will also get access to employment through the Multimedia Super Corridor, and the new electronic government is a natural career path for students who will have mastered the VU content and methods of delivery.

Where's the Courseware?

When surfing the web, it is nearly impossible to miss the myriad of courses available via distance learning. Universities across the world are touting new courses, programs, and degrees—from chemistry to theater and dance—all accessible by the touch of your fingertips.

The company's objective for the first phase of the VU was to provide packaged (precanned), multimedia courseware with limited interaction (mostly asynchronous instruction). The Malaysian client scoffed when the Project Team suggested the need for courseware *development*. While technology transfer—the transfer of courseware design and development know how—was clearly part of the long-term plan, the corporation's management had difficulty accepting that the desired courseware simply did not exist in the form they wanted.

When finally convinced (although half-heartedly) that it could not buy a ready-made VU, the corporation decided to forge alliances with universities that offer distance learning courses, bringing international recognition and facilitating the technology transfer. The selection of partners has been based on the evaluation of the institution's experience in the field and its resources for courseware development and training. The VU hopes to acquire and adapt existing courses and courseware, as well as develop courseware custom designed for VU students. Members of the academic community in Malaysia will review and approve all course content, instructional design, and the multimedia product.

In developing and adapting the initial courseware, the VU will tap into three sources of content: a) traditional classroom courses that contain a distance learning component; b) courses designed for distance education (print, video, electronic) and c) course concepts designed for the VU but not yet developed. Depending on the level of electronic development and the degree to which they meet the VU's requirements, some courses will need little adaptation, while others will require a significant time and financial investment.

As the Foundation Year program was developed, the project team met with several U.S. and Canadian university providers to evaluate their existing online materials as well as their capability for developing further distance learning resources. The costs were astronomical, especially when multimedia was involved. This presented problems as the Malaysian clients were and still are skeptical of investing in a product they can't see until completion and one they don't feel completely comfortable evaluating. While the clients have been presented with numerous instructional alternatives from one American university provider in particular, they remain hesitant to sign an agreement. Issues of ownership and copyright have also entered the picture.

English as a Foreign Language (EFL)

For the purposes of this case study, the authors have chosen the English courseware development process (although far from complete) to illustrate the issues encountered in designing and adapting instructional materials for the VU. In the case of business and science courses, the process was different. Many university providers already have all or portions of this type of courseware, and customization and ownership were the key issues involved. The English courseware was chosen for this case study because it will be the model for future courseware developed in Malaysia.

"Manglish." To begin the language situation in Malaysia presented the project team with many complexities. During the initial needs assessment, one of the case study authors sat in on an accounting class at a two-year degree vocational college. Although the language of instruction was Malay, the class textbook was in English (British published) because according to the instructor there were no sufficient accounting textbooks written in Malay. During the class, the teacher was holding the book in one hand and sight translating the text orally while writing it on the board. Although she was speaking in Malay, almost half of the terms she was using were English. Students spoke in a mixture of Malay and English.

English is considered a second language in Malaysia. One can easily find English language television, radio, newspapers, books, and magazines throughout the nation. Nevertheless, since the 1970s when Malay became the official language of instruction, English has been taught in secondary schools as a foreign language. What has resulted is a country of fossilized learners who can understand and express themselves in English but who suffer from weak grammar and writing skills. Listening to Malaysians speak, one might hear an offshoot of English that the natives call "Manglish," a mixture of English and Malay.

On several occasions, the client toyed with the idea of translating all or some of the VU courses into Malay. There were concerns regarding language acquisition prior to the introduction of academic courses. After much convincing, however, English was chosen as the language of instruction for several reasons. For one, within the U.S. and abroad, accredited academic institutions have a consistent language of instruction. Straying from this norm could affect international recognition. Second, if English was not the sole language of instruction, students would not be sufficiently prepared to work in the English-speaking business world and global economy—one of the main missions of the VU. Third, the quality of the courses would be sacrificed if they were translated. Individual courses would ultimately become a mix of English and Malay, perpetuating the language problems that plague the country.

The FY program includes a trimester of English I, English II, and English III, respectively, beginning with a basic intermediate integrated skills course (reading, writing, speaking, and listening), and moving toward more advanced academic reading and writing courses. Despite the decision to make English the language of instruction, the concerns over language proficiency were legitimate. Therefore, it was decided that students will take an English language placement test upon acceptance to the VU and be placed in either a local Intensive English Program (IEP) or English I. The IEP will mix traditional instruction with Computer Assisted Language Learning (CALL), thereby building students' language proficiency and preparing them for their role as distance learners. After students complete a trimester of the IEP, they will be re-tested to determine whether or not they are prepared for English I. The VU content experts will advise the IEP on the syllabus, CALL software, and the necessary preparation for English I.

Commercial Software and Web-Based Courseware. Initially, the project team set out to identify commercial software or pre-existing courseware which might meet the VU requirements. EFL specialists researched and evaluated CALL software products and web-based courseware through attendance at conferences, meetings with distributors and faculty, browsing the World Wide Web, and visits to area language labs.

As anticipated, the project team could not find what it was looking for. While some educational institutions' web sites claimed to have online integrated skills courses, they were in fact only writing courses or traditional courses simply listed online. The team found several glitzy commercial software programs that might keep the attention of students, but they dealt with the four skills on a relatively superficial level not sufficient for an academic course. Numerous web sites designed for EFL students were identified, but they are transient and would have to be monitored regularly.

Although no one product met the VU course requirements, some substantive quality content was identified. The project team concluded that creating a course consisting of a mix of resources—commercial software, custom-designed and web-based materials, portions of existing online courses, international email projects—would fit the bill. The major work would be to design a framework for the course: methodology, objectives, assignments, tests, interaction, and so on.

When searching for a potential EFL courseware provider (a university interested in developing the courseware), the reaction from faculty and content experts to teaching a language at a distance was mixed. Members of the project team encountered extreme resistance when they met with one local EFL program director in particular. She did not believe that an EFL integrated skills course could be successful without significant face-to-face interaction and expressed serious doubts about the possibility of learning a language through distance education. She likened our mission to trying to learn an instrument via the computer. "Where is the human being in all of this?" she continually questioned.

Assembling a Team of Experts. Since the integration of technology in language learning seemed to be controversial in many university departments, the Project Team decided to assemble its own group of faculty members and software consultants to create the three English courses for the VU. Throughout its research, the team had met several content experts who expressed a great interest in the project and a willingness to work as consultants.

The English Content Team was identified and asked to write a proposal for the first-term course, English I. The faculty members involved in the project have expertise and degrees in EFL, as well as knowledge of instructional design and the integration of technology in language learning. One of them taught EFL in Malaysia for a number of years and is familiar with the challenges facing the Malaysian language learner.

The content experts have proposed to be involved in the design and online presentation of the course. They will design a prototype unit and prototype lessons and then work with the system integrator's instructional designers to create a unit template (a unit is made up of several lessons.) The content experts will work side-by-side with the instructional designers and multimedia experts to advise on matters such as visual presentation and transitions. This process will also facilitate the technology transfer to Malaysia, as English I will likely be created in the U.S., and English II and III will be done in Malaysia.

The English courseware proposal was submitted to the client, and the English Content team members met with the Malaysian delegation in its Spring 1997 visit to the U.S. While the proposal has not been officially accepted, it is the only proposal under consideration, and it is presumed that it will be adopted at some point.

The Design of English I. The English I course will be an intermediate, integrated-skills course consisting of original and customized online instructional and interactive materials supplemented by the most appropriate commercial software available. Technological applications will include multimedia, video, voice mail, email, and the Internet. The course design will include objectives, a daily syllabus, study guides, testing, and built-in interaction between students and teachers.

For illustration purposes, a session of the VU English I course may look something like this: The student logs onto the intranet and chooses the English I icon. The student consults the syllabus and proceeds with the appropriate study session assignment, which may include a reading and comprehension questions (custom designed for the Malaysian market), a grammar exercise (focusing on the student's problem areas), a pronunciation activity (using voice-activated commercial software), and a writing assignment (submitted to the instructor via email).

The content will draw upon Malaysian references and at the same time raise students' awareness of the global environment. The objectives for each unit and lesson will be clearly stated in a theme-based syllabus based on four topics. There will be a daily syllabus for students and teachers listing each study session activity, homework, and options for further practice.

Students will have three one-hour study sessions (time will vary depending on student's pace) per week, which can be completed at their discretion. Students taking this course will likely spend six to eight hours online weekly: three one-hour sessions and three to five hours of homework. Students will have built in options to explore at their individual level.

As language is a tool for communication, the course will create an interactive learning environment online. Although most VU courses will be self-contained at a distance, English I will require students to occasionally work face-to-face with one or two classmates in order to refine their speaking and listening skills.

Instructor- or tutor-student interaction will be optimized through the use of email and voice mail. Students will be encouraged to produce videotapes and audiotapes for submission. Instructors will arrange one-on-one synchronous chat sessions four times during the course with the aim of assessment and counseling to maximize the learning process. There will be full-class synchronous chat sessions and opportunities to chat and email to destinations abroad.

Computer-based tests in the form of quizzes and more formal examinations will be for both diagnostic and evaluation purposes. Based on the test results, the student will be guided to work on problem areas through branching routes in the material. The instructor's manual will provide guidelines as to how homework assignments, quizzes, and tests should be evaluated. All feedback will be timely in order to help students measure their progress.

Western Distance Education Principles in Southeast Asia

Cultural, financial, technical, and decision-making issues are clearly magnified in the context of this international interdisciplinary project. While a core group of about ten people interact regularly by phone, by email, or in meetings, communication between and among American and Malaysian counterparts was strained due to differences in working culture and communication styles.

It should be noted that the communication problems did not only stem from differences in nationality but also from differences in discipline. Within the project team, there were often disagreements over the driving force behind the VU, whether it be academics, technology, or money. There were also conflicts over what should be discussed, with whom, and how. For instance, when some of the American educators decided to create an unmonitored electronic discussion list, some members of the team were totally opposed. It appeared that each culture, Malaysian, American, academic, business, and engineering, envisions the need and content of communication quite differently.

The communication and cultural problems within the project team were only compounded when the team tried to apply Western principles of distance education to the Malaysian context. The existing models for developing distance training are well known, and the initial VU project plan integrated the guiding principles discussed in this book. The Malaysian client wanted American distance education, and the process of analysis and design was enthusiastically embraced and certainly maximized the Team's efforts. The following discussion highlights the gap between theory and reality, and typical challenges faced while applying the "guiding principles."

Analyze Business Needs

The analysis of business needs, which in this case are also supposed to be the needs of the nation, was carefully conducted. However, identifying primary business goals turned out to be a controversial task. The impact of outside influences on Malaysian corporations is quite stronger than that on American corporations.

The political stakes are high, and what is and what should be depends on many external issues that have nothing to do with the business need. For example, technology training is clearly an important goal for the corporation. However, when the political situation called for the integration of a national history course and an elementary school teachers training component because of a recent trend, the corporation suddenly redefined its needs. Keeping up with each passing trend hindered the development process. In addition, decision-making in Malaysia can be slow, unpredictable, and precarious.

The VU project has certainly suffered because the business needs are always fluctuating. The project team often struggled with the issue of whether or not to follow the directions of the corporation or stick to the needs already defined. There's a fine line between pleasing the client and fighting for the survival of the project.

Of course those involved in international partnerships must be at least aware of these cross-cultural business issues. However, even with access to modern communication technologies on a regular basis, cross-cultural training sessions, and many trips between the two countries, the importance of sticking to the defined requirements—with slight modifications when necessary—was never sufficiently communicated. The face-to-face interaction (that we try to convince learners is not absolutely necessary) has been the most efficient way to address the communication problems.

Identify Strategic Distance Training

The instructional analysis of the primary components of the distance learning process, which include the learner, instructor, learning environment, instructional delivery technology, and organizational culture, has probably been the most challenging for the project team.

Learners. The VU learners will have to make significant adjustments. From classroom-based to CBT, from memorization in Malay to critical thinking in English, from acquiescent to independent learners, the role of the student is clearly being redefined. To answer the concerns of the education consultants, the project team decided that the learning skills methodology course has to be a requirement.

Instructors. Identifying instructors presents other challenges: most come from a traditional background, and very few have access to technology. In addition, contrary to American practices, it is not simple to hire qualified teachers in Malaysia. There are very few available teachers, and it is not politically correct to hire ("steal") instructors who already work at a national institution.

Finding qualified instructors and training them could turn out to be a major hurdle. Not only are there very few qualified teachers, but even fewer want to be trained to teach through technology. For example, during a workshop with teachers who might be involved in the VU, one of the authors of this case study noticed that the teachers were basically pressured by their management to come to the workshop. The decision was coming from the top with no consideration for the attitudes of the employees. The Western concept of selection, hiring, and training of teachers needed to be redefined with consideration of the Malaysian situation.

Learning Environment. The existing learning environment was analyzed, and it was obvious that the transition to a virtual environment was even more complex than anticipated. In many Malaysian classrooms, students do not interact freely with each other or their instructor, and they are not encouraged to express personal opinions or even ask questions. Students occasionally work in groups to help each other memorize.

Outside the classroom students rarely socialize. Male and female students rarely socialize with each other. They appear to be quite shy and passive compared to American standards. Very few students have access to a PC. The nation debates about whether corporal punishment can or cannot be administrated by an instructor. Overall, the Malaysian environment appeared quite traditional to the American educators who were eager to show all the progress that could be accomplished through the VU, while their Malaysian counterparts were more interested in discussing how to prevent students from cheating on exams.

Instructional Delivery Technology. The learning environment and the instructional delivery technology may be influenced or even defined by the existing infrastructure. Since very few students have easy access to computers and high speed digital Internet connection lines from their home, there was talk of creating over twenty study centers. However, because of time, space, and financial constraints, that would be as impossible as actually creating a traditional university. Therefore, it was decided that enrollment had to be capped.

The solution is to have the learners spend their first year mostly at the study centers and then move on to studying from home or the office. This plan, however, may turn out to be flawed if the communication infrastructure does not change radically. While the corporation had hoped that the VU could embrace the ideal of self-paced learning or learning on demand, reality is that access is restricted in most countries by infrastructure and technical limitations.

The project team was periodically informed that if the government wanted the project to succeed, buildings would be found, and T1 lines would be available. In the meantime, the project team decided to scale back the number of students and study centers that, in turn, had marketing and financial impact.

Organizational Culture. As an extension of a corporation, the organizational culture of the VU is unique: the VU is not part of the Malaysian academic world but is not quite a business either. The Malaysian corporation developing the VU already has a vocational school and would like to apply the same organizational structure to the VU. For example, the instructors in that school have to punch time cards and cannot leave their office until five, even if they are not teaching any class. They must follow the corporate culture. The incentive to teach for the VU is minimum when potential instructors imagine spending eight hours a day in front of a terminal with neverending instructional periods and then punch out. The concepts of flexible hours, telecommuting, or even research time are not being considered.

Identify and Select Technology

The identification and selection of technology in the initial concept was left entirely to the education specialists on the project team. As discussed previously, the information technology infrastructure limited the selection of instructional technology. Nevertheless, a variety of technologies were recommended. Proposed courseware designers were to identify and select the appropriate teaching and learning tools. However, pressures to design all course materials in a computer-based format were obvious as the Malaysian corporation had given its information technology department the lead for the VU project. The American system engineers were more aware of the principles at stake, but it eventually became clear that the corporation was not interested in some technologies, regardless of their pedagogical value. Voice mail, videos, and fax, for example, were not to be included unless courseware designers could convince the corporation that any of these were absolutely necessary.

The negotiations over technology are ongoing. However, reality is that even if a variety of media is better, in countries where they are most needed they are not all available. For example, in Malaysia, phone and fax are not as reliable and as easy to acquire as one might think. On the other hand cell phones are ubiquitous. Textbooks and books in general are not in great supply, and bookstores and libraries cannot fulfill the needs of the student population. On the other hand a student is more likely to have a Pentium computer than to have ever seen a 386 PC, probably one of the most common computers on American campuses! What is low-tech and high-tech is relative.

A Look into the Future

The main issues facing the project team before the project stalled completely were the shrinking time frame for the implementation of the systems, the precarious requirements, the technology transfer, the training of the VU staff, and the unstable financial situation in Malaysia.

Many lessons have been learned and will continue to be learned throughout the development and implementation of the VU. There is a new awareness among the project team that the Western guiding principles of distance learning are loaded with cultural values. When the clients tell us they want to apply American distance education strategies, what do they really mean? As we continue to work on the VU in Malaysia and embark on other distance education projects in Southeast Asia, special attention must be given to realistic expectations for distance education in a non-Western culture.

Issues and Lessons Learned

Thus far, this case study has recounted a number of issues related to the international and multidisciplinary nature of the project team and the creation of a distance education institution. Interspersed throughout the chapter is an analysis of various problems and their underlying causes and consequences. This final section explores key issues encountered and lessons learned during the developmental process of the VU that may be applicable to other distance education projects.

What Went Wrong?

- Cross-cultural issues. Many cross-cultural issues were addressed too superficially and too late. The multicultural team was not prepared to handle the complex issues that arose throughout the course of the project.
- Time. The timeline for the VU opening was never properly addressed. Timelines were set solely by upper management and based on marketing goals rather than on education and technology development goals. The project team was constantly working under unrealistic deadlines, cutting corners, and losing time trying to explain to upper management why the timeline was unrealistic.

- Money. A lack of communication about finances—who was paying for what—at the time the project was conceived resulted in a series of misunderstandings and crises that frequently slowed down the project.
- Training. There was never a real understanding that technology integration does not replace the need for staff and training. Human resources was not the priority it should have been.
- Information sharing. The policy of sharing information only on an as-needed basis was certainly not appropriate for an educational project but imposed by the strong business culture leading the project.

All of these problems are indicative of the fact that there were two different agendas at play. Some players privately viewed the VU as a marketing tool, one that could be used to enhance the political and economic stature of the principals. Others believed based on the rhetoric of the principals that the VU was to be a model distance education institution based on methodical planning and development. The friction created between these conflicting agendas stalled the VU development.

What Went Right?

- Qualified partners. Academic institutions asked to assist with the planning and development of the VU were enthusiastic and qualified and offered their time generously. In most cases, American academic partners were open to the VU concept and saw their involvement as an opportunity to share and apply their knowledge.
- Transfer of knowledge. Initially, the Malaysians looked to American educators for guidance on planning the VU academic program. The transfer of knowledge, a stated goal of the project team, was successful as the Malaysian educators eventually took more ownership of the project and were able to mold the American concept of distance education development into a sustainable Malaysian concept.
- Phases of development. The strategy of incremental academic program development versus the "big bang" approach was eventually accepted by upper management. While the initial concept plan included several undergraduate and graduate degrees, later plans were to start by developing a few computer-based courses to be used in conjunction with other delivery modes such as video, print, and face-to-face.
- Language of instruction. While politically charged and therefore extremely controversial, the decision to use English as the language of instruction was eventually accepted at the highest level of the management team. The plan to export the instructional materials re-enforced the choice of language.

Lessons Learned

Relevance of Cross-Cultural Communication. Within a few months of working on the VU project, it became clear that when working on a virtual and internationally staffed project, coherence and understanding of goals and strategies as well as knowledge of the political/cultural contexts are more important AND more difficult to achieve than in any other project.

Significance of Internet-Based Technology. The team had to make difficult choices about which educational technologies to emphasize based on the current infrastructure and available finances. However, it now seems to be an inefficient use of resources to support modes of delivery that do not incorporate use of the Internet or other sophisticated interactive information technologies. Modes of delivery may include fax technology or video but only if they are leveraged by use of the Internet. With limited resources, distance educators need to be forward-thinking and invest time, energy, and funds into learning what works through Internet-based education services.

Key Education Issues to Address when Developing a Distance Education Institution Abroad.

- Identify and establish mechanisms for regular and substantial communication between American educators and educators from the target culture.
- Identify ways to present models and modes of distance education course materials so that the client can make informed decisions.
- Raise awareness and comfort levels among educators about the use and limitations of communication technologies.
- Raise awareness of the crucial training needs that arise when integrating technology into education.
- Raise awareness of the issues involved in the long-term sustainability of distance education programs, such as hiring qualified instructional designers and providing ongoing training to instructors and staff.
- Develop a framework to evaluate the use of technology in the target culture's education system.

An Experiment in Learning

Underlying the VU project was a fundamental belief that the latest information technologies, particularly those affording multi-direction interactivity, can be powerful tools for increasing the efficiency of the teaching and learning environment.

However, much needs to be learned about how to use these new tools to foster better learning.

In essence, the VU project was an experiment to learn when and how information technologies can best be employed by a company to answer the educational needs of its employees and the nation. The project was also an experiment to learn when and how an international and multi-disciplinary team can best perform using the latest communication tools.

In writing this chapter, the authors hope that presenting the VU project's key components, its obstacles, pitfalls, and sources of strength provides guidance to those adapting distance education and training in settings involving a broad coalition of international partners.

CHAPTER THIRTEEN

THE VALUE OF BUILDING SKILLS WITH ONLINE TECHNOLOGY: ONLINE TRAINING COSTS AND EVALUATION AT THE TEXAS NATURAL RESOURCE CONSERVATION COMMISSION

Scott Walker

The Training Academy of the Texas Natural Resource Conservation Commission (TNRCC), a state environmental regulatory agency based in Austin, Texas, develops, contracts, and delivers all aspects of in-house training for the agency. This training ranges from policy training to management training to highly specialized technical training. Of the approximately 3,000 member staff, nearly 700 are situated in fifteen regional offices around Texas. One regional office is even in another time zone and closer to the California-Arizona border than it is to the headquarters offices.

Business Problem

With employees dispersed across such a wide geographical area, equitable training delivery is difficult and costly. At the same time, travel funds consistently declined for staff to travel to headquarters to participate in training or for TNRCC trainers to travel to regional offices to deliver training. Nearly all out-of-state travel and most intra-state travel became restricted to high priority events. Training seldom falls under the category of high priority when pitted against things like hazardous waste spills and public hearings.

Traditional training delivery at the TNRCC not only fell victim to reduced travel funding as just mentioned, it has associated "soft" costs such as overtime compensation and lost work time or "windshield time" for training staff riding from one town to another. The agency reached the point where regional field inspectors were telling stories of learning about new environmental legislation and environmental management techniques from the regulated community rather than firsthand from knowledgeable sources in the agency. Likewise, some problems had been encountered along the Texas-Mexico border as related to general cultural awareness and protocol. A solution was needed to address the shortage of travel funds, reduce overtime, and to quickly provide up to date training.

First Attempt

In order to facilitate the delivery of training to regional employees, we tried a variety of options. Our initial effort in distance training was with a two-day video conference of an agency introduction class held in cooperation with a regional university's statewide video conference system. The Texas legislature had appropriated funds to the university specifically for the purpose of spawning cooperative efforts of this nature; therefore the video conference equipment and rooms were of no cost to us.

This agency introduction class was previously a classroom event in which speakers representing various parts of the agency were invited to come and present their division's functions. This was supported by a lengthy course reference manual that had details on all of the division's functions, responsibilities, publications, and contact phone numbers. The primary audience was any employee who had been with the agency less than one year. The secondary audience was any employee who wanted to know more about the functions of the agency and how it worked. Since this very successful class (more of a "dog and pony show") was only held at the agency's headquarters offices, the regional staff was ranting that it was not receiving equal training and agency information, which was true.

Owing to our inexperience with video conferencing this was the class we picked to pilot video conferencing in our agency—a monumental effort no doubt, since we had to coordinate sites across the state. We used a two-way video conference system at each of ten locations. Fifteen speakers presented over the two days. Speakers had the opportunity to use computer slide presentations and videotapes that would play directly into the system. They could also display still images, maps, diagrams, or topic outlines with a document camera. Most chose to do a lecture presentation supported by a combination of printed material or video. Since the videoconference system had voice activated cameras, participants had the opportunity to simply speak up to ask questions. However, since we delivered this class to nine university branches located near TNRCC regional offices around the state, we had to be careful not to lose control of who was speaking, lest the voice activated camera technology run rampant with too many locations trying to speak at once. To keep this control we asked each site to keep its unit muted (basically turning the microphones off) while we took questions in a round robin fashion. As you might imagine, it took a long time to address questions from so many sites, and the participants soon became frustrated by having to wait to get their chance at asking questions. Although necessary for control, having to wait to ask a question diminished the quality of interaction and ranked as the worst part of the training in our end-of-class evaluations by participants.

While the overall class was successful and useful to regional staff, the time and effort to coordinate such an event proved to be extremely time consuming for our training staff. Two members worked nearly full-time for a month to meet the demands of such an endeavor. As an example of the difficulties encountered, simply obtaining university parking permission for our regional employees and distributing university maps proved cumbersome to coordinate. Further, such efforts as coordinating nine video conference sites on separate campuses outside of our realm of control in a heavily used video conference network eventually led to the elimination of this distance training option after a second class was delivered.

Later I did research and attended demonstrations with the intention of gathering background information for the promotion of the agency procuring our own dedicated video conference system to deliver training, but the costs were considered too prohibitive by agency management at the time, and the idea was dropped.

Second Attempt

The second effort to provide distance training was through CD-ROM driven computer based training (CBT). The idea was to procure CBT and have training CDs available for check out from the agency library. The unforeseen problem was that the computers in regional offices could not properly run the CBT software without major upgrades. Fortunately, the following year's budget included enough funding to purchase high-end computers to distribute one CBT-capable computer to each of the fifteen regions. With this fortunate change, the regional offices had a better chance to obtain additional technical training in the absence of a live trainer on site.

The CBT titles we chose were off-the-shelf technical training in the areas of drinking water, wastewater, air, and municipal solid waste regulations, as well as safety training. We chose these because they fit the needs of regional staff. Moreover, national regulatory and safety training materials usually only change with legislation, thus they are not very dynamic. Likewise, most of these topics are on a national scale and do not have to be tailored to the agency. The most requested titles were those pertaining to occupational health and safety training since each year regional staff doing industrial inspections must have an eight-hour refresher in order to enter industrial sites. While CBT is a solution to distributing training state wide, it does not cover dynamic topics or agency-specific training; thus a training gap remained.

Move to the Internet

I continued to research many of the options for expanding our distance training program and continually ran into roadblocks. Video conferencing was out due to the costs involved, both in time and infrastructure. Satellite broadcasting, which was available through a local community college, was even more expensive. To put together our own satellite uplink or broadcast station, the capital costs would have run in excess of $600,000. We did have satellite broadcast receiving equipment at headquarters and at two of our larger regions, but the antennae were fixed, and we could only receive broadcasts from one source, the Air Pollution Training Institute. I checked into adjustable satellite antennae and the related equipment so the regions could tune in to other satellite broadcasts, but the cost was over $5,000 for each of the fifteen regions. This did not include the cost of the actual broadcast subscriptions themselves, some of which cost over $400 per event for specialized technical training or proprietary management training.

As the agency moved toward Internet and intranet use, I started looking at pre-packaged web-based training (WBT) as a potential option for delivering training to our regional offices. As it turned out, WBT amounted to nothing more than CBT delivered via the World Wide Web. Most of this training was poorly developed, yet developers were touting it as the latest revolution in training delivery. I found little use for WBT in the TNRCC.

As the Internet became more popular in the media, employees were continually coming to me looking for classes on using the Internet and browser technology to aid them in their work. At the time only the agency's "electronic elite" knew how to send an email outside the agency or gather information from what was then an infant World Wide Web. At the same time staff needed to be aware of basic Internet etiquette and the new agency Internet-use policy because using the Internet at work was almost taboo for staff and rumors about using the Web and getting fired were running amuck. Managers were restricting access due to horror stories of "surfing" the net during work hours and great myths of pornography at every turn of a web page. A basic training to dispel Internet legends, while aiding staff in using the Internet for work, was overdue. I also saw it as an opportunity to deliver facilitated training to regional employees if I could just sell it to the management.

In consideration of the agency's environment of hesitation at anything Internet related, I needed to do more than just sell Internet-facilitated training. I needed to document the training needs in order to justify developing training on using the Internet for work. I suddenly received a request from my management that the agency needed to have training on using the Internet right away. They wanted a classroom type of workshop, without computers, so large numbers of people could quickly be trained. This was more a political move and knee-jerk reaction on the part of agency management, but it set me up to pursue the Internet as a training delivery medium. In trying to stick as close to the ISD (Integrated System Design) model as possible, I developed a five-question survey regarding Internet training needs, objectives of a potential training, and related cost factors. I sent the survey via email to a sample of agency section managers and all regional managers. The survey yielded a 31 percent response rate, which immediately indicated a desire on the part of managers to have basic Internet training made available. The survey suggested that 87 percent of managers wanted their staffs to learn to use the Internet, but moreover be familiar with associated policies in such a tightly controlled work environment.

As a result of the survey I contracted with a local computer-training vendor to deliver a basic Internet seminar for staff and managers. Unfortunately, we were limited to a prepackaged training that did not include any actual use of the Internet, only lecture and demonstration with overhead transparencies. Additionally, the training did not cover agency-specific policy regarding web and Internet email use, nor did it overcome the travel barrier for regional staff.

Online Training: Net Tools for Work

To solve the problem of delivering Internet training to the regions, I began the development of the first Internet-based course in the history of the state of Texas. "Online Training: Net Tools for Work" was designed to be delivered 100 percent over the Internet and to test delivering training to regional offices. Since the target audience had little if any experience with the Internet, the training had to start small and expand to the use of listservers, telnet, file transfer protocol, browsers, associated plug ins, and more. Unlike the previous Internet workshop I contracted out in response to my manager's requests, the target audience for this was our staff in regional offices.

The broad training objectives for "Online Training: Net Tools for Work" were to (a) help participants understand the structure of the Internet, (b) explain the acronyms and abbreviations used when referring to the Internet, (c) explain and practice using a browser, file transfer protocol, telnet, and so on, (d) show participants how they could use the Internet for work, and (e) allow participants to experience using the Internet and their newly acquired skills. These objectives were designed to be met at the participants' own pace, at their convenience within a given time frame, at home or at work, without any travel costs, and without additional cost to the agency.

The training was scheduled for a five-week duration. All of the materials for the training were available on the web. The training was also developed and facilitated by one person in a short period of time. No physical training facilities were required for the training nor was any travel. The class was advertised over the agency's email system, and the limited number of participants were sent instructions on how to subscribe to the agency's email distribution list, often referred to as a list or listserv. From my email I could see who successfully subscribed to the list since I was the list moderator. Upon everyone's subscription, I sent the first assignment via the list. After the participants became familiar with the email system, we moved on to the web. I continued to make assignments through the list, but the sources of information participants needed to complete the assignments were on the web. As an example, one of the first assignments was to learn to search the web. I pointed the class to web pages that explained how to search and how to find web directories. The participants then replied with the web addresses of sites they deemed useful for their work. I could randomly check these addresses, or URLs, to be sure they were successfully finding web sites. At the pace of the participants yet within a given time frame, we moved on to other topics such as downloading and installing the latest beta version of a browser, posting files to the agency's FTP site, and so on.

Yet since this was a pilot class for what was considered an unconventional method of delivery for a conservative state institution, I needed to document the benefits and costs, as well as the ability to transfer knowledge and information via the Internet to demonstrate that this was a viable method of training delivery. I started the evaluation from the very beginning of the training, while an online colleague from Australia evaluated my evaluation techniques as part of her doctoral program on open and distance learning.

Evaluation Strategy and Analysis

I evaluated the class on five levels. Levels one through four were based on Kirkpatrick's classification of training evaluation (Phillips, 1991). Level five was an analysis of the return on investment of the training. One step above a cost-benefit analysis, the return on investment quantifies how much an institution actually gains out of a training event.

Although the evaluation techniques presented in this case study are specific to an online training on the topic of using the Internet, other trainers could conduct a similar evaluation on a different training topic by applying these techniques and methods. I would not recommend doing five levels of evaluation for every training class you produce. Rather I would recommend going this distance for each new type of training delivery medium adopted or for each new course type adopted (for example, technical, personnel, management, and so on). Likewise, institutions may find a level one to level five evaluation useful to evaluate training over time.

Level-One Evaluation

This was an evaluation of the participant's reaction to the class. This type of evaluation is commonly seen in training and education environments. In this case I simply sent our standard training evaluation form by email at the end of class and asked participants to return it by email. In order to achieve 100 percent compliance, I did not distribute course completion certificates until I received a completed evaluation.

The following results are the averages from the level-one evaluation. This format could be modified and applied in many situations to aid a course facilitator in learning about the participant's perceptions and opinions of a class. The level-one evaluation results are summarized in Exhibit 13.1.

This form of evaluation should be used for each presentation of an online training as a minimum. While the information does not objectively measure any learning, class improvements can be made for future delivery of similar training based on the participant's input.

Level-Two Evaluation

This is an evaluation of the participant's learning of principles, facts, techniques, and skills as presented in the training. Several different measures can be used online at this evaluation level including tests, skill practice, and simulations. In this

EXHIBIT 13.1. LEVEL-ONE EVALUATION RESULTS.

The course content satisfied my expectations.
<u>17%</u> Strongly agree   <u>83%</u> Agree   _____ Disagree   _____ Strongly disagree

The class examples, activities, or demonstrations helped me to learn.
<u>33%</u> Strongly agree   <u>67%</u> Agree   _____ Disagree   _____ Strongly disagree

The course materials were useful.
<u>20%</u> Strongly agree   <u>80%</u> Agree   _____ Disagree   _____ Strongly disagree

The audio/visual aids enhanced the course.
—— Strongly agree   <u>100%</u> Agree   _____ Disagree   _____ Strongly disagree

The trainer(s) seemed knowledgeable about the topics.
<u>83%</u> Strongly agree   <u>17%</u> Agree   _____ Disagree   _____ Strongly disagree

The trainer(s) encouraged participation, provided clear feedback, and summarized the main points.
<u>83%</u> Strongly agree   <u>17%</u> Agree   _____ Disagree   _____ Strongly disagree

The topics presented in this course will help me do my job.
<u>67%</u> Strongly agree   <u>33%</u> Agree   _____ Disagree   _____ Strongly disagree

The course improved my skills and knowledge.
<u>67%</u> Strongly agree   <u>33%</u> Agree   _____ Disagree   _____ Strongly disagree

Overall, I was satisfied with this course.
<u>50%</u> Very satisfied   <u>50%</u> Satisfied   _____ Unsatisfied   _____ Very unsatisfied

online training the participants practiced several skills such as searching the web, downloading helper applications, retrieving files from an FTP site, and so on. I then evaluated the products they produced as a result. For example, I would assign participants different files to retrieve from our FTP site. They would then have to send me an email message with the first sentence of the word processing file they were assigned. In the following example I asked the class to report back with a list of web addresses they found in a search, similar to the way your high school math teacher had you "show your work" on a quiz or assignment. Having participants show me where they had been on the web demonstrated their ability to actually find a site of interest by searching. The level-two evaluation activity is presented in Exhibit 13.2. In the preceding activity I simply checked the email list to see if the participants completed the activity. I could then respond to any problems they encountered by direct email and evaluate where the participant stood in relation to the other participants and his or her own progress. The "five-minute paper" helped me find the weak spots between my facilitation and the participant's understanding of concepts.

EXHIBIT 13.2.   LEVEL-TWO EVALUATION.

Use one of the search engines or directories found at the web address above to find additional web sites related to your job. When you are done, do the following:

1) Take five minutes to write your thoughts on the class so far. Include any problems you faced in your web search and how you overcame those problems. Note any outstanding problems you could not overcome.

2) Write the URLs of at least five web sites you found in this activity. Please include a brief (one line) explanation of these new site(s).

3) Post the above to the discussion list with the subject "Activity Three."

In this online training each participant completed the skills outlined in each activity at 100 percent of what I expected. I kept track of who completed the activities and the completion dates in a simple chart similar to a grade book.

Level-Three Evaluation

This is an evaluation of the participant's increase in skills on the job as a result of the training. Since the whole point to training is to improve skills or knowledge related to a job or task, this is an important evaluation step. However, many training events are not designed to capture this type of information. At this level some forethought must go into the design and sequence of the training event, and a method must be adopted to capture the information in a useable fashion.

An improvement in skills can be measured with before and after skill or knowledge comparisons: observations from supervisors, peers, subordinates; statistical comparisons; and long-range follow up. To evaluate at this level I made before and after comparisons based on the participants' own comments. At the onset of the class I asked participants to post an email introduction of themselves as the first activity. I asked that they answer certain questions I had preselected as evaluation points and also asked them to write anything additional they thought might be important by way of introducing themselves. This activity actually served two purposes. First it helped build a sense of community and collaboration among the class participants so they could learn from one another. This set the stage for an activity to come later in the class in which participants would have to pick partners and work together. Second, I could get an idea of where each person stood related to the course objectives. The questions I asked were not asked directly in the context of an evaluation or quiz. Rather, I "disguised" the evaluation as a simple introduction and was later able to compare their answers to the level of learning each achieved at the end of class.

Some of the questions I asked in the introduction included the following: What is your current level of Internet use? Have you ever used a listserver, FTP, browser, Telnet, and so on? I asked questions related to their preclass knowledge of the Internet and computer competence. Finally, this exercise allowed me to find out what types of computers the participants were using, which is essential when you are trying to find certain applications across platforms such as Macintosh, Windows, and UNIX. Now it would help to know which version of Windows a participant has, thus helping the facilitator guide participants through setting up freeware, viewers, or helper applications. Moreover, this technique could be applied to any online training if a facilitator were to treat participants' introductions of themselves as a structured activity that is actually a camouflaged pretest.

The advantage to online training is that all discussion traffic between participants and facilitator is electronic. One can easily capture and store introductions until the end of class for a comparative analysis. Selected responses to participant's introductions, labeled "before," and comparisons after class and how I used them are presented in Exhibit 13.3.

Applied in a different training situation, the training facilitator should conceive of questions related to the skill or knowledge set she or he wants to impart to the participants or have them learn on their own, then ask directly or watch for clues on how participants apply those skills. An advantage to an online training that is conducted over several weeks, such as this course, is that new skills can be applied immediately at work and reported back before the class is over. Such information is not easy to capture in a one-day classroom situation when the instructor never sees the participants again.

To take this type of evaluation to a higher level, a facilitator could follow up several weeks or months later with the participants or participants' supervisors with comparative questions designed to measure on-the-job application of skills and knowledge. A qualitative presentation of the increase in on-the-job tasks could then be made for the purpose of reporting the value of the online class to the organization or institution.

Level-Four Evaluation

This is an evaluation of the results of the training program in regard to organizational improvement. Organizational improvement can be measured in several ways, including cost savings, work output improvement, and quality changes. In the case of this training, the evaluation results were presented three ways: (a) travel savings, (b) expected participant time savings, and (c) course development/administration time and cost savings.

EXHIBIT 13.3.   LEVEL-THREE EVALUATION.

Before – "I am moderately familiar with the Internet. I use it at work regularly and my computer is a . . ."

After – This participant ended up instructing other employees in Internet usage in the Houston regional office. I found this out through day-to-day correspondence with the participant and noted it in his records.

Before – This participant had no knowledge of setting up an Internet e-mail list.

After – He set up his own e-mail list sharing information between hazardous waste spill coordinators throughout Texas. He also taught a coworker how to set up a list. This comparison demonstrated an increase in on the job skills directly related to the training.

Before – "My familiarity with the WWW is extremely limited."

After – This participant expected to save about six hours a week because of new knowledge of the Internet and because his job required accessing data that he discovered available on the web. Previously he had to use the library. Although this expectation in time savings is high, he also expected to "be able to keep up with the latest developments in [his] career field" of State and Federal environmental regulations.

Before – "I occasionally access the Internet at work using Netscape."

After – This participant later reported being able to gather more information at her desk before conducting a field investigation. She was also able to access regulations needed for work without having to spend time in a library.

Before – "From time to time I need to retrieve information [from the web] for purchasing purposes. And knowing the correct way of accessing the information, would make my job a lot easier."

After – This participant was later able to download purchasing information and was able to locate landowner data for field investigations by using the Internet.

Travel Savings

Since online training goes to the participant and the participant can stay at his or her desk to complete the training, the cost of travel by the regional employees was eliminated. I gathered the following data from participants at the end of the training, which was based on the best information available.

For an equivalent face-to-face class of sixteen hours, the total travel cost for eight participants would have been $4,596, had they traveled from their regional offices to a training site in the capital. I based this travel estimate on the participants' estimates of their potential overnight hotel and other expense rates, automobile fuel or airfare expenses, compensatory time converted to dollars per hour, and time away from the office while in transit converted to dollars per hour. Since some of this information is sensitive I had the participants send information related to salaries and costs directly to my private email so no one would hesitate to divulge pay levels. Likewise, I had initially made it explicitly clear in the advertisement of this class that it was a pilot training and the participants would be "guinea pigs," so to speak. I brought this up again as I asked them to give me information that would lead to figuring out their earnings.

Participants' Time Savings

Since the training facilitated the learning of new skills for using new technological tools, I asked the participants to estimate how much time they thought they could potentially save in the future due to their newly acquired skills. Although a study of how much time each participant actually saved due to using the Internet would be ideal, it was not feasible due to time and budget constraints. The evaluation method I used here was the best method available given the circumstances.

The participant's estimated average potential time savings came to 4.6 hours per week. I found this estimate to be a bit extraordinary, so I arbitrarily reduced it to 1.5 hours per week (two-thirds less) to be on the conservative side. I then converted this to dollars based on the salary and benefit data I acquired from the participants. The adjusted average savings came to $120 per week per participant. Although a rough and difficult-to-quantify estimate, it was an estimate nonetheless on potential time savings converted to a hard currency figure that is easily understood by managers or anyone needing this level of evaluation.

Development Time Savings

Since "Online Training: Net Tools for Work" was conducted solely via the Internet, the course materials already existed on the web, and training room space was not used. I compared the costs of this class with other classes I facilitated near this same time period, as well as the comparable face-to-face Internet class previously held.

I should note here the importance of keeping data related to training development time and costs, administration, and other descriptive statistics related to your training if you intend to evaluate in such a manner. If this data were not captured for other training events the training academy previously held, a comparison could not be made, thus rendering this powerful evaluation technique useless. It may be the case that you will have to go through several months of previous training information to put this type of data together.

The total cost of this class was $301 with a start to delivery time of forty-eight days, which included me working on other projects simultaneously as I developed the class. A similar but face-to-face class on the topic of the Internet cost

$2,312 per class and took me sixty-four days from assignment to delivery due to state bid procedures. Another sixteen-hour specialized technical training class I contracted for cost over $10,500 and took fifty-six days to implement and deliver due to contract writing and managing. Finally, another sixteen-hour classroom class cost $4,325 and took forty-nine days from start to delivery. Put in this context alone, the cost evaluation of this particular training delivery begins to show promise as a viable training option.

Return on Investment (Level Five Evaluation)

The Return on Investment (ROI) for a training program is based on the benefit-cost of the program and the net cost of the program divided by the cost. I have outlined a description of the benefit-cost and ROI for this class.

Benefit/Cost

The totals from these tables were used to figure a benefit-cost ratio for this training, where the benefit figure is divided by the cost.

TABLE 13.1. TRAINING BENEFITS.

Benefits	
Travel cost saved	$4596
Estimated participant time savings over a one-month period	$4320
Room use cost saved	$300
Facilitation expenses & materials cost saved	$1362
Development & contracting cost saved	$651
Total	$11,229

TABLE 13.2. TRAINING COSTS.

Costs	
Development & presentation	$300
Participants' computers amortized (estimated)	$30
Facilitator's computer amortized (estimated)	$4
Internet connection total	$4
Participants' time converted to dollars	$2660
Total	$2998

EXHIBIT 13.4.   BENEFIT/COST RATIO.

$$\frac{\text{Benefit}}{\text{Cost}} = \frac{\$11{,}229}{\$2998} = 3.75{:}1$$

EXHIBIT 13.5.   RETURN ON INVESTMENT

$$\text{ROI} = \frac{\text{Net Benefits}}{\text{Cost}} = \frac{\$8231}{\$2998} = 275\%$$

The ROI is the difference between the benefit-cost (net benefit), divided by the total cost.

Thus, by presenting "Online Training: Net Tools for Work" the Texas Natural Resource Conservation Commission gained benefits of more than twice the total outlay for the training. Additionally, each time this training is presented in the future, the agency will receive the same benefit, but the cost of the training will be reduced due to the lack of development time, bringing the potential ROI up to 313 percent.

Intangible benefits should also be taken into consideration at this level of evaluation, but they may be difficult to quantify. I suggest noting the intangibles in an evaluation report and leaving it at that. However, if you can find a way to attach a dollar figure to the intangible, do so. The intangible benefits directly related to this online training could include the following:

- Promotion of training interdependencies among peers due to the collaborative nature of the training.
- Opportunity for learning-on-demand, often referred to as just-in-time training.
- Sharing of expertise among individuals who would not normally have contact with one another.
- Reduction between the perceived division of learning and working.
- Increase in technological awareness and use of technological tools.
- A single computer platform is not required (the Internet works interchangeably with Macs, Windows, and UNIX computers).
- Participants could learn at their own pace and skip material they already know; thus the training is more individualized and job related, leading to participant satisfaction.

- Course materials can be reviewed at any time since they were all found on the Internet.
- Course updates, modifications, or adaptations can be made quickly by the facilitator.

Conclusion

This evaluation process was followed to assess if online or web-based training would be a viable option for the Texas Natural Resource Conservation Commission. The evaluation itself took a significant amount of time yet validated the concept of using the Internet in a government workplace to deliver training. This depth of evaluation should not by any means be performed for each class or course developed. Again, I suggest any new method of distance training delivery be evaluated as such and possibly be compared to other methods of distance training delivery.

I should also note that online training development takes some specialization in a trainer's skills. It may be the case that someone could develop online training at a reasonable cost yet be only marginally effective in transferring skills or knowledge in this medium. In the case of the TNRCC Training Academy, although the class presented here was extremely successful and was delivered four times, much of the agency's staff was not ready for such an extreme change in training delivery methodology.

However, two other online courses on different topics did follow this Internet class. They were "Working on Texas/Mexico Border Issues" and "How to Develop On-the-Job Training." The audience for these two courses was limited, so they too were short-lived. However, they did meet the specific needs of regional staff located across the state, which was the intended outcome of our online training effort.

Overall, what we learned is that many potential solutions are available for delivering training to regional offices to eliminate travel costs, yet each training topic is different, and the appropriate distance training method and media must be appropriately selected. In the case of technical training, video conferencing is difficult over numerous sites. At the same time it is expensive and time consuming to develop, especially when you are dependent upon an established university video conference network. Computer based training (CBT) works well for standardized subject matter that is not too susceptible to change, such as occupational safety training. However, the hardware must be available in each remote location. Nowadays, off-the-shelf computers are sufficient for most CBT yet must be available to the training audience. Prepackaged web-based training has the same limitations as CBT; it is only delivered in a different manner. Facilitated training over the

Internet can work as a solution to dynamic or agency- or institution-specific training yet may be met with some skepticism. At the same time, proactive and planned evaluation can help establish Internet-based training as a viable distance training method that saves time and money, as well as addressing just-in-time training needs.

Technical Information

"Online Training: Net Tools for Work" was initially delivered using an email list server that existed within the agency's standard email software and with a newsgroup set up by our computer staff. The main concern with this medium was trying to help participants organize their activities (lessons) in a useful manner. Email archiving soon became a lesson in itself after I found that most of the participants did not know how to fully utilize our email system. Likewise, email lists do not provide any sense of conversational flow. For example, if I send a message to the list, then someone else sends another message on a different topic, then people start replying, the original message(s) can get lost in the deluge of email replies. The newsgroup helped add some structure and flow to the activities and conversations, yet there was the absence of being able to control the structure from the facilitator's point of view because you are dependent upon the participant to place his or her reply message in the right place, rather than start a new "conversation."

This situation of class structure was overcome in the later classes by the use of a web-based conference on the agency's web server. The conference software we used was a freeware UNIX-based conference system by the name of COW (Conferencing on the Web). This type of web-based interface is relatively easy to operate, as the course facilitator can establish a hierarchy of activities, post messages, receive messages, set up classes, remove messages, and more. The interface is through a web browser once the UNIX implementation has been made. A limited knowledge of HTML is useful but not required for such a conference.

We also practiced using a CGI-script (Common Gateway Interface) "whiteboard" for some lessons, but the participants preferred the web-based conference. Again, the structure of messages and replies was lost, as the whiteboard structure was very similar to that of a newsgroup. Nonetheless, each time I delivered this class it was done using an asynchronous method of Internet communication. I found the available synchronous delivery options such as web chat boards, MUDs (Multiple User Domains), and IRCs (Internet Relay Chat) to be considered "playing" by the participants. Likewise, they had to work out specific times to meet if they wanted to conduct business. If they wanted to discuss something in real-time they felt they could use the POTS (Plain Old Telephone System) and simply make a phone call or leave a voice mail message. So, I dropped the synchronous media from the class until desktop videoconferencing becomes the norm.

CHAPTER FOURTEEN

BUILDING INTRANET COURSEWARE USING MULTI-DISCIPLINARY TEAMS: THE STORY OF QUANTUM SOLUTIONS, INC. AND COLUMBIA/HCA HEALTHCARE CORPORATION

Ann D. Yakimovicz

What do people with education and work experience in journalism, art history, music, English as a second language, computer science, landscape architecture, and instructional design have in common? We were the IDL (Interactive Distance Learning) team, the group that built courseware for delivery on the corporate intranet of Columbia/HCA Healthcare Corporation, the largest healthcare delivery system in the United States.

Using multi-disciplinary teams to design and deliver products has become the normal practice in many work environments, from manufacturing to professional services. Typically, the team consists of people with different areas of expertise working together to develop products and services more rapidly and competitively than if each discipline was involved sequentially to design, develop, and market the product. However, this multi-disciplinary approach is new to the training arena, especially since the skills needed to effectively work in web-based courseware development are still emerging. Formal education and research to support these skills has not yet become a discipline.

One such multi-disciplinary group in a small company began developing web-based training (WBT) courseware in Austin, Texas, in 1995 and continued after the company was purchased by a Fortune 40 company in 1996. The ever-changing technology on the web coupled with the shifting organizational culture caused us to critically consider the necessary skills and roles needed for web-based development.

Background

First, let's take a brief look at the company and its mission and how that affected the role of the IDL team.

The Quantum Beginning

The IDL team began in the fall of 1995 when Quantum Solutions, Inc. hired me as a instructional designer to build the first of a series of courses for hospital executives to be offered for sale on Quantum's web site. Quantum was a management consulting firm specializing in health care. The company culture was one of dialogue, in which every activity and product was discussed and debated at length by everyone in the company before being acted upon. The company had developed two systems thinking models for use in dialogue with its clients, the Tetrahedron and Systems Leverage, and used both models internally as well.

Initially Quantum planned for courses to be developed in partnership with several state hospital associations. The associations would provide needs assessment, assist with pilot testing, and market to their members; Quantum would provide content, course development, and web site administration. The vision was for course products to be modeled on problem-based learning, a discovery learning model composed of real-life problems, small group learning, and a tutorial dialogue used with some success in medicine and dentistry for over twenty-five years, most notably at McMaster University Medical School in Toronto, Canada.

The Situation at Columbia

In mid-1996, Quantum was purchased by Columbia/HCA Healthcare Corporation, a Fortune 40 company and one of the largest employers in the United States. With the purchase by Columbia, the IDL team shifted focus. Now we needed to develop courseware targeted at specific performance improvement needs in the organization. Quantum became Columbia Planning, Education, and Consulting, with responsibility at the corporate level for organizational transformation. To do that we used a two-part approach for education and training: (a) content that encouraged the use of systems thinking for innovating healthcare and (b) learning technology to unite an organization of 285,000 people stretched all across the United States in a conglomeration of 347 hospitals, 118 ambulatory surgery centers, 530 homecare agencies, and various ancillary services.

The learning needs in such an organization were enormous. While individual hospitals continued to provide health and safety training, patient education, and staff development, more was needed. Groups of hospitals in regions and markets were working together to provide a broad range of patient services, looking for training in new ways of working together. Other corporate departments were building common systems for behind-the-scenes hospital functions—food services, supplies, billing and collections, and medical records—and wanted training assistance.

Technology needs were also large. Because the company had experienced widespread growth in a short period through acquisition, there was limited consistency in the technology. Various systems for communication and data collection and transfer were acquired along with the hospital facilities. Unlike manufacturing and high-tech industries, health care has concentrated on technology investments to support physicians' delivery of quality services rather than on infrastructure. Thus, the IDL team faced a very different environment as we began to work as a corporate department within Columbia/HCA Healthcare Corporation: an organizational change strategy, more product and process stakeholders, and limitations in technology.

Building a Courseware Development Team

By the time I arrived at Quantum Solutions in 1995, an initial course topic had been chosen, and content was being developed by independent experts with backgrounds in health care administration from the University of Houston Clear Lake. The staff consisted of a project manager coordinating the work of the experts, two administrative assistants, and a computer programmer, each of whom was learning some HTML.

My first task was to develop an instructional design model that could adapt the problem-based learning approach to the web, reframing the small group and tutor roles. To help the company understand concepts such as chunking content and allowing users to navigate in more than one way through a hypermedia learning environment, I filled the walls of my office with mind maps and Post-It™ notes in every color of the rainbow. In the usual Quantum way, these models were discussed, dissected, debated, and analyzed. Everyone on the team had a chance to learn more about instructional design theory, consider the model in connection with his or her personal learning experiences, and provide input into the design.

The final model for the first series of courses, Practice-Based Self-Managed Learning, resulted. Given the limited web experience of the team (and indeed most people in 1995), the model was text-based, starting with a hospital problem to be solved by the learner accompanied by realistic tables and charts and supported by theoretical text. The model concluded with a systems thinking analysis of the problem, learner dialoguing with a "canned" expert. Using this model, we reworked the content, translated material to HTML, added programming for course registration, pre-tests and post-tests, checked the on-screen behavior of the course in multiple browsers, hired graphic artists to design computer-generated icons and banners, and were ready for our first "beta" testing with real users in mid-December 1995.

Early Lessons Learned

Our own systems thinking models were perfect for reviewing our work on the first course. We used an ad hoc approach with team meetings and email and memos rather than a formal evaluation process. So what did we learn about our own work in developing the first course?

- We were continually stumped by the technology and our production skills. Web development was limited in 1995. Attempts to include the amount of interaction and feedback found in computer-based training failed because we could not produce it using simple HTML and CGI scripting.
- The production team really was learning "on-the-job." With a team working impossible hours building HTML skills to produce the courseware, I deliberately simplified the instructional design in order to meet the committed deadline for testing the product.
- Third, team members became more and more aware that they had not worked together as a team before. Two of the four people directly involved with creating the product reported to different managers. Both administrative assistants had word processing, receptionist, and presentation development responsibilities in addition to the project; the programmer also had responsibility for administration of the company web site. In fact, only the instructional designer was assigned full-time to the project.

What did we discover in the early beta testing with users? Access, skills, and tools were the limiting factors.

- Some parts of the market were not yet ready for online learning. Many of our target audience in health care did not have Internet access at home; hospitals were just beginning to get connected.

- Health care executives were not comfortable working with computers; they had few skills using keyboards and a mouse.
- And even though Netscape was releasing its 2.0 version of the Navigator browser, learners were getting online with a variety of very limited tools, which caused our courseware to behave differently. Beta testers found problems with the password-protected course access, with the operation of our icons, and with the presentation of on-screen colors in different monitors.

First Expansion of the Team

Learning these lessons, we made adjustments to the courseware. We also needed additional staff, including telephone customer service, to answer learner questions about courseware and to provide help desk support for tools learners were using. We discovered a real need for greater understanding of how learners, especially non-technical people and skilled professionals, would use the computer, as well as a need for stronger programming skills. What was most important for the team, however, was an ability to communicate, to share information in such a way that listeners from other disciplines really understood and could build, expand, and create from this understanding. For example, telephone customer support could provide valuable insights from users about confusing instructions in the password assignment process. To develop effective courseware, no team member needed to have all the answers, but we needed to consider a substantial range of issues important for end-user success. Communicating well with each other was the best way to do that.

We began recruiting in the spring of 1996, finding that the number of people with basic web development skills and knowledge of HTML was increasing. By the time the company was purchased by Columbia/HCA Healthcare Corporation six months later, we had hired two additional HTML writers and a customer service representative, and we had developed substantial relationships with independent graphics and instructional design consultants working in web media.

The Courseware Development Process

To build a web-based course when all of the decisions about the product from topic to subject expertise to marketing approach are made within a tightly knit group of thirty people takes one process. To build the same course as a small team within a 285,000-employee organization is something else entirely! The course development process had to shift quickly once we became part of a larger organization. We needed to change our approach to content development, to technology, and to teamwork.

Content and Organizational Strategy

Perhaps the first area in which we noticed a change was in the development of content. Columbia had an Education Task Force that investigated training needs in eight broad areas identified as key leverage points for company improvement. As we moved forward with continued courseware development, these training needs were used to determine course topics. In addition, corporate sponsors were identified. A sponsoring department had responsibility for planning and providing opportunities for improvement within a particular set of hospital processes. For example, one sponsoring department was Operations Support, Business Office, which directed overall company efforts to standardize admissions, billing, collections, and business office management for the hospitals.

Content Sponsorship and Stakeholders

For new courseware, we began a different way of working in content development. For step one, a project lead with health care experience and a project lead with an instructional design background met with the appropriate managers in a sponsoring department to detail each course. During several meetings, the day-to-day contacts were identified; clear learning objectives were created; specific subject matter experts were assigned to the project; and timelines were developed. We obtained agreement from the sponsors at each stage of the process, and we began documenting each project in a project management process heretofore omitted.

Step two was the actual development of content. The subject matter experts wrote the first several drafts for review by the sponsors and their internal oversight committees of experienced field staff or stakeholders. For example, content for a health information management course was reviewed by both corporate staff and a content committee with broad representation at the division and local levels in the company. The instructional designer also participated in the content development efforts to ensure that the content mapped to the learning objectives.

Once content was available and acceptable, the instructional designers could go to work creating the course materials. At this stage the content was chunked into manageable learning activities, along with graphics and other illustrations which were provided by the stakeholders. At the same time the production team began creating possible screen designs for sponsor review. The project leads had responsibility for communicating progress to the sponsors, especially during production when nothing visible seems to be happening.

The next opportunity for sponsor input came in preparation of the testing for the courses. While the Columbia network had a sophisticated database adjunct to the intranet server, not every sponsoring department selected to test in the same way. One course was designed to introduce employees to the new discrimination skills they would need when using electronic medical records, so ability to use online searching and reference materials was an important goal rather than specific scores. Another course was designed to test incrementally, following each module, with scores reported to the supervisor for ongoing coaching. Test design, operation, and review was a stakeholder function. In addition, sponsors worked with Human Resources to determine how employee records would be managed at the hospital level.

Sponsors also participated in the courseware piloting and roll-out process. Alpha testing was mainly for instructional design and online functionality, using a peer review and a user think-aloud check. At this point, the course was still on our server in Austin, and we could assign limited access for sponsors to take their first look at the course online. Following the alpha testing the course was moved to the Nashville server for beta testing. At this point, sponsors were highly active in the process, identifying groups or regions where volunteers could be gathered for testing, introducing the course at a test site, and handling field questions about the intent of the education or training intervention. Once the courseware was ready for roll-out, sponsors again took the lead to market the course, writing notices for the company newsletters, presenting demonstrations to senior management, encouraging employees to enroll in the course, and mailing completion certificates and continuing education unit awards to those who completed the course.

The Information Technology Connection

Besides corporate sponsorship, the Information Services Department was the other critical connection for achieving successful courseware development within Columbia. At the same time that we were creating courseware, an intranet development team of people from software technology, network security, distributed systems, interactive marketing, and other areas began to meet to build intranet use. The IDL team participated in weekly conference calls with this intranet team as we discussed both planning issues that would affect future courseware and handled troubleshooting of daily operations.

Courseware does not work independently of the other information systems in this environment. Collection of test scores and transfer to the database for reporting may seem simple, for example. However, questions persist about how many employees may have records stored, for how long, and what access and reporting needs influence the size and type of database storage system, departmental budgets and resources requirements for management and maintenance.

At Columbia, one vital connection was the established link between Information Services in Nashville and the Directors of Information Services at the Division and hospital levels. The field people were directly responsible for installing the network connections, computers, and browsers that allowed employees to access the intranet. Our ongoing communication with this group allowed us to learn the status of the intranet company-wide, to plan more effectively for pilot testing sites, and to set acceptable roll-out dates and locations. We could also share future plans for target audiences of employees so that computer installation could be budgeted and could occur in advance of course demands.

This established connection with Information Services is a crucial factor in making smooth transitions from one hardware or software system to another. This occurred most recently in the spring of 1997, when Columbia moved from Netscape Navigator as the suggested browser standard to Microsoft Internet Explorer as the required standard and from a UNIX-based to an NT-based operating system for the intranet.

By the time Information Services decided to make the switch, we had seen more than 5,000 employees take our courses on Koala, averaging 25–30 percent of the intranet usage. We could track access times, peak loads, and types of systems in use. And, we had some good anecdotal evidence about how employees were using the browsers and network access. With this information, we developed a plan for minimal interruption of service to existing courses and for a rapid shift to the new development platform. We shifted time frames for development of several courses so that they would be completed only for delivery on the new operating system.

A New Day for Teams

As Quantum Solutions, we had a very loosely constructed team with the entire company having input into our projects. As part of Columbia/HCA this was no longer true. Many of our fellow employees traveled most of the time with little opportunity to participate in dialogue about courseware in the way they had previously. The IDL team, at that time with six people under twenty-six years of age, missed the company input.

As we discussed what was happening, we recognized we needed to become more self-reliant as a team within the old Quantum structure, but we also needed to reach out. We identified several new roles within the team: project and client management, internal marketing, instructional systems design, and quality control.

First, we needed to educate our partners about courseware development processes. Our department within Columbia was considered a revenue center, which meant that we needed to market our services, create demand, and find other departments that could support development of a course within their budgets. We had begun establishing relationships with some departments even before Quantum's purchase by Columbia. So we needed to make sure that those internal customers were happy. And we wanted to change our internal approach, too. Being part of a specific organization meant we could target performance improvement. To do that well, we wanted to use the Instructional Systems Design (ISD) process to identify training needs, develop measurable learning objectives, and write content mapped to those objectives with the active participation of sponsors and stakeholders. On a temporary basis, we expanded by using outside consultants to fill some of these new staffing needs. Meanwhile, technological issues and quality control moved to the forefront.

Developing on an Intranet

With the purchase by Columbia/HCA, we faced a new issue—developing for delivery on an intranet, the web-like delivery system which operates on a limited-access system within a company, rather than for delivery on our own web-connected server. Columbia's intranet, called Koala, was in the beginning stages of development at the time of Quantum's purchase with an "official" roll out in the summer of 1996.

In fact, one of the first activities put online was the Quantum course Leading the Transition to Integrated Healthcare Delivery, our first course as adapted for Columbia. Most of our Columbia work on this course consisted of changes to the content, developing problems simulations which were more typical of hospitals in the Columbia health care systems rather than independent facilities. Because we had been using a UNIX-based system for courseware delivery, and this was also the Columbia approach, we made only minor technology changes to the courseware.

We discovered that working internally made one part of the job easier. Columbia had decided to use one browser, Netscape Navigator, as the company standard, which solved many of our early problems with tools, making screen appearance more controllable. Many other changes needed to be made in how we worked with technology though.

We found that the development process needed to be altered, for reasons of location and security. Columbia's corporate headquarters and the intranet server were in Nashville, Tennessee, while we remained in Quantum's location in Austin, Texas. This meant preparing course files and testing them could be accomplished in Austin. However, we needed to move courses using ftp (File Transfer Protocol) to Nashville via T1 line.

In addition, the courses used C programming for more complex operations such as registration, calculation of test scores, and collection of courseware management data for transfer to a database. This program code is compiled or translated into machine language in slightly different ways depending on the operating system. While we were all working in UNIX, variations in UNIX abounded, and the Austin and Nashville servers used two slightly different operating systems and compilers.

Limitations on Distant Development

- Sometimes files did not transfer smoothly and needed server-side editing. This created a bottleneck in our development process since only one person in our office initially had security access to reach and edit the files on the Nashville server.
- Programming could not assume the code was fully operational if compiled and tested in Austin; it had to be recompiled and retested in Nashville. This created a second bottleneck, again laid at the feet of programming.
- One additional handicap in development came as we conducted quality checks in the courseware. When the final version of the on-screen text has to be typed without benefit of a word processing program's spell-check function, mistakes occur. As we reviewed the courses online, we discovered that the limited access to the Nashville server precluded editing of this text by anyone except the permitted programmer, further slowing our completion time.

Courseware Maintenance on an Intranet

The first course was targeted at the top four hospital executives—Chief Executive Officer, Chief Financial Officer, Chief Nursing Officer, and Chief Operations Officer. With 347 hospitals, our target population was about 1,400 people. As employees began using the first course, we discovered three course maintenance areas in which limited access to the files created customer service problems.

The simple database we had developed to register people for courses, track usage, record test scores, and note course completion was an integral part of the early courses. Without full access to the database, the customer support representative could not identify and fix user problems, most of which were forgotten passwords.

We further discovered that the quality of web-based courseware is totally dependent on the robustness of the program code and the stability of the links. If a post-test for example worked well for 100 users yet failed on the 101st, it was usually due to some combination of keystrokes or test entry selections that the programmer had not anticipated. Regardless of the cause the "customer" inferred that the course was not high quality. Both development slow downs and customer service perceptions could be controlled through restructuring security arrangement to allow the team to perform course development in Nashville. However, this led us to one more discovery about courseware development: version control.

Version control is a file check-out system used in document management to ensure that the most recent version of a master file is used by everyone working on the same file. We discovered that with files stored out of sight in Nashville and with team members in different offices instead of shared cubicle space, we were duplicating each other's efforts and hampering our production. A version control system was the answer.

Most importantly, we learned that the dialogue process we practiced as part of the Quantum systems thinking approach continued to be useful in the larger corporate environment. We had to communicate especially by listening carefully and intently to understand the broad technical initiatives under way within Columbia and to determine how we could work within those initiatives.

Building a New Kind of Team

As the Director of Courseware Development and the team manager, I had the responsibility for building the new Columbia courseware team. I first developed a set of competencies necessary for continuing creation of courseware for the intranet. These competencies included

1. *account management*—for client relationships
2. *project management*—for project-specific client contact
3. *instructional design*—all competencies needed to complete the ISD model, from needs assessment to level four evaluations
4. *user interface design*—human-computer interaction issues
5. *information design*—navigation, cognitive overload and flexible content organization
6. *HTML writing and editing*—skills in HTML markup language
7. *online proofreading*
8. *simple programming*—CGI, JavaScript, basic networks
9. *complex programming*—C, C++, PERL, sophisticated networks
10. *database design and administration*—records management

11. *telephone help desk and customer service*
12. *computer-generated graphics*
13. *computer-generated audio/video*
14. *paper-based illustration* (to be scanned)
15. *quality assurance.*

Using this competency list, I identified those skills we already had in our present team members, those that might be developed internally, and those we needed to add through recruiting or outsourcing. Our first priority was to develop internal skills, which would not only increase our productivity and internal capacity but would also help our employee retention efforts.

To build internal skills we used a two-part approach. We began a series of weekly cross-functional training sessions. Each week, one team member would research and present information on a new topic. We started by building software skills. One of the HTML editors demonstrated the software which automatically translated text documents into HTML; the customer service representative discussed the nuances of the database used at the help desk. In addition, team members wanted to learn on their own. Columbia supported this learning with the purchase of books and manuals on web page development, user interface, and software systems. Team members worked individually and in pairs to gain additional competency in JavaScript, CGI programming, and graphics, including animations. We also sent several team members for classroom-based training on new network systems.

After several months, however, we encountered a roadblock. Much of the additional competency we needed in areas such as human-computer interaction, programming, and software quality assurance could not be developed from basic training or books. Nor could we develop additional competency using a master-apprentice approach because we did not have in-house experts who could serve as coaches and trainers.

We needed to find outside expertise, and we did so through recruiting and outsourcing. By the fall of 1996 we needed an additional instructional designer and a replacement for our programmer who resigned. I actively recruited for both positions from companies that were well-established and had strong quality programs in place, looking for employees with experience in quality development processes and finding two great candidates to begin work in the early spring of 1997. I also contracted with outside consultants for instructional design, user interface design, and some programming work. With up to twenty-five years' experience each, these consultants were invaluable in providing ideas from other companies which could be adapted for use in our courseware development.

Team Reactions

Team members were concerned about the competency-building process. First, team members viewed hiring externally as a threat. They could not see that their limited work experience prevented them from finding the best solutions to problems. It was only after consultants with expertise in our weak areas had worked with the team for some time that team members recognized this expertise could not be gained overnight and was a valuable part of producing high quality work.

Second, team members had become comfortable working with a very loose structure of work assignments. Using outside contractors meant that work assignments and time spent needed to be more closely tracked to manage all parts of the budget. Team members found themselves being asked to change, and they were uncomfortable with the change, especially one which added structure and procedures to their work.

We finally added additional training in teamwork, in which the outside consultants participated. From this training, the team discovered that much of the angst they had been experiencing was typical of different stages of team development. It was amazing to watch the sudden recognition that the team was going through a growth process, especially when the team quickly moved to a stage of high performance following the training.

The Team at Work: Organizational Transformation

The trainer's dream is to link education and training efforts to company goals and objectives. The Columbia intranet initiative was a dream come true for those of us in the IDL team, charged with organizational transformation. We faced five major challenges in transformation:

1. Limited network connections within hospitals,
2. Limited numbers of and access to desktop computers,
3. Limited computer literacy among employees,
4. Numerous organizational cultures from acquisition of existing hospitals, and
5. Market forces driving the need to create new ways to deliver quality health care.

The Strategy

The company decided that training and education delivered over the corporate intranet could be a substantial tool in meeting these challenges. By making the intranet the primary resource for information and knowledge sharing, we could not only build competence in using the technology we could build skills in cross-company interaction, leveraging company expertise across the continent. Our strategy was four-fold:

1. Identify change agents
2. Target top-level training needs
3. Deliver training seven days a week, twenty-four hours a day
4. Make it fun!

In any organization, some people are more likely than others to support new initiatives. We identified four groups of people who would influence the adoption of intranet-based training in Columbia and began to plan how to work with each group.

Senior Management. We started with this group. Their positions as decision makers and role models in the hospitals were important to gain financial support for new equipment and to serve as role models for broader employee acceptance of the initiative. We determined that this group was most likely to have desktop computers and network connections to the intranet. We knew that this group tended to be highly competitive division by division and that their decisions were influenced by financial considerations.

In the fall of 1996, we rolled out three courses for this group, focusing on their immediate learning needs related to changing health care delivery. These courses were introduced as a competition. Each division was encouraged to get as many of its top four hospital executives to enroll as possible. An incentive was given to the top division at the end of the enrollment period. A second phase of the contest was to get as many of these enrollees to finish courses as possible. At the end of the completion period, a second incentive prize was given. Through this promotion, approximately 5,000 Columbia executives enrolled in at least one course, with 40 percent completing a course within the promotion period.

Managers and Supervisors. Managers and supervisors were a second target group, since they were the ones responsible for releasing employees to training and for determining the organizational value of the training. Training was targeted for this group for 1998. In the meantime, we were developing front-line staff training for which we wanted their support. To accomplish this, we made sure that direct supervisors and managers were actively involved in the stakeholder committees developing course content. We asked them to participate in alpha testing and designed a level four evaluation (Do they use what they learned?) to be sent to this group ninety days after their direct reports participated in intranet training.

Employees. We knew that employees might fear online training for several reasons. They might be concerned about their ability to use computers; they might worry about having to learn new skills in order to learn online; they might worry about losing their jobs if they did not participate. As we developed the first courses for employees, we took these worries into consideration four ways:

- Identifying employees to participate in beta testing, drawing from those who might be reluctant as well as those who were enthusiastic,
- Developing classroom train-the-trainer programs so more experienced employees could assist others at the local hospital level,
- Including noncomputer activities such as recommending paper-based note taking in the instructional design,
- Using humor, color, quick cartoon-like graphics, and simple games in the courseware so that it was fun to learn yet definitely work-focused.

Training Departments. We also knew that training departments with varied responsibilities from hospital to hospital would be concerned about loss of local control and potential loss of staff if training was provided in other ways than the stand-up training methods in use. In order to begin dialogue about local training concerns, we partnered with the corporate Human Resources Department in June 1997 to hold an education summit. Three representatives from each of Columbia's forty divisions were invited to come to Nashville for three days of conversation about education and training issues. Attendees had the opportunity to attend two separate sessions about web-based training, which included a demonstration of upcoming courses, a discussion of new training roles such as delivering train-the-trainer sessions and moderating online conferences, and a presentation on new company-wide software for collecting outcomes data. In addition, the IDL Team had been testing new NT conferencing software to replace the custom programming used in three courses for discussion forums. Following the education summit, I set up and moderated a health care educators forum on the intranet to continue summit conversations and build company-wide training department discussions.

Outcomes Attained

Initial objectives for the intranet training included evaluation of our work on a regular basis using a "balanced scorecard" approach popular in the management literature. Within our department, the balanced scorecard looked at four quadrants of organizational results: (a) financials, (b) customer satisfaction, (c) development, and (d) operations. The following paragraphs describe the outcomes attained for the first three courses offered via intranet, with data available through June 1997.

In terms of financials, we calculated that the average cost to send one executive to a twelve-hour seminar cost approximately $2,200, considering travel time, travel expenses, and tuition. Educating 1,400 senior hospital executives online saved $308,000.

We measured customer satisfaction using an online twenty-question form at the end of each course and increased the response rate by faxing the survey to those who did not respond online. We measured customer satisfaction in four areas based on whether the material was relevant, useful, worthwhile, and fun to learn. Among the respondents, the average rating across the four categories was 4.1 on a scale of one to five, with one being "Strongly Disagree" and five being "Strongly Agree."

In terms of development, we used an online level two evaluation. Each course contained a multiple-choice post-test of twenty-five to thirty questions, which a learner could take no more than three times. A learner needed to pass the post-test with a score of at least 70 percent in order to complete the course successfully. Test questions were developed as a larger bank based on the learning objectives for the course. A random set of questions, in random order, was presented each time. Of the 2,000 who completed at least one course, the average score was 89 percent.

Operational results were not available. We planned to compare operations results by division, since we collected user and completion data by division. However, reports could not be completed prior to the closure of our department.

The Value of Multi-Disciplinary Teams

Providing informational support for learning environments begins to highlight the complexity issues in web-based design. In addition to references and links to useful corporate information, the web allows us to actually create organizationally customized courseware. The intranet has the potential to provide hands-on practice with implementing company processes, such as a benchmarking methodology, by launching a form or spreadsheet from within the training itself. Running synchronous "chat" sessions or asynchronous discussion forums online in conjunction with a course, such as we did for the first three courses, or as follow-up discussion to encourage transfer of training, such as we developed for a fourth course, allows web-based training to move into extended organizational learning.

We can provide education and training opportunities that tie directly into company information systems in ways that allow simulation and hands-on experience. Learners can explore, experiment, and interact with online training materials in ways that suit their time, their learning styles, and their immediate needs for information and knowledge. They can deepen their understanding of organizational operations, improving both individual performance and the performance of the whole company.

So how do we get to that kind of training? It is no longer enough to put together a trainer and a subject matter expert, developing a product using a software design package that makes many of the decisions for the designer. As we worked in our multi-disciplinary team, we saw many chances to create meaningful training that would improve the organization. Not only that but the quasi-team members—the stakeholders and the Information Services employees—began to think differently about training as well. They looked again at processes and procedures they knew were not satisfactory, and they saw the possibilities for change using web-based training delivered on the intranet.

New Roles and Responsibilities

A multi-disciplinary team to create the courseware by itself is not enough. We found that the most critical role in creating effective corporate training in web environments is that of the project manager who ensures that the process is followed, provides guidance on quality standards, facilitates dialogue and communication among highly disparate team members, coordinates testing, and provides resource links such as outside contractors. The project manager also ensures that organizational stakeholders and direct users are involved in the process from the beginning, resulting in greater early acceptance for this new type of learning.

From a teaching or training perspective, the second critical role is that of instructional designer. Often in training the instructional designer is also the teacher, the expert, and the knowledge "maker." Or a subject matter expert works with a designer to develop the instruction. The instructional designer still becomes quasi-expert on the topic and creates not only the instructional flow but also the materials. Presentation or "knowledge making" is usually conducted by the subject matter expert or by the designer-trainer. The learning product is developed by a single person or a very small group, whether the training medium is classroom or CBT/CD-ROM.

In the Columbia courseware development process, we were all part of a much larger team, with everyone actively involved in making decisions throughout the project. While the instructional designer can take the lead and ensure that decisions continually tie back to the learning objectives and desired outcomes, many creative ideas and results come from other team members. The instructional designer must be able to recognize valuable instructional solutions and strategies presented by nondesigners.

New Kinds of Expertise

In custom web-based courseware design, broader technical expertise is required to code the HTML for screens and hyperlinks, to develop graphics that appear complex but transmit simply, to write computer code such as C, CGI scripts, JavaScript, and others which allow automated customization to learners, and to make testable decisions about user interfaces. We had to recognize that web-based development requires substantial depth of expertise in the technology, often expertise gained from "playing around" with the technology rather than from formal education, and we had to allow time for this experimentation.

In addition, web-based courses are both primitive and complex compared to CBT. CBT can include complex program functions, substantial audio and video, and high quality graphics, but its structure is linear. Web-based training, on the other hand, relies much more on text but has great flexibility in the order in which the learner sees pages. Clear, well-supported decisions on instructional strategies need to be made. The designers must be capable of making those choices and of leveraging the expertise of the other team members to develop the most creative, successful learning opportunities possible.

In addition, working in a multi-disciplinary team of experts with varying viewpoints required new expertise in facilitation. This was especially important in team discussions, in which members tended to yield to the logical arguments of the programmers, and in meetings with the stakeholders, when great ideas often came from people less closely involved with the day-to-day production. Facilitating groups was not a competency identified early, yet it became one of the most valuable skills used by the team to reach a stage of high performance. We learned the instructional designer is often the best person to take on this additional responsibility.

New Process

Models for the instructional design process typically follow a linear path from needs and task analysis to content development, materials development, testing, and revision. We found that our concepts of the process needed to be reframed. The process is more an iterative one across the broad team, with continual dialogue and negotiation in making decisions continually focusing back on the learner. Like the design process used by landscape architects, architects, interior designers, industrial designers, and others, this process is more circular than linear. It moves back and forth between team members involved in the detailed components of the courseware and those who are working with a broader view of how the training fits into organizational initiatives and strategies.

Summarizing What We Learned

In short, the experience of our team at Quantum and at Columbia/HCA Healthcare Corporation reveals that the multi-disciplinary teams can be very successful in developing web-based education and training courseware to meet private sector needs for individual and organizational learning. We learned six valuable lessons in this experience.

- First, teams designing training for the web need to benchmark the experience of manufacturing companies such as Ford Motor Company and Lockheed Martin, companies that have used multi-disciplinary teams to transform industrial design.
- Second, web-based training development is similar to software development, with quality controls and rapid prototyping processes. Team structures and processes created by software companies can be used for web-based training teams.
- Third, web-based courseware is a living document, linked to continually changing company databases for current information and performance measures. As such, a maintenance plan involving course stakeholders and Information Services is an integral component in the final product.
- Fourth, as individuals we have to constantly learn new skills, changing as the technology changes. If we become too comfortable with what we know, we can hold back the team.
- Fifth, each team member is responsible for keeping imagination alive in the team so that cross-disciplinary ideas and creative solutions to problems flourish.
- And sixth, the most outstanding result of our experience was learning to communicate across disciplines. We discovered that education and experience in a particular discipline bring with them a set of assumptions about how the world works. Being able to consider the ideas and views of someone from another discipline is crucial to recognizing and reframing our assumptions to achieve common goals.

In short, we found that the multi-disciplinary team approach was what made the web-based training initiative successful, first within Quantum and then within the Columbia/HCA behemoth.

Note: Due to corporate restructuring and shift in strategy, Columbia/HCA Healthcare Corporation closed its Planning, Education, and Consulting department and eliminated the IDL team described here.

PART THREE

CHANGING ATTITUDES AND ENHANCING MOTIVATION

CHAPTER FIFTEEN

ELICITING COMMUNITY BELIEFS AND CHANGING ATTITUDES THROUGH EDUCATION: INNOVATIVE DISTANCE LEARNING AT THE COLUMBUS CENTER

Regina Bento, Cindy Schuster, Alberto Ramirez and Tamara Salganik

Hundreds of years ago, Christopher Columbus set sail for a journey that took him to lands he didn't know existed. As we prepare to enter the twenty-first century, an exciting journey is also taking place under the tent-like roof of the Columbus Center, designed to resemble massive ship sails and symbolize the mission of this new science center for marine biotechnology research and education, perched on Baltimore's inner harbor. Like their famous predecessor, the participants of this modern journey reach across space and time to touch communities they have never met before. But different from the original Columbus, these modern adventurers do so without ever leaving port. Using a combination of fiber optic interactive video, intranets and the World Wide Web, this interdisciplinary team of scientists, educators and information technology specialists are exploring new frontiers in distance training.

The goal of this chapter is to take an in-depth look at a particular distance training event in order to illustrate why and how the center is "going the distance" in using technology to fulfill its dual education and research mission.

A unique aspect of distance training in the Columbus Center is that it was not an afterthought. While the center was still being constructed, a Bell Atlantic Distance Learning Lab was integrated into the award-winning design of its Hall of Exploration. Distance training was integrated just as seamlessly into the design of the center's business strategy, representing a critical element in fulfilling the center's mission in marine biotechnology research and education.

In the next section, we will provide an overview of the center's mission, structure, and activities and of how distance education fits into the overall organization. We will then move on to describe and analyze a particular distance training event, in which the center quickly responded to a regional outcry for scientific information about the cause and consequences of fish lesions in Chesapeake Bay, possibly associated with the pfiesteria microorganism. Finally, we will discuss how the lessons learned from this particular example relate to the broader role of distance training in contributing to the dual research and education mission of a modern science center.

Columbus Center

The Columbus Center (*http://www.columbuscenter.org/*) is a new private nonprofit national center for marine biotechnology, one of the fastest growing fields of science. What makes it unique as a research institution is that it includes public education and workforce training as part of its primary mission. The center's purpose encompasses not only marine research but also education, interactive public exhibition, economic development, and marine environmental preservation.

Of the four interrelated components of the Columbus Center, two are dedicated to research and two to public education. In 1995, the newly constructed Columbus Center became the home of University of Maryland's Center of Marine Biology (COMB), a world-class research center in biotechnology, molecular biology, and molecular genetics of marine life. Two years later in 1997 this scientific nucleus was joined by a second research component, the new Food and Drug Administration Division of Seafood Safety Center.

The two educational components of the Columbus Center are the Science and Technology Education Center (SciTEC), and the Hall of Exploration. SciTEC provides advanced hands-on science experiences to students, teachers, and families and is designed to prepare up to 2,500 students annually for science and technology-related careers. The Hall of Exploration opened in May 1997 is a new prototype for public science centers, with its interactive exhibits designed to "break down the barriers that exist between science and the public."

Throughout the Columbus Center, stylized representations of DNA in sculptures, windows, brochures, and other places remind visitors of the importance of biotechnology to understanding and preserving marine life. The interlinked spirals of DNA can also be seen as powerful symbolic representations of the connect-edness between the research and public education sides of the Columbus Center and of how the combination of both can have profound economic and societal impact. The Hall of Exploration exhibits are based on marine biotechnology research being conducted in COMB labs and include several hands-on public science labs where visitors participate in authentic research experiences. SciTEC programs are based on COMB current research, and a COMB researcher has the formal role of providing an active liaison between COMB scientists and SciTEC educators. SciTEC not only translates COMB research into biotech educational programs for middle and high schools but also creates a new model for urban education and workforce training. SciTEC is involved with an innovative program to provide basic job skills for Baltimore's inner-city teenagers. SciTEC is also meant to link COMB scientists to the business and technology communities, through short courses, seminars, and conferences.

Distance Training Site Planning

The Columbus Center Distance Learning Lab started operations in May 1997 when the Hall of Exploration opened and has been from its inception an integral part of the operations of the center. The main technology used for its distance training programs is an interactive video system, which allows participants in different electronic locations to interact with audio and video signals in real time through the use of telecommunications.

While the Columbus Center was still under construction, Bell Atlantic came to the planners with a prototype classroom and the idea of how a distance learning classroom would help the center in reaching its goals of community outreach, public awareness, and follow-up learning. The decision-makers perceived a strategic fit for the Distance Learning Lab (DLL) in their vision for the Columbus Center, and thus the DLL became part of the $13.5 million Bell Atlantic initiative to build a Maryland Interactive Distance Learning Network (MIDLN), an effort to connect every public school, community college, and four-year college in Maryland.

The decision of using MIDLN for distance training was an easy one for the Columbus Center because a large portion of its primary audience (K-12 schools) already had MIDLN classrooms, as did community colleges and university sites throughout Maryland. Although the decision to have a distance learning lab was made while the center was still under construction, a few constraints were already in place. For example, the DLL room had originally been planned as a lab area, and the basic design could not be changed. Because of that the DLL is one of the smallest MIDLN rooms, seating ten participants with interactive

microphones. There are also two benches that can seat an additional ten participants and temporary chairs that can be added to the room when necessary.

The small size of the DLL room works well for the Columbus Center. Most
of the time the DLL is the originating host site, disseminating information and
learning for large audiences who participate in the various DLL outreach and
follow-up training programs from various remote locations. Classroom size would
be an issue if the DLL were located in a different type of institution, such as a university wishing to accommodate large classes in the transmitting site.

MIDLN is one of two educational interactive video networks in Maryland,
together with IVN /ELVIN (IVN for the University System of Maryland, ELVIN
for Maryland community colleges). MIDLN is a private, fiber optic transmitted,
interactive video network. MIDLN uses a "codec," but the bandwidth supplied
(fiber optic – T3) makes the audio and video signals seamless. This network has
also incorporated the use of a variety of multimedia that enhance the distance
learning environment. The network is currently limited to Maryland and is broken
into LATAs (similar to telephone area codes). There is an additional monthly cost
to cross LATAs. The provider and coordinator of this system, Bell Atlantic, do-
nates the original equipment to education and nonprofit institutions. The
institutions agree to pay a monthly tariff and may purchase optional technical
support.

The Bell Atlantic package includes a furniture unit encasing the first three
front monitors, an audio system, and "codec," a document camera and cabinet
to store other inputs, instructor and student microphones, a personal computer, a
Crestron panel and remote, a furniture case with monitors for the back of the
room, and full installation and training (including both informal training and a
formal workshop by a distance education consultant). Room furniture (desks
and chairs), a teachers' workstation and chair, audio panels, a VCR, a telephone,
a fax machine, and a printer are not supplied. Any room enhancements (related
to lighting, cabling, and so on) are also the responsibility of the site.

The Columbus Center DLL has introduced several adaptations and innovations to the prototype design of a typical Bell Atlantic MIDLN classroom.
One of the most interesting features of the Columbus Center DLL is that it has
two glass walls, matching the multistory glass walls and the open look of the
Hall of Exploration. No one was sure how this would work, but not only does it
work it also allows the remote sites to take a virtual field trip of the Hall of
Exploration. From the DLL room one can see the adjacent science lab, as well
as the eye-catching exhibits in the public area. The glass walls and the bright
colors create an exciting learning environment. Blinds can be lowered when
needed; combined with carpets they help create a sound dampening effect.

Auxiliary Equipment

Since the Columbus Center is a scientific training site, additional enhancements have been made to the distance learning lab to customize the usual MIDLN setup to the specific needs of the center. In the front area of the DLL room a wet lab table was added for the performance of live scientific experiments in distance training programs; thanks to the high-end camera above the wet table remote audiences can observe the experiments down to the smallest detail.

Another important modification was the redesign of the Crestron touch panel that controls the cameras, audio levels, and additional inputs to the system. The panel was redesigned to allow for two document cameras (the original one that came with the room and the one for the wet lab table) and for additional audiovisual inputs. One such input of particular importance for the Columbus Center is a digital microscope camera that captures the images being observed under the microscopes in the science lab adjacent to the DLL and allows them to be directly transmitted to audiences in remote locations. A student in a remote site can see exactly the same live images a scientist is seeing through his or her microscope, as well as images that the scientist might have observed and video-taped beforehand. The combination of four video microscope cameras and video taping prior to the distance learning session also allows scientists to show a particularly interesting time sequence of events in a shortened and edited time span (for instance, cell division). All this of course is done in addition to other traditional uses of video taping. Like other MIDLN sites, the Columbus Center uses the recording capabilities of the MIDLN system to make unedited videos and backups for emergency use and also to create a reference library of special sessions.

Direct access to the Internet is another important element the Columbus Center DLL added to the typical MIDLN room. Using a graphical browser to access the World Wide Web, live transmissions from the web can be incorporated in the distance training programs of the DLL. Scientists can easily integrate information and images from the Columbus Center home page and numerous other web resources into their discussions and demonstrations over the interactive video network. The center staff hopes to implement the use of underwater camera and satellite in the future.

The microphones used in the Columbus Center DLL have also been adapted to serve special purposes. In order to accommodate the hands-on approach of distance training sessions, the two instructor microphones that come with the MIDLN system were replaced by headset microphones. This leaves the instructor's hands free to conduct experiments, write on a paper in the document camera, or manipulate other inputs on the panel controls. The audio quality is excellent. In addition to the regular student microphones, an upright microphone was installed in the DLL room to permit easy and practical access to participants in wheelchairs.

Distance Learning Instructors and Instructional Materials

The recruitment and selection of the right staff for the new educational programs of the Columbus Center were seen as even more strategic than the technological decisions. From the very beginning, the center realized that an interdisciplinary team approach would be critical for its ability to successfully integrate technology, science, and education into a synergetic whole. The center searched for people who were not only proficient in their respective fields but also had the talent and spirit for doing things differently, going beyond the "normal" approaches to research and teaching.

The resulting interdisciplinary team brings together professionals with all kinds of different backgrounds and skills. The DLL Project Manager, for example, has a background in film and video with extensive experience in distance training; the presenters in the distance training programs are scientists from COMB who have learned how to use DLL technology, put together a presentation, and deliver it as an interactive "performance" rather than a boring lecture.

Distance Learning Programs

Since May 1997 the DLL facilities have been used for distance training events in which students and teachers in remote locations throughout Maryland learn about science and technology from the Columbus Center specialists. Presenters and participants at the DLL transmitting site can have live video and audio two-way interactions with four remote sites simultaneously, while broadcasting to up to ninety other MIDLN sites (270 in the future). The phone, fax, and email capabilities of the DLL room allow participants in these latter sites to still play an active role in live programs even though they cannot be seen by the audience in the host DLL site or in the main interactive locations.

Programs can also be sent by cable TV to an unlimited number of broadcast locations, which has inspired the idea of special programs for DLL's first winter: on days when snow forces the schools to close, homebound students will still be able to learn science through the Columbus Center special "Snow Shows" on their cable TV!

The DLL was designed to be closely integrated with the other elements of the Columbus Center. For example, distance training expands the reach of onsite programs beyond their usual time and space boundaries. The DLL can be used to prepare teachers and students more fully before they come for their school visits to the Hall of Exploration education programs. Later on, after teachers and students get the initial hands-on experience from the onsite visit, follow-up DLL programs can help them to continue learning through ongoing interactions with the Columbus Center.

The DLL can also contribute in multiple ways to COMB, the scientific research nucleus of the Center: DLL's multimedia capabilities make it possible for current research to be presented in rich and vivid detail (such as the microscope camera) for both training (distance learning) and research purposes (video conferences among scientists). The combination of the microscope camera with the recording capabilities of the MIDLN system enables scientists to capture and save time-sequence observations for future reference. In using MIDLN as a low-end recording studio to capture observations, the Columbus Center provides easy to use equipment to its scientists, at no additional cost to the center. Moreover, DLL can be used as a receiving site for externally generated programs, facilitating the continuous professional development of Columbus Center scientists and educators.

In addition to the regularly scheduled training programs, the DLL is positioned to play an important part in some special initiatives of the Columbus Center. For example, the inner-city teenagers in the Columbus Center Youth Alive program for job skill development will be able to use the DLL to interact with their counterparts in sixty-eight other science centers. Another special initiative involves the trip to Asia of the "Pride of Baltimore II." A teacher aboard the ship will send data and video tapes throughout the journey, which will be used not only for Columbus Center onsite programs but will also be more broadly shared through the DLL.

During the Distance Learning Lab dedication ceremony in May 1997, the CEO of the Columbus Center said that DLL should provide "scientifically accurate, up-to-date and understandable educational materials keyed to breaking stories in life sciences, health, the Chesapeake Bay, and the environment, as well as other current events." An excellent example of how DLL is fulfilling this mandate is the special distance training event discussed next.

Distance Training Event

Just a few months after the Distance Learning Lab started operations it offered a distance training event that epitomized its strategic role in the Columbus Center mission. At the height of a crisis affecting the fish of the Chesapeake Bay, the Distance Learning Lab received a request for a distance training event on how the pfiesteria microorganism might be contributing to fish lesions in the Bay. In this section, we will discuss in detail this training event, in order to illustrate how the DLL uses distance training technology to serve the needs of Columbus Center stakeholders.

Problem Statement

The Columbus Center is located in Piers Five and Six at Baltimore's inner harbor, at the headwaters of Chesapeake Bay, the nation's largest tidal estuary. During the summer and fall of 1997, lesions found on fish in the Chesapeake Bay waters led to widespread public concern about seafood safety and the waters of the bay. The possibility that the lesions could be linked to the "Pfiesteria piscicida" microorganism and that humans could be adversely affected soon developed into a "pfiesteria hysteria" blown out of all proportion by media hyperbole and public misinformation (see *http://www.columbuscenter.org/hall/pfiest.html*).

Even though there was no scientific evidence of danger to the public, Chesapeake Bay seafood disappeared from supermarket shelves and restaurant menus throughout the state of Maryland; seafood prices plummeted; and the whole industry suffered. While the media concentrated mostly on the graphical images of the fish lesions, some politicians hurried to propose legislation that would respond to public pressure to "do something" about the problem, even in the absence of scientific evidence of the efficacy or necessity of those measures, and in spite of the profound economic effects for other industries.

In the middle of all this turmoil, the Health Department of Maryland's Worcester County, one of the areas most directly hit by the "pfiesteria hysteria," contacted the Columbus Center about the possibility of developing a special training program on the latest scientific research about pfiesteria and delivering it through the Distance Learning Lab to students in various high schools in Worcester County.

In the space of only three days the pfiesteria presentation was developed by two COMB scientists, Dr. Bill Jones (the researcher who serves as liaison between COMB scientists and SciTEC educators) and Mr. Adam Frederick (the marine biologist who later presented the program through distance training), with support from the SciTEC and DLL education and distance training specialists.

Populations Served

The pfiesteria program was developed to directly serve the information needs of high school students and teachers in Worcester County, Maryland. But the DLL hoped to indirectly reach an even broader public through subsequent dissemination of such information to the families and friends of program participants.

Given the scope of the problems generated by the misinformation about pfiesteria around the state, this type of educational program should serve the needs not only of the school communities directly involved in the distance training events but also of other stakeholders of strategic importance for the Columbus Center, such as local and state government and the commercial seafood industry.

Intended Outcome

The challenge facing the Columbus Center was to develop over a short period of time a one-hour program to be delivered through distance training at the Distance Learning Lab. At the cognitive level, the program should transmit the most relevant and recent information about the pfiesteria microorganism and why and how it could possibly affect fish or human beings. This should be done using language that would be both scientifically correct and appropriate to capturing and sustaining the interest of high school students.

At the emotional and attitudinal level the program was intended to elicit the beliefs and feelings of the participants about pfiesteria, the fish lesion problems and their broader societal impacts; allow them to examine these feelings in a supportive environment; and contrast their own emotions and feelings with the latest existing scientific evidence.

At the behavioral level, the program should help students, teachers, and their families and friends to make informed decisions about their own use of Chesapeake Bay seafood and waters. It should also motivate and enable students and teachers to later seek on their own further information about the subject.

Initial Presentation

The live presentation opens with Mr. Adam Frederick, dressed in informal clothes and with the hands-free microphone around his neck, asking the students and teachers in the remote sites if they can hear him well. With this question he not only gains needed feedback, but also motivates the remote audiences to use their microphones and get into the interactive mode of the program.

Mr. Frederick then announces that he will give the audience a few minutes to write the answers to five questions meant to identify what they may or may not know about pfiesteria. The image on the screen shifts to the document camera, showing a piece of paper with written questions ("What type of organism is pfiesteria?" "How long does it take a lesion to form?" "What does pfiesteria eat?" "Has anyone gotten sick from eating seafood contaminated with pfiesteria?" "Is pfiesteria contagious?"). The document camera zooms in, and the questions on the paper take up the whole monitor screen, vivid and clear, handwritten in print with a dark marker against the white paper background.

Mr. Frederick remains silent for several minutes, the questions still the only image on the screen. After a while, he asks if the audience is ready, and several voices from the remote sites answer "No!" A few minutes later, the question is repeated and the answer comes back "Yes!" The image shifts back to show Mr. Frederick, who with a straight face declares "Now I have an essay I would like you to write . . ."—and, looking at the dismayed student faces on the monitors, smiles and says "Just kidding . . ." Relieved laughter from the remote sites shows that he had really scared the students . . .

Audience Responses

These initial interactions accomplish several results. The questions provide a set of learning objectives that span the content of the whole presentation and make the students realize how little they actually know. This prepares them to suspend their fears and emotions for a while and receive information, in accordance with Lewin's (1951) recommendations about the need to "unfreeze" past attitudes and perceptions in order to achieve learning and change.

The questions direct their attention to key aspects of the presentation so that when the information is provided they will recognize it as important. Moreover, the questions motivate students to "get it right," almost like gaining points in a Jeopardy game. They also put students in the frame of mind of scientific inquiry, in which asking the right questions drives the whole process of discovery. Stimulated to frame their own inquiry, students ask numerous and relevant questions in later parts of the program. When at the end of the program the presenter repeats the initial questions, each student can assess how much he or she has objectively learned.

Writing the answers to the initial five questions gives students the opportunity for individual reflection and for ownership of the learning, protects their privacy by not embarrassing them with a possible public display of their misinformation on the subject, and avoids competitive feelings toward those who know more. By presenting the questions in written format and asking the students to write down the answer, the presenter allows time for introspection and accentuates the interactive nature of the experience. His silence and his absence from the screen are an early indication that in this mode of learning the focus is not on transmission of the instructor's knowledge but on the students' learning. This is reinforced by the fact that the presenter respects the students' request for more time, indicating that they set the pace of the program and that this is not a proforma exercise.

The presenter's joke about asking the students to write an essay not only uses humor to relax the atmosphere but also shows that he appreciates their effort and will not abuse their cooperation.

Guiding the Learner

Mr. Frederick starts the lecture by saying that before getting down to the "nitty gritty" he wants to show students some thought-provoking things. The image shifts again to the document camera, where Mr. Frederick starts placing several cartoons that have recently appeared in the press about pfiesteria, fish lesions, and the drastic reactions of supermarkets and restaurants. The cartoons give the presenter the ability to summarize in a short time, using the combined power of symbols and humor, the significance and societal impact of the subject while implicitly sending the message that "it's okay to be concerned about this; lots of other people seem to be, but what are the real facts?"

After the audience reacts to the cartoons, Mr. Frederick starts the exposition by saying that a big part of the problem is perception and asks: "Where do you get your information from?" The answers come fast from the remote sites: TV, newspapers, the Internet, other people. Mr. Frederick then prompts the students to question the factual basis of their beliefs and feelings by asking "Do you think these sources have done a good job in giving you the correct perceptions?" Without giving students the opportunity to provide an answer that would prematurely "refreeze" their attitudes, he quickly adds "You decide if they are right or wrong after you hear the information."

The cartoons are followed by newspaper articles shown under the document camera. Zooming the image in and out, the presenter alternates between details of the text and an overall view of the articles. He then comments that interest in pfiesteria has spawned the creation of several web sites. The image being transmitted to the remote sites shifts again, this time directly displaying the DLL computer screen and providing a clear view of a web page. Mr. Frederick starts with the Columbus Center web page (*http://www.columbuscenter.org/*), and follows the link to a page about pfiesteria (*http://www.columbuscenter.org/hall/pfiest.html*).

Next he goes to the web page of pfiesteria researchers from North Carolina State University, demonstrating how the Internet makes it easy to obtain firsthand information from the most qualified sources. For a sharp contrast, the image on the screen shifts back to the document camera, where Mr. Frederick once again displays newspaper clippings that show how much the media has dwelt on fears and emotions, rarely paying attention to available scientific facts.

The contrast is accentuated when the image on the screen shows a scientific document and zooms in to show a picture of pfiesteria taken with an electron microscope. Mr. Frederick starts describing the shape of the microorganism, dispelling the misconceptions about its nature (not a bacteria, not a microbe) and reinforcing the students' pride in the information they're acquiring by saying "Only one-tenth of 1 percent of the population knows this; you'll be unique." He then uses the document camera to display maps of the United States and of

Chesapeake bay to show where similar problems have occurred and that the present situation is not unusual or unprecedented.

Next, the image on the screens shifts to show a computer-based presentation created by a scientist from the University of Maryland's Sea Grant Extension Program, "A Threat to the Chesapeake." The presentation includes pictures (fish lesions, pfiesteria, media articles) and text produced with a presentation software in vivid colors and with bullet listings of the basic points. Mr. Frederick's voice-over explains and expands each slide, clarifying the meaning of scientific terms and providing a full, detailed analysis of the main facts currently known about pfiesteria and how it relates to fish and humans.

Anecdotes, photos, and personal stories about the researchers studying pfiesteria enliven the presentation and help students to personalize and understand the process of scientific discovery.

Feedback to the Learner

Throughout the program, questions from the audience are always addressed with respect and encouragement: "Good question," "I don't think anybody has studied this point yet, but it sure would be interesting to investigate." New pieces of information are anchored by questions that help students relate them to their prior knowledge and experience ("What life cycles have you studied?" "Frogs!" "How do frog life cycles compare to this slide that shows the pfiesteria life cycle?").

Juxtaposing explanations and questions, Mr. Frederick guides student reasoning so that each new piece of information serves as a basis for the next set of concepts. When illustrating the role of mucus in the fish lesions, Mr. Frederick makes sniffing noises and the audience laughs: the visual and audio metaphor of nasal mucus is powerful and summarizes information in a way that students will remember.

The computer-based presentation helps students develop a broad basis of knowledge on pfiesteria. They then get a direct look at the microorganism when the projection switches to show images captured with the video microscope camera. What the students see on the screen is exactly what a scientist can see on the microscope. For even more detail, Mr. Frederick switches back to the document camera to show a picture of images seen with electron microscopes by Florida scientists. Images from web pages follow, which go into more depth into the possible causes and implications of observed fish lesions.

Mr. Frederick moves on to discuss the facts behind stories about possible health effects for humans, explaining the special circumstances surrounding the documented cases, the mechanisms leading to different effects, and the possible long- and short-term consequences.

Mr. Frederick then goes back to the initial question sheet and considers each one in turn. The questions now seem "easy," but Mr. Frederick carefully highlights how each question relates to specific types of information covered during the session. Throughout the program he stays by the wet lab table in a relaxed posture so that the camera does not have to chase him around the room. The hands-free instructor microphone allows him to make gestures to stress important points and to manipulate the control panel in an entirely smooth and unobtrusive way.

When the presentation is over, Mr. Frederick looks directly at the camera and says "Now I turn it over to you." The image on the screen then switches to show the students in the remote sites. Many hands are quickly raised, and the camera focuses on each questioner as he or she uses one of the microphones built into the audience desks.

The questions are excellent as Mr. Frederick frequently acknowledges. Students discuss several aspects of the "pfiesteria hysteria" and ask questions of obvious personal relevance ("Is it safe to swim in the river where I live?"), which Mr. Frederick addresses with particular care ("Where do you live? Let's look at the map and . . ."). The images switch back and forth between the students and Mr. Frederick.

The program concludes with an invitation for continuous learning: "If you'd like to learn more, here is the address of the Columbus Center web site, and here are our direct phone numbers." The information is displayed on the document camera. The program concludes with final good-byes and images from the various sites.

Outcome

This chapter was completed only a very short time after the pfiesteria distance training, which precludes the analysis of long-term outcomes. But it was immediately clear that the intended cognitive outcomes had been achieved: at the end of the program, the answers to the initial questions and the incisive intelligent new questions posed by the students made it obvious that a large volume of relevant little-known information had been learned in a relatively short period of time (about one hour of live transmission).

From an emotional and attitudinal point of view, the tone and nature of the interactions throughout the session also indicated that students had gone through the various phases of the change process as described by Lewin (1951): unfreezing (questioning their initial beliefs and emotions), change (combining prior and new information, contrasting it with their own and other people's fears and perceptions), and re-freezing (constructing a novel knowledge structure and relating attitudes to that new knowledge).

The interactions and questions also suggested that the intended behavioral outcomes had been achieved: students left the session with the ability and motivation to make more informed behavioral choices, to inform others, and to keep learning more from other available sources.

Discussion

Community Impact

The pfiesteria distance training event had a direct impact on the community it targeted. Worcester was the hardest hit county in the "pfiesteria hysteria" that spread throughout Maryland. The people of Worcester County not only had to worry whether the fish on the dinner table was safe; they also had to deal with the economic impact on Worcester's fishing industry, the health concerns of living in the area where the fish were dying, and possible environmental problems.

The students' questions and concerns during the program made it clear that the impacts from the pfiesteria scare were being felt at all levels of the community. The dinner table conversations for these students were not about what was happening "out there" but about what was happening in their own homes.

By putting together in a few days the pfiesteria distance training event, the Columbus Center stepped right into the middle of this traumatized community, educating and probably relieving not only the students but also their families. Through the use of multimedia and distance training technology, the students received timely and accurate information, while the organizers were able to avoid the logistical complications and costs of transporting so many people across the considerable geographic distance between Worcester County and the Columbus Center.

The Columbus Center experience with distance training and the particular case of the pfiesteria training program help illustrate the guiding principles discussed throughout this book.

Fit with Business Needs and Alignment with Nonprofit Mission

The Columbus Center is owned and operated by Christopher Columbus Center Development, Inc. (CCCD), a private non-profit corporation. The construction of its $160 million complex was made possible with support from federal, state, and local government, as well as private support from businesses and other entities. The budget for the center's initial operations included a combination of earned revenue from the Hall of Exploration and affiliated organizations located in the building, programs and projects grants, membership, and annual giving.

The first months of operation of the Hall of Exploration did not bring in as many visitors as expected, and the revenue contribution potential of the DLL became even more important, not only in terms of distance training events but also for developing public awareness about the center and attracting more visitors to the Hall of Exploration. Plans were formulated for using the DLL for business purposes, such as video conferencing and fee-based special events, but its initial operations concentrated on the primary mission of producing and delivering research-based training.

Distance training is a crucial element in the center's ability to serve the needs of a broad array of stakeholders and to fulfill its dual education and research mission. The pfiesteria program is a good example of how the center used distance training to respond quickly to the needs of local communities (through the health department request for training for Worcester County high schools) and build goodwill through the provision of training based on state-of-the-art research.

By requesting the pfiesteria program from the Columbus Center, the Health Department of Worcester County took a proactive step to deal with an important issue affecting the whole community. The quick response of the Columbus Center provided Worcester County with the best scientific information available, thus establishing a powerful basis for political advocacy of county interests in the statewide debate about measures to be taken to deal with the pfiesteria problem.

This type of program should also help the Columbus Center in obtaining grants from government and other research funding organizations because it used distance training to demonstrate to a large number of constituents how the research being conducted in the center is relevant to the economic well-being of the region as well as to science in general. Moreover, the content of the pfiesteria program was of direct relevance to Maryland residents, to the seafood industry, and to a variety of local businesses (supermarkets, restaurants, and so on).

Strategic Distance Training

Being able to use distance training to respond quickly to a rapidly-developing, highly visible, and socially relevant issue puts the Columbus Center in a special class among research centers. The pfiesteria program is a prime example of this type of applied scholarship. The challenge was to develop in a very short period of time a program that would showcase the latest research being done on pfiesteria and fish lesions in order to achieve the cognitive, emotional, attitudinal, and behavioral outcomes discussed before.

The success of the program illustrates the synergy generated by a good articulation of the primary components of the distance learning process:

- The learners: high school students living in an area that was directly affected in multiple ways by the "pfiesteria hysteria" and who were far enough from the center to make a field trip unpractical;

- The instructor: a scientist who combined sophisticated knowledge of the topic with mastery in the use of distance learning technology and who appeared to the audience as being entirely comfortable in the distance learning environment;
- The learning environment: two-way interactions, just-in-time information driven by student needs, specialized production, customization, and a team-based approach (see Table 2 in Berge's "Conceptual Framework" chapter in this book);
- The instructional delivery technology: smooth and seamless articulation of all technological capabilities of MIDLN as adapted to the Columbus Center DLL's particular circumstances;
- The organizational culture: the Columbus Center's distinctive commitment to combining education and research, as demonstrated in the content and form of its distance training programs, as well as the interdisciplinary teams that develop and deliver them.

Conceptual Frameworks of Learning and Distance Training

Everywhere in the Columbus Center one sees evidence that the educational model that drives all activities is the transformation model as opposed to information transmission (see Chapter 2, Conceptual Frameworks in Distance Training and Education). From the onsite exhibits to the distance training programs, there is a constructivist emphasis on individual thinking, construction of meaning, experiential learning, creative framing of novel structures of knowledge, and personalized avenues of inquiry (Bentley, 1993; Joyce and Weil, 1996).

There is also a pervasive influence of social constructivism as demonstrated by the emphasis on ongoing multi-layered interactions between teams of learners and instructors, as well as the strategic importance of creating and sustaining interdisciplinary teams to develop and deliver the distance training programs (Bandura, 1971).

Technology

The Distance Learning Lab achieved a unique style of product development and delivery by using and expanding the technological capabilities of MIDLN classrooms, as described before (interactive remote sites, camera over wet lab table, video-microscope cameras, document camera, computer with Internet access and presentation software, hands-free instructor microphone, student microphones, and customized control panel).

The pfiesteria program is a model of how various technological elements can be seamlessly combined to produce an interactive multimedia distance training program that engages the minds and hearts of the remote audiences while dealing with a complex topic shrouded in fear and misinformation.

Instructional Materials

The instructional materials used in the pfiesteria program are a good example of what the Columbus Center strives to achieve in its distance training. The development of instructional materials was customized for the occasion and driven by the center's trademark combination of research and education and its learning model of information transformation.

As discussed in the "process" description of the pfiesteria program, the instructional materials questioned the learners' prior mental models (for example, the written questions that opened the program), elicited critical reflection (such as the cartoons and newspaper clippings), facilitated the construction of new frameworks (for example, the information about pfiesteria life cycles and forms of interaction with other life forms, the discussion of causes and consequences of fish lesions, the views from the video-microscope camera), and encouraged pursuit of further learning (such as the references to web pages with multiple pathways for knowledge building). The information was provided at a level that was compatible with the students' level of scientific sophistication but expanded and enriched it.

Implementation Support

The Distance Learning Lab is fully integrated with the other components of the Columbus Center. As discussed before, an extraordinary emphasis was placed since its very inception on assembling an interdisciplinary team driven by a common desire to innovate and experiment with new ways to combine education and research. For example, the pfiesteria presentation was developed and delivered by scientists proficient in distance training supported by education and technology specialists.

The easy relationship between the members of this team allows them to continuously push the boundaries of what is possible. During one meeting of the authors of this chapter, a scientist walked into the Distance Learning Lab and asked its Project Manager "Do you think we can use the microscope camera to video tape the images I am seeing right now in my microscope? I would like to capture them to use later in a presentation." The Project Manager answered without hesitation. "Sure, why not; let's try." They immediately started experimenting with the equipment. The glass walls between the DLL and the adjacent science lab enabled face-to-face communication with the scientist using the microscope and facilitated detailed adjustments and exchange of opinions about how to capture the best images. In the space of a few minutes, they had successfully used the technology to expand a little further the integration of research and teaching.

Implementation and Evaluation

The Distance Learning Lab is a brand new part of a new organization. The prevailing philosophy is "we're learning as we go," which fits well within the Columbus Center's culture of innovation and experimentation. Its first months of operation highlight the importance of a good choice of technology ("buy top-of-the-line equipment whenever possible; it's worth it in the long run"); of adapting packages such as the MIDLN classroom to the particular needs of the organization (the camera over the wet lab table, the hands-free microphones, the live Internet access, the video microscope cameras, the wheelchair-accessible audience microphones); of turning constraints into opportunities (the glass walls that were part of the original plan did not cause the audio problems that were feared and enabled an open feeling of integration with the surrounding environment and adjacent lab and exhibit areas); and of bringing together a highly qualified interdisciplinary team (experts in science, education, and technology sharing the same spirit of adventure and commitment).

There is a pervasive belief in the Columbus Center that "without information technology one can't do modern science." The distance learning lab fits into this philosophy. Still in the early stages of the DLL life cycle, the Columbus Center is firmly convinced that "going the distance" is one of the best ways to combine the powers of research and education to break the barriers between science and society.

Conclusions

Several lessons can be learned from the pfiesteria distance training event. First, if a science center wants to be an active member of its community, helping the public understand and influence "breaking stories" of great scientific and societal impact, it cannot limit its sphere of influence to on-site programs. Interactive video technology enabled the Columbus Center to be at the forefront of societal debate on a scientific issue with profound economic implications.

Second, the speed and timeliness of the center's response was made possible not only by its technology but by its interdisciplinary team of specialists in distance training, science and education, who in three days were able to develop and deliver a thoroughly professional presentation.

Third, the medium was proven to be appropriate for attitudinal, behavioral, and motivational change, as well as for the more traditional cognitive objectives of transmission of information. The highly interactive nature of the medium combines with the vividness of the experience it delivers to form an environment where learners are stimulated to address fears and concerns as well as ideas and information.

Last but not least, the impact of the experience was magnified by the fact that the presenter was thoroughly comfortable with the technology, moving seamlessly from document camera to video microscope to direct web access to face-to-face interaction. He was also a masterful teacher, able to use these very modern technologies to motivate students to ask and answer the age-old questions of scientific inquiry and education: Why do things happen the way they do? What do I really know? How do I know I know it? How can I find out more?

The distance training programs of the Columbus Center allow it to "go the distance" in reaching constituencies far beyond its walls in pursuit of a mission of scientific discovery, dissemination, and dialogue.

CHAPTER SIXTEEN

MEASURING ATTITUDES TO ASSESS TRAINING: THE INTERACTIVE DISTANCE LEARNING GROUP LOOKS AT LEARNING AND TRANSFER FROM SATELLITE TRAINING

Joan Conway Dessinger, Kenneth G. Brown, Martha N. Reesman, and Lauri E. Elliott

Background

The history of this case study is really the history of The IDL Group Inc., an alliance of corporations who are jointly developing and transmitting manufacturing-focused satellite distance learning courses. The vision of The IDL Group is to cost effectively supplement training at participating organizations by collaboratively developing the necessary infrastructure for technology-supported education and training.

The IDL Group, Inc. is a subsidiary of the National Center for Manufacturing Sciences (NCMS), a non-profit organization that focuses on multi-company research and development. The IDL Group's roots lie deep in an NCMS project that took place from 1994 to 1996. The project focused on how to provide effective distance training courses that rely on state-of-the-art instructional principles and are highly interactive so trainees do more than sit and watch a television screen. The label for this type of training and the company that creates it became one and the same—Interactive Distance Learning (IDL).

The companies that participated in the project included Eastman Kodak, EDS, Ford Motor Co., General Motors, Lockheed Martin, NIST-Manufacturing Extension Partnership, U.S. Air Force, Center for Optics Manufacturing, Cadkey, Texas Instruments, and RWD Technologies. The objectives of the project were to (a) pilot the use of interactive distance learning across multiple companies, (b) develop a business case for the use of IDL by individual companies as well as consortia of companies, (c) develop a "best of the best" understanding of instructional design for IDL, (d) evaluate the effectiveness of IDL for providing instruction to the employees of the participating firms, and (e) evaluate the effectiveness of IDL for providing training to small- and medium-sized companies. One outcome of the project was the formation of The IDL Group by the NCMS Board of Directors at the request of General Motors and Texas Instruments. Another outcome was the development of guidelines for designing, developing, delivering, and evaluating IDL. The third outcome was the commissioning of a series of courses based on needs that were identified by The IDL Group's guiding partners. The IDL Group then selected partners to help it design, develop, deliver, and evaluate the courses based on the IDL guidelines and chose two courses, Understanding Cycle Time and DFMEA for the first and second broadcast in the series. The current case study discusses the evaluation that was created to study the effectiveness of these two courses.

IDL Guidelines

Since the IDL guidelines are such an integral part of all courses developed by The IDL Group, the authors would like to take a moment to discuss those guidelines. As part of the original project, participating organizations were asked to provide copies of their instructional systems design or distance learning design guidelines. Material was provided by Eastman Kodak, Ford Motor Company, General Motors, EDS, Texas Instruments, and the United States Air Force. Using this material and current research on distance learning, Dr. William Walsh of Mei Technologies partnered with The IDL Group to write a set of guidelines based on both traditional Instructional System Design (ISD) and "strikingly new approaches to learning and training design" (Walsh, 1996). The focus of the IDL guidelines is on the learner and how instructional designers and trainers can build effective IDL learning environments, with particular emphasis on increasing interaction and participation during training.

The guidelines were developed to serve as a "how to" guide for the participating companies' training departments. Specific objectives for the guidelines are

1. Project managers are able to tell whether the process being used by their team is adequate and will provide the excellence they expect in a course.

2. Instructional designers are able to look up activities, principles, and methods to apply to projects.

3. Subject matter experts get better insight into what is expected of them and how their collaborations and contributions are transformed into a course through the instructional design process.

4. Media specialists recognize some principles to follow in tailoring their products for distance learning applications.

5. Instructors begin to understand why distance learning courses are structured the way they are and how they play a critical role in making each course successful.

The guidelines are organized so that users can progress from a general understanding of the fundamental issues regarding IDL instructional design to more specific applications of design principles. The guidelines begin with a discussion of learning and how learning can be affected by distance. There is a comparison of distance learning with traditional classroom teaching. This gives designers a chance to shake off some old stereotypes and to make use of what they have been doing throughout most of their careers. The focus is on the IDL student and devising ways of building effective IDL learning environments for students.

Exhibit 16.1 is an excerpt from *Instructional Design Handbook for Interactive Distance Learning* (Walsh, 1996, Section X). This section focuses on the effectiveness of the IDL Instructor.

Problem Statement

The purpose of this evaluation case study was to study the effectiveness of two IDL-sponsored satellite courses, Understanding Cycle Time (UCT) and Design Failure Mode Effects Analysis (DFMEA). The problem faced by both the designer/developers and the evaluators was twofold:

1. How can we design evaluation of distance learning courses to capture multiple training outcomes?

2. What model can we use to ensure that the knowledge and skill acquired during a distance learning course is transferred to the workplace?

Applying evaluation to distance learning is complicated not only by the time and technology parameters of the new medium but also by popular views of evaluation itself.

EXHIBIT 16.1.   IDL INSTRUCTOR CHECKLIST.

While developing an IDL course, keep in mind the IDL instructor. Review the IDL course using this checklist to make sure that the instructor is effective. Any **"No"** answer indicates that learning is in jeopardy. The IDL course should be revised to account for the missing element.

	Yes	No
• The instructor is not always *on camera?*	☐	☐
• The instructor maintains *eye contact* with the camera?	☐	☐
• The instructor remains within camera range at all times, i.e., doesn't move around?	☐	☐
• Instructor gestures are planned, rehearsed and deliberate?	☐	☐
• Instructor handwriting is clear and readable?	☐	☐
• The instructor is comfortable with the technology, i.e., doesn't panic when something unexpected happens?	☐	☐
• The instructor pauses sufficiently for students to respond to questions?	☐	☐
• The instructor isn't the source of all course information?	☐	☐
• The instructor asks probing questions and respects student answers?	☐	☐
• At appropriate times the instructor is willing and plans to let the students have control of learning?	☐	☐
• The instructor makes students concentrate on how to get the right answer not what the right answer is?	☐	☐

Source: Walsh, 1996, p. 64.

Knowledge and Skill Acquisition

Research has clearly shown that learning is the result of complex interactions among the training strategy, the training content, the trainee and the context (Gagne, Briggs, and Wager, 1992; Yelon, 1996). As a result, evaluation of learning should seek to identify effective training strategies and isolate problems with training materials, particular groups of trainees, and if applicable, the media interface. This requires evaluation that takes place during all phases of training, including design. (Dessinger and Moseley, 1998)

Popular opinion of evaluation does not match our perspective. Evaluation is often regarded as an effort to determine whether after a course is designed and administered it succeeded or failed. This simplistic perspective is exacerbated by a concern that effective evaluation is too complex or costly for most organizations (Phillips, 1991). Ultimately, these popular opinions give rise to a win-lose mentality and what we will call "evaluaphobia." Organizations, training sponsors, instructional designers, and trainers are afraid to evaluate the course for fear that after their effort they will discover that it did not work! As a result, evaluation design is often (a) left to the last minute, (b) dropped from the radar scope when time pressure arises, or (c) limited to a "smile sheet" that focuses on trainee satisfaction with the course. These "smile sheet" evaluations continue today despite increasing evidence that trainee satisfaction has a small relationship to learning outcomes, including transfer (Alliger and others, 1997)

Transfer

In the last few years increasing market pressures from global competition has raised the need for companies to continuously improve the performance of their workers. Training is often regarded as a critical component of this effort because it is the most frequently used method to improve workplace performance (Broad, 1997). Unfortunately, there is little evidence that the gains from training translate back to behavior on the job (Baldwin and Ford, 1988). One estimate suggests that as much as 80 percent of the investment in training is ultimately wasted because trained skills fail to transfer back to the workplace (Broad and Newstrom, 1992). The "transfer of training problem," requires that training experts take a serious look at evaluating the success of their programs both in terms of learning and in terms of transfer.

In addition to assessing transfer, training designers should consider how training efforts may be modified to ensure that knowledge and skill learned in training will be applied. Training strategies that facilitate transfer are available (Garavaglia, 1996), and they should be adjusted so they can be used effectively in the satellite medium.

The Bottom Line?

Another common measure for evaluating training is cost efficiency as assessed by return on training investment. Unfortunately, efforts to evaluate the cost effectiveness of training often neglect the impact that training has on the individual learner (Hall, 1997). To completely capture the value of a particular training program, return on investment should factor in individual learning gains that occur as a result of training. In the ideal case, these changes would be assessed both at the end of training and back on the job. Whenever possible, evaluation should involve tracking trainees back to the workplace to ascertain whether changes in knowledge and skill were maintained over time and whether these changes generalized to situations that were not explicitly covered in training (Baldwin and Ford, 1988). As learning and transfer are rarely assessed systematically, we felt our efforts should concentrate on the learner, learning, and transfer rather than on generating cost analyses.

Summary

To summarize, effective training evaluation requires a perspective on evaluation that is generally overlooked or ignored. The perspective we advocate here occurs during all stages of training and focuses on the process by which transfer occurs, rather than on terminal training outcomes. Thus, in this case study we focus on learner assessment rather than cost effectiveness or training efficiency. While we do not suggest that the latter outcomes are unimportant, we do feel strongly that neglecting learning can lead to misunderstandings regarding effectiveness and efficiency.

Target Population

The UCT and DFMEA courses were designed and developed for the employees of The IDL Group's partners, specifically engineers and other technical employees of large manufacturing firms with locations across the country and around the world. When the broadcast catalog is published anyone from the Group's partners may sign up for a course(s). The companies whose employees participated in the first course, UCT, were General Motors, Raytheon TI Systems (formerly Texas Instrument Defense Systems and Electronics Group), Goodyear Tire and Rubber Company, Delphi Packard Electrical Systems, and Hughes. The second course, DFMEA, included participants from the following companies: General Motors, Raytheon TI, Goodyear Tire and Rubber, Delphi Packard, Kinefac, and Quantum Consultants.

Desired Outcomes

During this case study we set out to demonstrate that it is possible to conduct an evaluation of satellite courses that will evaluate multiple training outcomes and assess transfer. At the same time we also wanted to determine the effectiveness of an instructional technique that is targeted at facilitating the transfer of knowledge and skill to the workplace. This technique, which we call APPLY, is based on the relapse prevention model of behavior change (Marx, 1982).

Marx (1982) created a transfer-enhancing intervention using principles from relapse prevention. Relapse prevention is the teaching of cognitive and behavioral strategies to maintain behavior change, similar to techniques employed by Alcoholics Anonymous and other addiction treatment programs. The logic behind this approach is that (a) old ways of doing things at work are habitual much the same as an addiction and (b) individuals need support and encouragement to get through a successful change of behavior. The relapse prevention intervention includes identifying transfer barriers, developing strategies to overcome these barriers, and setting personal goals for transfer. The basic concepts behind relapse prevention intervention are reflected in the use of an "action plan", but relapse prevention goes a step further, suggesting that trainees discuss and practice strategies for maintaining behavior change.

Relapse prevention is a useful tool because it approaches the transfer problem in a number of different ways. First, it seeks to increase trainees' motivation to transfer. Second, it provides training design that increases learning not only of content skills but also of secondary support skills that can improve the application of new knowledge. Third, it prompts trainees to be active in changing their work environment so that it is more conducive to positive transfer.

After reviewing the research by Marx (1982), we decided to create our own version of relapse prevention training. The intervention we present includes an expanded focus on opportunities for transfer as well as barriers, but both interventions contain many of the same main features. The intervention is designed to provide trainees with procedures and skills that they can use to apply new knowledge and skill to work and increase their resiliency against negative work environments. Consequently, the intervention is called *Application Procedures Providing Learning Resiliency* or APPLY. (Brown, Ford, and Milner, 1998). The major features of APPLY are depicted in Exhibit 16.2. Constraining factors during course design prohibited the full use of the APPLY model, so not all features were employed. Footnotes on the table indicate which portions of the model were used for each course.

Description of Pilot Course Process

The Performance Consulting Group Inc. (PCG) developed UCT, the pilot course for this case study, in late summer and fall of 1997. The first broadcast of the course took place at the General Motors studio in early October.

Design/Development

Course design followed traditional instructional systems design (Goldstein, 1993) and the guidelines created by The IDL Group. The course design incorporated a number of interactive exercises including structured time when trainees could (a) ask questions, (b) offer specific comments and observations, and (c) work on and report on exercises. The designers also incorporated the following instructional strategies from the APPLY model to facilitate the transfer of training: (a) discuss the importance of applying trained skills, (b) identify application opportunities and obstacles, (c) discuss strategies for overcoming obstacles, and (d) set action plans.

Delivery

The technology for delivering the Understanding Cycle Time course included an on-camera instructor, one-way video, two-way audio, and the OneTouch data

EXHIBIT 16.2. MAJOR FEATURES OF THE *APPLY* INTERVENTION.

At the beginning of training
Discuss importance of trained skill[1,2]
During training
Identify relevant skill and set application goal
Identify application opportunities and obstacles[1]
Commit to goal by considering consequences of applying and not applying trained skill
At the end of training
Discuss effective goal setting techniques
Review goals set during course, revise two or three
Review obstacles and opportunities
Discuss strategies for overcoming obstacles, creating opportunities[1]
Practice relevant strategies
Set action plan or behavioral contract[1]
Discuss effective self-monitoring techniques
After training
Provide multiple forms of post-training support

[1] Feature used in the UCT course
[2] Feature used in the DFMEA course
Source: Brown, Ford and Milner, 1998, p. 10.

response system. The technology uses satellites and analog phone lines to provide live IDL to multiple sites that are geographically dispersed.

One-way video means that the trainees may see the instructor or visual aids on a TV monitor; however the instructor does not see the trainees. The visual aids for this course included overheads, slides, and video. Two-way audio communication was conducted between the instructor and the trainees during and between classes. Two-way audio allowed both the instructor and the trainees to ask questions, provide feedback, make comments, and generally interact with each other.

One Touch keypad technology enhanced the interactivity and made it possible to gather and capture responses for both instant and later analysis. For example, after the trainees answer a question using the One Touch keypad system, the instructor could project a histogram showing the class response. In this way, both the trainees and the instructor received immediate feedback.

The instructor used a semi-scripted instructor guide, and the trainees used a participant manual as a course guide and study aid. The participant manual included copies of the slides, additional information, structured note taking, tests, forms, and other material required for the UCT course. After the course was over, the manual helped the trainees to apply their new knowledge and skill back on the job. The course was broadcast from a General Motors studio in Warren, Michigan. The studio is equipped with an instructor's podium that has a touch screen computer, a computer tool that allows the instructor to annotate the on-screen graphics, and an overhead document camera. The company receive sites varied somewhat but are generally located in a classroom that is equipped with a television monitor (minimum of 27 inch) and One Touch keypads. The sites have site coordinators whose primary function is to turn on the equipment and distribute course materials.

Evaluation

Evaluation was ongoing and included both formative and summative phases. We conducted formative evaluation during both the design and development of the UCT course. Summative evaluation took place after the course was over and focused on the results of the training.

Formative Evaluation. This phase of the evaluation covered the content, design (including interaction, media, and instructional strategies), and materials developed for the course. We set up a plan to evaluate the design elements of the course at no less than two points within the development process: (a) draft development and (b) pilot version of the course materials.

The primary techniques used for conducting the formative evaluation of the drafts were reviews by senior instructional designers, an experienced distance learning instructor, and content area experts. The pilot was a walkthrough involving the instructor, producer, senior designer, developer, graphic artist, and representatives from The IDL Group. Formative evaluation results were gathered, analyzed, synthesized, and integrated into the *Instructor Guide, Participant Manual,* and visual aids throughout the development process.

It is important to recognize the importance of the first broadcast of a course and the overlap between formative and summative evaluation that occurs during that broadcast. During a first broadcast, we gather summative feedback from trainees on their satisfaction with the course and the new knowledge or skill they acquired as a result of the course. This feedback is then used as formative evaluation to revise the course if necessary for future broadcasts.

Summative Evaluation. In order to evaluate how well the training worked, we planned to focus on the learner and evaluate changes in knowledge, skill, and attitude that occurred as a result of training. We also wanted to track trainees back to the workplace to ascertain whether those changes were maintained over time and whether the changes influenced performance on the job.

Our overall strategy was to assess change in knowledge and attitudes through pre and post-testing. At the beginning of the broadcast we intended to ask trainees to fill out a background and attitude questionnaire, followed by the knowledge pretest. At the end of training, we planned to administer attitude and knowledge post-tests and ask trainees about their intentions for applying newly acquired knowledge and skill. We also planned to begin follow-up interviews with the trainees approximately ten weeks after the course was over. The purpose of the follow-up interviews was to capture information on training transfer.

Outcome Taxonomy. In deciding which outcomes to select for evaluation, we employed a training outcome taxonomy developed by Kraiger, Ford, and Salas (1993). The Kraiger, Ford, and Salas (1993) taxonomy focuses on cognitive, behavioral, and affective training outcomes. Similar to work by Gagne, Briggs, and Wager (1992), this view of training outcomes expands the measures typically employed to evaluate training and explicitly depicts the importance of measuring multiple outcomes both at the beginning and end of training. The particular outcomes assessed depend in large part on the objectives of the training program. First, we decided to assess cognitive outcomes using traditional tests of verbal knowledge. While tests of verbal knowledge have been criticized for being unable to discriminate among trainees at higher levels of expertise, they are useful during early stages of skill acquisition (Kraiger, Ford, and Salas, 1993). In our case study we put tests of verbal knowledge on slides and in the participant manual and asked the trainees to answer the questions using the One Touch keypads. For the UCT course we developed a fifteen-item multiple-choice test. Each item contained three distractors and one correct answer. The same test was to be used before and after training.

Second, we looked for ways to assess skill-based outcomes by reviewing performance on training activities. One-way video does not allow observation of skilled performance. It is also possible to collect evidence of certain skills either verbally by asking trainees to answer a question or in written form by having trainees fax or email written activities back to the instructor. Unfortunately, none of these options were viable given the limited time available in these courses or the site setups, for example, inconsistent access to fax machines. Third, we wanted to assess affective or attitudinal outcomes. The traditional measures of affect in training evaluation are satisfaction or liking of the course (Kirkpatrick, 1974). Recent research has made it quite clear that such measures are not highly correlated with learning, nor are they predictive of transfer (Alliger and others, 1997; Warr and Bunce, 1995). As a result, while "smile sheets" are useful for assessing trainee satisfaction from a customer perspective, they are not useful for predicting learning or transfer. There are other attitude measures that predict transfer. Research on self efficacy, an individual's belief in his or her capacity to successfully perform a particular act or behavior, suggests that high self-efficacy is essential for transfer. Bandura (1997) suggests that individuals who believe that they can successfully perform a given behavior are more likely to engage in and persist with that behavior. Research also shows that self-efficacy predicts the maintenance of new skills (Gist, Stevens, and Bavetta, 1991). Finally, in a meta-analysis of training outcomes, Alliger and others (1997) demonstrate that the perceived utility of training for subsequent job performance is related to both learning and transfer. This type of attitude is reflected in questions regarding the perceived relevance or practicality of training. We decided that because of its relationship with learning and transfer, we would assess utility perceptions. Finally, we looked at how to assess transfer of the new knowledge and skill acquisitions. To assess transfer, we planned telephone interviews with trainees eight to ten weeks after completing the course. Trainees would be asked to self-report their experiences applying the content along with their reactions to the course.

To facilitate transfer, we also incorporated an action plan into the course. The instructor presented the action plan as one of the course objectives, and discussed the action plan form throughout training. At the end of the course, trainees were asked to fax the action plan to IDL for review by the evaluation team.

Summary. In summary, our evaluation plan was focused on cognitive and affective training outcomes as well as transfer of training. We planned to generate and collect data that would capture verbal knowledge, utility perceptions, self-efficacy, transfer intentions, and course satisfaction. Table 16.1 summarizes the constructs measured and sample items. We knew that the specific method of assessment is affected by the training medium and that in this case study the methods would be limited by one-way video and two-way audio. Later in the chapter we will discuss how the choices made for evaluating satellite training were also limited by time.

TABLE 16.1. MEASURES FOR UCT COURSE WITH SAMPLE STATEMENTS AND QUESTIONS.

Measures	Sample Statements/Questions
Demographics	• How long have you worked for your current employer? • What is the highest level of education you have achieved? • How many courses have you taken that use technology similar to that being used today?
Knowledge test	Which of the following methods is the preferred method for calculating Cycle Time? (a) Interview, (b) Little's Law, (c) Sampling, (d) Historical Data.
Course satisfaction	I enjoyed this course.
Self-efficacy	I am confident that I have learned the material offered in this course.
Transfer intention	I intend to use the information presented in training back on the job.
Utility perception	If I do not learn this material, I may have difficulty performing my job well.
Opportunity to use	To what extent were you able to apply the following concepts and skills from the course?
Knowledge/skill gain	How have the following knowledge and skills changed from before the course?
Change in job performance	How has your overall job performance related to _____ changed from before the course?

UCT Course Outcomes

Technical difficulty with the course eliminated all pretesting measures. In addition late release of the IDL catalog reduced course attendance to twenty trainees. Of these twenty trainees, only eight provided complete data through One Touch.

Given the small sample size of the UCT course, it is impossible to meaningfully discuss differences among individuals on the knowledge test. In addition, missing pretest measures eliminated the possibility for assessing change in knowledge or attitudes that occur as a result of training. As a result, the only measures available for analysis were post-test knowledge scores, content self-efficacy, utility perceptions, transfer intentions, and course satisfaction. Table 16.2 presents descriptive data which may be used to analyze the UCT course outcomes.

Learning and Attitudes

Scales for the course satisfaction, self-efficacy, perceived utility, and transfer intentions were created by averaging the items designed to tap each construct. Factor analysis is inappropriate with so few trainees, but internal consistency reliabilities suggest that each scale is relatively reliable (coefficient alpha 5 .76, .69, .80, and .91 respectively). Correlation analysis revealed that related constructs, such as utility and transfer intention, were more highly related to each other than to course satisfaction (r 5 .91 versus r 5 .27 and r 5 .31 with course satisfaction, respectively). Interestingly, performance on the knowledge test had small or negative correlations with the attitudinal outcomes. Descriptive statistics reveal that trainees perceived the course positively.

With regard to the action plan, all trainees had time to complete the form at the end of training. The instructor asked the trainees to fax the plans to IDL at the end of training, or within forty-eight hours. IDL received one of twenty action plans. The limited number of action plans prohibits any prediction of who is likely to submit that plan. However, the low base-rate is a notable finding.

Transfer

The quantitative data collected during the interviews is presented in the bottom two rows of Table 16.2. Descriptive statistics reveal that trainees felt their knowledge and skills had changed but only slightly. Similarly, reported changes in related aspects of job performance were small. Change in job performance was

TABLE 16.2. UCT DESCRIPTIVE STATISTICS AND INTERCORRELATIONS.

	Mean	SD	Test score	Course satisfaction	Self efficacy	Transfer intention	Utility perception	Knowledge and skill gain	Change in related job performance
Test score[a]	8.00	1.77	(.65)						
Course satisfaction[b]	4.00	.58	2.05	(.76)					
Self-efficacy[b]	3.83	.71	2.04	.71*	(.69)				
Transfer intention[b]	3.96	.86	.23	.59	.68*	(.91)			
Utility perception[b]	3.64	.84	.03	.56	.83*	.91*	(.80)		
Knowledge and skill gain[c]	1.38	.91	2.31	2.08	.05	2.24	2.15	(.82)	
Change in related job performance[c]	1.29	1.25	2.42	2.04	.41	.05	.30	.67	—

N 5 8 for top six rows of matrix (test score to utility perception)

N 5 7 for bottom two rows of matrix (gain to change in job performance)

* $p < .05$ (2-tailed), numbers in parentheses are reliabilities

[a]Number correct out of 10

[b]5 5 "high," 3 5 "neutral," 1 5 "low"

[c]3 5 "much better than before training," 0 5 "no difference," 2 1 5 "worse than before training"

Source: Brown, Ford and Milner, 1998, p. 21.

TABLE 16.3.   UCT QUALITATIVE FOLLOW-UP DATA.

Questions	Response Themes and Examples[a]
Please tell us about your experiences applying concepts and skills taught in the class back on the job.	Have not had the opportunity to use the material yet, will be soon (4) ex. "I plan to use these things but I haven't had a chance" Have used the material on the job (3) ex. "I've been able to use basic concepts daily and had success."
What part of the course did you find most useful?	How to do the line analysis (3) ex. "The line analysis problem because it used an example" The training manual/guide (2) ex. "The manual is very helpful and had good descriptions."
How do you think the course could be improved?	Provide more detail and examples (2) ex. "Good overview, but if trainees have more exposure then they need more detail. With any previous exposure, the front part of the course could be shortened."
Do you have any other comments?	Instructor good at getting participation (2) ex. "The instructor was very good. She was active and called on people when she didn't get answers."

[a]Numbers in parentheses reflect the number of individuals whose answers were classified into that theme.

Total *N* 5 7.

Source: Brown, Ford and Milner, 1998, p. 23.

positively related to self-efficacy and utility perceptions although these correlations are not significant given the small sample size.

The qualitative data collected during the interviews was coded for themes. The questions asked and the themes generated from the responses including examples are presented in Table 16.3. Numbers in parentheses indicate the number of individuals who expressed opinions that were classified under this theme. For the question regarding application, there was a fairly even split between trainees who were able to use course-related knowledge and skill and those who were not. When queried about the part of the course that was most useful, trainees focused on the most complex aspect of the course, the line analysis, and on the participant manual, which provided take-home materials. Suggestions for improving the course focused on providing more detail and examples. An open-ended question at the end of the interview revealed that the trainees liked the instructor because she was good at generating participation during the broadcast.

Discussion

This discussion will cover technical problems, time factors, and the evaluation process. A few weeks after the UCT broadcast, the evaluators had a chance to apply lessons learned on the Cycle Time course to DFMEA, the second course in the series. We will also discuss the design and outcomes of this "second chance."

Technical Problems

IDL courses are live television. Technically, things can and do go awry. The Understanding Cycle Time course was technically cursed and provided a good example of the difficulties in real world evaluation research. Two events occurred during the broadcast that had never previously happened since the studio began operation.

Prior to the broadcast there is a one-hour test period. Suddenly the hour turned into a time of pandemonium because the fiber connectivity to the up-link wasn't working. The problem (someone had unplugged a cable and not reconnected it) was discovered during the test period, and the course began on time. However, the up-link problem eliminated all pretraining measures and the possibility for analysis of knowledge gains. As a result the only measures available for analysis were post-test knowledge scores, self-efficacy, utility perceptions, transfer intentions, and course satisfaction.

The second event occurred part way through the broadcast, when the One-Touch host "froze" and had to be restarted. This was obvious to the trainees who had to relog in to the system and may have affected the collection of data and the attitude of the trainees toward the class.

Time Problems

The course was scheduled to last for three hours, and the broadcast itself was three-hours including a ten-minute break halfway through. The content for the course was developed from two full days of training. This created time pressure with regard to content, even before the evaluation measures were embedded. A number of suggested measures were cut, including midcourse attitudes and learning process.

In addition, due to timing issues we were not able to include the full complement of strategies outlined in the APPLY model; therefore we were not able to evaluate the results of these strategies. Instead of focusing on how to facilitate transfer by using the APPLY Model, the focus of the case study evaluation became the influence of individual differences on learning activity and outcomes.

Administration Problems

Given the time limitations, we sought to use a simple pre-post test strategy that would take place before and after the broadcast. Unfortunately, course administration difficulties reduced the effectiveness of this design.

Also, rather than a simple training versus control study, we initially wanted to compare alternative training strategies by randomly assigning trainees to receive different training strategies and tracking trainees through the learning process. However, the UCT course was only offered once in the fall, so multiple versions of the course to compare alternative training methods were not available.

Finally, due to late distribution of the IDL catalogue by the companies, only twenty trainees signed up for the course. Of these twenty, only eight trainees logged in to the One Touch system and provided answers to the questions. Given the small sample size of the course, it is impossible to meaningfully discuss differences among individuals on the knowledge test.

Evaluation Process

During this case study, evaluation became an integral part of the whole IDL process from design to delivery. However, the evaluation strategy used for this course was less than ideal due to limitations imposed by the characteristics of the IDL course and the system.

Formative Evaluation

Involving an instructional designer, developer, media specialist, trainer, and subject matter experts in the formative evaluation process increases the effectiveness of the process if all team members are on board from the start of the project. This was reinforced when the media specialist and several subject matter experts did not become involved until the second draft.

The result was revisions that could have been made in the first or second draft or might not have been necessary at all if the content issues had surfaced earlier in the design and development process. In addition, last minute revisions have an adverse effect on instructor preparation time and rehearsals. The problem was exacerbated when scheduling conflicts with the studio made it impossible to conduct a pilot run-through of the course with trainee feedback prior to the first broadcast.

Summative Evaluation. Throughout this case study, the evaluation process took a decidedly cognitive orientation and focused on assessing learning impact rather than assessing cost effectiveness or training efficiency. While we do not suggest that the latter outcomes are unimportant, we do feel strongly that neglecting learning can lead to misunderstandings regarding effectiveness and efficiency. After all, training efficiency cannot be calculated solely on training costs, such as instructional development and travel.

The value of a particular training program should factor in changes in individual knowledge and skill. This requires targeted learner assessment. Further, changes in knowledge and skill should be assessed for their impact on outcomes in the workplace, the classic transfer issue. Thus, program evaluation requires learner assessments in order to present a full picture of costs and benefits. While a method to factor learning into program-level evaluation is beyond the scope of this case study, the need to do so underlines the importance of our focus.

DFMEA: A Second Chance

A few weeks after the Cycle Time broadcast, we were able to apply some of the lessons learned to the second course, DFMEA. The DFMEA course was developed by General Physics in the fall of 1997 and was broadcast in the middle of October. The response rate for the DFMEA course was somewhat better; thirty-five of thirty-seven trainees logged into One Touch, and we were able to obtain almost all of the evaluation data that we planned to collect.

A nineteen-item multiple choice knowledge test was created for the DFMEA course. Again, there were some time problems. The length of the course precluded the use of both a pretest and post-test. Instead, the instructor used six of the test items during the course as review items at the end of each module and dropped the remaining items as time ran short. We used the same affective outcome scales for the DFMEA course as we did with the Understanding Cycle Time course. While ensuring that data will be collected, the lack of multiple scores prohibits any analysis of change.

Scales for the post-training course satisfaction, self-efficacy, perceived utility, and transfer intentions were created by averaging the items designed to tap each construct. Table 16.4 presents reliabilities, descriptive statistics, and intercorrelations. Reliabilities for these scales were somewhat lower than those in the UCT course. Correlations indicate that related constructs—utility and transfer intention—were more highly related to each other than to course satisfaction although

TABLE 16.4. DFMEA COURSE DESCRIPTIVE STATISTICS AND INTERCORRELATIONS.

	Mean	SD	Test score	Course satisfaction	Self efficacy	Transfer intention	Utility perception	Knowledge and skill gain	Change in related job performance
Test score[a]	4.25	1.06	(.57)						
Course satisfaction[b]	4.00	.67	.09	(.81)					
Self-efficacy[b]	3.96	.62	.23	.68*	(.85)				
Transfer intention[b]	3.98	.61	.12	.42*	.65*	(.58)			
Utility perception[b]	4.23	.56	2.13	.53*	.53*	.58*	(.62)		
Knowledge and skill gain[c]	1.71	1.25	2.04	.57*	.21	.12	.42	(.97)	
Change in related job performance[c]	2.00	.93	.35	.71*	.33	.29	.57*	.93*	—

$N = 28$ for top rows 1–5 of matrix (test score to utility perception)

$N = 15$ for bottom rows 6–7 of matrix (gain to change in job performance)

*$p < .05$ (2-tailed), numbers in parentheses are reliabilities

[a]Number correct out of 6

[b]5 = "high," 3 = "neutral," 1 = "low"

[c]3 = "much better than before training," 0 = "no difference," –1 = "worse than before training"

Source: Brown, Ford and Milner, 1998, p. 24.

intercorrelations were all high. Again, test score was not highly related to attitudinal outcomes.

Overall, trainees rated this course positively particularly the utility. One reason for high utility perceptions in this course is the nature of the content. The course focuses on the use of a particular form that is frequently used at GM and other companies. These forms are often required during product design, so the information contained in this course will almost surely be used on the job. The extent to which the course helped trainees use the form on the job will be assessed with transfer interviews.

Consistent with this explanation, quantitative transfer data indicates greater change in job performance than that reported for the Cycle Time course. All of the attitudinal outcomes were associated with greater improvement in course-related skills and job performance, but course satisfaction and utility perception were the best predictors.

Qualitative data from the interviews was coded for themes. When asked about their experiences applying knowledge and skill, trainees reported very different experiences because of differences in their reasons for appearing in training. (See Table 16.5.) One group of trainees (N 5 4) took the course because they serve as assessors that review the DFMEA process and paperwork. Nearly all of these individuals mentioned how useful the course was in broadening their understanding of the process. Another group of trainees (N 5 7) engaged in projects using DFMEA was less positive about the course. Three trainees from this group specifically mentioned that greater detail and more examples would be necessary to improve the course. Another group of trainees (N 5 5) indicated that it was planning to use the DFMEA process in the future. Two individuals noted that they were taking the course not to learn the material but to familiarize themselves with the course for other reasons.

When asked which part of the course was most useful, the majority of trainees said the information on how to fill out the form (N 5 10). Two trainees did note the overview was useful. Suggestions for improving the course centered on providing greater detail (N 5 8) and more participation (N 5 4). Unlike the UCT course, the instructor of this course was criticized for not using the medium to stimulate participation.

Lessons Learned

We learned a number of lessons from this case study with regard to evaluating interactive television courses. The lessons learned dealt primarily with issues related to needs assessment, time, and site coordination.

TABLE 16.5. DFMEA QUALITATIVE FOLLOW-UP DATA QUESTIONS.

Questions	Response Themes and Examples[a]
Please tell us about your experiences applying concepts and skills taught in the class back on the job.	Have not had the opportunity to use material yet, will be soon (5) ex. *"I didn't expect to apply any of this stuff right away. I may be able to apply it in the future."* Have used the material on the job (4) ex. *"We're using this for particular projects right now."* Material needed to be more specific in order to be applied (3) ex. *"I think the training could have included more specific information to make it easier to apply."* Using information as an assessor/auditor (4) ex. *"I'm an assessor, so I audit forms to see if they are filled out correctly. The course gave me a better understanding. I know more about what to look for when auditing."*
What part of the course did you find most useful?	How to fill out the form (10) ex. *"Applications of the process; stuff about form."* Overview (2) ex. *"Explanation of the process, not just the form."*
How do you think the course could be improved?	Increase detail, including better examples (8) ex. *"Examples need to be more specific and more complex; current examples are too hard to apply to what we are doing."* Increase participation (4) ex. *"Instructor could have forced more interaction from participants and pressed people to get involved. If no one answered a question, he would often provide the answer and move on."*
Do you have any other comments?	Instructor could be more effective (2) ex. *"The instructor could have come up with better ways to encourage participation."*

[a]Numbers in parentheses reflect the number of individuals whose answers were classified into that theme. Total *N* 5 18.

Source: Brown, Ford and Milner, 1998, p. 26.

Needs Assessment

Conducting an up-front needs assessment may have identified the different types of trainees who appeared in the DFMEA course and pinpointed content needs.

Tailoring activities and examples to the needs of trainees can improve course outcomes, but this requires some knowledge of trainees' backgrounds before the course begins. Unfortunately, in consortium environments the unpredictable nature of course sign ups is unavoidable. One method for improving future courses would be to use knowledge generated from this type of evaluation and modify course materials to incorporate examples for different types of participants. For example, the next iteration of the DFMEA course could include examples for both engineers and auditors. The instructor could focus on the material that best matches the course composition.

Time

Knowledge and skill tests take a great deal of air time, and air time is costly. Despite our best intentions to measure change in knowledge and skill by having multiple measures, we did not obtain multiple measures from either course. Embedding evaluation measures directly into training helps to ensure that technical difficulties or late arrivals do not interfere with data collection. The problem with this solution is the loss of change measures. One possible solution is to lengthen course time while maintaining the same satellite time. Each of the current courses was advertised for three hours, and the broadcast lasted three hours. If the courses had been advertised as four hours, and thirty minutes were used before and after for evaluation, then response rates may have increased. In order to do this effectively, site coordinators would have to take on greater responsibility.

Site Coordination

While action plans are a useful way of encouraging transfer, it may be difficult to collect them in a consortium environment, and without seeing the plans it is difficult to say how effectively trainees used them. The collection rate may be greater if the plans are collected during or directly after the broadcast either electronically or through the use of site coordinators. Also, Broad (1997) provides some ideas on how action planning may extend beyond the timeframe of the broadcast to include maintenance activities, for example, involving supervisors or developing performance contracts.

One possibility for future evaluation efforts is to have on-site data collection and to expand the role of site facilitators. The geographically dispersed nature of consortium-sponsored training makes this difficult, however, by developing new opportunities for gathering site data and by expanding the role of site training facilitators a number of additional assessing opportunities would arise. For example, on-site fax machines and email capabilities would make it easier to collect data and training site facilitators in group processes would make it possible for trainees to engage in role plays or other group activities.

The practical advantages of satellite training arise in part from the use of only one content expert, the instructor, who can only be one place at one time. The question is whether site coordinators can be trained to help with data collection and other coordination duties without significantly increasing course costs. While moving to full video conferencing may alleviate this problem somewhat, effective site coordination is likely to be a critical issue regardless of the technology.

IDL Guidelines

Based on lessons learned, we are drafting revisions to the IDL guidelines that address both changes in evaluation and changes in instructional design and development and delivery that can benefit the transfer of satellite-based training. While transfer is in large part determined by the work environment, in recent years there has been increased research attention to how instructional designers and trainers can facilitate transfer through training efforts. A sample of these efforts is discussed by Broad (1997). The bottom line for enhancing transfer, according to Broad, is to actively involve stakeholders in the transfer process. Specific activities that can be conducted during training include providing job-relevant exercises and helping trainees develop action plans.

CHAPTER SEVENTEEN

UNANTICIPATED ATTITUDINAL CHANGE: THE PROGRESSION TOWARD SELF-DIRECTED DISTANCE TRAINING AT H.B. ZACHRY COMPANY

Larry M. Dooley, Kim E. Dooley and Keith Byrom

Advances in science, telecommunications, information processing, and dissemination technologies are accelerating the rate of human knowledge (Hefzallah, 1990). This is affecting growth, restructuring, and the need for information dissemination and technology transfer for a trained workforce. Industries are facing difficulties with meeting the needs of a changing and increasingly technological society. Constant retooling and training has become the reality for corporations all over the world. The sheer size of the new generation of job seekers in need of training is staggering. No longer can potential workers assume that the jobs they begin today will survive until retirement.

Right-sizing, down-sizing, reengineering of the company—all are terms that frighten today's employees. In November 1997 film giant Kodak announced it would lay off 10,000 workers, about 10 percent of its international workforce. Kodak was not alone, however, as that same day apparel maker Fruit of the Loom announced 2,900 cuts or about 9 percent of its workforce; electronics parts maker Kemet said it would cut 1,000 jobs or 10 percent of its workers; and fashion purveyor Donna Karan said it would shed 285 employees or 15 percent of its workers (Strauss and Maney, 1997).

The Training Solution

As companies are paring down their workforces, the discriminators between employees seem to boil down to a portfolio that includes education and training. Managers today must engage in some type of distance training if they are to narrow the education and training gap of all their employees. In industry, especially where some job sites have restrictive entry unless certain safety and other certifications can be verified, trainers employ distance delivery to satisfy this training need.

Prior to the introduction of *Reframing Organizations* (Bolman and Deal, 1991) and *The Fifth Discipline* (Senge, 1990), companies spent little time with the overall growth of the employee. Instead, they believed that if training was not tied directly to the "bottom line" then it was not something that concerned them. One only had to look at the training budgets of companies as a percentage of the total budget to see where the real commitment lay. However, in recent years, the commitment to training of the total employee by management has seen a sharp rise.

The total development of people is therefore essential to achieving a goal of corporate excellence, according to Bill O'Brien, president of Hanover Insurance (Senge, 1990). It is very important that businesses go about the job of training the workforce because employees with high levels of personal mastery are more committed to the industry, more important to the company, and will take on more initiative. They have a broader and deeper sense of responsibility in their work, and they learn faster. For all these reasons, many organizations espouse a commitment to fostering personal growth among their employees, believing it will make the organization stronger (Senge, 1990).

Senge introduced into the workplace a commitment to the total employee that training directors have been advocating for many years. In some organizations, training directors are being invited to join CEO executive staff meetings. Training is finally being correlated to an increase in profits and a way to increase competitive advantage.

Current Training Methods

Since most employee training takes place on the job site, corporations are now reevaluating the potential and exploring the effectiveness of a variety of instructional settings for human resource development. Corporations that can afford a training division typically use formalized instruction in a classroom setting, designed and delivered by in-house training staff. Simply put this is the easy way out and requires the most minimum allocation of training resources. But this kind of training alone cannot keep pace with the growing demand. Large companies purchase almost 40 percent of their formal training from outside providers, with small employers outsourcing nearly all of their formal training (Carnveale and Carnveale, 1994). The expenditures on American corporate training are estimated to be over $40 billion per year, which is comparable to the total funds spent on universities (Moore and Kearsley, 1996). This may sound very high, but placed in perspective, training budgets rarely exceed five cents for every dollar spent. The answer lies in telecommunications and distance education.

Distance Education as a Training Tool

Distance education has become a strategic means for providing training, education, and new communications channels to business, educational institutions, government, and other public and private agencies (Dooley and Greule, 1995). Can distance education reach more people, save time and money, and also provide effective learning experiences for students? Hundreds of media comparisons have shown there is no significant difference in the educational effectiveness of media (Schlosser and Anderson, 1994). The media simply serves as a communication channel. The fundamental concept of distance education is simple enough; employees and trainers are separated by distance and sometimes by time. If this is true, it becomes necessary to introduce some form of communication medium that will deliver information and also provide a channel for interaction between them (Moore and Kearsley, 1996).

A consideration of training at a distance forces a reexamination about the ways people learn and are trained (Albright and Post, 1993). Corporate employees in the future will need to take control of their own growth and development, demanding training time and money as part of their rewards for supplying their services. Adult education principles of self-directed and life-long learning will become a major part of compensation packages. Collective bargaining agreements in the future will probably require levels of training for employees that do not exist today. Companies desiring a competitive advantage will "jump on the band wagon" and establish policies and procedures to take advantage of distance learning to deliver these services.

The rapidly changing workplace of the future will demand that trainers move toward this vision with a spirit of adventure. Training professionals at all levels will need considerable imagination, common sense, and creativity to cope with the changes that undoubtedly await us. Corporate success depends upon having and keeping talented people. The shortage of such people is widely accepted, and training (including distance education) at long last is beginning to be recognized as part of the solution. The difficulty is not in converting training materials into an electronic format but in trying to change corporate tradition and attitudes.

Corporate Attitudes

In 1988, Douglas K. Smith and Robert C. Alexander authored a book titled *Rumbling the Future: How XEROX Invented, and then Ignored, the First Personal Computer* (Smith and Alexander, 1988). This book chronicles the activities of the Palo Alto Research Center and its development over ten years ahead of anyone else of the personal computer. These researchers had completed a prototype of the personal computer complete with hardware and software. Why did corporate management not act on this discovery? Could it be that XEROX was beginning to lose market share; was top-management operating in a non-risk culture? Did change require a protracted period of testing and review before change could be initiated (Connick, 1997)?

The construction industry is one of the least likely of businesses to be accepting of the change required to move toward technology-assisted training. Essentially, construction companies are in the business of building things, usually on a very time-conscious budget. Taking the time to train individuals, especially on what the training industry calls soft skills, will take time away from the project currently underway. Moreover, the cost of this training must be absorbed somewhere or on some project budget. Therefore, it is usually when profits begin to drop or the industry becomes increasingly competitive that companies will look inward to find ways to gain more of the market share. Only when all other training modalities either fail or are less cost effective will technology-integrated training be considered.

Corporate History

H.B. Zachry Company is a privately owned general contractor with construction projects throughout the United States and in many foreign countries. Corporate headquarters are in San Antonio, a conservative community in southern Texas. It should be noted that Texas is a right-to-work state and most construction is performed "open shop" without an agreement. H.B. Zachry Company hires most of its labor directly, subcontracting only a small portion of workers. This would seem to indicate that the company is not as concerned with employees as with profits. However, Zachry began as a small family-owned company and has not lost this heritage as it has grown. Respect for and care of their employees has always been a high priority.

As with other companies during their formative years, the labor pool was rich with numbers, and employee training was not considered valuable to the job unless labor shortages were acute and the return on the investment directly correlated to the income generated by that particular project. Projects currently range in size from employing fifty to eight hundred employees and vary in nature from the construction of roads, dams, and power generating facilities to the maintenance and construction of chemical plants, refineries, and pulp and paper mills. These projects are very labor intensive and use unskilled and semi-skilled labor. Supervisors typically have minimal training and education. Traditionally, supervisors often learn both their technical trade and supervisory skills through on-the-job training. Because most of this labor pool is short-term in nature, skilled and craft training is the majority of training conducted; soft-skilled or personal development training is seen as unnecessary.

Proposed Outcomes: Training for Standardization

Because most Zachry projects are in remote areas away from San Antonio, supervisors have a great deal of autonomy and responsibility to complete the job within budget and on time. Obviously supervisory training is a vital element in the corporate strategy to ensure supervisors manage in accordance to corporate custom, regulations, and guidelines. (However little attempt has been previously made to ensure training files are kept up to date). Customs and procedures training for supervisors include corporate history, culture, required behaviors, and procedures for hiring, discipline, termination, benefits, labor law compliance, and human relations.

Zachry Training Prior to Distance Learning

However, training for standardization had taken a backseat in the company due to the rising cost of travel and other factors in transporting employees to and from training sites. In most cases, the training site was the company headquarters in San Antonio, Texas. The remoteness and complexity of the projects coupled with the traditional high turnover experienced in the industry had created almost insurmountable barriers to effective training. In this context and in an attempt to deliver this training in the most economically feasible way possible, company-sponsored training took three basic forms:

- *On The Job Training (learn it as you go):* In this case, supervisors were "on their own" to learn the proper ways to respond to the work environment. They were not introduced to *customs and procedures* and they were *not* rewarded for training, since there was no specific evaluation of training. Generally, experienced supervisors passed on experience and information to new supervisors, likened to an apprenticeship. Unfortunately, the wrong way to do it was often passed on along with the right way, and managers were continually constructing and reconstructing processes. So what was the right way or the company way? With no formal evaluation or supervisor to observe the process, the training did not take place with any degree of consistency or regularity.

- *Job Site Training (make it up as you go):* On certain projects and in certain situations, customs, procedures, and guidelines had been developed and were passed on to employees. On these occasions, the project director would provide training for supervisors, who would then train the workers. The instructors (supervisors) usually did not have any background in how adults learn (andragogy), nor did they have any background in teaching strategies or instructional design. As a result, there were no retention and transfer exercises and documentation-assessment procedures to ensure consistency among and between projects. No research was conducted to assess whether the training was right for the particular task concerned. Confusion would result when employees and supervisors would be transferred to other projects. Documentation of training was not kept up to date to follow employees, so new supervisors had no idea of what training had taken place. Benchmarks for individual training had not been established.

- *Corporate Training (pay as you go):* Some projects had the foresight and initiative to take advantage of corporate training programs and resources available. These programs and resources were limited to the basics and were generally conducted in locations where the numbers were sufficient enough to bring people together for traditional stand-and-deliver classroom training. Very little interactive training was conducted. Subsequently, *only supervisors* on large projects or projects in metropolitan areas were trained and *only projects* that were willing to pay for these costs received this training. Moreover, company incentives were not in place to reward this training; this merely exacerbated the problem as it created a division between the "haves and have nots." Although the training was carefully designed to present the preferred company customs and procedures, the training still varied from other projects that either received no training or that had personnel who had trained supervisors themselves. Since each project must pay for the training from the project budget, training did not always take place project by project.

Effects of Lack of Training

Zachry recognized the inefficiency that resulted from this lack of consistency and standardization of custom and procedures among its supervisors, notably high employee turnover. Lack of a steady workforce placed great strain on the company's ability to staff projects in areas of low labor availability. Some areas of Texas have an unemployment rate of less than 5 percent. As an example of how this affects Zachry projects, a project with a peak of one thousand employees and a turnover of 100 percent (on average the turnover on a large industrial project is 240 percent) means that the contractor must hire two thousand people to complete the project. It is clear that a reduction of turnover not only reduces the cost of employing the additional one thousand employees but it also becomes a competitive advantage when bidding the next project. The intention is not to have each project stand on its own but to have the projects provide a fluid workforce. Management believed based on exit interviews that the improvement of supervisory behaviors was the key to reducing turnover. The standardization of training on customs and procedures and enhanced employee training was one way to reduce the costly turnover. The business imperative for training affected the bottom line. Moreover, if the company was to make an immediate impact in this training and make inroads into systemic change in the training inventory, an intervention strategy had to be devised whereby impact could diffuse throughout the company.

Description of the Process

In order to address the need for standardization, a series of videotapes and a student handbook were developed in 1984 (the *Supervisor Video and Workbook*). The curriculum and student-trainee assessment was based on predetermined competencies by the training staff with requirements for specific levels of mastery on each set of competencies before moving on to the next. It was further decided that each project would have autonomy to facilitate multiple teaching and learning strategies, such as classroom training or a self-study approach. In other words, the company left it up to the individual employee to complete the training. There was no other incentive (merit pay, promotion incentive, job security, and so on) to complete training other than employee loyalty.

Over the next twelve years, the *Supervisor Video and Workbook* became the foundation piece for all supervisory training in the company. The program was designed to facilitate training and provide consistency and competency assessment. The videos and workbook were sent to the projects and sites for dissemination.

Although no research was conducted to assure validity or reliability, all other training programs in the company were built on this basic orientation. It was assumed that this was a prerequisite for further training. By 1996 however, with little attention given to the reasons why, the number of supervisors who had taken the course had dropped to 34 percent. An evaluation of the program revealed that it was used only on projects that had asked for corporate assistance. In other words, it was being conducted only when a member of the corporate training staff would personally go to a site and teach in a classroom setting and usually as part of a more advanced training program. (Therefore, it was not done in remote areas where budgets for projects were very lean.) In these circumstances, little was gained as far as corporate standardization of customs and procedures across the company. In fact, in a classroom setting with an experienced trainer, the video was not even necessary to present the information. Turnover remained unacceptably high. Thus, corporate management demanded another examination of the problem and recommendations for solutions.

Extensive interviews of trainers, management and supervisors were used to develop the following assumptions about the existing training program: a) In spite of verbal commitment to the contrary, training of supervisors took a low priority among corporate and project management; b) operations managers did not understand training and education theoretically or technically, yet they were always called upon to design and approve training; c) there were no processes for providing the instruction required for the company; and d) training was typically assessed on the basis of how well it was received (liked) rather than how much was retained or transferred. No training professionals provided assistance in this company requirement. Projects were too remote, the numbers too small, and the cost too high to employ a sufficient number of qualified trainers to go around the country to conduct traditional classroom training. The stage was set for distance learning!

Intervention of Distance Education

The change started when the Director of Training for the H.B. Zachry Company enrolled in a graduate class at Texas A & M University, Introduction to Distance Learning. This survey course was taught over the Trans-Texas Videoconference Network (TTVN), an interactive videoconference network from College Station, Texas, to San Antonio, Texas, and introduced students to all the differing modalities of delivery that define the field of distance education. This provided a mechanism for the exploration of strategies to solve Zachry Company's training problem. Alternative delivery systems (correspondence, audio, video, computer-based training, multimedia development, interactive video, and so on) were examined as part of this course, and each spurred interest and enthusiasm as training solutions for Zachry Company. Although Zachry Company was looking for one single best mode of delivery, the answer became clear by the end of the semester: multiple modalities. "The test is always to use new technology in meaningful ways to take advantage of multiple media in combinations that make the most sense in terms of the needs of the learner, the needs of the instructor, the needs of the institution or organization, and the cognitive needs of the learning tasks involved" (Chute, 1997). There is no one best way to deliver training, but numerous modalities can be deployed separately and strategically to meet specific needs of multiple cost sensitive projects and the individual student.

A presentation was made by the course instructor to company managers suggesting intervention strategies to be adopted by the company to alleviate this training dilemma. Emphasized in this presentation were not only policy changes that would be necessary but attitudinal changes as well.

For large projects in a metropolitan area, traditional classroom training might be the best methodology. After all, one third of the company was adequately receiving training in that way. Additionally, computer-based training (CBT) might be best on those remote projects with few supervisors, where sending corporate training for didactic instruction is not practical. On the other hand, on remote projects where computers are not available in abundance, text-based self-study may be the answer. Some students depending on the available time for study might choose self study over classroom training.

Regardless of the modality chosen, the appropriate delivery system must be student- and subject-matter sensitive, as well as cost effective. As an example, interactive video might be best for courses on sexual harassment and human relations, whereas computer-based training (CBT) might be best suited to craft or skills training. Moreover, there are instances where a trainer or supervisor cannot enter the job site unless he or she is certified in another training program such as those sponsored by the Occupational Safety and Health Administration (OSHA). The added expense to the company to send trainers and supervisors for these certifications so they can enter the job site to teach or to advise supervisors caused additional contemplation about distance learning as a possible solution.

Slowly management began to sense that a real change was beginning to evolve. Attitudes began to change, old paradigms began to be dissolved, and an increased optimism for the future began to emerge. The authors representing Texas A & M University were invited to attend a board meeting of the Associated General Contractors (AGC) in Florida for the purpose of presenting to them the same material on distance learning presented to the Zachry Company managers. AGC is a professional organization of all general contractors nationally. They were in the beginning stages of considering distance learning as a vehicle for delivering training to the industry. This was an opportunity to plant the seeds for long-term change in an industry not accustomed to change. The authors believe this was the time when attitudes shifted and distance learning won its initial support.

Attitudinal Change

These proficiencies require more than a *shift in duties* but also a *shift in attitudes*. Attitudinal change—how people perceive and react to new technologies and methods—is far more important than structural and technical obstacles in influencing their use. It requires a change strategy, incorporating and empowering all divisions in the decision-making process. The change to distance delivery of training if it is to be accepted must be espoused by the organization, and it must come from the very top of the organization. If the transfer to technology integration is expected to succeed, then one must look at the strategic intent to see if technology is mentioned in the corporate strategic plan.

In an effort to solidify this initiative with management, the vice president for Human Resources attended several middle management introductory sessions on distance learning to lend his visual support to the sessions. His presence added instant credibility to this effort and laid the groundwork for changing attitudes in this area.

Contemplating the utility of distance education for a construction company, Zachry Company began to realize the ramifications of multiple delivery systems on corporate training. Rather than a focus on oral presentations, trainers would need to develop a written curriculum or script, and interactive teaching and learning strategies would need to be implemented. Most corporate trainers are comfortable presenting but have little or no experience with storyboards, presentation software, Hyper-Text Mark-Up Language (HTML), or more advanced authoring programs. Trainers of the future will also need to develop proficiencies in differing distance education technologies, instructional design, competency assessment, needs assessment, and matching prerequisite skills and knowledge and learning styles to the context of the training environment or project, including student evaluation and accreditation. This would require the trainers themselves to be re-tooled!

Selling the Concept

The next step was to convince and solicit support from the corporate executive responsible for training and employment. From his vantage point, a change in direction was both welcomed and needed. Having gained needed skill through correspondence schools while in the Armed Forces, the vice president of Employee Relations immediately recognized the utility of distance education. He also questioned the tremendous cost of transportation of trainers to remote sites to conduct traditional classroom training.

While agreeing to become an advocate, he also recognized the objections that would be legitimately voiced by other senior managers of the organization. For example, what is the business imperative for training? What are the benefits of such a program relative to the costs? How will the success of the program be evaluated, measured, and modified if required? To answer these questions, the vice president of Employee Relations spent almost a week in one-on-one conversations with executives from the Center for Distance Learning at Texas A & M University. During these sessions, he studied the concept of multiple modality, the newest technology, and methods of measuring return on investment for distance education.

The next step was to present the concept to senior management. This was a much more difficult sell. Not being training experts and only marginally interested in training, they were understandably skeptical about expenditures on new technology and a new training paradigm. Their thoughts and questions included, "The material might be over the heads of some supervisors, many of whom have not graduated from high school. Some supervisors might consider the material irrelevant to their job. The subject of human relations might not be of interest to some of the more senior supervisors. Assuming that interaction is the key to effective training, how will the existing training be diminished in a distance education venue?"

Fortunately, the vice president of Employee Relations had been tutored by the Center for Distance Learning (CDLR) and was able to articulate an argument for topics such as human relations. In addition, he was able to show research supplied by the CDLR that interaction and motivation enhance retention of material and that students can learn equally well either in a classroom or in a distance situation.

The next step therefore was to announce this new direction in training to the training staff. This new vision for training was outlined and supported with distance education literature and the business imperative or necessity of decreasing the cost of training while increasing access for supervisors in remote locations. The organization, it was pointed out, could no longer be competitive in the global environment with so many untrained supervisors. Moreover, the company could not afford all of the trainers needed for traditional delivery. Upon hearing his new vision, the training staff just sat there with a look of disbelief and apprehension.

Although the training staff remained skeptical, after eight months and a constant restatement of the vision, the staff finally supported the distance learning concept. Even then they had a tendency to move toward traditional delivery systems rather than multiple modalities. Change did not come easily for this traditional, conservative, family-owned company. The construction industry is not known for its innovations in training; innovations in construction techniques, yes, but not in training. Training was seen as a management technique not something associated with moving the individual construction project forward. They were not accustomed to this type of change, especially rapid technological change. They wanted to slow down and study it for a while, a typical response given the situation.

Getting Buy-In

Getting buy-in from the training staff was a challenge but doable. The real test, and as the saying goes "where the rubber meets the road," came when we attempted to gain approval from the operations managers. As pointed out in the assumptions, their endorsement was essential for the implementation of any new program. Additionally, as per company policy, operations managers have budget approval responsibility. Their support and endorsement was mandatory. The strategy, therefore, had three objectives: a) provide training and exposure to the multiple modalities of distance learning technology, b) demonstrate the business imperatives for distance education, such as the reduction of training costs, the increased access to remote sites, and the return on investment that would accrue, and c) focus on multiple modes of delivery for the future of training for the Zachry Company.

Proof of Concept

To accomplish these objectives, the company would need a proof of concept and successful test case. If an extensive plan was attempted and failed, the chance to infuse distance learning into the training function and into the Zachry Company proper might never come to fruition. To attempt to convert an existing skills training curriculum to a distance education delivery from scratch would be too large of an investment for the operations committee to approve. Additionally, if it took too long or if the skeptics could not see early successes, our entire operation might have been in jeopardy. The company decided to try a small project, one that could almost guarantee success, but it did not appear that way to the rest of the company.

Since the *Supervisor Video and Workbook* had already been developed and tested although it had primarily been used in a classroom, it could easily be converted into an asynchronous independent-study learning model. In addition, soft-skills training could be designed quickly and would help ensure an early victory in this market. Moreover, work had already begun on revising these materials to make them current so start-up costs would not be necessary.

Once the modification was complete with the assistance of the Center for Distance Learning Research at Texas A & M University, one thousand videos and workbooks were reproduced at $3.00 each. The video and workbook were modified to include additional competencies such as human relations, cost and scheduling, understanding differences, and total quality management.

Additional Curriculum Development

These were courses that had already been developed and taught in the organization for many years. However, when the instructors were asked to submit a written curriculum for the purpose of conversion to a distance learning format, it was discovered that a written curriculum and course materials did not exist. These instructors had successfully delivered these types of programs in a classroom but had not considered other types of delivery formats. A cost analysis suggested that it might be more cost effective and produce better quality to obtain an existing curriculum from another source rather than to convert our existing curriculum to a distance education format. Through the Center for Distance Learning, a curriculum was identified from within the construction industry. The Associated General Contractors (AGC), Carolinas Chapter, had a comprehensive and well developed curriculum containing the competencies Zachry required for its supervision course. The chapter had become interested in distance education technology but did not possess the technical capability of converting its curriculum. After careful negotiations around quality control and copyright, the AGC, Carolinas Chapter, H.B. Zachry Company, and the Center for Distance Learning entered into a partnership by which they allowed Zachry to utilize the curriculum in exchange for conversion of the curriculum into a self-study distance learning format. The cost of the conversion would be born by H.B. Zachry Company, and the CDLR would make the distance conversion using graduate students. This type of collaborative effort is unprecedented.

To make it really effortless, a letter of introduction, a Scantron test, and even a Zachry pencil were included in a shrink-wrapped package that was mailed directly to all supervisors. The total cost was $8.25 per package. The *Supervisor Video and Workbook* orientation was completed and distributed in May of 1997. As of September 1997, six hundred and two of the company's seven hundred and three supervisors or 85.6 percent had completed the video training program as compared to 32 percent when the program began. The training gap was reduced from 66 percent of the supervisors who had *not* received the training to 15 percent in just three months. In our first pilot project, six hundred and three supervisors had been trained in fifty-seven different locations on their own time, without travel, and without seeing an instructor in less than three months at a cost of $8,250. It was estimated that to train the same number of people at the same locations in a traditional face-to-face format would have cost $42,000 in travel and expenses for the instructors alone. More significantly, the training would have required an estimated twelve months of full time effort by the training department to complete. Included in this estimate is the down time of trainees while they traveled to the training site, as well as the development of the materials and the cost of duplication and evaluation of the examinations.

Team Effort

This team effort was accomplished through the Center for Distance Learning Research (a partnership between Texas A & M University and the GTE Corporation). The mission of the Center for Distance Learning Research (CDLR) is to provide timely and appropriate information on the development, application and maintenance of information technology systems through demonstrations, training, publications, and technical assistance. The CDLR is divided into four divisions: a) Network Management, b) Multimedia Development, c) Training, and d) Research and Information Services.

The divisions within the CDLR address two primary goals: a) access to information and b) workforce development and training. The world is undergoing a dramatic shift from an industrial-based society to an information-based society. One key reason for this shift has been the "information superhighway" or Internet. The Internet provides a resource for up-to-the-minute information and fast inexpensive global communication. The principles of distance learning are founded on the concept of transferring information in a variety of media. The CDLR concentrates heavily on the technology that enables the transference of this information and the human resources necessary to ensure this transference occurs.

Multimedia Conversion

With all this institutional capacity, it made sense for H.B. Zachry Company to partner with the CDLR and Texas A & M University. Therefore, Zachry funded two graduate students to convert the existing video- and text-based curriculum into HTML for conversion into a CBT program and multimedia presentation, including a CD-ROM that was interactive with video clips and multimedia graphics. (Each job site was to provide a computer workstation with a CD-ROM drive capable of running at least 133 MHz.) The program was to be self-paced with competency testing at various intervals. The employee could start and stop at will; however he or she could not receive credit for the module until at least 80 percent mastery had been achieved on all items. Once this was achieved, the COMPLETED button would become active. By pressing the button, the file would be saved with the employee's identification number and be ready to upload to the master employee file in the employee relations department of corporate headquarters.

These portions of the course were placed on the World Wide Web as they were developed so that Zachry could advise on content quality. In two months, the CBT versions of *Supervisor Orientation* were complete and downloaded to stand-alone site computers. This allowed new supervisors to receive the training at the time of hire. Since these versions were also on the Internet, they became accessible to those that also traveled constantly. Subsequently, the training gap was reduced to 5 percent by November of 1997.

Implementation

The purpose was to work as a development team to redesign and standardize the training program for multiple modality distance delivery. Faculty and graduate students with an expertise in distance education, multimedia, and instructional design worked with the Training Director and content experts at Zachry to create a new way of delivering the necessary content.

The instructional designers and media experts used the literature on effective design principles. Moreover, the training director acted as a sounding board as to what would be acceptable and not acceptable to the company. The importance of understanding the limitations and strengths of each piece of technology and to match media, methods, and objectives to the content was emphasized (Dooley and Greule, 1995; Farr and Schaeffer, 1993).

In designing a video and workbook training series, it was critical that instructors and facilitators in the distance education environment also considered the lack of non-verbal cues, the need to build rapport, and stimulation of student motivation (Dooley and Greule, 1995; Driscoll, 1994). Students therefore are more likely to be anxious about the training than in a traditional program and, as one would expect, at the same time find it more difficult to express these anxieties to the trainer (Moore and Kearsley, 1996). It was critical to the Zachry Company that the instructional designers address these questions up front. The intervention of distance delivery on this training project with the H.B. Zachry Company was deemed a great success.

Conclusion

H.B. Zachry Company has made great strides in moving into the distance learning arena. The greatest victories however are those that are not seen but result in major shifts in attitudes and enhanced motivation of the entire workforce. It took patience to allow the company to move at its own pace and not try to accelerate it to our pace.

Along the way, many lessons were learned regarding both the successful initiation of change efforts and the institution of distance education in a business organization as well. These included research and development, preparation of an advocate, breaking the paradigm, sustainability, transfer of the technology, and collaborative efforts. Each will be summarized individually.

Research and Development. While technical organizations such as Zachry often invest in R & D for technical subjects, investments in R & D for training and education is a relatively new phenomenon. In this case rather than sending its training director to a popular "flavor of the month seminar," the company sent him to get a Ph.D. in Education. In this case the classroom experience and the relationships developed in the classroom led to a dramatic business intervention.

Preparation of an Advocate. Quite often training directors will return from seminars enthusiastic about new and revolutionary ideas, only to see the new ideas fail and their enthusiasm about any new idea diminish because of a lack of support from their immediate supervisor. In this case the immediate supervisor became an effective advocate because he believed in the idea and because he was willing to get additional information. In this case he received the additional information from the Center for Distance Learning Research. As a result he was able to articulate the business imperative for additional short-term expenditures for conversion of curriculum to a distance education format. This business imperative not only included the traditional cost and benefit analysis but the theoretical basis for the change as well.

Breaking the Paradigm. Although everyone believed that he or she understood the new training paradigm, unconscious resistance still remains. Months after the initiation of the change even trainers find themselves reverting to old ways. The tendency over time is to use distance learning technology in a "stand and deliver" setting. Management must remain diligent in restating the goals, objectives, and philosophies of distance learning.

Sustainability. The key to any successful intervention is sustainability. In the case of training, distance education provides the best vehicle for continued use and development by providing a modality that can be delivered in remote locations to a single individual. It is more easily updated than print or video materials.

Transfer of Technology. Rather than being hindered by the state of technology at Zachry, the implementation of distance education created a practical need that had the effect of increasing its use and understanding throughout the organization. Supervisors who had previously never attempted to utilize a computer very quickly became expert in the use of CD-ROM and the Internet.

Collaborative Efforts. In the beginning it appeared that Zachry simply did not have the resources to create a distance education program. It did not have the technical expertise and as it turned out did not have a curriculum. It was the innovative partnership between Zachry, AGC of Carolina, and the Center for Distance Learning that provided the elements to make the new training initiative a success.

Once the distance program was implemented, the company discovered many benefits and training interventions that had not been previously considered. For example, the Zachry Company is enlarging its international operations. Traditional training requiring travel across the world would be cost prohibitive. Distance delivery solves that problem! Zachry is also developing programs to address cultural traditions and language using expatriates across the world. In addition, the new training and distance delivery systems provided needed professional development for overseas workers.

Although the company was able to save time, travel, and expense, it was most impressed with the ability to reach large numbers of employees at one time. The flexibility of conducting training asynchronously allowed for success when other avenues had failed. Just-in-time training has always been an advocate of adult learning and distance education, and this case is no exception.

Telecommunications and computer technology have also encouraged the collaboration of teams that did not exist before, a result that was not anticipated but applauded by management. Management and labor are "talking" together, which transfers to higher productivity. Zachry was also able to have technical experts available for all employees through the training without the added cost of travel and time.

Another benefit of this university-corporate partnership was an increase in quality of the training materials. Zachry Company discovered that collaboration with experts in the field of distance learning improved the current and future training programs. As evidenced by this case, future training will be able to reach audiences not possible before, and the saturation of training can be complete.

There were also many challenges to introducing this technology, including technophobia to an industry that is not accustomed to high technology. When this project began, computers were not a standard item of equipment at the production worker level. In fact, there was initial concern that supervisors would not have access to a computer to complete the training. Additionally, when the Center for Distance Learning Research suggested a web site to post the training schedule, Zachry was concerned about access to their server, where "hackers" could enter the proposal database.

Another challenge was the major instructional modifications that had to be made to the supervisory training module. An instructional designer did not develop the original training; rather it was designed by an individual in the construction industry. Therefore, changes had to be made to the method of delivery as well as the evaluation necessary to guarantee mastery of the concepts.

There were not many instances of misapplication of technology; however there were suggestions as to which modality of delivery would be best in each situation. In all cases the company agreed, and problems in this area were kept at a minimum. It would be easy to see when the recommendation of technology would be met with resistance due to cost or availability.

The coordination of technology and on-site technical support for the pilot project have not been an issue, due to the low support necessary for the workbook and video tape project. However as more complicated equipment is utilized for additional interventions into training, these authors see the need for formal policies and procedures to be in place prior to proceeding.

The introduction of the CD-ROM training also had a very important side effect: management became comfortable with the technology and decided to try other modalities of distance learning, such as video conferencing. It was discovered that T-1 lines were already leased to send and receive construction data. With a prepaid T-1 half the battle is won on delivery costs. Managers quickly found the additional benefits of video conferencing for such applications as construction conferencing, continuing education for key management personnel, administrative applications, association meetings, and taskforce meetings.

Management has decided to work more closely with the Center for Distance Learning Research to design additional training programs that can be delivered on the job site. The authors are convinced that this is only the beginning to a long and successful relationship that will position the H.B. Zachry Company to the forefront of construction training at a distance.

CHAPTER EIGHTEEN

UTILIZING TELELEARNING AS STRATEGIC MEDIA CHOICE TO ENHANCE EXECUTIVE DEVELOPMENT AND AFFECT ORGANIZATIONAL PERSPECTIVE: THE U.S. NAVY'S BUREAU OF MEDICINE AND SURGERY (BUMED)

Jim Suchan, Alice Crawford

The widespread popularity of telelearning programs particularly given the significant resources spent on equipment suggests there exists common understanding of what these technologies mean and how they should be used. However, as Karl Weick has pointed out, technologies are not mere artifacts whose use is self-evident; they are equivocal and open to interpretation, and the interpretations organizational members ascribe to a technology influence both thinking and its use (Weick, 1990).

Not surprisingly, administrators, training directors, and instructors have often interpreted telelearning technology in fundamentally different ways. For example, many administrators, squeezed by decreasing budgets but increasing education and training demands, focus on cost benefits (reduction of instructor labor costs and learner per day and travel costs) and the possibility of penetrating new markets. On the other hand, instructors may see the technology either as a threat, an increase in workload, and an impediment to close interaction with learners or as a new opportunity to exert their influence on a larger number of learners, a curious tool they would like to experiment with, and a way of transforming instruction and learning by giving students access to multiple information sources.

What contributes to divergent interpretations of a new technology such as telelearning is the lack of models for understanding its potential capabilities and uses. Models provide a common language that frames thinking about, attitudes toward, and, ultimately use of technology. This chapter describes a model we developed to reframe thinking about telelearning in the Navy's Bureau of Medicine and Surgery (BUMED) as it wrestled with determining which forms of distance education could be used to educate physicians, nurses, and medical service corps officers being groomed for high-level executive positions. Our goal for this model was two-fold: to serve as an analytical tool that guided thinking about how to use telelearning for executive development and to change the nature of the discussion about learning, interactivity, and the capabilities of new technological media in the BUMED community.

This chapter first provides an overview of the BUMED organization and the factors that caused it to consider distance education as a solution to its education and training challenges. Next, we describe the mental model about communication and training prevalent in the organization that framed administrators' interpretations of telelearning. Subsequently, we introduce the model that focuses on the relationship between instructional content based on learning outcomes, the instructional techniques required to support the learning outcomes, and the media that will support the levels of interactivity that the pedagogies require. Finally, we describe how we implemented the model and the experience we had offering a BUMED module using a two-way video, two-way audio tele-education system (VTE).

The Organizational Problem

The Navy has a worldwide health care system designed to meet the health care needs of active duty personnel, their dependents, and retired military members. Until the early 1990s physicians, nurses, and medical supply corps officers were required to assume top management positions in hospitals and their surrounding clinics, commonly called medical treatment facilities (MTFs), with minimal if any managerial training and education. When time permitted physicians might attend commercially provided management development programs such as the Physicians in Management (PIM) program or several in-house management programs. However, those who did attend were unable to systematically take courses that progressively developed their management abilities; furthermore, program content in the PIM program and its counterparts was not tailored to the uniqueness of managing a MTF. Not surprisingly, the managerial results were less than ideal: resources were not managed as carefully as they should be, and patient needs were not being met in a timely manner—complaints about long waits to receive care and even the inability to receive needed care were being forwarded to legislators. Adding to the health care complexity, Navy medicine was transitioning to a managed care delivery system complete with its accompanying financial complexities (for example, capitation budgeting and contracting for services) as well as integrating the three military services into one health delivery system. To help ensure that military hospital administrators had the tools to manage this increasingly complex environment, Congress passed legislation that mandated that senior managers, specifically Commanding Officers and Executive Officers of these MTFs, must demonstrate managerial competence before they can assume these senior-level positions.

To provide the education necessary to demonstrate that competence, the Navy Bureau of Medicine and Surgery (BUMED) in partnership with the Naval Postgraduate School Systems Management Department (SM), created an Executive Management Education (EME) program tailored to the needs of Navy health care professionals. To design this curriculum, selected SM faculty conducted an extensive two-part needs analysis. Over 100 semi-structured interviews at fifteen hospitals across the country were conducted with physicians, nurses, and administrative support staff to determine the managerial, administrative, and leadership capabilities senior executives must possess to do their jobs well. These qualitative data were then used to develop a questionnaire designed to measure the gap between the capabilities health care administrators currently had and the level they needed to be effective senior-level MTF administrators. The questionnaire was administered to all senior officers in the medical community.

The curriculum resulting from this two-part needs assessment consists of fifty-three modules, most lasting from four to sixteen hours, of graduate-level management education on topics ranging from health resources allocation and administration in areas such as financial management and facilities management to managing change, formulating strategy, and improving organizational communications in the general management and organizational behavior areas. These modules reflect the gamut of desired learning outcomes, ranging from knowing principles, concepts, procedures, and rules (for example, the financial management and contracting modules) to exercising judgment in the face of uncertainty and changing habits of mind (the strategy, change, and communications modules).

Initially, these modules were to be taught at the major MTFs. This on-site module instructional plan was developed because it is not feasible for health care personnel to leave their jobs to enter a resident program. However, program administrators soon discovered that this delivery method would not provide modules fast enough to officers who needed them. Furthermore, because officers frequently transferred to other MTFs, EME program administrators would have difficulty ensuring that modules officers needed were available at the MTF where they were stationed. Finally, faculty could "burn out" from extensive travel and the need to perform resident teaching, secure research funding, publish research in the open literature, and provide service to the department, the school, and their professional organizations.

To solve these problems, late in 1994 EME administrators began examining the feasibility of using various forms of videoconferencing systems to deliver EME modules. To provide EME administrators with guidance to formulate a workable instructional delivery plan that does not compromise learning, we (the authors) were asked to assess the lessons learned from telelearning research. After an initial survey of literature to determine best practices, we expanded the scope of our inquiry to include the development of a model that captures the complex interrelationships between instructional content, learning outcomes, instructional strategies, and media choice. Furthermore, we developed a matrix that links specific BUMED EME modules with viable instructional media. At the heart of this model and its matrix is that instructional media choice is a complex strategic activity influenced by interrelated factors such as learner needs, organizationally and individually based learning outcomes, the interactivity required to meet those outcomes, the repertoire of pedagogical techniques instructors use to reach those outcomes, and the relative media richness of the instructional technology that enables it to support the teaching strategies and interactivity required to reach learning objectives. Developing models is one thing; getting an organization to apply that model in a rapidly changing severely budget constrained environment is another.

Factors Shaping EME Administrators' Thinking About Distance Learning Technology

As indicated earlier, technologies can be equivocal, resulting in multiple interpretations and hence lack of shared understanding of how they can and should be used. Several factors cause these multiple interpretations within an organization. As Deborah Schreiber points out in the introduction chapter, the organization's distance learning technological capability level (OTC) reflects the degree of shared understanding about how various distance learning technologies can help the organization meet performance outcomes that are aligned with business strategy, vision, and mission. Organizations at an early or immature stage of OTC have limited understanding of the strengths and weaknesses of distance learning technology and limited knowledge of the degree to which it can support training or educational learning outcomes, let alone how that technology can further the organization's strategy and thus meet stakeholders' needs. Consequently, these organizations rely on their former mental models to shape their interpretation of new distance-learning technologies' uses.

Clearly, BUMED EME was at an immature stage of OTC development. Administrators saw telelearning technology primarily as a means of cutting training costs; initially they wanted to offer all EME modules via two-way video, two-audio teleconferencing (VTE). That EME administrators interpreted telelearning use almost entirely from an economic perspective is understandable. Since the end of the cold war, the Navy budget had been cut over 40 percent in real dollars. These reductions have been felt throughout every Navy organization, particularly those engaged in training and education. Consequently, cost savings colored administrators' interpretation of virtually everything, particularly the perceived value and use of new technologies.

In addition, BUMED EME administrators felt political pressure to implement some high-tech form of telelearning. They were keenly aware that the Navy's training organization, Center for Naval Education and Training (CNET), had been using for several years various forms of telelearning—primarily two-way audio and somewhat less than full motion (twenty to twenty-five frames per second) two-way video to *train* successfully enlisted personnel and junior officers at multiple locations in celestial navigation, base security, fiber-optic repair, and a number of other areas with lower-level learning outcomes (Simpson, 1993; Simpson, Wetzel, and Pugh, 1995; Wetzel, 1996). And word had reached BUMED that the Air Force Institute of Technology (AFIT) had successfully conducted training using a relatively inexpensive one-way video, two-way audio videoteletraining (VTT) system.

The perceived success of these training programs prompted BUMED to conduct a one-week Instructor Effectiveness training program using two-way video, two-way audio links to approximately ninety learners at nine different sites. Despite equipment problems and difficulty generating interactivity among learners at different sites, administrators believed the experiment was a success. This perception was based on a one-page report written by a low-level administrator who attended parts of the program that stated the instructor was an excellent lecturer and the students seemed to be engaged in the material. This brief experiment suggested that VTE technology could serve as an instructor multiplier and that significant travel and per diem costs could be reduced by using this technology.

The Navy like all military organizations pays careful attention to the beliefs and actions of its most senior leaders. Consequently, the Navy Surgeon General's attitude toward technology would also steer EME administrators' beliefs about the value of telelearning. The new Navy Surgeon General was a very strong technology advocate, which he made very clear from the outset. He disliked paper, preferring email to written correspondence and expecting computer-generated briefings with the briefer providing him with a disk rather than a hard-copy of the briefing "viewgraphs." Further, he planned to curtail his extensive travel and that of his subordinate officers through use of video teleconferencing. This attitude toward technology represented a dramatic shift in the BUMED organizational culture. The Surgeon General saw technology as an important tool to cut costs and improve efficiencies. And as one BUMED administrator commented, "what interests my boss fascinates the hell out of me."

Soon EME program managers, initially a Navy captain and then a commander, began discussing with NPS Systems Management faculty ways of converting and translating face-to-face EME modules to video tele-education (VTE) versions. Also, the discussion focused on the logistics of transmitting and delivering the face-to-face instruction to remote locations and the technological capabilities (equipment interoperability issues, bandwidth capabilities, and so on) of doing so. The primary concern was to determine to how many remote locations EME modules could be delivered. Cost effectiveness was the watchword. Unwittingly, EME administrators saw VTE as an automation technology that could replicate at numerous locations the instructor and instructional aids such as computer-generated viewgraphs and video clips. The metaphors that we highlight are telling because they reflect an implicit mental model about communication, technology, and learning that influenced thinking about how telelearning technology could be used.

The conversion, translation, transmission, replication, and delivery metaphors signaled that EME administrators implicitly viewed communication and learning as information transfer and the telelearning technologies as mere conduits that delivered information. This view obviated the possibility that various forms of telelearning technology represented strategic media choices and that these choices were dependent on the assessment of factors such as the interactivity needs of highly skilled professional learners, the modules' varied learning outcomes, and the type and level of interactivity that must be generated to achieve those outcomes. In fact, concepts such as strategic media choice, interactivity, and learning outcomes were not part of EME administrators' language; consequently, recognizing let alone seriously considering these factors was beyond administrators' horizon of possibilities. This lack of a critical language to discuss these important issues resulted in BUMED EME administrators being unable to ask important questions that could align distance learning technologies with desired organizational outcomes.

Given the organizational context within which BUMED is situated, this prevailing view of communication, technology, and learning is not surprising. BUMED is embedded in a bureaucratic Navy hierarchy and culture that emphasizes the need to follow clearly defined rules, regulations, and procedures. This focus is warranted given the technical and high risk nature of the work, such as operating nuclear power plants on ships and submarines and launching and landing jets on aircraft carriers. Within this environment, where focus is on support of the Navy mission of readiness and combat effectiveness, there is limited tolerance for ambiguity and a strong bias for disciplined, structured problem solving.

The Navy culture in turn drives perceptions of both enlisted and officer development toward an institutionally controlled training framework in which learners acquire standardized material through a didactic process and instructors merely deliver information already provided them by a team of instructional designers. In short, information is generally seen as a commodity that needs to be transferred and media as a conduit to transfer that information.

The pervasiveness of Navy culture and the implicit assumptions about communication helped create a teacher or expert-centered preference among BUMED EME administrators. This view of learning was made clear in 1996 when the ranking BUMED EME program manager wanted to convert the entire EME program to digitized video discs (DVD). DVD is a form of computer-based instruction that provides structured learning heuristics that are anticipated and devised by subject matter experts. Learners engage with a multimedia system to progress through multiple sequences of learning. Thus, learners interact with the system not with each other. Clearly, DVD closely mimics the training processes that are the Navy's norm.

Although DVD could be a viable distance learning approach for a limited number of EME modules, this technology was not suitable for all modules. Fortunately, this EME program manager rotated to a different position (as mentioned earlier, naval personnel change jobs every two to three years).

The Model and Its Impact on Telelearning Assessment

This model is composed of four primary factors and their relationships with each other:

1. Analyze the needs of the learner and the organization to determine the appropriate instructional content.
2. Link instructional content with learning outcomes, that is the performance expected as a result of the learning experience.
3. Select instructional techniques that support specific learning outcomes. Instructional techniques vary in the levels of interactivity they attempt to generate.
4. Choose instructional media that will support the levels of interactivity that the selected instructional techniques require.

Next, we examine each of these factors in detail and show the interrelated influences that make telelearning media choice a *complex, strategic* activity. This complexity is partly caused by differences in control of these factors: organizations may have difficulty ensuring that learner and organizational needs are aligned; learning outcomes may be determined by administrators, instructors, learners, or combinations of these groups; instructional techniques are generally determined by the instructor, but that choice may be limited by organizational training norms; and media technology availability and use is often determined by administrators and technology experts. These differences in control make it challenging to align learning needs, learning outcomes, and instructional techniques with distance learning media choice.

EME Participants' Learning Needs

As indicated earlier a needs assessment was conducted to determine appropriate instructional content for the BUMED EME program and to determine the learning styles and classroom expectations of its participants. Interviews revealed that the EME program audience consisted of highly sophisticated learners who were acutely aware that fundamental structural changes in the military health care delivery system required new knowledge, strategies, and skills to balance effective use of health care assets with high quality care. The physicians, nurses, administrators, and other health professions represented had high expectations for the relevance of learning to their jobs and clear ideas about how learning should occur and their roles in this process. They eagerly took responsibility for their learning, desired autonomy, and most importantly wanted to share what they knew as well as learn from their colleagues' experiences.

Research on adult learning demonstrates that adults generally learn more deeply and permanently with instructional approaches that give them the opportunity to use their own initiative as compared to traditional teacher-oriented classroom approaches (Savery and Duffy, 1995). This can occur only if instructors construct environments that create opportunities for learners to interact easily with each other. In fact, Knowles (1984) argues that for many kinds of learning, adult students not instructors are the richest learning resources for one another. And both Senge (1990) and Nonaka and Takeuchi (1995) claim that *significant* organizational learning occurs only when individuals have the opportunity to place their insights, experiences, and best practices within the larger pool of group or collective experience and test the organizational applicability of those insights and practices. Through instructor-facilitated discussion, dialogue, and even role plays, the individual and group not only can explore complex issues from multiple perspectives and gain insights unavailable from individual self-reflection and analysis but also forge new shared collective understanding that can reshape organizational thought and behavior.

Discussion, dialogue, case analysis, and role play require an instructional environment that enables significant verbal and non-verbal interactivity and allows for rich feedback. Furthermore, these student-centered modes of learning require instructors to function as process facilitators. Consequently, if a new instructional technology were to be used to reach these professionals, that technology must be capable of supporting not only these interactive, communication rich modes of learning but also the facilitation role (and the communication requirements that define that role) instructors must play.

Although we have made a strong case for the creation of instructional environments that enable BUMED health-care professionals to be responsible for and direct their learning, two fundamental questions arise: to what extent do these learners need to be involved in their learning and given the large number and wide range of EME modules, does this degree of involvement apply to *all* learning situations? In the next section we show that distinct learning outcomes, based on modifications of Gagne, Briggs, and Wager's (1992) taxonomy, do exist; and to achieve each outcome, instructors must use different instructional techniques and strategies and the right combination of instructional media to support those techniques.

Learning Outcomes and Instructional Strategies

Educators and learners have goals often called learning outcomes that are achieved through various communication methods commonly called instructional techniques and strategies or pedagogies. Given the Navy training culture discussed earlier, BUMED EME administrators were not aware of the higher-level learning outcomes required of many of the EME modules, let alone the interactions among instructors and learners needed to reach those outcomes. Consequently, providing EME administrators with a learning outcome taxonomy was essential to differentiate modules from each other by goal and the instructional techniques required to reach that goal. Borrowing heavily from the work of Gagne, Briggs, and Wager (1992), we created four distinct learning outcomes and the instructional techniques that define their pedagogical environments.

Know and Supply Information

This category includes knowledge of facts, principles, concepts, procedures, and rules that can serve as a building block for more advanced outcomes. This type of knowledge can also have a pragmatic function: mid- or senior-level health care administrators can supply executives or decision makers with the knowledge to understand a concept, procedure, or rule before taking appropriate action.

When learning basic concepts in an unfamiliar discipline, learners are dependent on the instructor's knowledge and ability to clearly communicate that information. Consequently, knowledge of these basic concepts can in a sense be transferred by lecture, question and answer, and limited discussion from instructor to student.

Apply Information within Structured Situations

This outcome requires the learner not only to know but also to do. The student learns what knowledge, principles, concepts, rules, and procedures to apply to structured problem solving and decision making situations. For example, BUMED EME professionals would be able to apply the correct contract regulation to a procurement request, to know how to perform the Total Quality Leadership plan (do, check, act, process), or to select the appropriate accounting principle for a financial management decision. Although there may be some degree of uncertainty in these situations, this learning outcome deals primarily with correct and incorrect processes, problem solutions, and decisions. In other words, there is great likelihood that knowledgeable managers would implement the same (or similar) process, solution, or decision.

Exercise Judgment in the Face of Uncertainty

This outcome develops in health-care professionals the ability to exercise judgment when faced with complex, messy, and sometimes career-threatening problems of strategy, change management, program management, ethics, and leadership. Judgment is defined broadly to include problem analysis, assessment of internal and external stakeholder needs, determination of system-wide implications of implementing a problem solution, and a variety of other activities that require executives to analyze and synthesize both "hard" and "soft" information. Unlike the previous two categories, this outcome specifies performance in the absence of firm rules and guidelines for applying learned knowledge and skills. For example, though ethical frameworks can be taught as a basic concept within the "know and supply information" category, ultimately health care professionals make ethics-based decisions under very equivocal circumstances that require them to draw on their deep understanding of organizations based on both education and experience.

Understand and Change Habits of Mind

This last outcome attempts to make health care professionals self-conscious about the strategies they customarily use to assess complex problems and to be aware of the assumptions that are at the foundation of these strategies. Sometimes called double loop (Argyris and Schon, 1978) or generative learning (Schon, 1983), the results of this outcome may not immediately be a better repertoire of strategies but professionals who are more aware of the way they typically attack problems, the sources—professional, educational, and personal—of the problem-solving strategies they customarily use, and the strengths and limitations of their approaches. This awareness or heightened self-consciousness may eventually lead to new patterns of thinking that can result in breakthrough interpretations of organizational situations and novel approaches to organizational problem diagnosis.

Media Characteristics

BUMED EME administrators' initial desire to offer all EME modules via two-way video, two-way audio teleconferencing and then through DVD indicates the implicit belief that media are mere conduits that transfer knowledge from instructors to learners. These administrators lacked a theory of media richness to analyze the capabilities of telelearning media, particularly various forms of VTE, to support various types of communicative interactivity needed to deploy instructional strategies and techniques to attain various learning outcomes. In short, media choice was not seen as a strategic activity.

Media choice researchers have demonstrated the need to link communication task requirements with media that have capabilities to meet those requirements. These media capabilities can be classified and then grafted on a continuum from lean to rich. Relatively lean media have sufficient information-carrying capacity to fulfill structured routine communication task requirements, such as the information exchange or knowledge transfer interactions required to achieve the first two learning outcomes. However, more unstructured and ambiguous tasks, such as strategic planning in a dynamic environment or determining organizational change strategies, require rich media that enable learners to generate multiple interpretations of available information, explore different solution scenarios, and come to sufficient agreement about the meaning of the problem, the interpretation of the data, and the steps to take (Lengel and Daft, 1988). Consequently, a key requirement is that instructors have available media that are rich enough to support the instructional strategies (the communication task requirement) needed to achieve desired learning outcomes.

Three interrelated factors determine the relative leanness and richness of media: the capability of the medium to support various levels of verbal and non-verbal interactivity, the type and timeliness of feedback a medium can provide, and the relative degree of perceived interpersonal presence that the media can enable. Interactivity is a medium's ability for senders and receivers to notice and respond to each others' communication cues. There are verbal and nonverbal components to interaction: language, speech rate, voice pitch, and intonation and eye contact, proxemics (use of space), gestures, and body language in general. Different media support to varying degrees one or more of these components, thus enabling different types and amounts of interaction. Feedback is a subcategory of interaction. We define feedback as a specific type of interaction that has as its purpose the development of individual, group, or organizational learning. Finally, interpersonal presence is the media's ability to communicate the personal feelings and emotions that accompany many face-to-face communication interactions (Daft, Lengel, and Trevino, 1987).

How well and easily a medium supports a particular component of interactivity influences the extent to which the component is used. For example, if an instructor using a two-way video, two-way audio VTE system finds it too difficult or cumbersome to cut from a long shot of the class to a medium close-up of a learner asking a question, that technological limitation will steer the instructor into relying on long shots. That reliance will affect the interactivity between instructor and learner. The instructor will be forced to focus merely on the language of the question not the student's facial expression, the tilt of the head, and the position of the body. The limited interactivity because of the need to focus merely on language will influence the content and tone of the instructor's response, the likelihood of follow-up questions and responses, and even the possibility that the questions could open up a rich discussion among other learners. In essence, limited interactivity could also decrease the amount and type of learning-enhancing feedback between the instructor and students.

Linking Media with Instructional Techniques and Learning Outcomes

To make strategic media choices, BUMED EME administrators must be able to link media with the interactivity requirements instructional techniques demand to meet desired learning outcomes. In discussing this linkage, we focus on the minimum richness requirements a medium must possess to generate the needed interactivity. In addition, media must be capable of supporting the highest level outcome and the most communication-rich strategy the instructor is trying to realize. Finally, new media such as DVD and VTE have more traditional media embedded in them (for example, text and visuals); consequently, these technologies occupy a range on the richness scale. The location on the range depends on how effectively instructors and learners make full use of a technology's capabilities.

Know and Supply Information

This learning outcome requires minimal instructor-learner interaction, and learners generally require limited feedback. Consequently, relatively lean media can be used to attain this outcome. The lean media requirements enable administrators to focus on cost-saving technologies such as video-taped lectures or multi-point (a number of linked sites) VTE that can reach a large number of students. In fact, emerging, relatively low-cost technologies such as the Internet can be piggy-backed onto any one of these previously mentioned media to supply not only information contained in home pages but also to provide student feedback via email.

If the content or procedures to be learned remain relatively stable and the instruction must reach large numbers, then professionally developed, digitized video discs (DVD) or video taped lectures (VHS format) with high production values delivered by a dynamic speaker will enable students to meet this learning outcome. The drawback of extensively using lean media to train mature adult learners with high growth needs is decreased motivation. As mentioned earlier seasoned professionals, particularly executive-level healthcare officers, often demand control over their learning and expect instruction that requires them to interact with colleagues. Lean media concentrate the locus of control in the instructor or the technology itself.

Apply Information Within Structured Situations

This outcome requires low to moderately interactive instructional techniques such as question-answer and instructor-focused discussion. To support these techniques, media located at the mid-level of the richness scale are needed.

VTE systems have the capability of supporting the communication these instructional techniques require. In fact, one-way video/two-way audio VTT systems, a significantly less costly alternative to two-way video/two-way audio systems, are communication rich enough to support the instructor-learner interaction and feedback. Although one-way video makes it impossible for instructors to respond to multiple learner cues (visual and spatial), the structured nature of this learning outcome may require only verbal interaction between instructor and learner.

Exercise Judgment in the Face of Uncertainty

This outcome requires highly interactive feedback-intensive instructional techniques such as learner-centered discussion, case analysis, and role plays. These techniques require rich communication media. Obviously, face-to-face instruction is the richest medium. However, a cleverly designed full-motion two-way video/two-way audio VTT system may be able meet the richness criteria. This system would require state-of-the art equipment at the originating and remote sites. To employ highly interactive feedback-intensive instructional techniques, instructors would need to use the equipment to its maximum communication capacity. This use requires technical and graphics support. However, even the most sophisticated satellite broadcast systems have a voice transmission time lag that makes conversation awkward. This time lag significantly affects routines for entering and exiting conversation that instructors and learners unconsciously use. Consequently, the free-flowing dynamic exchanges that characterize well-run case analyses and role plays are difficult to duplicate in the VTE environment and virtually impossible if multiple site locations are used.

Although these and other factors dampen interaction and limit feedback, we do not know to what extent these differences affect learning or how much they may be mitigated as a result of instructors' and learners' changing communication behaviors as a result of continuing use of and greater familiarity with VTE systems. Clearly, the limitations these factors create require that instructors use special, VTE-unique interaction and feedback techniques for activities such as case analysis and role plays. We believe these techniques may partially mitigate the dampening effect VTE has on interaction. In short, VTE use causes a trade off between the amount of interaction as well as the quality of feedback and cost effective access to learners. Given financial constraints the tradeoff may be worth it.

Understand and Change Habits of Mind

This outcome requires instructional techniques that are highly interactive and feedback intensive. Furthermore, instructor interpersonal presence is key to establishing a safe, trusting learning environment in which executives can not only step outside their job roles and the habits of mind that accompany them but also avoid the defensive routines that protect them from the embarrassment and threat of exposing their own thinking and making clear the assumptions and weaknesses behind that thinking. Even the most sophisticated VTE systems cannot duplicate the complex interplay of visual, spatial, tactile, and olfactory cues that generate interpersonal presence and enable the facilitator to create a safe learning environment.

Applying and Testing the Model

We surveyed NPS BUMED module instructors to determine the learning outcomes of each of their modules, the instructional techniques they used to achieve those outcomes, and the expected stability over time of the content of their modules. These data were compiled in a matrix that links these factors with the media rich enough to help achieve the desired learning outcomes. The criteria used to link the modules to media are discussed below.

DVD Criteria

We used two criteria to assess DVD module use: stability of module content and amount of interactivity required to meet module learning outcomes. Module content stability was divided into five categories that represent the amount of change in content a module would undergo within three years. Module developers determined the percentage of change in module content by checking the appropriate category.

DVD technology would be cost effective only for modules whose content remained relatively stable for an extended period. Stable content is operationalized as a 20 percent or less change in module content within three years. The high cost of initial DVD preparation would make modules in which content changes even relatively quickly (more than 20 percent per three-year period) poor candidates for DVD application.

DVD provides learners with structured learning heuristics that are anticipated and devised by subject matter experts. Consequently, DVD technology well supports learning outcomes that reflect knowledge acquisition (for example, knowledge of accounting concepts and contracting regulations), structured processes (following the correct hazardous material disposal procedures), and even some complex decision processes when there is sufficient information to use a structured process for making a decision (constructing a stakeholder map). These outcomes are reflected in the know and supply information and the apply information to structured processes categories. In addition to the content stability criteria, we also stipulated that at least 50 percent of a module's learning outcomes must reflect these two categories for a module to be considered a potential candidate for DVD application.

VTE Criteria

The type and amount of interactivity a module required was the primary criterion used to determine VTE module applicability. This amount, which varies from module to module, was implicit in the instructional techniques module developers used to achieve specific learning outcomes. Module instructors who rely on lecture and question-answer require less interaction between themselves and students and between and among students than instructors who use discussion, cases, role plays, interactive exercises, and other forms of experiential learning.

In addition, since learning outcomes desired should influence instructional techniques, we examined the data to determine if there was a relationship between a module developer's determination of learning outcomes for a module and the instructional techniques used to achieve those outcomes. Except for two modules, there is a very strong relationship in the expected direction. Instructors teaching modules focusing on "know and supply information" and "apply information to structured processes" outcomes depend heavily on lecture and question-answer techniques. On the other hand, instructors who aim for the "exercise judgment and change habits of mind" outcomes use more interactive pedagogies.

The earlier discussion of VTE implies that using the medium for specific applications is not a simple yes-no choice. Because interactivity is a continuum, we suggest three categories of VTE-module "fit": excellent, satisfactory, and high-risk candidates for VTE use.

Excellent candidates for VTE are modules that use 50 percent or more lecture and discussion and focus 50 percent or more on the "know and supply" and "apply information to structured processes" learning outcomes. These modules lend themselves to VTE because they do not require extensive interaction to attain their learning outcomes. Consequently, the dampening effect that VTE systems have on more complex interpersonal interactions is not an issue when the interaction is highly structured and often instructor directed.

Modules in this category may also be suitable for multipoint delivery or may be offered via one-way video/two-way audio VTE systems. This type of system would significantly reduce delivery costs.

Satisfactory VTE candidates are modules whose instructors use 50 percent or more of highly interactive instructional techniques and focus 50 percent or more on the "exercise judgment and change habits of mind" learning outcomes. Modules meeting these criteria are considered only satisfactory candidates because the VTE technology may be unable to support the levels of interactivity required of instructional techniques used to attain these higher-level learning outcomes. Literature we reviewed on the Navy's use of VTE to conduct leadership education indicates frustration on the part of instructors and some learners when VTE is used where extensive interpersonal interaction between and among participants is required (Wetzel, Simpson, and Seymour, 1995). While there is still insufficient research to determine the actual impact of VTE use on interaction and learning outcomes, there appears to be some risk of a decrement in learning and learner satisfaction, particularly among senior managers, if VTE is used for higher-level learning outcomes.

High-risk VTE candidates are modules that focus 75 percent or more on highly interactive learning techniques or the "exercise judgment and change habits of mind" learning outcomes. The lack of research and experience in using VTE to achieve such complex learning outcomes suggests that a large-scale VTE investment for such learning may waste resources and undermine the learning that BUMED officers require to be skilled MTF executives.

Testing the Model

We began testing the model by determining if there were differences in learning outcome, learner satisfaction, and interactivity between face-to-face and two-way video, two-way audio VTE version of the "bottom line and high-impact health care communications" module. This eight-hour module, which provides health care executives with instruction and practice in organizing and writing effective managerial documents, focuses primarily (over 50 percent) on the "know and supply and apply information to structured processes" outcomes though module sections require learners to exercise judgment in applying the communication concepts to specific organizational situations. Three instructional techniques are used to attain the learning outcomes: lecture, discussion, and document analysis. The module requires a moderate level of interactivity; consequently, it was classified as an excellent VTE candidate. We provide a brief overview of the participants, the VTE equipment and its setup, the instructor's strategies to generate interactivity, and the experiment's results.

The face-to-face (FTF) module was taught in a one-day session at the Bethesda Naval Hospital in Bethesda, Maryland and the Bremerton Naval Hospital in Bremerton, Washington. The two-way video/two-way audio VTE instruction originated from the Naval Postgraduate School (NPS) distance learning classroom; there were no live students at this location. The two VTE remote sites were located in San Diego, California and Portsmouth, Virginia. The module was divided into two four-hour blocks taught on consecutive days. Listed next are the number of participants at each site:

SITE	PARTICIPANTS
Bethesda (FTF)	12
Bremerton (FTF)	18
San Diego (VTT)	14
Portsmouth (VTT)	12

The two-way video/two-way audio NPS site used a PictureTel 4000 video-conferencing system communicating through three ISDN lines. One ISDN line has a bandwidth of 128 kbps for a total of 384 kbps on three lines. This system could broadcast and receive about twenty-five frames per second of video, which is fairly close to full motion.

Room designers assumed instructors would operate the VTE equipment to reduce labor costs; consequently, most of the equipment (for example, control panels, touch screens, and phone dial ups) was located at the front of the room on a raised platform. This equipment partially blocked student view of the instructor; the instructor was visible only from the chest up, which limited instructor shot selection to medium close up and close ups. Also, this setup limited significantly instructor range of movement; instructors must remain close to the equipment to operate it. Unwittingly, designers created a classroom setup that promoted lecture. Indeed, instructors who have used the room have almost always lectured, choosing a medium close up of themselves and a long shot of the remote students. Generally, they only altered these two shots to show information on the document viewer or their computer-generated "viewgraphs."

At the two remote locations, learners sat in four rows, four to five learners per row. This arrangement was caused by the camera, monitor, and microphone setups. At both locations there were two thirty-five inch monitors located at the front of the room, one that showed the instructor and another that showed what the instructor was seeing. The remote location cameras could not be controlled from NPS because of equipment compatibility problems; consequently, a technician at the remote site controlled the camera. Finally, at Portsmouth each student had a microphone and a switch that had to be pressed before the microphone could be activated. When the student pressed the microphone switch, the camera automatically panned to the student and zoomed to a medium close up. At Balboa, students shared voice activated microphones that were not linked to camera movement. As we will discuss later, this room setup affected interactivity.

At the NPS location the instructor, one of the authors of this chapter, had to modify significantly customary use of the room to generate learner engagement with the material so that learners would be primed to interact when posed questions. To be engaged with the material, particularly during mini-lecture segments, learners require visual and auditory variety. The instructor wanted to create that visual variety through different shot selections and by using a variety of non-verbal strategies (body position, hand movement, and so on) to emphasize lecture or discussion points. To achieve these results, the instructor used a VTE equipment operator to vary shot selection (the instructor and operator preplanned four different shots and specific floor locations the instructor would need to hit for the shots to be effective) and abandoned the raised platform with its banks of VTE equipment blocking learners' view of the instructor in favor of the classroom desk space. This area looked more informal, enabled the camera operator to significantly vary shot selection so that remote learners could see the instructor in various positions and types of shots, and allowed the instructor to establish eye contact with the remote students by constantly focusing on the camera.

If the instructor had operated the equipment, he not only would have been trapped on the platform behind the VTE equipment but also would have suffered from cognitive overload caused by concurrently operating the equipment, speaking to the camera, scanning the remote students to determine their level of understanding, thinking of questions to pose to generate discussion, and planning ahead as to what he was going to say or do next. Clearly a team approach is necessary during actual VTE instruction if learners are to be provided with the visual variety necessary to engage them with the material and thus be ready to interact.

The instructor, who had read a number of reports on VTE instruction, varied significantly his teaching preparation and style for the VTE module. Rather than plan in twenty to thirty minute blocks as he did for face-to-face classes, the instructor planned in six to eight minute blocks for the VTE class to ensure there was no dead camera time and to attempt to create the impression of a well choreographed seamless experience for the learners. He also had to slow his speaking speed, enunciate more carefully, and most importantly, pause after asking a question to account for the time delay between sites. This delay significantly altered the dynamics of typical question-answer exchanges and the implicit rules of entering and exiting conversations during discussions. At the beginning of the VTE class, the instructor cold called on learners initially to get them involved with the equipment and the class; cold calling became unnecessary after about forty-five to sixty minutes of instruction.

To meet the constraints of video being transmitted at twenty-five frames per second (less than full motion), the instructor had to avoid quick movements because they would appear jerky and disjointed at the remote sites. Furthermore, because he was being seen on a thirty-five inch screen, he had to tone down his hand, body, and head movements, and to some extent match his nonverbals with the shot selection. For example, if the operator had a tight close up on the instructor, he could only use head movement and facial expression to emphasize points. Finally, the instructor had to simultaneously look at the camera to establish eye contact with remote students and scan the monitor located above the camera to gauge remote students' reactions to the material. Assessing learner reaction to the material and to open-ended questions was difficult because the camera washed out many visual cues, particularly of learners located in the third and fourth rows.

Study Results

We measured differences between FTF and VTE sites in learning outcome, learner assessment of the instructor and the module, and amount and type of interactivity. The difference between a pre- and post-module assessment exercise, which was graded on a ten-point scale using criteria derived from the module content, was the learning outcome measure. This assessment required participants to diagnose organizational and stylistic problems in a document and then revise it to ensure it was well organized and readable. The same assessment was used for the pre- and post-assessments. Learner evaluation of the instructor was measured using four questions (instructor knowledge of material, ability to explain module concepts, effectiveness in encouraging participation, and presentation style) on a ten-point scale; learner evaluation of the module was assessed using eight questions. Interactivity was measured by an interaction scheme created specifically for this experiment. A research assistant at the learner sites coded the interactions in real time; she also tape recorded the interactions and reviewed the tapes to ensure that the coding was accurate. We provide a brief overview of the data, focusing primarily on the interaction data. The data and analyses from this study will be more fully reported in a subsequent paper.

Statistically, there were no significant differences in learning outcome between the FTF and VTT sites. However, a follow-up study with a larger sample size may produce different results. Because of the small sample size, which should be considered as we review the results, we view the data as exploratory.

Although FTF students gave slightly higher evaluations to the instructor and the module, these differences were not statistically significant. The novelty of the VTE experience and Navy officers' biases in favor of new technologies may have skewed the VTE results. On their post-module assessments, officers stated that VTE was "outstanding," "a wonderful learning environment," "dazzling in its capabilities," and a "great asset that we should use."

Ironically, the instructor felt he was significantly more effective in the FTF than the VTE classes. Furthermore, he felt a lack of connection with the remote learners, causing the VTE experience to feel cold and somewhat unsatisfying. Finally, teaching the VTE module required significantly more preparation and was more tiring than the FTF modules.

The interaction data though tell a different story. Although there were virtually the same number of interactions between the FTF and VTE sites (113 and 105, respectively), there were statistically significant differences in the *types* of interaction. Specifically, the difference between sideline interactions (FTF 5 32; VTT 5 9) was significant. Sideline interactions reflect discussions between two or more students without the instructor intervening; in short, learners control the discussion, and the instructor facilitates. Clearly, there were far more learner-centered interactions at the FTF sites.

In addition, there were statistically significant differences between the number of two-person instructor-learner interacts: FTF 5 37; VTT 5 61. These are rather isolated interactions, often generated by the instructor's question. Not surprisingly, there were significantly more three-or-more-person interactions at the FTF than the VTT sites: FTF 5 70; VTT 5 33. Finally, there were significantly more learner comments that were not prompted by an instructor question at the FTF than the VTT sites: FTF 5 41; VTT 5 8.

Clearly, the VTE environment caused learner interaction to be instructor focused and seemed to discourage learner-to-learner interaction. Rarely in the VTE modules did the instructor facilitate a learner-centered discussion or did learners on their own generate questions or comments, while this occurred fairly often at the FTF sites. Learners at the VTE sites noticed the interaction differences. During informal discussions after the modules were completed, they commented they felt compelled to interact with the instructor because the technology arrangement, particularly the monitors, directed attention to him. Furthermore, the remote site learners discovered that if they quickly commented on points another learner made (particularly at the Portsmouth site where they had to press a microphone button to be heard), the instructor often could not see them when they spoke because the remote cameras weren't able to pan and zoom in quickly enough on them. Consequently, remote site learners varied their interaction patterns to complement the VTE technology's capabilities.

Conclusions

EME administrators did not have a complex enough interpretive framework to determine the appropriate kinds of telelearning technology for senior-level executive education modules. These administrators focused almost exclusively on perceived telelearning cost advantages, viewed executive education from an institutionally controlled training perspective, and saw telelearning media as merely conduits that transferred information from instructors to students. Clearly, there was need for a richer framework to influence EME administrators' decisions about the types of telelearning technologies that would support senior-level executives' learning needs. In addition, administrators needed a new language about telelearning and management development—concepts such as media choice, media richness, interactivity, learning outcomes, and adult learner needs—that would interrupt current organizational routines about technology and training, thus potentially creating more carefully thought out possibilities for telelearning use.

To create that framework and language, we developed for BUMED The Strategic Media Choice for Telelearning model described in this chapter, linked the model's factors to EME modules, and began testing the model's predictive power. To date, the model's affect on EME administrators' thinking appears to be limited. Although feedback about the model from the EME program manager was very positive and the model has been used to determine which modules are "reasonable risks" for transformation to various forms of telelearning, we haven't seen evidence that EME administrators are using a more complex framework to think about telelearning technology: discussions still focus on telelearning cost advantages and ways to transfer face-to-face modules to either VTE or network based instruction (NBI) versions. However, our model—more specifically our continual discussion and dialogue about the model with Naval Postgraduate School Systems Management faculty teaching EME modules—has affected their thinking about telelearning technologies. They have begun asking substantive questions about the extent to which various forms of telelearning can support the teaching techniques they use, the ability of telelearning technology to generate the interactivity required to meet their instructional goals, the type of administrative and technical support needed to teach in a telelearning environment, and so on. These module instructors may influence EME administrators' interpretive framework about telelearning as they force administrators to confront concepts about telelearning use before these instructors agree to transform a face-to-face module to a telelearning version.

Ironically, our own model explains the limited effect we have had on EME administrators' thinking. In essence, we were attempting to change EME administrators' habits of mind about technology, learning, and communication. That change requires more than the technical reports we have written—a medium far too lean for the change required—and the briefings we have given. What was needed to start this change process was a communication-rich forum in which we facilitated discussion about EME administrators' expectations about telelearning technology, their implicit attitudes about adult learning, their understanding of communication and interactivity, and their strategy for using telelearning to reach the learner performance outcomes needed to manage and lead a medical treatment facility. In short, we needed a process for EME administrators to put on display their mental frameworks, their habits of mind about telelearning and to recognize the "blind spots" those customary ways of thinking created. Only then could the elements of our model be introduced and fully discussed as a potential way of generating different ways of thinking about telelearning as a strategic media choice decision.

CONCLUSION

CHAPTER NINETEEN

BEST PRACTICES OF DISTANCE TRAINING

Deborah A. Schreiber

Trainers and education specialists traditionally have looked to developments in communications technology to deliver distance learning. As is often the case with complex phenomena, however, no one solution provides a silver bullet. It appears that the most effective strategy for meeting the needs of distance education and training is to employ a variety of forms of instructional technology and electronically mediated instruction. Deciding what technology to use, however, and how to use it effectively continues to pose great challenges to organizations as they attempt to design delivery of distance learning.

It is recognized that many companies procure new technology but often see limited return because they do not know how best to employ it. And for the organization that is mature in its technological capabilities, effective implementation of distance learning events may occur; however, the company wrestles with how to institutionalize its efforts so that distance training becomes part of the profile of the organization.

Designing and implementing distance training that contributes strategically to the organization requires not only a new organizational chart but often a transformation of the corporate culture itself. Maximizing the use of technology to deliver distance and distributed learning is not dissimilar to reengineering processes in that there is a redefining of roles and responsibilities. Further, significant collaboration among diverse experts becomes critical to ongoing maturation by the organization for technological capability to support distance training.

To understand the impact that such diversity may have on the interdisciplinary efforts necessary for successful distance training, one must examine the various roles and personalities of information systems and human resource personnel involved. It is also necessary to understand corporate and government cultures, as they greatly influence policy and management issues regarding an organization's technology capability for distance learning.

Distance and distributed education and training represent a process composed of multiple and diverse elements. These elements or components are interrelated and include (in addition to organizational culture and the diverse experts collaborating to develop distance training) the delivery technology itself, the learner, the instructor, and the learning environment. To understand the instructional and technological needs of a distance training event or program, it is necessary to understand the associated impact of each component on intended business-driven performance outcomes. A systems processing model for distance training can provide a mechanism of checks and balances to account for these components.

Even with the availability of prescribed models for design and implementation of distance training, often there is continuing difficulty on the part of employees and organizations to participate in cooperative efforts that are systematic and logical. This can be due to the phenomenon of group dynamics associated with interdisciplinary teams as well as the complexity and parameters normally associated with operating at an organizational level. The result is distance learning applications that are defined by a specific department or function, rather than business goals and objectives of the organization. Such a distance training event may be implemented effectively from a procedural perspective, but it contributes minimally to the organization's strategic gains.

Overcoming barriers to interdisciplinary and organizational-level efforts however, is critical to successful implementation and institutionalization of distance training. To help address these issues, the case studies in this book identify a number of best practices for avoiding pitfalls and rising above limitations to develop and deliver distance training to meet business goals and objectives of corporations, government agencies, and nonprofit organizations. The lessons learned provide valuable insight into how to overcome organizational and technical barriers to maximize use of technology for distance learning and ultimately make distance training a part of the profile of the organization.

The following paragraphs identify practices which work best to facilitate strategic distance training. These strategies manifest the guiding principles described in the Preface and include discussion of the following phenomena: (a) the impact of corporate culture on interdisciplinary and organization-level distance training efforts, (b) the existence of conceptual frameworks which provide parameters for diverse types of learning at a distance, and (c) the need to correlate instructional methodologies and delivery technologies to maximize learning at a distance.

Impact of Corporate Culture on Distance Training

As discussed earlier in the book, distance training makes strategic contributions when driven by organizationally recognized business goals and objectives. However, an institution's previous attitudes about training, as well as its organizational chart and division of labor, often make it difficult to initially engage in a conversation at this level. The contributing authors recognize this phenomenon and suggest soliciting support from one or more individuals in the organization who may positively influence change and facilitate innovation regarding training strategies.

Engage Champion or Change Agent

Contributing authors Klueter (Chapter 6) and Howard (Chapter 5) strongly advise engaging a champion or change agent to facilitate initiation and institutionalization of distance training efforts. Breaking down departmental silos, integrating staff responsibilities, rethinking budgets, and changing processes demand strong leadership and commitment. For distance training to ultimately become part of the profile of the institution or agency, the organization must evolve beyond individual championship. However, upon start up this focus is critical.

The role of the change agent or champion for distance training is twofold: the individual aids in broadening perspectives for innovative instructional strategies, and he or she establishes procedures for uncharted and nonroutine training programs.

When considering who or what type of individual may serve effectively as champion or change agent, Suchan and Crawford (Chapter 18) caution that the role of consultant (internal or external) is not the same as that of change agent. Consultants may facilitate reshaping perceptions about use of telelearning technology for distance training as well as aid in the integration of interdisciplinary efforts. However, it is an organizational change agent (who possesses the needed direct interaction with key organizational administrators) who can secure operational and budgetary support for initiation of distance training efforts.

Describe ROI in Strategic Terms

Soliciting support of a champion or change agent for distance training requires demonstration of significant return-on-investment (ROI). A cost-benefit analysis results in a strong ROI when the contribution is strategic. Distance training that contributes strategically to an organization is implementation that enhances the company to work smarter, innovate faster, and ultimately perform stronger than the competition.

Several of the case studies in this book describe cost-benefit analyses that demonstrate strong returns and strategic gains from distance training (Chapters 6, 7, 9, 10, 11, 17, and 18). As part of aligning distance training to organizational business goals and objectives, the contributing authors identify several attributes they strongly suggest practitioners consider when costing out return-on-investment and strategic gain from distance training. These include rate of delivery of the distance training, the size and diversity of the population accommodated, and consistency or standardization of the instruction that results.

For example, Dooley and others explain in Chapter 17 that it is the standardization of training on management customs and procedures that reduced costly turnover of general staff and supervisory personnel. Mortlock and Dobrowolski describe in Chapter 9 that with downsizing, right-sizing, and reengineering, distance training took center stage in aiding thousands of individuals in redirecting their knowledge and skills to new applications. And finally, the case study by Suchan and Crawford (Chapter 18) illustrates a significant rate of delivery of instruction at a distance with a videoconferencing strategy whereby ninety learners participated at nine sites simultaneously.

Boost ROI: Beware of Marginal Costs

A common pitfall for practitioners is overlooking marginal costs associated with distance training. Marginal costs include nondocumented overhead or embedded costs that are not accounted for when costing out return-on-investment. The outcome is that the marginal costs must be covered by existing budgetary line items associated with the estimated cost of doing the business of distance training. The result is a projected ROI for distance training that is significantly lower than anticipated.

The recommendation for readers is to use a proven analysis strategy when costing out distance training applications and strive to identify non-documented associated costs. (See Chapter 3, Steps Three and Four of the IDM-DT, for further discussion of marginal costs and cost justification of distance training.)

Some of the marginal costs to look for when costing out distance training include the time and dollar expenditures associated with pedagogical applications and instructional personnel. Regarding interactive video teletraining, Payne and Payne (Chapter 10) and others explain that the cost of course conversion by commercial contractors is varied and potentially the largest (underestimated) expense to a telecourse program. Some organizations acknowledge that the alternative is to engage content instructors on staff to complete course conversions. Beware, however, the time investment is significant and often undoable with other current commitments (Chapter 8 and others).

Similar circumstances exist for using staff content experts to develop computer-based training applications and online course materials. Marginal costs (in lost productivity) may be associated with these instructors attempting to convert and design course materials for distance learning while concurrently working to complete other assigned tasks (Chapter 12 and others). Significant to both media, employing in-house staff to convert, customize, or design distance course materials may also result in individuals trying to overcome teaching styles and pedagogical perspectives idiosyncratic to classroom instruction and which may be inconsistent with the new delivery media (Chapter 8 and others).

Finally, marginal costs may also be incurred when distance training applications look to in-house computing services and broadcast personnel to provide technical maintenance and support. As distance training competes for use of various equipment within the organization (as well as auxiliary hardware and software) along with other technological applications within the corporation or agency, support services become significant marginal costs of distance training unless specifically outlined and documented. Several contributing authors recognize this phenomenon (Bento and others, Dooley and Byrom, Howard, and Payne and Payne). Evidence from the case studies suggests that one way to avoid the pitfall of such marginal costs is to negotiate site facilitators and network management services through current contract agreements with telecommunications vendors and equipment distributors and resellers (Chapters 10 and 15).

Please note that the point of this discussion is not to suggest that course development and support services for distance training must be contracted outside of the organization. The point is that if in-house development and support are employed, it must be documented and accounted for as core costs of doing the business of distance training. Thus, marginal costs will be avoided; core costs will be accurately identified; and the estimated ROI from distance training will be strengthened.

Establish Interdisciplinary Core Team

Marginal costs are most often incurred when individuals and independent organizational functions work in isolation to deliver distance training activities. One technique that strengthens development and delivery strategies is support from an interdisciplinary core distance learning team. The team should include members from various functions within the organization, including senior management, information technology, network services, broadcasting and communications, instructional design, training, and performance consulting areas (Chapters 6, 12, 14, 15, and 17). Floating members of the team may include subject matter experts and end users or individuals representing a specific target audience.

The goal of the interdisciplinary core distance learning team is to facilitate cross-company interaction and leverage company expertise across functions for training at a distance (Chapter 14). Core team efforts may include developing instructional materials for distance training, facilitating remote site planning (for interactive video teletraining events), and identifying audience member technology capabilities to support online courses or web-based CBT (Chapters 6, 12, and 15). Depending on the size and composition of the distance learning team, it may also provide content instructors, guest speakers, or clinical advisors (Chapter 11).

The success of a core distance learning team depends on its perceived credibility and actual capability to support distance training. The case study by Yakimovicz (Chapter 14) suggests that credibility and capability evolve initially when the distance learning team targets its efforts. The team should focus on a sponsor that has a need for specific distance training events. (The concept of a sponsor is different from the champion or change agent identified earlier. The sponsor is a user group or intended audience for the distance training event.)

The capability of the distance learning team to respond to a sponsor depends on the team skills possessed by its members. The dynamics of group work are complex and must be accommodated. Contributing authors who discuss interdisciplinary distance learning core teams recommend that a dual lead be identified to strengthen the group's efforts. The dual lead consists of an instructional designer and a subject matter expert (Yakimovicz, Chapter 14). Using a dual lead is one way to overcome some of the diversity and personality conflicts inherent to interdisciplinary teamwork.

Participate in DT to Improve Attitudes About DT

The establishment and use of core distance learning teams represent a step forward in an organization's evolution to maximize use of technology for training at a distance and institutionalize distance training efforts. However, individuals will not buy into and support distance training (DT) if they do not understand the process or they lack confidence in the facilitators of the activities. Further, some individuals in an organization are simply more inclined to support new initiatives than others.

Shifting paradigms from traditional, classroom-based, instructor-led delivery to distance delivery is often necessary. To do this, several contributing authors illustrate that actually engaging individuals to participate in distance training events and processes increases knowledge and understanding about learning at a distance and improves attitudes toward distance training (Chapters 6, 8, 17, and 18). In Chapter 17 Dooley and Byrom illustrate that engaging company individuals in distance training changed attitudes; classroom-based instructor-led training is no longer the only training approach acceptable to Zachry staff and managers.

In addition to enlisting general staff members to participate in distance training to enhance motivation to use and support learning at a distance, content specialists and instructors may also need to be encouraged to participate. An organization which traditionally relies heavily on instructor-led classroom-based delivery may experience fear or resistance to distance training by the highly skilled onsite instructors (Klueter and Kalweit, Chapter 6). Payne and Payne (Chapter 10) recommend inviting instructors into the broadcast studio, encouraging them to interact with touch screen monitors and facilitating group discussions with telecommunications staff as well as instructional designers skilled in developing distance training.

Participating in distance training improves attitudes about distance training because it provides shared experiences with new terminology and learning events. Cultural traditions and language associated with training begin to shift (Chapter 8). And as Dooley and Byrom confirm in Chapter 17, using telecommunications and computer technology to deliver training throughout the organization encourages collaboration of teams that did not exist before, management and labor who are talking and technical experts who suddenly are available!

Conceptual Frameworks for Types of Learning at a Distance

As described in Chapter 2, essentially there are two frameworks from which to view education and training at a distance. Content and knowledge may be determined by someone else and transmitted to the learner, or a learner transforms information received, generating hypotheses and making decisions about the knowledge he or she is constructing. Learning successfully occurs at a distance when the instructional events are consistent with the characteristics of the selected learning model.

The case studies in this book illustrate that no topic is unteachable at a distance. Whether it is increasing knowledge and understanding, building skills (such as creative thinking skills or mechanical skills) or changing attitudes, all types of learning may be facilitated by distance training events or processes. A key to effective distance training is to align content topics to the type of learning desired.

Align Content Topic to Type of Learning Desired

Several case studies demonstrate that distributing information to increase knowledge is the most appropriate type of learning to facilitate at a distance when time and application are critical (Chapters 4, 5, 6, 7, and 8). The content distributed may relate to marketing information, operational processes, new business regulations, and life-saving techniques and other health issues. The body of information transmitted should include facts, names, principles, and generalizations.

Skill-building at a distance may include development of intellectual skills, motor skills, or interpersonal and communication skills. Case studies by Mortlock and Dobrowolski (Chapter 9), Walker (Chapter 13), and Yakimovicz (Chapter 14) describe distance training of intellectual skills including the application of rules and solving problems as well as the development of cognitive strategies for self-learning and independent and critical thinking. Content topics may include programming languages, customer service, and organizational management strategies.

Building manual or psychomotor skills at a distance involves facilitating coordinated and accurate execution of muscle-controlled performances. Chapters 10, 11 and others, present case studies that illustrate successful distance training in production and maintenance of machines and electronic systems and performance of healthcare procedures, respectively.

Interpersonal and communications skills (often considered intellectual skills) may also be taught at a distance. The case study in Chapter 12 illustrates that appropriate content in which to build these skills includes the application and interpretation of verbal and nonverbal cues for social and political implication. Similar to the case studies in Chapters 9, 13, and 14, the distant learner is transforming information and generating hypotheses about how to apply rules and solve problems.

The final type of learning at a distance which the case studies demonstrate is that which is designed to change attitudes or enhance motivation for desired behaviors. An attitude is defined as a personal or emotional perspective, preference, or value. Attitudes guide social and organizational interactions and affect performance. Case studies in Chapters 15, 16, 17, and 18 illustrate that enhancing motivation of staff is appropriate when personnel and business perspectives are adversely affecting overall productivity of the company or agency.

Design Learner-Centered and Reality-Based Experiences

Regardless of the type of learning to be facilitated, learning successfully occurs at a distance when the instructional events are consistent with the characteristics of the selected learning model. Contributing case studies suggest that instruction delivered at a distance and intended for training adults may be teacher-led or student-driven, but it should always be learner-centered (Chapters 7, 11, and 14).

As previously stated, content and knowledge may be determined by someone else and transmitted to the learner. The case studies in this book elaborate, stating that the associated instruction should be designed so that the learner can receive related materials on facts, principles and generalizations in a manner consistent with his or her learning style. If it is intended that the learner will transform information received, generating hypotheses and making decisions about the knowledge he or she is constructing, then instruction should be designed so that the learner can explore, experiment, and simulate organizational experiences to increase understanding and improve performance (Chapter 14).

Several of the case studies in this book discuss the impact of simulations and reality-based experiences on learning and strongly suggest that they be part of the design of distance training events. Monahan (Chapter 7) and Place, Stephens, and Cunningham (Chapter 11) describe how reality-based experiences significantly increase transfer of knowledge and application of skills to the workplace. The case study in Chapter 7 describes a two-week module on sales techniques for loan originators and includes a lesson on how to handle telephone rate requests. Part of the final assessment is an actual phone call from an online expert.

The case study in Chapter 11 describes a distance training design that facilitates participants' practice of prescribed health care procedures right in their own health departments. There is considerable variation between geographical regions with regard to health concerns. How the learner's skills apply depends on the priorities and client demographics of each area health department. The instructional design of the distance training events facilitate the application of learner skills early to the real health department clientele. The result is a significant experience by the participant with increased knowledge and understanding and transfer of analytical skills to the workplace.

Correlation of Instructional Methodologies and Distance Delivery Technologies

To facilitate adult learner-centered distance training experiences based on real life and practical exercises, practitioners must fully understand instructional goals and performance objectives, as well as the strengths and weaknesses of available delivery technology. Live interactive video conferencing, for example, enables two-way audio and one- or two-way video. This technology may be selected to deliver distance training to both visual and verbal learners. A primary strength of the interactive video technology is real-time communication with visual interaction and observation of physical demonstrations which fosters cultural indoctrination, common language building and immediately available feedback to and from the instructor and students.

In contrast, the Internet (as described in Chapters Two and Three) is another distance training technology that delivers instruction. However, Internet-based online training engages learner interaction in an environment that does not require students and instructors to be present together at a specific time or geographic location. Access to the technology is flexible, and use is maximized by instructional events that facilitate social interaction and constructivist learning.

The case studies in this book describe a multitude of technologies that may be used to deliver distance training. These include the Internet (intranet/extranet), satellites, fiber optics, CD-ROM, and laser disks (DVD [digital video disks]), as well as audiotapes and videotapes. The associated instructional applications include (a) web-based CBT and online courses, (b) electronic performance support systems, and (c) interactive video teletraining.

All technologies possess unique capabilities. And the strengths and weaknesses of a technology to deliver distance training may be best described by the medium's "usability" characteristics.

Usability characteristics represent criteria used to determine the strengths and weaknesses of various organizational technologies for communication and training at a distance. Some of these criteria are (a) type and level of interactivity, (b) costs for development and implementation of associated materials, (c) user access to the distance learning technology, (d) learner style, and (e) type of intended learning outcome (for example, knowledge acquisition, skill-building, or attitudinal change). (See Chapter Three for further discussion of *usability criteria*.)

Regarding the question of which technology to choose to deliver distance training, the case studies in this book suggest that the answer depends on the integration of three phenomena associated with learning at a distance: the instructional goals and performance objectives, the instructional design of the distance training events, and the strengths and weaknesses of the delivery tool itself.

Use Multiple Technologies

Although the answer to the question "which technology is best to deliver distance training" is not straightforward, contributing authors do concur that practitioners should entertain the use of multiple technologies to maximize interaction and facilitate diverse learning outcomes. No one technology is a silver bullet in the struggle to deliver distance training that contributes strategically to corporations, government agencies, and nonprofit organizations.

The case studies presented in this book illustrate implementation of distance training using diverse technologies, including online courses, live interactive video teletraining, electronic coaching, or electronic performance support systems, and one-way video satellite broadcasting. Following is a brief description of delivery practices that worked well for contributing authors Monahan, and Bento and others, as they implemented various strategies.

The online courses which the Mortgage Bankers Association of America used (see Chapter 7) were supplied by an outside contractor and distributed by a private network provider. Traditional seminar instructors served the role of online experts, and a course facilitator engaged students to complete skills-based exercises in a collaborative setting. The associated instructional design of the distance training permitted flexibility and enabled the opportunity to respond to teachable moments, such as big news topics related to the content.

Bento and others submitted a case study that describes use of audio and video two-way interaction for just-in-time distance training regarding the pfiesteria microorganism. The goal was to report on the latest scientific evidence available and motivate informed decisions about the use of Chesapeake Bay seafood and waters. The live two-way interaction enables participants to look directly at the microorganism, while concurrently enabling the instructor to observe participant reaction and body language.

In addition to the primary technology employed in the case studies described in preceding paragraphs, the Internet, listservs, fax, and voice mail were used to enhance delivery and communication.

As an organization's distance training program evolves, instructional methodologies design in the simultaneous use of multiple technologies to deliver distance events. The case study in Chapter 9 illustrates the use of several technologies for learning at a distance, including computer-based training on CD-ROM, the Internet, business television, and video teleconferencing. Business television and video teleconferencing were used to distribute information and begin the process of "reskilling" efforts. Newer computer technologies, with the capability to display sophisticated graphics at a distance, were used to teach instructional concepts that are difficult to grasp.

A similar situation was experienced at NYNEX as its distance training program broadened its delivery options to include not only CBT (text and graphics), but also business television, multimedia (CBT with text, audio and video), two-way video conferencing, Internet-based electronic performance support systems (the *electronic coach*), and transitional systems (including conversion of broadcast videotapes to CD-ROM based multimedia).

Driving the use of multiple technologies are the goals to increase learner access and maximize interaction.

Maximize Planned Interaction

The case studies in this book acknowledge that interaction is needed to effectively facilitate adult learning at a distance. Furthermore, the contributing authors recommend this interaction should be planned, and not left to chance!

Interaction includes verbal and nonverbal dialogue. Interactivity is the extent to which instructors and participants observe and respond to one another's communication cues. Interactivity may be student-directed or instructor-led and occurs between instructor and student, student and student, and student and environment (including technological interface).

Several strategies may be employed to maximize planned interaction during distance training. These strategies and techniques are specific to individual delivery technologies. Case studies in Chapters 7 and 10 describe techniques for strengthening interaction during participation in online training, as well as one-way video, two-way audio teletraining (respectively). Case studies in Chapters 13, 15, and 18 describe techniques for strengthening interaction during participation in audio and video two-way interactive conferencing.

In Chapter 7 Monahan describes an instructional methodology for increasing student to student interactivity during participation in online seminars. The instructor assigns job-related tasks, and the participants post answers and accompanying work to the online classroom. Students are mandated to interact among themselves and discuss peer findings and conclusions. Interaction with the online expert is encouraged but is considered secondary to student-student interactivity.

The designers of the Mortgage Bankers Association's online seminars feared that mandating student-student interaction may force the participants to disengage from the learning experience. However, the reverse occurred, and for the majority of the students, the increased interaction helped to spawn more interactivity. (Note: the interaction described in this case study is both synchronous and asynchronous.)

Maximizing interactivity during one-way video broadcasts is illustrated by the case study in Chapter 10. Two interactive devices were integrated as part of the instructional design of the distance training events: one is the use of a viewer response system, the other is the use of a traditional audio (telephone) conferencing system. With the viewer response system, each participant has a simple keypad that allows the individual to talk to the instructor and with learners at other sites. An individual can talk over the system when the instructor opens the learner's microphone, but only two learners at one time can have their microphones opened. Viewer response systems also enable learners to respond to instructor questions by inputting yes-no, true-false, multiple choice or numeric answers. In contrast, the audio conferencing system represents traditional conferencing via telephones and does not support electronic collection of response data.

This case study states that upon completion of the teletraining courses, there were no significant differences between the classes in learner satisfaction or in learners' perceived level of interaction. However, participants using the audio conferencing system had a significantly higher level of verbal interaction, while the participants using the viewer response system had a significantly higher level of overall interaction.

As a final note, Payne and Payne comment that interaction during distance training is the instructor's responsibility. To maximize the instructor-student interactivity, the instructor must make eye contact with the camera and ask questions targeted to specific individuals.

The last technology to be examined regarding interactivity in distance training is interactive videoconferencing. This technology enables live two-way audio and two-way video communication.

The most striking finding from the contributed case studies describing live interactive videoconferencing is that the number of remote sites participating in the distance training event must be limited if the strength of the technology is to be realized. Case studies in Chapters 11 and 14 suggest that maximum interaction occurs between instructor and student and among students across sites when the number of remote sites total six or less (with approximately eighteen to twenty learners per site).

Walker, the contributing author of Chapter 13, confirms, noting that an attempt to coordinate nine videoconference sites outside of a propriety dedicated system (in a heavily used videoconference network) led to grave difficulties in site coordination and scheduling with little benefit to interactivity and overall learning. Not only was interactivity among sites not heightened by the increased number of participating locations, the interactivity between the instructor and learner actually decreased.

Recognizing an optimum number of remote sites that maximizes interaction during live interactive video conferencing, Suchan and Crawford, authors of Chapter 18, focus on ways to plan or design in interactivity.

Suchan and Crawford found that close-up camera shots of students verbally responding at remote sites significantly affects interactivity between instructor and student, enabling communication to be embellished with a tilt of the head, facial expressions, and body positions. These authors also found that if the distance training instructor finds it too difficult to manipulate the equipment to secure a close shot of the participant speaking at the far site, then the communication is merely language and interactivity is less than maximized. Consequently, the live interactive communication capability of the two-way video conferencing technology goes underutilized.

Accommodate Diverse Audience Experience with Technology

While many distance training events attempt to enhance interactivity by way of email, listservs, fax and voice mail, some participants may not have access to these organizational technologies. In Chapter 11, Place, Stephens, and Cunningham acknowledge that regional health department staff may have Internet and email access at home but that it is not currently in every workplace.

Several contributing authors note that intended audiences for distance training are often interdisciplinary, cross-cultural, and multi-generational (Howard; Monahan; Mortlock and Dobrowolski; and Yakimovicz). Significant differences can exist among audience members regarding experience with or access to computers and telecommunications technology (examples of distance training delivery tools). The lesson learned from the case studies in this book is to be aware of the potential diversity among audience members regarding experience with distance delivery technology and design instructional strategies that accommodate this diversity.

Monahan, the author of Chapter 7 describes her organization's target audience for distance training as one in which "computer expertise varies widely among the participants." Some students had never downloaded files prior to registering for the online seminar courses. The author accommodates this diversity by securing support services from the contractor who owns the conferencing system on which the online seminars are delivered.

Other case study authors, Mortlock and Dobrowolski (Chapter 9), caution to beware of connectivity issues with online and web-based training. The case study by these authors describes early attempts to provide computer-based training courses over corporate intranets. Individuals anxious to participate in the training began downloading through 9.6K modems. Accessing the distance training materials took several hours, tying up phone lines while they waited.

Chapter 14 confirms that connectivity can be a problem. Yakimovicz found that the quality of web-based courseware is dependent not only on the robustness of the program code, but also on the stability of the connectivity. Hyperlinks, fundamental to interactivity in computer-based training, must work; and if they do not, it may be due to problems with a particular audience member's connectivity, rather than a combination of keystrokes that the programmer did not anticipate. Regardless of the origin of the problem, the user finds fault with the online training course.

Finally, Walker, in the case study of the Training Academy of the Texas Natural Resource Conservation Commission in Chapter 17, notes that an attempt to use self-contained CD-ROM driven computer-based training can even be unsuccessful if some field offices possess insufficient memory or incompatible computer platforms to run the CBT software.

Integrate Off-Line Learning Experiences

One final lesson learned from the case studies in this book is that distance training efforts are strengthened when off-line learning experiences are integrated into the overall instructional design strategy. Off-line learning experiences are those activities that occur in the absence of *live* audio and video interaction.

Off-line learning experiences have always been a part of asynchronous computer conferencing and self-paced computer-based training. A misconception exists among many distance training practitioners, however, that live interactive communications can not effectively support off-line experiences. Paying telecommunications transmission rates drives many distance trainers away from off-line activities because it is perceived as down time or wasted time.

Case studies by Monahan, and Dessinger and others dispel this notion. Dessinger, and others, in Chapter 16, describe an effective instructional methodology for distance training via one-way video and two-way audio whereby planned times are prescheduled for asking questions and providing comments and observations as well as completing off-line tasks and participating in work-related exercises. Place, Stephens and Cunningham in "Delivering Clinical-Based Training in a Public Health Setting," describe a distance training strategy consisting of a four-day didactic live interactive course, followed by an off-line clinical practicum facilitated by a clinical advisor.

The key to effective integration of off-line exercises (whether as part of computer-mediated instruction or live distance training communication) includes the following processes: (a) design in accountability for the off-line experiences, (b) set dates for submitting work, (c) provide ongoing synchronous and asynchronous communication in support of task completion, and (d) schedule live discussion and/or demonstration of outcomes.

Off-line activities strengthen and reinforce reality-based experiences and should be designed into both online and live interactive distance training events.

Next Steps

The next few years will prove pivotal to the evolution of distance training that contributes strategically to meet the business needs of corporations, government agencies, and nonprofit organizations.

Currently, there is an understanding that distance and distributed education and training represents a process composed of multiple and diverse elements. And designers and developers are beginning to understand the instructional and technological needs of a distance training event or program, including the associated effect of each component on intended business-driven performance outcomes. However, while practitioners focus on terminal training outcomes, minimal attention is being paid to the process of transfer of learning from distance instructional events back to the workplace.

Contributing authors caution that evaluation of distance training for transfer of knowledge and skills is in its infancy. Case studies in Chapters 13 and 16 demonstrate that a lack of formative and summative evaluation is resulting in misunderstandings regarding effectiveness and efficiency of distance training. For example, it is now understood that participant satisfaction with distance training events does not necessarily translate into increased understanding and new skills which are transferred to applications in the workplace (Dessinger and others, and Walker).

It is recommended that further research and clinical assessment occur in two areas: (a) continued evaluation of business-driven performance outcomes accomplished through distance training and (b) assessment of transfer of distance learning to workplace applications.

Some techniques that may facilitate this future work include embedded evaluations of distance training and instruction, content-specific knowledge and skills tests, and action plans. Embedded evaluations represent formative assessment; content-specific tests represent summative assessment; and action plans represent contracts for ongoing maintenance of skill development and application transfer.

Today's business environment is one of increased training need and lifelong learning. A century of dramatic change and innovation in organizational and instructional hardware and software has positioned distance and distributed instruction as a primary resource in meeting this demand. The goal is to maximize utilization of technology and institutionalize an organization's distance training efforts.

GLOSSARY[1]

Contributing resources for this Glossary include: Berge, Z. L. and Collins, M. (1995). Editors. *Computer Mediated Communication and the Online Classroom*. Cresskill, New Jersey: Hampton Press, Inc. / Brooks, D. W. (1997). *Web-Teaching: A Guide to Designing Interactive Teaching for the World Wide Web*. New York, NY: Plenum Press. / Cooke, C. (1997). Graduate Assistant. University of Maryland Baltimore County / Picard, D. (1996). "The future in distance training." *Training*. November. pp. s5–s10. / Portway, P. and Lane, C. (1994). *Teleconferencing and Distance Learning*. 2nd Edition. Livermore, CA: Applied Business teleCommunications. / Schaaf, D. (1997). "D.T. comes home." In Distance Training, a special editorial section in *Training Magazine*. Minneapolis, MN: Lakewood Publications, October. / Schreiber, D. A. (1995). *Introduction to Distance Learning*. Published by the American Association of Retired Persons [AARP]/Learning Center. Staff/Volunteer Development Newsletter. Third Quarter.

Analog Technology. A technology type that is based on continuous measurement, for example, sound, which is continuously varying air vibrations and is converted into analogous electrical vibrations resembling the original sound. Current TV and radio signals are analog, as are many telephone lines. Analog technology is now being replaced by digital technology.

[1]For additional online Glossary resources, refer to the following:
http://mason.gmu.edu/~epiphany/docs/fgglossary.html, and
http://www.wentworth.com
c/o LBEM-L@STAR.UCC.NAU.EDU
Subject: [LBEM-L] Internet Glossary

Asynchronous. Transmission by individual bytes, or packets of bytes, not related to specific timing on the transmitting end. When used to described computer-mediated communication, it indicates that communication can take place without both parties being logged on at the same time, as messages can be left for subsequent reading. Often used for low-speed terminal links.

Audioconferencing. Two-way electronic voice-only interactive conference among two or more groups or three or more sites.

Audiographics Conferencing. Connection of graphic display devices to allow participants to view high-resolution, still-frame visuals (including facsimile, slow-scan television and 35 mm slides) at different sites. In more sophisticated systems, participants can manipulate and change as well as view the visual or collaborate on the development of new files or documents.

Bandwidth. Derived from the traditional term used to describe the size or "width" of the frequencies used to carry analog communications such as TV and radio, bandwidth (for purposes of the Internet) is essentially a measure of the rate of data transfer. It is best visualized using the "pipe analogy" in which a pipe four times the diameter (or width) of another pipe can pass four times the amount of data in a specified period of time. Internet service providers are essentially bandwidth retailers—they buy large bandwidths at a wholesale price and then resell that bandwidth in smaller widths to multiple individual users. Bandwidth is usually stated in bits per second (bps), kilobits per second (kbps), or megabits per second (mps). A full page of English text is about 16,000 bits. A fast modem can move about 15,000 bits in one second. Full-motion full-screen video would require roughly 10,000,000 bits per second, depending on compression. A rule of thumb is that the higher the bandwidth, the better the video looks, the better the audio sounds, and the faster data loads and transfers. Maximum Bandwidth Specifications: 14.4 Modem: 1.4 Kilobytes/second; 28.8 Modem: 2.8 Kilobytes/second; ISDN Modem: 8K or 16 Kilobytes/second; T1: 187 K/second; and T3: 5.6 MB (5,600K)/second.

Bridge. Device which interconnects three or more telecommunication channels, such as telephone lines. A telephone conference audio bridge links three or more telephones (usually operator-assisted). A meet-me audio bridge can provide a teleconference direct dial access number. Both connect remote sites and equalize noise distortion.

Broadcast Site. The site from where the instructor is transmitting. For the students at this site, it is viewed as their classroom site.

Bulletin Board System. [BBS] A type of electronic communication using the Internet or intranet whereby messages can be posted and read over a period of time. Usually BBSs focus on a theme and facilitate debate and discussion.

Business Television. [BTV] Typically one-way video broadcast via satellite from corporate headquarters to branch offices. Primary applications of BTV include information dissemination (critical, just-in-time, or need-to-know) and motivational.

CD-ROM. Compact Disc-Read Only Memory. A storage medium. Discs which can store a variety of data types, including text, color graphics, sound, animation, and digitized video that can be accessed and read through a computer. A disc can store up to 600 megabytes of data, much more information than can be stored on a 3.5 inch computer disk, which holds up to 1.4 megabytes. This makes CD-ROM an inexpensive medium for storing large amounts of data. Because CD-ROM was not designed to store digitized, full-motion video, compression technology is important in compressing data to fit on a disc as well as decompressing data for playback. (Note: A CD-ROM provides enough storage for five encyclopedias on a 4.75-inch disc and is read by laser technology.)

CODEC. Acronym for coder-decoder, the hardware that codes outgoing video and audio signals (converting and compressing analog information into digital form) and decodes incoming ones (decompressing the digital information and recoding it into analog form).

Compressed Video. When the vast amount of information in a normal TV transmission is squeezed into a fraction of its former bandwidth by a codec, the resulting compressed video can be transmitted more economically over a smaller carrier. Compressed digital video [CDV] transmits live video and audio simultaneously over special phone lines (Integrated Services Digital Network or ISDN lines), switched-56 kilobit lines, or T-1 lines (large "pipes" consisting of twenty-four 64 kilobit channels). The interactive communication between sites is two-way audio and two-way video. No special production studios, equipment, or satellites are required.

Compression/Compressed File. A file in which wasted space has been removed by using a computer application that replaces current bits and bytes with new ones. Formulas or algorithms allow duplicate or empty space removal, and also permit reconstruction of the original file identically (lossless compression) or nearly identically (lossy compression).

Computer-Assisted Instruction. [CAI] See computer-based instruction [CBI].

Computer-Assisted Learning. [CAL] See computer-based instruction [CBI].

Computer-Based Instruction. [CBI] Refers to using computers to instruct human users. CBI includes computer-assisted instruction [CAI] (tutorial, review and practice, simulation, and so on); computer-managed instruction (diagnostic and prescriptive testing functions); and electronic messaging (which is generally associated with networked computer classrooms).

Computer-Based Training. [CBT] The use of interactive computer or video programs for instructional purposes. Often refers to the actual instructional materials delivered as CD-ROM or web-based programs.

Computer Conferencing. A distance learning method using computers. Computer conferencing participants leave messages for each other (asynchronously) and do not usually access the conference simultaneously (synchronously).

Computer-Mediated Communication. [CMC] Refers to the entire range of electronic networking activities and includes electronic mail, computer conferencing, informatics, and computer based instruction. See computer-based instruction [CBI].

Desktop Conferencing. Using a desktop computer to send and receive video, audio, and text in real time via the Internet. Most appropriate for small groups or individuals. Many desktop conferencing systems support document sharing. Desktop conferencing that includes live two-way video transmission is often referred to as desktop video conferencing.

Digital Technology. A form of information (discrete bits) which is represented by signals encoded as a series of discrete numbers, intervals or steps, as contrasted to continuous or analog circuits. This method allows simultaneous transmission of voice and data. Can be sent through wire or over the air.

Distance Education. A formal process of distance learning, with information being broad in scope, for example, college courses.

Distance Learning. The acquisition of knowledge and skills through mediated information and instruction, encompassing all technologies and other forms of learning at a distance.

Distance Training. Business practitioners' reference to distance learning. A more customized or targeted learning experience; content is focused to facilitate performance outcomes that meet business needs.

Document Sharing. A computer program feature supported by many desktop video conferencing systems that allows participants at both ends of a video conference to view and edit the same computer document.

Downlink Site(s). The training site where students are viewing the instructor via monitors. The instructor is located at the broadcast site. Often times referred to as the remote site.

Electronic Education. Similar to distance learning; a broad concept implying distance learning which utilizes multiple and diverse forms of technology to meet education and training needs at a distance. See case study by Barry Howard in this book.

Electronic Mail. [Email] A means of sending text messages to individuals or groups of individuals using a computer network. The sender inputs a message to the computer via a terminal, and the receiver also uses a terminal to read and respond to messages. This is one method of transmitting information in distance learning.

Electronic Performance Support System. [EPSS] An integrated computer program that provides any combination of expert system, hypertext, embedded animation, CAI, and hypermedia to an employee to enhance performance with a minimum of support and intervention by others. Examples include help systems, electronic job aids, and electronic expert advisors.

Extranet. A web site that is made available to external customers or organizations for electronic commerce. Although on the Internet, it generally provides more customer-specific information than a public site. It may require a password to gain access to the more sensitive information.

Fiber Optics. The technology that transmits voice, video, and digital information using light waves through thin glass strands. Fiber optics uses a fraction of the space and energy required by conventional copper cable. A strand of fiber optic cable has a bandwidth of ~2b hertz versus twisted pairs of copper wire which possess ~500 hertz.

HTML/Hypertext Markup Language. The language used to mark up text files with links for use with World Wide Web browsers.

HTTP/Hypertext Transfer Protocol. Text linked so that the user can jump from one idea to another, usually by clicking on the text.

Hyperlink. A highlighted word or picture within a hypertext document that when clicked takes one to another place within the document or to another document altogether.

Hypermedia. A program that links different media under learner control in a way similar to hypertext linkage of text. Hypermedia links media such as text, graphics, video, voice, and animation. For example, the learner can choose video when available, see a related video sequence, and then return to the program.

Hypertext. Text that includes links or shortcuts to other documents, allowing the reader to easily jump (browse) from one text to related texts, and consequentially from one idea to another, in a non-linear fashion. Coined by Ted Nelson in 1965.

Integrated Services Digital Network. [ISDN] A digital telecommunications channel that allows for the integrated transmission of voice, video, and data at speeds up to 128,000 bits-per-second over regular phone lines. It is anticipated that ISDN technology will become increasingly important in distance learning and may replace current telephone lines.

Interactive Distance Leaning. [IDL] A mode of delivering distance learning and distance training that connotes one-way video satellite transmission and two-way audio via telephone lines. IDL may include an automated electronic input device (for example, One-Touch system) to accommodate participant responses.

Interactive Multimedia. [IMM] A multi-level multimedia presentation that allows access to information randomly and non-sequentially. Often sophisticated, large-memory computer-based training programs.

Interactive Television. [ITV] A mode of delivering distance learning and distance training that employs one-way video satellite transmission and two-way audio via telephone lines. ITV may also include an automated electronic input device (such as the One-Touch system) to accommodate participant responses.

Interactive Video. A mode of delivering distance learning and distance training that employs two-way video transmission between two or more sites. (Two-way audio is included.) Transmission can be either via satellite or compressed technology.

Internet. An electronic data network that enables infinite numbers of computers to send text and graphics to one another over phone lines. A worldwide network of networks that all use the TCP/IP communications protocol and share a common address space. First incarnated as the ARPANET in 1969, the Internet has metamorphosed from a military internetwork to an academic research internetwork to the current commercial internetwork. It commonly supports services such as email, the World Wide Web, file transfer, and Internet Relay Chat.

Intranet. A private network that uses Internet-related technologies to provide services within an organization. Compare *extranet*.

LAN/Local Area Network. A group of computers at a single location (usually an office or home) that are connected by phone lines or coaxial cable. This represents a private transmission network. MAN—Metropolitan Area Network. WAN—Wide Area Network.

Laser Disk. An optical disk used for full-motion video. Laser disks have been used for interactive training as well as for home theater, where its higher resolution is noticeable on larger screens. For the most part, CD-ROMs have replaced laser disks for training, and it is expected that DVDs will replace the laser disk as well as VHS tape for movies.

LISTSERV. LISTSERV is the software that manages electronic discussion groups or computer conference distribution lists. These discussion groups are often called lists because using what is called a "mail exploder" and a subscription list of electronic mail addresses, LISTSERV sends messages directly to the electronic mailboxes of many subscribers. Participants subscribe by sending a message to the LISTSERV hosting the list of interest. Eric Thomas originally wrote the LISTSERV software for IBM mainframes, but there is now a similar program that runs on Unix systems.

Multipoint. More than two linked sites that can collaborate on an activity, connected by a computerized bridge to allow full interactivity.

Multipoint Conference. Interactive video conference or teleconference in which more than two sites are linked.

Online Training. In technology-based learning, information currently available for direct access. Usually implies linkage to a computer.

Originator Site. See broadcast site.

Protocol. A formalized set of rules governing the format, timing, and error control of transmissions on a network. The protocol that networks use to communicate with each other. TCP/IP is an example of a network protocol.

Remote Access. The ability to access one computer from another from across the room or across the world. Remote access requires communications hardware, software, and actual physical links. This link may be as simple as a telephone line.

Remote Site(s). The training site where students are viewing the instructor via monitors or desktop. The instructor is located at the broadcast site.

Satellite Communications. Distance training is sometimes delivered over *satellite*. A satellite is an electronics retransmission device placed in orbit around the earth in a geostationary orbit for the purpose of receiving and retransmitting electromagnetic signals. It normally receives signals from a single source and retransmits them over a wide geographic area. Domestic communications satellites operate on two frequency ranges designated C and Ku band. Each requires specific electronic equipment. C-band is less expensive and operates at 4 kHz. Ku-band operates at 12 kHz.

Special Interest Group. [SIG] Brings together members who have common interests and backgrounds. Some groups get together to learn new skills or sharpen existing ones. Others focus on keeping up with the state of the art in a particular field or discipline.

Synchronous. Data communications in which transmissions are sent at a fixed rate, with the sending and receiving devices synchronized. Synchronous communications occur in real-time, for example, with two or more users communicating at the same time to one another.

T1 Line. A high speed, high bandwidth leased line connection to the Internet. T1 connections deliver information at 1.544 megabits per second.

T3 Line. A high speed, high bandwidth leased line connection to the Internet. T3 connections deliver information at 44.746 megabits per second.

Telecommuting. Working at an alternate site instead of commuting in the traditional style; the alternate site may be the worker's home. Typically involves the use of a computer for communications with the organization and transmission of work.

Teleconferencing. Two-way electronic communication between two or more groups or three or more individuals in separate locations. Includes group communication via audio, audiographs, video, and computer systems. Loosely, a meeting where the participants are at separate locations. A telephone call with three parties would be a very simple teleconference. A teleconference can arrange to provide two-way communication.

Telemedicine. Using videoconferencing for medical diagnosis and treatment. A specialist can monitor the patient remotely taking cues from the general practitioner or nurse that is actually examining the patient.

Teletraining. Teletraining is a human performance system that integrates telecommunications into planning, designing, and delivering training programs. Methods may include one or all of the following techniques: audio-only, audio-graphic, computer-conferencing, one-way video broadcast, one- or two-way video with audio interaction, and desktop video-conferencing. (See interactive television [ITV] and interactive video.)

Video Conferencing. Communication across long distances with video and audio contact that may also include graphics and data exchange. Often this communication is via satellite. Also, a meeting involving at least one uplink and a number of downlinks at different locations. Communication is often one-way video and two-way audio.

Video Teleducation. Similar to video conferencing, utilizing one-way video and audio via satellite and two-way audio via telephone.

WAN/Wide Area Network. A private long distance network, typically the intercity network that covers an area larger than a single building or campus and uses leased lines to connect computers or LANs. A MAN (metropolitan area network) generally covers a city or suburb.

Web-Based Training. [WBT] Computer-based training delivered via the Internet.

WWW/World Wide Web. A hypertext-based, distributed information system created by researchers at CERN in Switzerland. It allows users to create, edit, or browse hypertext documents. Different systems highlight hyperlinks differently—some put link in boldface or in color; others underline the link. The clients and servers using the WWW are easily accessible and available.

REFERENCES

Abrams, N. "Technology in Corporate Training: Now and in the Future." Unpublished article, 1997.

Adams, M. [maadams@connectinc.com]. "Strategies for Changing Management Education at Xerox Corporation." Contributors: Lida Henderson, Xerox Management Institute; Randi Smith, Smith and Associates, Inc. 1995.

Ajzen, I. "The Theory of Planned Behavior." *Organizational Behavior and Human Decision Processes,* 1991, *50,* 179–211.

Albright, R. C., and Post, P. E. "The Challenges of Electronic Learning." *Training and Development,* 1993, *17*(8), 27–29.

Alessi, S., and Trollip, S. *Computer Based Instruction: Methods and Development.* Englewood Cliffs, N.J.: Prentice Hall, 1991.

Alliger, G. M., Tannenbaum, S. I., Bennett, W., Traver, H., and Shotland, A. "A Meta-analysis of the Relations among Training Criteria." *Personnel Psychology,* 1997, *50,* 341–358.

America Demographics. "The Outlook for Home Improvement." *America Demographics, Marketing Power Supplement, 12* Nov. 1996.

American Council on Education. *Distance Learning Evaluation Guide.* Washington, D.C.: ACE Central Services, 1996.

American Council on Education. *Guiding Principles for Distance Learning in a Learning Society.* Washington, D.C.: ACE Central Services, 1996.

American Red Cross Biomedical Services. "ARCBS Web Page." [http://www.arcbs.org]. 1997.

Americans With Disabilities Act of 1990, Pub. L. No. 101-336. U.S. Government Printing Office, Washington, D.C.

Andleigh, P. K., and Thakrar, K. *Multimedia Systems Design.* Prentice Hall PTR, 1996.

Argyris, C., and Schon, D. A. *Organizational Learning.* Reading, Mass.: Addison-Wesley, 1978.

Armstrong, A. G. *Net Gain: Expanding Markets Through Virtual Communities.* Boston, Mass.: Harvard Business School Press, 1997.

Avis, J. "Post-Fordism, Curriculum Modernisers and Radical Practice: The Case of Vocational Education and Training in England." *Vocational Aspect of Education,* 1993, *45*(1), 3–14.

Bagnara, S. "Organizational Requirements for Educational Technologies Development and Use." In R. J. Seidel and P. R. Chatelier (eds.), *Learning Without Boundaries: Technology to Support Distance/Distributed Learning.* New York: Plenum Press, 1994.

Baldwin, T. T., and Ford, J. K. "Transfer of Training: A Review and Directions for Future Research." *Personnel Psychology,* 1988, *1*, 63–105.

Bandura, A. *Social Learning Theory.* New York: General Learning Press, 1971.

Bandura, A. *Self-Efficacy: The Exercise of Control.* New York: W. H. Freeman, 1997.

Barnard, J. "The World Wide Web and Higher Education: The Promise of Virtual Universities and On-Line Libraries." *Educational Technology,* May–June 1997, pp. 30–35.

Barret, E. *Sociomedia.* Cambridge, Mass.: MIT Press, 1992.

Bedard, M. D. *Structures Housing Knowledge and the Memory of Experiences.* 1989.

Bellini, J. "Foundations of Rehabilitation." *Rehabilitation Education,* 1997, *3*(11), 155–160.

Bentley, M. L. "Constructivist Pedagogy." [http://www.chias.org/www/edu/crcd/crcdcon.html].1993.

Berge, Z. L. "Electronic Discussion Groups." *Communication Education,* 1994, *43*(2), 102–111.

Berge, Z. L. "Changing Roles in Higher Education: Reflecting on Technology." *Collaborative Communications Review 1996.* McLean VA: International Teleconferencing Association. 1996a, pp. 43–53.

Berge, Z. L. "Where Interaction Intersects Time." *MC Journal: The Journal of Academic Media Librarianship,* 1996b, *4*(1), 69–83 [http://wings.buffalo.edu/publications/mcjrnl/v4n1/berge.html#mk].

Berge, Z. L. "The Role of the On-Line Instructor/Facilitator." [http://star.ucc.nau.edu/~mauri/moderate/teach-online.html]. 1996c.

Berge, Z. L. "Instructional Design from a Constructivist Perspective." *EDUC 671 Syllabus: Principles of Training and Development,* University of Maryland Baltimore County, Spring Semester, 1997.

Berge, Z. L., and Collins, M. P. "Technology and Changes in Higher Education." Paper presented at the International Professional Communication Conference (IPCC), Savannah, Ga., September 27–29, 1995a.

Berge, Z. L., and Collins, M. P. *Computer-Mediated Communication and the Online Classroom,* Vol. 2: *Higher Education.* Cresskill, N.J.: Hampton Press, 1995b.

Berge, Z. L., and Collins, M. P. (eds). *Computer-Mediated Communication and the Online Classroom.* Cresskill, N.J.: Hampton Press, Inc., 1995c.

Berner, R., and Oscar, S. "Home-Improvement Leaders Leave Rivals Little Room." *Wall Street Journal,* Feb. 5, 1997, B7.

Boettcher, J. V., and Conrad, R-M. "Distance Learning: A Faculty FAQ." *Syllabus.* June 1997, pp. 14–17, 54.

Bolman, L. C., and Deal, T. E. *Reframing Organizations: Artistry, Choice, and Leadership.* San Francisco: Jossey-Bass, 1991.

Borg, W. R., and Gall, M. D. *Educational Research.* White Plains, N.Y.: Longman, 1989.

Bower, G. H., and Hilgard, E. R. *Theories of Learning.* Englewood Cliffs, N.J.: Prentice Hall, 1981.

Bridges, W. *Surviving Corporate Transition.* New York: Doubleday, 1988.

Broad, M. L., and Newstrom, J. W. *Transfer of Training.* Reading, Mass.: Addison-Wesley, 1992.

Broad, M. L. "Overview of Transfer of Training: From Learning to Performance." *Performance Improvement Quarterly,* 1997, *10,* 7–21.

Brown, J. S., Collins, A., and Duguid, P. "Situated Cognition and the Culture of Learning." *Educational Researcher,* 1989, *18*(1), 32–42.

Brown, K. G., Ford, J. K., and Milner, K. R. *The Design and Evaluation of Distance Learning Courses.* (Technical Report, Part I, for NCMS/MVAC Research Grant: The IDL Evaluation Project.) Lansing, Mich.: Ford and Associates, February 1998.

Brown, S. (ed.). *Open and Distance Learning: Case Studies from Industry and Education.* Stirling, Va.: Kogan Page Limited, 1997.

Bruner, J. *Toward a Theory of Instruction.* Cambridge, Mass.: Harvard University Press, 1966.

Bruner, J. S. *The Relevance of Education.* Cambridge, Mass.: Harvard University Press, 1971.

Campbell, J. P. "An Agenda for Theory and Research." In I. L. Goldstein (ed.), *Training and Development in Organizations.* San Francisco, Calif.: Jossey-Bass, 1989.

Carnveale, A. P., and Carnveale, E. S. "Growth Patterns in Workplace Training." *Training and Development,* 1994, *48*(5): S22–S28.

Carpenter, W. J. *Learning by Building: Design and Construction in Architectural Education.* New York: Van Nostrand Reinhold, 1997.

Chacon, F. "A Taxonomy of Computer Media in Distance Education." *Open Learning,* Feb. 1992, pp. 12–27.

Christensen, C. R., Garvin, D. A., and Sweet, A. (eds.). *Education for Judgment: The Artistry of Discussion Leadership.* Boston, Mass.: Harvard Business School Press, 1991.

Chute, A. G., Sayers, P. K., and Gardner, R. P. "Networked Learning Environments." In T. E. Cyrs (ed.), *Teaching and Learning at a Distance: What it Takes to Effectively Design, Deliver, and Evaluate Programs.* New Directions for Teaching and Learning, no. 71. San Francisco: Jossey-Bass.

Clark, R. E. "Media Will Never Influence Learning." *Educational Technology Research and Development,* 1994, *42*(2), 21–29.

Clark, R. C. *How to Plan, Develop, and Evaluate Training.* Phoenix, Ariz.: Clark Training and Consulting, 1993.

Clement, H. "Home Renovation and Retailing in Quebec." *Marketing,* Maclean Hunter, 1996, *101*(July 22–29), S14.

Collins, A. "Cognitive apprenticeship and instructional technology." In L. Idol and B. F. Jones (eds.), *Educational Values and Cognitive Instruction: Implications for Reform.* Hillsdale, N.J.: Erlbaum, 1991.

Connick, G. P. "Issues and Trends to Take Us into the Twenty-First Century." In Thoman E. Cyrs (ed.) *Teaching and Learning at a Distance: What It Takes to Effectively Design, Deliver, and Evaluate Programs.* San Francisco: Jossey-Bass, 1997.

Connick, G. P. [connick@maine.maine.edu]. "Sources of Information about Distance Learning." The Education Network of Maine, 1996.

Cook, D. "Open Learning in Reuters." In *Open and Distance Learning: Case Studies from Industry and Education.* Stirling, Va.: Kogan Page Limited, 1997.

Cooney, M. "A Real Network Fixer Upper." *Network World,* 1994, *11*(47), 21–24.

Cronin, M. J. *Doing Business on the Internet.* New York: Van Nostrand Reinhold; Thomas International Publishing Company, 1994.

Cullen, J. C. "Telecommunications: A Shifting and Changing World." *Ed Journal of USDLA's ED: Education at a Distance.* May 1997, pp. J9–J11.

Cunningham, D. J. in *Constructivism and the Technology of Instruction: A Conversation.* T. M. Duffy and D. H. Jonassen (eds.). Hillsdale, N.J.: Lawrence Erlbaum Associates, 1992.

Daft, R. L., Lengel, R. H., and Trevino, L. K. "Message Equivocality, Media Selection, and Managerial Performance: Implications for Information Systems." *MIS Quarterly,* 1987, *11,* 355–366.

Defense Technical Information Center. "Potential Benefits of Using Video Teleconference at ALFC/HW to Conduct Training." 1988.

Deleuze, G. *Cinema 1.* Minneapolis, Minn.: University of Minnesota Press, 1986.

Dessinger, J. C., and Moseley, J. L. "360° Appraisal of Training." In P. Dean and D. Ripley (series eds.), *Performance Improvement Pathfinders,* Vol. 2: *Classic Training Interventions.* Washington, D.C.: The International Society for Performance Improvement, 1998.

Deutsch, R. W. "The Window of Opportunity Opened after a Door Closed." In Jerry Knight (ed.), "Washington Investing." *Washington Post,* Aug. 4, 1997.

Dewey, J. *Experience and Education.* New York: Henry Holt, 1963.

Dick, W., and Carey, L. *The Systematic Design of Instruction.* (1st ed.) New York: Scott, Foresman and Company, 1978.

Dick, W., and Carey, L. *The Systematic Design of Instruction.* (4th ed.) New York: Scott, Foresman and Company, 1996.

Dillehay, B. H. "Foundation for Change: Building a Technology Infrastructure in Virginia." *Ed Journal of USDLA's ED: Education at a Distance,* Apr. 1997, pp. J13–J16.

DiPaolo, A. "Moving Toward Education Anywhere, Anytime in an On-Demand Environment." *Ed Journal of USDLA's ED: Education at a Distance,* Mar. 1996.

Dipboye, R. L. "Organizational Barriers to Implementing a Rational Model of Training." In *Training for a Rapidly Changing Workplace.* Washington, D.C.: American Psychological Association, 1997.

Dooley, K. E., and Greule, A. *Faculty Guidebook to Distance Learning: Interactive Video Edition.* College Station, Tex.: The Center for Distance Learning Research, 1995.

Driscoll, M. P. *Psychology of Learning for Instruction.* Needham Heights, Mass.: Allyn and Bacon, 1994.

Drubach, D. A., Kelly, M. P., Peralta, L. M., and Perez, J. "The Community Based Rehabilitation Program: A Model for Medical Rehabilitation in the Nineties." *Journal of Rehabilitation Administration,* 1996, *20*(1), 37–46.

Duncan, J. B., and Powers, E. S. "The Politics of Intervening in Organizations." In H. D. Stolovitch and E. J. Keeps (eds.), *Handbook of Human Performance Technology.* Washington D.C.: National Society for Performance and Instruction, 1992.

"Edward Hines Lumber's Customer Computer Design Center." *Chain Store Age Executive with Shopping Center Age,* September 1995, *65,* 57–59.

Ehrmann, S. C. "Ehrmann on Eval. (Parts 1–3). Asking the Right Question: What Does Research Tell Us about Technology and Higher Learning?" In AAHESGIT. [listproc@list.cren.net]. Jan.13, 1995.

Elangovan, T. "Developing Internet-Based Teaching Applications: A Personal Experience." *USDLA's ED: Education at a Distance,* Nov. 10–11, 1996, pp. 9–12.

Eskow, S. "Distance Learning and the Corporate Agenda: Linking Learning, Training, and Productivity." EUN (Electronic University Network) home page [http://www.wcc-eun.com/index.html], 1997.

Farr, C. and Shaeffer, J. "Matching Media, Methods, and Objectives in Distance Education." *Educational Technology,* July 1993, pp. 52–55.

Federal Aviation Administration. *Interactive Video Teletraining: Review of Responses to the Commerce Business Daily Training Aids and Devices—Potential Sources Sought.* Oklahoma City, Okla., 1994.

Federal Aviation Administration. *Interactive Video Teletraining Program Master Plan.* Oklahoma City, Okla., 1995a.

Federal Aviation Administration. *Interactive Video Teletraining: Review of Responses to the Commerce Business Daily Training Aids and Devices– Potential Sources Sought.* Oklahoma City, Okla., 1995b.

Federal Aviation Administration. *Interactive Video Teletraining Integrated Program Plan.* Oklahoma City, Okla., 1996a.

Federal Aviation Administration. *Cost-Benefit Analysis and Sensitivity Analysis of the Interactive Video Teletraining (IVT) Program.* (FAA Document Control Number D60014-01). Oklahoma City, Okla., 1996b.

Federal Aviation Administration. *Federal Aviation Administration FY 1997 Annual Training Report.* Washington, D.C., 1997.

Federal Aviation Administration. *Survey of Educational Technology.* Training Program Office, AHR-14. Department of Transportation, Sept. 1996.

Federal Register. 34 C.F.R. Part 361 and others. State Vocational Rehabilitation Services Program: Final Rule. 1997, *62*, 28.

Filipczak, B. "Distance Teamwork." *Training,* TECH TRENDS, Apr. 1994, p. 71.

Filipczak, B. "Training on Intranets: The Hope and Hype." *Training,* Sept. 1996, pp. 24–32.

Finney, M. "Harness the Power Within." *HR Magazine,* Feb. 1997, pp. 66–74.

Fluckiger, F. *Understanding Networked Multimedia.* Englewood Cliffs, N.J.: Prentice Hall, 1995.

Ford, J. K., and Weissbein, D. A. "Transfer of Training: An Updated Review." *Performance Improvement Quarterly,* 1997, *10*, 22–41.

Ford, J. K., Quinones, M. A., Sego, D., and Sorra, J. "Factors Affecting the Opportunity to Perform Trained Tasks on the Job." *Personnel Psychology,* 1992, *45*, 511–527.

Forrester Research. *Business Trade and Technology Strategies Report.* [http://www.forrester.com/press/pressrel/970725BT.htm]. 1997.

Fortenbaugh, B. "No Couch Potatoes! Ensuring Interactivity in Training Via Videoconference." Unpublished article. Baltimore Md.: UMBC, 1997.

Franklin, N., Yoakam, M., and Warren, R. "Distance Learning: A Guide to System Planning and Implementation." Chapter 1. "Introduction to Distance Learning." [http://www.indiana.edu/~scs/dl primer.html], 1996.

Friedan, S. "Is Anybody Out There Planning? Surviving the Future of Distance Learning." *Ed Journal of USDLA's ED: Education at a Distance.* Apr. 1997, pp. J19–J20.

Fritz, R. *Corporate Tides: The Inescapable Laws of Organizational Structure.* San Francisco: Berrett-Koehler, 1996.

Fukai, D. "PCIS: A Piece Based Construction Information System on the World Wide Web." *Journal of Automation in Construction,* Elsevier Ltd., 1997, *6*, 287–298.

Fulford, C. P., and Zhang, S. "Perceptions of Interaction: The Critical Predictor in Distance Education." *The American Journal of Distance Education,* 1993, *7*(3): 8–21.

Gagne, R. M. *Essentials of Learning for Instruction.* New York: The Dryden Press, 1975.

Gagne, R. M., Briggs, L. J., and Wager, W. W. *Principles of Instructional Design.* (4th ed.) Fort Worth, TX: Harcourt Brace Jovanovich, 1992.

Gagne, R. M., Yekovich, C. W., and Yekovich, F. *The Cognitive Psychology of School Learning.* (2nd ed.) New York: HarperCollins.

Garavaglia, P. L. "Applying a Transfer Model to Training." *Performance and Instruction,* 1996, *35*(4), 4–8.

Gardner, H. *Multiple Intelligences: The Theory in Practice.* New York: Basic Books, 1993.

Gist, M. E., Stevens, C. K., and Bavetta, A. G. "Effects of Self-Efficacy and Post-Training Intervention on the Acquisition and Maintenance of Complex Interpersonal Skills." *Personnel Psychology,* 1991, *44,* 837–861.

Gloor, P. *Elements of Hypermedia Design: Techniques for Navigation and Visualization in Cyberspace.* Boston: Birkhauser, 1997.

Goldstein, I. L. *Training in Organizations: Needs Assessment, Development, and Evaluation.* (3rd ed.) Monterey, CA: Brooks/Cole, 1993.

Gordin, D. N., Gomez, L. M., Pea, R. D., and Rishman, B. J. "Using the World Wide Web to build learning communities in K–12." [http://www.usc.edu/dept/annenberg/vol2/issue3/gordin.html].

Governor's Task Force on Health Objectives for the Year 2000. *Healthy Carolinians 2000,* Raleigh, NC: The North Carolina Department of Environment, Health and Natural Resources, 1992.

Graham, John R. "Making Dollar and Cents Out of the Internet." *Bank Marketing,* Jan. 1997, *29,* 24–29.

Green, K. C. "Drawn to the Light, Burned by the Flame? Money, Technology and Distance Education." *ED Journal,* 1997, *11*(6), J1–J9.

Griffiths, S. "Motorola's Use of Educational Technology for Training at a Distance." [sgriff1@gl.umbc.edu]. 1996.

Hackman, M. A., and Walker, K. B. "Instructional communication in the televised classroom: The effects of system design and teacher immediacy on student learning and satisfaction. *Communication Education.* 39(3), 196–206, 1990.

Hall, B. *Web-Based Training Cookbook.* New York: Wiley, 1997.

Hammer, M., and Champy, J. *Reengineering the Corporation.* New York: HarperCollins, 1993.

Handbook of Training Evaluation and Measurement Methods. (2nd ed.) Houston, Tex.: Gulf Publishing, 1991.

Hanson, R. A., and Siegel, D. F. "The Three Phases of Evaluation: Formative, Summative and Confirmative." Paper written for the 1995 meeting of the American Educational Research Association, 1994.

Harasim, L., Hiltz, S.R., Teles, L., and Turoff, M. *Learning Networks: A Field Guide to Teaching and Learning Online.* Cambridge, Mass.: MIT Press, 1995.

Harrison, N. "Practical Instructional Design for Open Learning Materials: A Module Course Covering Open Learning, Computer-Based Training and Multimedia." (2nd ed.) Online 1995.

Harrison, T. M. *Computer Networking and Scholarly Communication in the Twenty First Century.* State University of New York Press, 1996.

Hayword, P., and Wollen, T. *Future Visions: New Technologies of the Screen.* Online: BFI Publishing, 1993.

Hechinger Company Report. *Washington Post,* Business, 14:3.1997.

Hefzallah, I. M. *The New Learning and Telecommunications Technologies: Their Potential Applications in Education.* Springfield, Ill.: Charles Thomas, 1990.

Hellman, M. F., and James W. R. *Multimedia Casebook.* New York: Van Nostrand Reinhold, 1995.

Hellmich, N. "Buyers Learn Building and Design Skills." *USA Today,* July 13, 1989, 1:3.

Helsel, S. K., and Paris, R. J. (eds.). *Virtual Reality: Theory, Practice and Promise.* Westport, Conn.: Meckler, 1991.

Henderson, A. "The University of Niceness: Training Municipal Workers in Customer Service." *Governing,* Feb. 1996, *9,* 39.

Henkoff, R. "Why Every Red Blooded Consumer Owns a Truck, and a Five Pound Jar of Peanut Butter, and a Personal Computer, and a Tool Belt, and a Case of Energy-Saving Light-Bulbs, and Why It All Matters on a Nearly Cosmic Scale." *Fortune,* May 29, 1995, *131*(10), 85–100.

Herman, C. J., Tessaro, I. A., Kavee, A. L., Harris, L., and Holliday, J. "An Evaluation of Professional Education Efforts for Breast and Cervical Cancer: A Survey of North Carolina Public Health Nurses 1996." *Journal of Health Management and Practice,* forthcoming, 1998.

Hill, R. R., and Schroeder, F. K. *Joint RSA/CSAVR Vision and Strategies for Streamlining the Public Vocational Rehabilitation Service Delivery System: RSA and CSAVR.* 1996.

Himowitz, M. J. "Software for Hammerheads." *Fortune,* June 24, 1996, *133,* 151–155.

"Home Centers Building for the Future." *Chain Store Age,* June 1997a, *73,* 34–36.

"Home Depot Is Working to Put its House in Order." *Chain Store Age: The Extended Retail Enterprise Supplement,* June 1997b, *73,* A19.

"Home Sector Nails Third Place: Use of Consumer Enhancement and Development Tools." *Chain Store Age,* 1996, *72,* Jan. Supplement, Consumer Enhancement and Development, p. 50.

Horton, W. "How we communicate." Paper presented at the Meeting of the Rocky Mountain Chapter of the Society for Technical Communication, Denver, Colo., June 1994.

Horton, W. *Designing and Writing Online Documentation: Hypermedia for Self-Supporting Products.* New York: Wiley, 1994a.

Horton, W. *The Icon Book: Visual Symbols for Computer Systems and Documentation.* New York: Wiley, 1994b.

Hunter, B., Renckly, T., Smith, J., and Tussey, D. *The Effects on Student Achievement and Attitude of a Distance Learning Seminar Educational Program Compared to a Traditional In-Residence Program.* Washington, D.C.: Air University, Air Education and Training Command, U.S. Air Force, 1995.

Institute for Distance Education. "Models of Distance Education: A Conceptual Planning Tool Developed by the University of Maryland System Institute for Distance Education." [http://www.umuc.edu/ide/modlmenu.html], 1996.

"Iron Age New Steel." *Teaching Home Improvement and Steelmaking in Inland's Joblink 2000,* Feb. 1997, *13*(2), 50–55.

Ivey, M. "Distance Learning Collection. Long Distance Learning Gets an 'A' at Last." *Business Week.* May 9, 1988.

Jette, R. "Adopting Educational Technology." In AAHESGIT. [listproc@list.cren.net]. Aug. 17, 1994.

Johnson, D., and Johnson, R. *Cooperation and Competition: Theory and Practice.* New York: Interaction Book Company, 1989.

Johnson, G. *In the Palaces of Memory: How We Build The Worlds Inside Our Heads.* New York: Alfred A. Knopf, 1991.

Johnson, J. D. "On Use of Communication Gradients." In G. M. Goldhaber and G. A. Barnett (eds.), *Handbook of Organizational Communication.* Norwood: N.J.: Ablex, 1988.

Joint Center for Housing Studies. *The State of the Nation's Housing: 1996.* John F. Kennedy School of Government, Cambridge: Harvard University Press, 1996.

Jonassen, D. H. "Objectivism versus constructivism: Do we need a new philosophical paradigm?" *Educational Technology Research and Development.* 39(3), 5–14, 1991.

Jones, B. L., and Maloy, R. W. *Schools for the Information Age: Reconstructing Foundations for Learning and Teaching.* Westport, Conn.: Praeger Publishing, 1996.

Jones, S. *Computer-Mediated Communication and Community.* Newbury Park, Calif.: Sage, 1995.

Jones, S. G. *Cybersociety: Computer-Mediated Communication and Community.* Thousand Oaks, Calif.: Sage Publications, 1995.

Joyce, B., and Weil, M. *Models of Teaching.* (5th ed.) Boston: Allyn and Bacon, 1996.

Kalish, I. F., and Nelson, J. "State of the Industry: An Expanded Focus on Home Improvement Retailers." *Chain Store Executive,* Aug. 1992, *68*(8), Section 2, 36–37.

Kanter, R. M. *The Change Masters. Innovation and Entrepreneurship in the American Corporation.* New York: Simon & Schuster, 1983.

Katz, S., and Lesgold, A. in *Computers as Cognitive Tools.* S. Lajoie and S. J. Derry (eds.). Hillsdale, N.J.: Lawrence Erlbaum Associates, 1993.

Keegan, D. *The Foundations of Distance Education.* London: Croom Helm, 1986.

Keisler, S., Siegel, J., and McGuire, T. W. "Social Psychological Aspects of Computer-Mediated Communication." *American Psychologist,* 1984, *39*(10), 1123–1134.

Kempfer, L. "Home Improvement the AutoCAD Way." *Computer Aided Engineering,* Apr. 1995, *14*(4), 37–40.

Kincaid, S. "Presenting Difficult Content on the Internet." Paper presented at the 2nd annual Teaching in the Community Colleges Online Conference [http://leahi.kcc.hawaii.edu/org/tcc-conf/pres/kincaid.html], 1997.

Kirkpatrick, D. L. "Evaluation of Training." In R. L. Craig (ed.), *Training and Development Handbook* (2nd ed.) New York: McGraw-Hill, 1974.

Klaphaak, K. "Why Invest in Info Tech?" In AAHESGIT. [listproc@list.cren.net]. Dec. 5, 1994.

Knowles, M. *Andragogy in Action: Applying Modern Principles of Adult Learning.* San Francisco: Jossey-Bass, 1984.

Kojonen, T. *Self-Organization of Associative Memory.* (3rd ed.) New York: Springer-Verlag, 1989.

Kraiger, K., Ford, J. K., and Salas, E. "Application of Cognitive, Skill-Based, and Affective Theories of Learning Outcomes to New Methods of Training Evaluation." *Journal of Applied Psychology,* 1993, *78*, 311–328.

Lane, C. "Distance Education." In *Teleconferencing and Distance Learning.* (2nd ed.) Livermore, Calif.: Applied Business teleCommunications, 1994.

Lengel, R. H., and Daft, R. L. "The Selection of Communication Media as an Executive Skill." *Academy of Management Executive,* 1988, *2*(3), 225–232.

Lennon, C. A., and Payne, H. "A Comparison Between IVT and Resident Versions of FAA's Quality Assurance Course." *Teleconference,* 1997, *16*(3), 50–52, 68.

Levin, J. "Education and Society in the 21st Century: Networks, Diversity and Mediation." Presented at the American Educational Research Association (AREA) Meeting. Chicago, Ill., Mar. 24–28, 1997.

Lewin, K. *Field Theory in Social Science.* New York: Harper & Row, 1951.

Loftus, G. R. *Human Memory: The Processing of Information.* New York: Wiley, 1976.

Mackin, D., and Hoffman, J. "The Learner Interaction Model for the Design of Interactive Television." *Ed Journal of USDLA's ED: Education at a Distance,* Apr. 1997, pp. J9–J12.

Mann, R. L. "Institutional Applications of New Information Technology." In *Information Technology: Innovations and Applications.* San Francisco: Jossey-Bass Publishers, Sept. 1982.

Mantyla, K., and Gividen, J. R. *Distance Learning: A Step-By-Step Guide for Trainers.* Alexandria, Va.: ASTD Publications, 1997.

Markus, M. L. "Electronic Mail as the Medium of Managerial Choice." *Organization Science,* 1994, *5*(4), 502–526.

Marlow, E. *Web Visions: An Inside Look at Successful Business Strategies on the Net.* New York: Van Nostrand Reinhold, 1997.

Marx, R. "Relapse Prevention for Managerial Training: A Model for Maintenance of Behavioral Change." *Academy of Management Review,* 1982, *7,* 27–40.

McCormack, K. "Casualties of the War: The Carnage among Home Improvement Retailers Has Left a Bloody Mess . . . And a Few Opportunities." *Financial World,* May 20, 1997, *166,* 45–49.

McLaren, T. A. "Give Me a Place to Stand." *CBT Solutions Magazine,* May–June 1996.

Miller, R. L. "Learning Benefits of Interactive Technologies." *Editor and Publisher.* Falls Church, Va.: The Videodisc Monitor, 1990.

Millikin, M. "Practical Advice for Implementing Corporate Intranets." *Telecommunications,* Apr. 1996, *30,* 34–39.

Moore, M. G. "Three Types of Interaction." *The American Journal of Distance Education,* 1989, *3*(2), 1–6.

Moore, M. G., and Kearsley, G. *Distance Education: A Systems View.* Boston: Wadsworth Publishing Company, 1996.

Moore, M. G., Thompson, M. M., Quigley, B. A., Clark, G. C., and Goff, G. G. *Effects of Distance Learning: A Summary of Literature.* University Park, Pa.: The American Center for the Study of Distance Education, 1990.

Moreau, D. "How Can Home Depot Rebuild Its Faltering Rate of Growth?" *Kiplinger's Personal Finance Magazine,* Nov. 1995, *49,* 30.

Morrison, D., and Lauzon, A. C. "Reflection on Some Technical Issues of 'Connecting' Learners in Online Education." *Research in Distance Education,* 1992, *4*(3), 6–9.

Morrison, G. R. "The Media Effects Question: 'Unresolvable' or Asking the Right Question." *Educational Technology Research & Development,* 1994, *42*(2), 41–44.

Moshinskie, J. "Instructional Design Primer for Distance Education." [http://www.hsb.baylor.edu/html/moshinsk]. 1997.

Mullany, G. "Taking in the Sites: Home Improvement: On TV, Online." *The New York Times,* Aug. 19, 1996, D4:4.

Neibauer, A. R. "Home Improvement. Total Planning on Your Computer." *Que,* June 1995.

Newman, S. D. "Applying Total Quality Management to Interactive Distance Learning." *Ed Journal of USDLA's ED: Education at a Distance,* Feb. 1997, J17–J20.

Noblitt, J. S. "Top-Down Meets Bottom-Up." *Educom Review,* 1997, *32*(3), 38–43.

Nonaka, I., and Takeuchi, H. *The Knowledge-Creating Company.* Oxford: Oxford University Press, 1995.

Norris, D. M, and Dolence, M. G. "IT Leadership Is Key to Transformation." *Cause/Effect Magazine, 19*(1), 12–20.

North Carolina State Center for Health Statistics. *Access to Health Care in North Carolina: Indicators and Baseline Data.* Raleigh, NC, 1996.

Office of Educational Research and Improvement. "Technology and Education Reform." Washington, D.C.: United States Department of Education, 1997.

Open Learning Technology Corporation Limited. "Constructivist Theory." [http://www.oltc.edu.au/cp/04c.html]. 1996.

Ostendorf, V. *Interactive Compressed Video Distance Learning and the Adult Learner.* Nashville, Tenn.: Association for Educational Communications and Technology, Feb. 1994.

Parar, M. (ed.). [mparar@ glaeb.cc.monash.edu.au]. "Unlocking Open Learning." 1994.

Patrick, J. *Training: Research and Practice.* London/New York: Harcourt Brace Jovanovich, Academic Press, 1992.

Paulk, M. C., Curtis, B., Chrisses, M. B., and Weber, C. V. "Capability Maturity Model[SM] for Software." Version 1.1. 1993. *Technical Report CMU/SEI-93-TR-024.* Software Engineering Institute. Pittsburgh, PA.: Carnegie Mellon University.

Paulsen, M. F. "An Overview of CMC and the Online Classroom in Distance Education." In Z. L. Berge, M. P. Collins (eds.), *Computer Mediated Communication and the Online Classroom,* Vol. III: *Distance Learning.* Cresskill, N.J.: Hampton Press, 1995.

Payne, H. "Video Teletraining Course Conversion Costs: What Are They and Can They Be Controlled?" *Teleconference,* 1996, *15*(2), 17–19.

Payne, H. E. "Review of the Literature: Interactive Video Teletraining in Distance Learning Courses." In P. S. Portway and C. Lane (eds.), *Technical Guide to Teleconferencing and Distance Learning* (3rd ed.). San Ramon, Calif.: Applied Business Telecommunications, 1997.

Payne, L. W., and Payne, H. "Business Students Meet Business Television: An Introduction to Distance Learning for On-the-Job Training for Business Students." Proceedings of the Ninth Annual Association of Collegiate Business Schools and Programs, 1997, *9*, 51–60.

Pemberton, A. "CMC and the Educationally Disabled Students." In Z. Berge and M. Collins (eds.), *Computer Mediated Communication and the Online Classroom: Overview and Perspectives,* Vol. 1. Cresskill, N.J.: Hampton Press, 1995.

Peters, O. "The Iceberg Has Not Melted: Further Reflections on the Concept of Industrialization and Distance Teaching." *Open Learning,* 1989, *4*(3), 3–8.

Petrovic, O., and Krickl, O. "Traditionally-Moderated Versus Computer Supported Brainstorming: A Comparative Study." *Information & Management,* 1994, *27*, 233–243.

Phillips, J. J. *Handbook of Training Evaluation and Measurement Methods* . (2nd ed.) Houston: Gulf Publishing, 1991.

Phillips, J. J. *In Action: Measuring the Return on Investment.* Vol. 1. Alexandria, Va.: American Society for Training and Development, 1994.

Picard, D. "The Future in Distance Training." *Training,* Nov. 1996, pp. s5–s10.

Pisel, K. "An Analysis of Distance Learning Applications for Joint Training." *Journal of Interactive Instruction Development,* Summer 1995, pp. 12–23.

Piskurich, G. M. "Reconsidering the Promise of Satellites as a Distance Learning Technology." *Performance Improvement,* 1997, *36*(2), 19–23.

Porter, L. R. *Creating the Virtual Classroom: Distance Learning with the Internet.* New York: Wiley, 1997.

Portway, P. S., and Ostendorf, V. A. "Interaction in One-Way Video." In P. S. Portway and C. Lane (eds.), *Technical Guide to Teleconferencing & Distance Learning* (3rd ed.). San Ramon, Calif.: Applied Business Telecommunications, 1997.

Portway, P., and Lane, C. *Teleconferencing and Distance Learning* (2nd ed.) Livermore, Calif.: Applied Business teleCommunications, 1994.

Quinones, M. A., and Ehrenstein, A. *Training for a Rapidly Changing Workplace. Applications of Psychological Research.* Washington, D.C.: American Psychological Association, 1997.

Raggatt, P. (1993). "Post-Fordism and Distance Education—A Flexible Strategy for Change." *Open Learning,* 1993, *8*(1), 21–31.

Rakow, J. "Networking Multimedia Training." *Training*, Mar. 1997.

Reauthorization of the Rehabilitation Act of 1992, Pub. L. 99–506. U.S. Government Printing Office, Washington, D.C.

Reed, J. "Videoconferencing in the Classroom and Library: Instructional Strategies." [http://www.kn.pacbell.com/wired/vidconf/instruct/instruct.html]. 1996.

Rehabilitation Act of 1973, Pub. L. No. 93–112. U.S. Government Printing Office, Washington, D.C.

Reigeluth, C. M. "Instructional Theory, Practitioner Needs, and New Directions: Some Reflections." *Educational Technology*, 1997, *37*(1), 42–47.

Robinson, D. G., and Robinson, J. C. *Performance Consulting*. San Francisco: Berrett-Koehler Publishers, 1996.

Rogers, R. C. "Distance Learning: It Played Well in Peoria." *Training*, Nov. 1994, pp. 51–53.

Rohfeld, R., and Hiemstra, R. "Moderating Discussions in the Electronic Classroom." [http://star.ucc.nau.edu/~mauri/moderate/rohfeld.html]. 1995.

Ross, E. (1994). "Making Dream Homes Come True." *Christian Science Monitor*, Aug. 9, 1994, 11:2.

Roth, W. *Personal Computers for Persons with Disabilities*. Jefferson, N.C.: McFarland & Company, 1992.

Russell, T. "Television's Indelible Impact on Distance Education: What We Should Have Learned from Comparative Research." *Research in Distance Education*, Oct. 1992, 2–4.

Sabbagh, K. *21st Century Jet: The Making and Marketing of the Boeing 777*. New York: Scribners, 1996.

Saettler, P. *The Evolution of American Educational Technology*. Englewood, Colo.: Libraries Unlimited, 1990.

Salahaldin, A. "The Role of Training and Education in Technology Transfer." *Technovation*, Apr. 1991, *11*(3), 13–33.

Santoro, G. M. "What Is Computer-Mediated Communications." In Z. Berge and M. Collins (eds.), *Computer Mediated Communication and the Online Classroom: Overview and Perspectives*, Vol. 1. Cresskill, N.J.: Hampton Press, 1995.

Savery, J. R., and Duffy, T. M. "Problem Based Learning: An Instructional Model and Its Constructivist Framework." *Educational Technology*, 1995, *35*(5), 31–38.

Scardamalia, M. "Networked Communities Focused on Knowledge Advancement." Presented at the American Educational Research Association (AREA) Meeting, Chicago, Ill., Mar. 24–28, 1997.

Schaaf, D. "A Pipeline Full of Promises: Distance Training Is Ready to Deliver." *Distance Training*, Oct. 1997, A6–A10.

Schaaf, D. "D.T. Comes Home." In *Distance Training* (special editorial section in *Training Magazine*), Oct. 1997, A3.

Schlosser, C. A., and Anderson, M. L. *Distance Education: Review of the Literature*. Ames, Iowa: Iowa State University, 1994.

Schon, D. A. *The Reflective Practitioner*. New York: Basic Books, 1983.

Schreiber, D. *Interactive Video Handbook*. Washington, D.C.: American Association of Retired Persons/ Learning Center, 1995a.

Schreiber, D. *Introduction to Distance Learning*. American Association of Retired Persons/Learning Center, *Staff/Volunteer Development Newsletter*, 3rd Quarter, 1995b, 1–3.

Schreiber, D. "Business-Case Applications of Distance Learning: The Internal Corporate Interface." Unpublished article, 1996.

Seamans, M. C. "New Perspectives on User-Centered Design." Presentation at The Interchange Technical Writing Conference, University of Lowell, Mass., 1990.

Selinger, M. "Critical Communities through Computer Conferencing." [http://www.edfac.unimelb.edu.au/online-ed]. Apr. 11, 1997.

Senge, P. M. *The Fifth Discipline: The Art and Practice of the Learning Organization.* New York: Doubleday, 1990.

Senge, P. *The Fifth Discipline Fieldbook: Strategies and Tools for Building a Learning Organization.* New York: Doubleday, 1994.

Sheehan, B. S. (ed.). *Information Technology: Innovations and Applications.* San Francisco: Jossey-Bass Publishers, Sept. 1982.

Sheperd, J. M. *Be Your Own Contractor and Save Thousands.* (2nd ed.) Chicago: Dearborn Financial Publishing, Inc., 1996.

Sherry, L. "Issues in Distance Learning." *International Journal of Distance Education,* 1996, *1*(4), 337–365.

Shulz, D. P. "Omens Good for Home Centers as Key Spring Season Begins Improvement CAD." *Manufacturing Systems,* Mar. 1995, *12*(3), 13–19.

Shulz, D. P. "Wickes Thrives by Targeting Pros." *Stores,* Oct. 1995, *77*(10), 30–31.

Simpson, H. "Conversion of Live Instruction for Video Teletraining: Training and Classroom Design Considerations." TR-93-4. San Diego, Calif.: Naval Personnel and Research Development Center, Feb. 1993.

Simpson, H., Wetzel, D., and Pugh, H. "Delivery of Division Officer Navy Leadership Training by Videoteletraining." TR-95-7. San Diego, Calif.: Naval Personnel and Research Development Center, Aug. 1995.

Smith, D. K., and Alexander, R. C. *Fumbling the Future: How XEROX Invented, Then Ignored, the First Personal Computer.* New York: Morrow, 1988.

Smith, K. A. "Cooperative Learning: Effective Teamwork for Engineering Classrooms." *IEEE Education Society Newsletter,* Apr. 1995.

Smith, K. U. *Cybernetic Principles of Learning and Educational Design.* Austin, Tex.: Holt, Rinehart, and Winston, 1988.

Spears, L. (ed.). *Insights on Leadership: Service, Stewardship, Spirit, and Servant-Leadership.* New York: Wiley, 1998.

Sproull, L., and Keisler, S., *Connections: New Ways of Working in the Networked Organization.* Cambridge, Mass.: MIT Press. 1991.

Steward, J. "The Chevron Virtual Classroom, Satellite Experience." *Ed Journal of USDLA's ED: Education at a Distance,* Feb. 1995, pp. J1–J3.

Stewart, D. "One World, Many Voices. Quality in Open and Distance Learning." 17th World Conference on Distance Learning, online, 1995.

Strauss, G., and Maney, K. "Film Giant Kodak Cuts 10,000 Jobs." *USA Today,* Nov. 12, 1997, pp. A1, B1.

Streibel, M. J. "Instructional Plans and Situated Learning." In G. J. Anglin (ed.), *Instructional Technology: Past, Present, and Future.* Englewood, Colo.: Libraries Unlimited, 1991.

Stussman, H. B. (ed.). "Nonunion Training Reaches a Key Stage." *Engineering News Record,* Feb. 5, 1996, *30.*

Symes, C. "A Post-Fordist Reworking of Australian Education: The Finn, Mayer and Carmichael Reports in the Context of Labour Reprocessing." *The Vocational Aspect of Education,* 1995, *47*(3), 247–269.

Thornburg, D. D. "Campfires in Cyberspace: Primordial Metaphors for Learning in the 21st Century." [http://www.tcpd.org/handouts/thornburg/Campfires.pdf]. n.d.

Tice, C. "Home Improvement Retailing: Get Tough Time." *Chain Store Age,* July 1996, *72,* 93–99.

Tiffin, J., and Rajasingham, L. *In Search of the Virtual Class: Education in an Information Society.* London/New York: Routledge Publishers, 1995.

Trester, A. and Place, J. L. *Physical Assessment of Adults Clinical Advisor Manual.* School of Public Health, University of North Carolina at Chapel Hill. (Companion manual to the course curriculum). 1996.

Trevino, L. K., Daft, R. L., and Lengel, R. H. "Understanding Managers' Media Choices: A Symbolic Interactionist Perspective." In J. Fulk and C. W. Steinfield (eds.), *Organizations and Communication Technology.* Newbury Park, Calif.: Sage, 1990.

Tufte, E. R. *Envisioning Information.* Cheshire, CT.: Graphics Press, 1994.

Tufte, E. R. *The Visual Display of Quantitative Information.* Cheshire, CT.: Graphics Press, 1993.

Turkle, S. and Papert, S. "Epistemological Pluralism: Styles and Voices Within the Computer Culture." *Signs: Journal of Women in Culture and Society. 16.* 1990.

Turner, G. "Engaging Spaces: Cinematic Codes and the Architecture of Information." Unpublished Masters Thesis, Washington State University, 1996.

Twigg, C. A. "The Need for a National Learning Infrastructure." *Educom Review,* 1994, *29*(5), 17–20.

U.S. Department of Transportation, Office of Inspector General. *Interactive Video Teletraining.* Federal Aviation Administration Report No. R6-FA-6-003. Washington, D.C., 1995.

Vanderheiden, G. C. [gv@tracer.wisc.edu]. "Application Software Design Guidelines: Increasing the Accessibility of Application Software to People with Disabilities and Older Users." Trace R&D Center, 1994.

Vaske, J. J., and Grantham, C. E. *Socializing the Human-Computer Environment.* Norwood, N.J.: Ablex, 1994.

Visser, J. "Learning Technologies and Communication Environments for New Learning Communities." *ED: Education at a Distance,* May 1997, pp. 9–11.

Vygotsky, L. S. *Thought and Language.* Cambridge, Mass.: MIT Press, 1962.

Vygotsky, L. S. *Mind in Society: The Development of Higher Psychological Process.* (M. Cole, V. John-Steiner, S. Scribner, and E. Souberman, trans.). Cambridge, Mass.: Harvard University Press, 1978.

Waggoner, M. D. *Empowering Networks: Computer Conferencing in Education.* Englewood Cliffs, N.J.: Educational Technology Publications, 1992.

Wakeley, J. "From Pioneers to Settlers: The Abbey National." In *Open and Distance Learning: Case Studies from Industry and Education.* Stirling, Va.: Kogan Page Limited, 1997.

Walsh, W. J. *Instructional Design Handbook for Interactive Distance Learning,* National Center for Manufacturing Science, Inc. Ann Arbor, MI. 1996.

Ward, D., and Warm, T. A. *Evaluation of the AFS Distance Learning Demonstration Project.* Oklahoma City, Okla.: Federal Aviation Administration Academy, 1994.

Ward, D., and Warm, T. A. *Evaluation of the CMD Distance Learning Demonstration Project.* Oklahoma City, Okla.: Federal Aviation Administration Academy, 1995a.

Ward, D., and Warm, T. A. *Evaluation of the Aviation Medicine Distance Learning Demonstration Project.* Oklahoma City, Okla.: Federal Aviation Administration Academy, 1995b.

Warr, P., and Bunce, D. "Trainee Characteristics and the Outcomes of Open Learning." *Personnel Psychology,* 1995, *48,* 347–376.

Weick, K. E. "Technology as Equivoque: Sensemaking in New Technologies." In P. S. Goodman and L. S. Sproull (eds.), *Technology and Organizations*. San Francisco: Jossey-Bass Publishers, 1990.

Wetzel, C. D. *Distributed Training Project: Final Report*. TR-96-7. San Diego, Calif.: Naval Personnel and Research Development Center, Apr. 1996.

Wetzel, C. D., Simpson, H., and Seymour, G. E. "The Use of Videoteletraining to Deliver Chief and Leading Petty Officer Navy Leadership Training." TR-95-8. San Diego, Calif.: Naval Personnel and Research Development Center, Aug. 1995.

Wexley, K. N., and Baldwin, T. T. "Post-Training Strategies for Facilitating Positive Transfer: An Empirical Exploration." *Academy of Management Journal*, 1986, *29*, 503–520.

Willis, B. *Distance Education: A Practical Guide*. Englewood Cliffs, N.J.: Educational Technology Publications, 1993.

Wilson, B., Teslow, J., and Osman-Jouchoux, R. "The Impact of Constructivism (and Postmodernism) on ID Fundamentals." In B. B. Seels (ed.), *Instructional Design Fundamentals: A Review and Reconsideration*. Englewood Cliffs, N.J.: Educational Technology Publications, 1995.

Windstrom, S. H. "CD and Browser: What a Lovely Pair." *Business Week*, May 20, 1996, 17.

Wissman, G. "Home Improvement Retail: At the Apex." *Chain Store Age*, 1995, *71*(Aug.) 33–34.

Yelon, S. L. *Powerful Principles of Instruction*. White Plains, NY: Longman, 1996.

Yelon, S. L., and Berge, Z. L. "The Secret of Instructional Design." *Performance and Instruction*, Jan. 1988, 11–13.

Zelmer, A. E., and Zelmer, A.C.L. "Distance Education: No Apologies." Paper presented at TELETEACHING '93, Trondheim, Norway, 1993.

INDEX